"Weltbeziehung"

Bettina Hollstein is an economist and academic manager of the Erfurt University's Max-Weber-Kolleg. *Hartmut Rosa* is a sociologist and director of the Max-Weber-Kolleg. *Jörg Rüpke* is a religious scientist and deputy director of the Max-Weber-Kolleg.

Bettina Hollstein, Hartmut Rosa, Jörg Rüpke (eds.)

"Weltbeziehung"

The Study of our Relationship to the World

Campus Verlag
Frankfurt/New York

The publication is co-funded by the Deutsche Forschungsgemeinschaft (DFG, German Research Foundation) – SFB TRR 294 – 42463867 and GRK 2283/2 – 313147291 and the University of Erfurt.

The work, including all its parts, is subject to copyright protection. The text of this publication is published under the "Attribution-Share Alike 4.0 International" (CC BY SA 4.0) licence.

The full licence text can be found at: https://creativecommons.org/licenses/by-sa/4.0/legalcode.de

Any use that exceeds the scope of the CC BY-SA 4.0 licence is not permitted without the publisher's consent.

The images and other third-party material contained in this work are also subject to the aforementioned Creative Commons licence, unless otherwise stated under references/illustration index. Insofar as the material in question is not subject to the aforementioned Creative Commons licence and the usage in question is not permitted under statutory provisions, the consent of the respective rightsholder must be obtained.

ISBN 978-3-593-51820-6 Print
ISBN 978-3-593-45587-7 E-Book (PDF)
DOI 10.12907/978-3-593-45587-7

Copyright © 2023 Campus Verlag GmbH, Frankfurt am Main.
Cover design: Campus Verlag GmbH, Frankfurt am Main.
Typesetting: le-tex xerif
Typesetting font: Alegreya

Printed in the United States of America

www.campus.de

Contents

Researching *Weltbeziehung*: Interdisciplinary approaches to self—world relations between humans, objects, and beyond 7
Bettina Hollstein, Hartmut Rosa, Jörg Rüpke

I   Conceptual Perspectives

Property as the Modern Form of *Weltbeziehung*: Reflections on the structural change of possessive forms of relating to the world 19
Hartmut Rosa

Relationship to the Good: On the world-opening and world-connecting power of virtues 37
Kathi Beier, Dietmar Mieth

Three Types of Fatalistic Practice 63
Andreas Pettenkofer

Reconstructing an Impartial and Pluralistic Notion of Progress in Contexts of Diversity 101
Achim Kemmerling

II Comparative Perspectives

How Can Worldviews Be Compared? The pragmatic maxim and intellectual honesty 121
Hermann Deuser, Markus Kleinert

"Theorizing Across Traditions": Social science as a polyphonic encounter 129
Martin Fuchs, Antje Linkenbach, Beatrice Renzi

The Cultural Meaning of "Market" in China and the Western tradition: Worlds apart? 157
Carsten Herrmann-Pillath, Qian Zhao

Triumphant Utopia—Shabby Bourgeois World—Totalitarianism: Transmuting visions of real existing socialism in Eastern interpretations of Walter Benjamin's Marxism 189
Gábor Gángó

Relating to Other Worlds: Religious spatiality and the beyond of the city in ancient cities' dealing with the dead 215
Jörg Rüpke

III Practical Perspectives

Values of Exchange, Values of Sharing: The ambivalence of economic *Weltbeziehungen*, explained for the example of carsharing 235
Christoph Henning

The Transformation of the Refugee Category and the Dialectics of Solidarity in Europe 259
Nancy Alhachem

Living World Relations—Institutes for Advanced Study as places for resonant relationships 279
Bettina Hollstein

Researching *Weltbeziehung*: Interdisciplinary approaches to self—world relations between humans, objects, and beyond[1]

Bettina Hollstein, Hartmut Rosa, Jörg Rüpke

The research programme "Attraction, Repulsion, Indifference—a comparative cultural analysis of world relations" follows on from the interdisciplinary, historically comparative cultural and social science research that has been pursued by the members and fellows of the Max Weber Centre for Advanced Cultural and Social Studies *(Max-Weber-Kolleg)* over the course of the past twenty-five years. This collaborative research effort pursues the goal of opening up innovative perspectives with a specific approach first developed by Hartmut Rosa. It has its roots in interpretive sociology (Max Weber), theory of action, and a relational sociology that is shaped by concepts from Karl Marx's reflections on alienation, through phenomenological approaches like that of Maurice Merleau-Ponty thematizing corporeality and human bodies, to Bruno Latour's networks of things and humans.

Over the years, we have made an effort to overcome Eurocentric and presentist approaches as much as narrow functionalist or cognitivist views. This entails the challenging balance of employing and confronting philosophical analysis with universalist claims, with comparative studies of phenomena and their cultural contexts across epochs and continents. In this way, those involved in the programme and its various sub-projects—from groups studying medieval philosophy, early modern natural law and Kierkegaardian theology to larger research networks analyzing religious

---

[1] The editors are grateful to Linda Finnigan and Henry Jansen for proofreading the texts and to Isabelle Lamperti for editing the manuscript. The publication is co-funded by the Deutsche Forschungsgemeinschaft (DFG, German Research Foundation) – SFB TRR 294 – 42463867 and GRK 2283/2 – 313147291 – and the University of Erfurt.

© The author/s 2023, published by Campus Verlag, Open Access: CC BY-SA 4.0
Bettina Hollstein, Hartmut Rosa, Jörg Rüpke (eds.), "Weltbeziehung"
DOI: 10.12907/978-3-593-45587-7_001

individualizations, property orders, ancient and contemporary ritual or the nexus of religion and urbanity—want to go beyond cutting-edge research in their fields and disciplines in order to jointly make a contribution to the grand societal challenges of the present. In the 2020s, this includes understanding the role of material, ideal, social, and cultural conditions for successful coexistence in pluralistic societies, the creation of common languages for the narrative development of cultural heritage, and the understanding of essential value complexes in modernity guiding people facing the challenges of overboarding state-violence or climate change.

This book is part of this effort. It is a review of where we are and a reflection on where we want to go; it is an account of what the programme can achieve and an invitation to join this enterprise. In some detail, it demonstrates how the sociology of *Weltbeziehungen* permits new insights in different disciplines and how it can be made fruitful for various areas of application. Following this introduction, a first part examines some basic concepts that are of particular importance for modern societies and the way we relate to the world, such as property (Hartmut Rosa), attitudes and virtues (Kathi Beier and Dietmar Mieth), practices (Andreas Pettenkofer), and progress (Achim Kemmerling). In a second part, comparative perspectives come into play. Starting with a systematic question on the possibility of comparing worldviews (Hermann Deuser and Markus Kleinert), reflections on and examples of comparisons beyond Western modernity are presented, such as regarding the need for decolonising social science research, partly with reference to India (Martin Fuchs, Antje Linkenbach and Beatrice Renzi), the concept and cultural meaning of "market" in China (Carsten Herrmann-Pillath, Qian Zhao), an alternative interpretation of Walter Benjamin from an East European perspective (Gábor Gángó), and the handling of death in ancient cities (Jörg Rüpke). Practical conclusions for and from the cultural and social sciences are drawn in the third part, for example with regard to practices of sharing and exchange (Christoph Henning), the policies related to the concept of "refugee" (Nancy Alhachem), and the design of research sites such as Institutes for Advanced Study (Bettina Hollstein). We will outline the individual chapters in more detail at the end of our introduction.

So, what do we mean by *Weltbeziehung*? Part of any comparative programme is a confrontation of the very terms employed in such an interpretive endeavour. In the English language, "relations" and "relationships" are extremely broad concepts, too broad to speak for themselves. "Self—world relations", as we have phrased it on several occasions before, seem to presuppose a consolidated concept of the self that we have attempted to deconstruct in an earlier research programme on religious individualization and de-individualization. And "world" is a term laden in very different and frequently unsuitable manners. Thus, we propose to use the German concept of *Weltbeziehung* to point to the connectedness of self and world and the concept of self resulting from such relationships. At the same time, the term unequivocally calls for filling in the world-pole of the relation and relationships. Following classical phenomenology, we start from people but, in adding relationality, we do not overlook the agency of all that constitutes world and the mutuality of the relationships established. "Worlding" is as much what people do as what is done to people.

But let us start from the latter. People first find themselves physically placed in a spatial world that has meaning for them: before they have a worldview, they have a sense of the presence of a world. The way people feel related to this world, how they want to and can act in it and what they expect, fear, or hope from it depends, of course, simultaneously on their self-image, on their ideas of who they are and what their tasks, needs, possibilities, and goals are in the world. People are characterized by the fact that they are forced to take a position on the things and affairs of the world as positively or negatively significant. Subjects orient themselves in the world by means of a "map" that shows them what exists and how things relate to each other (Taylor 1989). At the same time, they locate themselves on this map and determine their direction of movement in biographical foresight and hindsight, to which they then react by attempting to "lead" their lives.

"Resonance" can be used as a specific analytical concept which describes a particular form of relationship between a subject and the "world." The world here might comprise other subjects, animals, plants, artefacts, but also "transcendent relations" with comprehensive entities such as space, time (and the temporalities of past or future), and what has been called "meta-persons" like gods and God or abstract concepts credited with enormous agency like cosmos or nature. Resonance then is defined by a two-way "loaded" connection where the subject feels touched, moved, or thrilled by some internal contact to an outer source, a connection which is not just causal or instrumental, but imbued with a deeper "meaning," even where this meaning remains unarticulated. At the same time, however, the subject is not just passively moved or touched, but answers with an active internal or external expression: he or she reaches out to respond to the "call" such that the relationship between subject and world takes on a responsive, proto-dialogical character (Rosa 2019, 2020). In many societies, this form of contact is ritualistically established and culturally engrained: for example, it might manifest itself between believers and a priest or an image, amulet, or sacrificial victim; it is institutionalized in "sacred ground" or the "kairos," the right moment of a concert or a "date" (Rüpke 2021a, 2021b). Such "axes of resonance," often closely entangled with specific materialities, and "second-order resonances" building on memories of mind-shaking experiences can be identified even for periods and contexts where adequate experiential data are lacking. Thus, it is the shared ambition and conviction of our research programme that resonant relationships can be analytically distinguished from other, e.g., purely causal or instrumental forms of *Weltbeziehung*, in which the relationship remains mute or silent (but perhaps fully operational and thus simply "indifferent") or is even experienced as hostile, as "repulsive."

What kinds of new perspectives and insights can we gain through the analysis of *Weltbeziehungen*? Phenomenological research by scholars such as Maurice Merleau-Ponty (1945), Otto Bollnow (1963), Herrmann Schmitz (1964–80), Iris Marion Young (1993) or Thomas Fuchs (2000) has shown that people perceive their own position in time and space in drastically different ways. They invariably situate themselves in relation to fellow human beings, animals and plants, artefacts, events, as well as invisible beings and powers and the world at large. But the process of positioning and relating varies significantly between individuals and between cultural traditions and social formations, as our own data on ancient and modern contexts, and the wide range of European and Indian practices and experiences demonstrate. This does not hinder but invites the comparative approach indicated above. After all, one of the most important intellectual starting points of the research programme is the idea that *Weltbeziehungen* constitute a pivotal cluster of factors not only in trying to understand individual actions but in explaining distinct cultural and social formations.

Empirical and historical analyses conducted so far have already led to substantial insights into the ways "resonance" is experienced and enacted by different actors and how practices are institutionalized that raise the probability of resonant relationships or narrow the field in which they are sought. Dispositional resonance is fundamentally important here as a basic, common and habituative attitude of a subject towards the world, being prepared to engage in resonant relationships, to face the world with receptiveness and confidence and to accept the necessary vulnerability of itself.

This relational approach has proven fruitful for a more nuanced appreciation of the formation and effects of rituals beyond the state of the art as demonstrated by the research consortium of the international graduate school based at the University of Graz and at the Max-Weber-Kolleg.[2] The analysis of resonant *Weltbeziehungen* allows us to enter the realm of concrete practices beyond the level of worldviews. This enables the emancipation of the corporeality of experience and the meaning of material objects and artefacts from the level of cognitive and propositional interpretations. In this way, the cultural spheres of resonance constituted or stabilised by ritual and cultic practices can be examined anew by looking at the specifically generated resonance sensitivities and the axes of resonance established by them. Our findings also suggest that resonant relationships are not fully created once and for all time but can become indifferent or are even completely lost due to individual or cultural factors in the whole range of self, social, object, and transcendent relations.

Ritual practices not only establish relationships to parts of the world like places, things, people, and transcendent entities, as the heuristic usage of the concept of resonance seems to suggest. Evidently, such practices *constitute* segments of the world at the same time, towards which attitudes of indifference or repulsion are generated. If the assumption is correct that resonance is only possible against the background of overwhelmingly non-transformable, alien, and indifferent or even hostile world segments, then in such practices individual and cultural *Weltbeziehungen* are configured in their entirety. The institutionalization of resonance practices inevitably harbours the danger of their solidification and reification: by making "resonances" ritually (and personally) available and bringing them under control, as it were, they inevitably threaten to turn into "mute" routine *Weltbeziehungen* in which the ritual practices lose their resonance-creating power. Again, analytical interests are therefore directed as much at the production of accessibility as at the preservation of uncontrollability—and at historical processes of corresponding transformations.

That said, we need to nuance the very concept of resonance. Rosa's starting point was a definition of resonance as a kind of "peak experience" that can

---

[2] More information concerning the International Graduate School "Resonant Self–World Relations in socio-religious practices" can be found here: https://www.uni-erfurt.de/en/max-weber-kolleg/forschung/forschungsgruppen-und-stellen/research-groups/igs-resonant-self-world-relations.

inform individual action as well as social structures. The mode of resonance qualifies *Weltbeziehung* in a specific way, according to which four characteristics must be fulfilled: namely *affection* (the subject is touched, moved or seized by a source experienced as independent); *self-efficacy* (the subject experiences itself as efficacious at the same time in the sense that it can reach or move the other side as well); *transformation* (in the experience of mutual reaching out and touching, both sides are transformed and emerge changed); and *uncontrollability* (the resonance relationship is uncontrollable as it can neither be forced nor excluded and is always open-ended).

Our volume develops within such a framework. The first part's review of fundamental *concepts* in the light of *Weltbeziehung* is opened by Hartmut Rosa's piece on property. (Private) property, he argues, is one of the most basic institutions of modern society. It produces a very specific form of relating to things, to other human beings and towards the self, and by doing this, it defines the modern *Weltbeziehung* in the objective, the subjective, and the social dimensions simultaneously. This property-induced form of *Weltbeziehung*, however, proves to be highly problematic under contemporary ecological, technological, and political conditions.

Kathi Beier and Dietmar Mieth, in turn, deal with virtues as a specific form of relationships with the "good." It is, they argue, the contribution of virtues to produce stable relationships of people with what is good and right that is fundamental for *Weltbeziehungen* that are resonant rather than indifferent or repulsive. Virtues form bridges between the personal and the social and demand institutional support, that is, space for training and exercising virtues that allow people to develop orientations which habituate such resonance. Virtues are, the authors conclude, making their demands not just on individuals but also on societies.

Andreas Pettenkofer discusses in his chapter "Three Types of Fatalistic Practice" how treating *Weltbeziehungen* as objects of social research helps go beyond some assumptions that current theories of society take for granted. His example are fatalistic modes of understanding (which are typically discounted, because our standard theories tend to assume that "modern" social practices are sustained by the idea of an open future). The chapter shows how the existence and the stability of several highly consequential forms of political activity become easier to explain if one recognizes that they are profoundly shaped by fatalistic ways of relating to the world.

In his chapter, "Reconstructing an Impartial and Pluralistic Notion of Progress in Contexts of Diversity", Achim Kemmerling analyses a key concept of modernity, namely progress and its temporal dimension within political decision processes. He reconstructs progress as a necessary idea for decision making in contexts of diversity. The idea of pluralistic and impartial progress can work as a tool for allowing policymaking under conditions of human diversity. But it requires special analytical considerations: a temporal dimension, a normative dimension, and a symbolic dimension. Kemmerling pleads for a notion of progress that is slower and harder to achieve but ideally avoids the typical pitfalls of standard tools in accelerated decision-making. In doing so, this contribution adds to our understanding of how to address global challenges in their own time.

In the second set of chapters, we look beyond the Western present in explicit *comparison*. Hermann Deuser and Markus Kleinert start with addressing the principal question: "How Can Worldviews Be Compared?" They use a pragmatist approach and exemplify the difficulty of comparing worldviews by the topic of faith and knowledge, in the comparison of religious and secular worldviews. They show an American and a European reflection on the problem of referencing and comparing worldviews associated with the names of William James and Max Weber and point to the role of intellectual honesty as a disposition for constant self-reflection, for the thematization of one's own worldview.

"Theorizing Across Traditions: Social science as a polyphonic encounter", by Martin Fuchs, Antje Linkenbach, and Beatrice Renzi, demonstrates the need and the potential of a conscious interaction and entanglement of different strands of thinking across a post-colonial divide. Engaging with decolonization as intellectual project, and starting from a reflection on the implicit Eurocentric biases of important strands of sociological discourse, they strongly advocate the "attempt of de-centring and pluralizing sociological discourses and conceptualizations cross-culturally." Seen from the perspective of *Weltbeziehung* the theoretical concept formation in the social sciences must be a result of a cross-categorial dialogue between Western and non-Western historic-intellectual traditions.

Carsten Herrmann-Pillath and Qian Zhao compare the cultural meaning of the term "market" in China and the Western tradition of the term and institution. They point to a long tradition of understanding economy as part of good statecraft. Relations established by practices of exchange are part and parcel of the good relations between individuals, families, and the society at large, which is also the object of good administration and government. Against this background the concept of the "socialist market" is traditional rather than revolutionary and certainly contradicting mainstream understandings of liberalist conceptions of market economy. Yet "Western" must not be equated with a narrow range of anglophone economic thinking: Chinese ideas of property as a means to ensure the commonwealth and European, in particular Hegelian, traditions do converge if the latter's embeddedness in a larger ethical framework of society and the state is acknowledged.

Gábor Gángó's chapter entitled "Triumphant Utopia—Shabby Bourgeois World—Totalitarianism" crosses perspectives not between (South) Asia and Europe but between Eastern and Western Europe. It deals with different interpretations of Walter Benjamin's Marxism from the early 1970s in two countries of the Soviet Bloc, East Germany and Hungary. Similar to the debates in the GDR of the early 1970s, also Sándor Radnóti's road to Walter Benjamin was situated within the context of the polemic between the Frankfurt School and the review *alternative* regarding the appropriation of Benjamin's work. In contrast to the German scene, Radnóti sought a third way by presenting Benjamin as a theoretical support of the political orientation towards democratic socialism. In comparison with the reception in the GDR, the contribution reconstructs the intellectual constellation that made Radnóti's decision possible as well as the subsequent "Frankfurtization" of Benjamin's interpretation, which absorbed the later approaches of the Budapest School to Benjamin as well. Radnóti's advocacy of collective culture as a vehicle of pluralist and resonant structures poses a challenge to the comparative theory of East European totalitarianism and its reverberations in current Critical Theory in the form of forced resonance.

Jörg Rüpke develops an analysis of cities of the ancient Mediterranean world. "Relating to Other Worlds" analyzes how religious practices shape *Weltbeziehungen* in urban contexts. The focus is on a relationship fundamental for all inhabitants, namely to the dead, and dead ancestors in particular. With a framework of relational analysis, the chapter demonstrates that religion offers a toolbox for establishing a complex web of relations, to spaces, to people, to a beyond that is conceptually combining distance and contiguity. Burial practices and funerary rites show the working of such relations within the framework of an urbanity that amply employs the continuous membership of dead family for claiming social positions and at the same time conceptually excludes them from urban space proper.

In the last part of the volume, more practical perspectives are developed: Christoph Henning shows in his chapter on "Values of Exchange, Values of

Sharing: The Ambivalence of Economic *Weltbeziehung*, explained for the example of Carsharing," how exchange relations, and sharing relations as their counterpart, shape *Weltbeziehung* in the economic world. He examines the different social imaginaries related to "good" or "bad" exchange and "good" or "bad" sharing. Using the example of car-sharing, he differentiates various types of ownership and related forms of *Weltbeziehung* resulting in different practical effects for the ecosystem. The comparison of these effects illustrates that sharing is not per se an alternative to property, but that some sharing practices limit the power of property, while others do not. In order to grasp the differences, it is central to differentiate property structures[3] involved in practices of sharing and their effects on the *Weltbeziehung* of the users.

The next chapter by Nancy Alhachem is entitled "The Transformation of the Refugee Category and the Dialectics of Solidarity in Europe." She reconstructs how the notion of "refugee," established about 70 years ago to protect Europeans who were fleeing Nazi-fascist regimes and the aftermath of the Second World War, developed to a concept that carries racist prejudices that became visible with the "refugee crises" following the summer of 2015 in Germany. As already mentioned, dispositional resonance is fundamentally important as a basic attitude of a subject towards the world, being prepared to engage in resonant relationships and to face the world with receptiveness and confidence. Alhachem shows for the field of refugee policy how these dispositions changed over time and how they shape lived everyday solidarity in practice.

The last contribution "Living World Relations—Institutes for Advanced Study as places for resonant relationships" by Bettina Hollstein uses the concepts of *Weltbeziehung* and "creativity of action" (Hans Joas) to analyse how resonant relationships can be created in the world of science through specific institutions, namely Institutes for Advanced Study (IAS). IAS were established to enhance inter alia independent research, interdisciplinarity, creativity, and innovation. They are characterized by collegiality, tranquility, and inter-relationality. Drawing on the example of the Max-Weber-Kolleg, Hollstein shows that resonant relationships allowing for creative interdisciplinary research can be observed and enabled, but not enforced.

---

3 Concerning this topic see also Rosa in this volume.

Works cited

Bollnow, Otto Friedrich (1963). *Mensch und Raum*. Stuttgart: Kohlhammer.
Fuchs, Thomas (2000). *Leib, Raum, Person. Entwurf einer phänomenologischen Anthropologie*. Stuttgart: Klett Cotta.
Merleau-Ponty, Maurice (1945). *Phénoménologie de la perception*. Paris: Gallimard.
Rosa, Hartmut (2019). *Resonance. A Sociology of Our Relationship to the World*. Cambridge: Polity Press.
Rosa, Hartmut (2020). *The Uncontrollability of the World*. Cambridge: Polity Press.
Rüpke, Jörg (2021a). *Religion and its History: A Critical Inquiry*. London: Routledge.
Rüpke, Jörg (2021b). *Ritual als Resonanzerfahrung*. Religionswissenschaft heute 15. Stuttgart: Kohlhammer.
Schmitz, Hermann (1964–80). *Das System der Philosophie*. 10 Bde. Bonn: Bouvier Verlag.
Taylor, Charles (1989). *Sources of the Self. The Making of Modern Identity*. Cambridge MA: Harvard University Press.
Young, Iris Marion (1993). Werfen wie ein Mädchen. Eine Phänomenologie weiblichen Körperverhaltens, weiblicher Motilität und Räumlichkeit. *Deutsche Zeitschrift für Philosophie*, 41, 4, 707–25.

1
Conceptual Perspectives

Property as the Modern Form of *Weltbeziehung*: Reflections on the structural change of possessive forms of relating to the world[1]

Hartmut Rosa

1. Introduction

Property is not simply one social institution among many that constitute the social formation of modernity. Rather, it forms one, if not *the*, basic institution on which not only the organisational structure of the economy and the world of work rest but also that of the welfare state and cultural institutions, family connections, education, and health care in equal measure. The acquisition and possession, securing and (re)distribution, transfer and conversion of property—be it material assets, financial assets, capital assets, or immaterial property titles—are at the centre of both the production and administrative operations of modernity. Both the sphere of consumption and that of production are organised and oriented in terms of property rights and forms of ownership. Precisely because this is so, the orientations, aspirations, and sensibilities associated with it are so deeply rooted, habitualised, and naturalised that not only the social sciences, especially sociology, but even society itself seems to be characterized by a peculiar "forgetfulness of property." This is evident at almost all levels of social life: when the Central and Eastern European states began to fundamentally change their economic form around 1989, to them, *the market* appeared to be the core of the (desired) capitalist economy. It became their top priority to set its dynamics in motion. The question of ownership distribution, however, seemed to them to be absolutely secondary: it was not important who owned the enterprises (workers' cooperatives, municipalities, small businesses, Western

---

[1] © The author/s 2023, published by Campus Verlag, Open Access: CC BY-SA 4.0
Bettina Hollstein, Hartmut Rosa, Jörg Rüpke (eds.), "Weltbeziehung"
DOI: 10.12907/978-3-593-45587-7_002

investors, large corporations), it was much more important to those in political power to set in motion the spiral-like productive dynamics of escalation that are central to capitalism.[2] To a certain extent, this even applies to China's economic transformation since Deng Xiaoping.[3] A very similar pattern of interpretation could be observed when the massive neoliberal privatisation of both the health and care sectors and the media sector took effect in Western countries at about the same time. The decisive factor was that the services should be provided efficiently and reliably; the question of ownership was secondary.[4] Similarly, the distribution disputes in capitalist societies routinely focus on income structures and thus on the remuneration for labour, while the increasingly unequal property and wealth relations are hardly ever the subject of debate or even consideration.[5] And even at the micro level of social life, it can be observed that property structures are strangely excluded or ignored compared to procedural questions of ownership and operation. One example of this is when couples are not at all clear about who owns what in the property relations established by them and between them (who actually owns what in a joint household?); however, these issues become highly relevant especially in the event of divorce.[6]

At the same time, however, there is an almost monomaniacal "obsession with property" under modern capitalist conditions when it comes to acquiring property titles at all possible levels of existence—to *buy* something, to *generate income*, to *obtain entitlement rights*. Regardless of that, however, it seems as if the basic background structure of modern society, its property form, is lost to view and forgotten wherever it is not directly contested and dynamically "liquidated"; where it forms structures that have coagulated, as it were, out of sight of the actors. This is as remarkable as it is deplorable because property is of enormous scope and significance for the self-understanding

---

2 This is the subject of sub-project B07 (Property concepts and property conflicts in the privatisation process), headed by Joachim von Puttkamer, of the Collaborative Research Centre "Structural change in property" at the universities of Jena and Erfurt. Cf. Peters 2023.

3 The sub-project C01 "Hybrid property order in state capitalism", led by Carsten Herrmann-Pillath, is conducting research on this, also at universities of Jena and Erfurt.

4 The results are being analysed in sub-project C05, led by Silke van Dyk, "Conflicts over the public sphere and the future of the commons: Property relations in the context of welfare state transformation."

5 Distribution and class conflicts are the subject of sub-project B05 ("Property, inequality and class formation in socio-ecological transformation conflicts"), led by Klaus Dörre.

6 This is a striking finding of sub-project B06 ("Property inequality in the private sphere") led by Kathrin Leuze and Sylka Scholz (Althaber et al. 2023).

of modern society and its dominant form of *Weltbeziehung*. The basic thesis of this article is that every social formation establishes a very specific way of "being-in-the-world" for the subjects, a very specific set of relations to the world *(Weltbeziehung)* that is formed out of characteristic ways of experiencing, acting in and connecting to the world. With the concept of *Weltbeziehung*, I am trying to describe a form of habitualised experience and orientation that is anchored in the body and largely exists below the level of cognitive operations, consisting of a specific field of sensibility (or focus of attention) and a correlating structure of will (or pattern of intentionality). *Weltbeziehung* thus means a specific form of (passive-receptive) experience of the world and (active-intentional) orientation to the world. These patterns are ultimately only fully revealed in an analysis of subjectivity such as that provided by phenomenology (Zahavi 2007, 73; 2002; on this now also Rosa 2023). The overall structure of such relationships then defines the basic relation to the world *(Weltbeziehung)* of an individual or a community.

At least for modern societies and dominant patterns of subjectivity in those societies, three specific dimensions of *Weltbeziehung* prove to be constitutive; namely *social relations, relations* to things or objects, and *self relations*. It is no coincidence that Jürgen Habermas and Karl Popper, for example, agree in dividing in an onto-epistemological way, as it were, what we encounter as world, into an objective, a social, and a subjective world (Habermas 1981, 149; Popper 1973).[7] The field of sensibility and the structure of the will of the subjects then differ accordingly, depending on which of these three aspects of the world they are confronted with. And here it becomes apparent that the institution of property is of cardinal importance for all three dimensions of *Weltbeziehung*. Property establishes a specific form of relationship to things or objects, a characteristic mode of *social* relation and a particular pattern of *self*-relation. In what follows, I would like to elaborate first on these three forms of *Weltbeziehungen*, in order to clarify in the next step how much and in how far these property-mediated patterns of relations are changing in late-modern contemporary society, and finally, in the last step, to provide some insights into what other forms of *Weltbeziehung* are conceivable as a result of an (ongoing) structural change of property.

---

7 Popper, however, does not speak of a "social world," but he does identify (alongside the subjective and physical worlds) a (socially) "objectified" world of human thought and action.

2. Property as a form of existence: social-, thing- and self-relation

In the first place, the institution of property obviously constitutes and configures a specific relationship to things. In making a thing my property by buying it, for example, I acquire largely unrestricted rights of disposal over it. Property thus characterises a form of placing the world at my disposal: *I can do what I want and when I want it* with my bicycle, my land, and my trousers. I can use them, convert them, lend them, sell them, destroy them, simply leave them lying around, etc., and at the same time, they are protected from *access by others*. I have them at my *free disposal*. Of course, we immediately see that this usually does not mean *unlimited* disposal: I am not allowed to blow my car up; I am not allowed to drive it anywhere I want. Nor am I allowed to build what and how I want on my land, etc., and even if I own a company, I don't have permission to do with it simply as I please. But, with these restrictions, we already are basically touching on the social relations and the social bond of property. Yet, as for the relation to objects, this does not change the fact that we make things available to us through the institution of property.[8]

In becoming "my thing" in this way, however, a second form of relation to objects is established at the same time, as Aristotle already knew, namely, a *relationship of care* (Aristotle, Politics, 1262b—1263a). Because this is *my* land, or *my* car, it is important to me that they remain intact, that they are not damaged, are preserved in their value and usability, or even for their own sake. For example, if someone knocks over our bike, we exclaim loudly, "Hey, that's my bike!". The things we have at our disposal as property tend to be "close to our hearts." However, it is important to notice that there are forms of (capitalist) property to which this does not apply at all, such as *shares*. The specific feature of capital ownership seems to be that precisely this conditional relation of care does *not* arise in this case.[9] I will return to this below.

---

[8] At this starting point, I will refrain from differentiating between possession and property, because it is, to begin with, irrelevant to the phenomenal perspective adopted here. Nevertheless, I agree with Emil Angehrn's observation that *possession* primarily defines a relation to a thing and thus also affects the relation to the self, while *property* primarily describes a social relation. I will return to this in a moment. Cf. Angehrn 1989, here especially 96 f.

[9] Georg Simmel elaborated on this difference between abstract and concrete value in a phenomenologically differentiated way in his *Philosophie des Geldes* (Philosophy of money (1989). Karl Marx and, in a different way, Max Weber also substantiated it on the basis of economics.

The paradigmatic example of such a property-like relation to an object, which has been used again and again in the economic and philosophical discussion of property since the time of John Locke, Adam Smith, and David Ricardo, is one's own plot of land and the little house or flat one owns. "My home is my castle" means that my dwelling is at my disposal, that I take care of it and look after it, that I "appropriate" *(anverwandeln)* it to myself (certainly in Heidegger's sense of "dwelling" *(Wohnen)* as well) (Heidegger 2022), and that it is protected from access by others, including the state.

With this, however, it is now obvious to what extent property simultaneously configures a social relation, or, rather, a whole network of social relations. Subjects encounter each other as owners and thus as competitors for scarce goods to which they want to acquire rights of disposal and custody. In this context, property primarily establishes relations of exclusion: if something is mine, others—individually and collectively—have no access rights to it. It is literally "no longer their business." They can, however, encounter me as customers or clients or as buyers or sellers with whom I do business—this involves the negotiation and redistribution of property, such as when I sell my car or my land (or my block of shares). A certain social obligation then arises in a quasi-natural way from the fact that my use (or misuse or non-use) of property has consequences for others. This includes ecological ones, such as when I let my car rust in the garden, and oil and petrol seep into the groundwater. But this does not change the fact that property first and foremost establishes an exclusive relation of disposal and care.

It is through these property-mediated relations to things and others, however, that a specific form of subjective self-relation is constituted, too: the field of sensibility and the structure of the will of the subjects is directed towards themselves as *owners of specific sections of the world*. In other words, property creates a possessive self-relation, the basic structure of which Hegel already explained in his *Philosophy of Right*. He sharply analyses how the social relations and the self-relation of modern subjects are intertwined when he states:

"The person, distinguishing himself from himself, relates himself to *another* person, and indeed both exist for each other only as owners. Their identity, which exists *as such*, acquires existence through the property of the one becoming the property of the other with a common will and preservation of their right—in the *contract*." (Hegel 1986a, 98)

And in his *Lectures on the History of Philosophy*, he pointedly states: "Property is a possession that belongs to me as this person, in which my person as such comes into existence, into reality" (Hegel 1986b, 126).

Strictly speaking, the property form of the self-relation already results logically from the property form of the relation to the other: self-relation and relation to the (outer) world are always directly correlated and intertwined; every self-relation takes a diversion, so to speak, via a relation to the world outside. This means that modern subjects not only encounter each other but also themselves as owners: *I am the one who owns this house, this car, this job, as well as this coat, this record of music, this book, this jug.* We extend ourselves, as it were, into the world through the things we own. My self-confidence and my self-perception are shaped, for example, by the fact that I live in this flat if I am its owner—but also by the fact that this flat belongs to me if I am its owner and do not live there. Although the effects of (permanent) ownership and property on the self-relation are not the same, they both have a formative influence. We can state that, as a social process, subjectification to a significant degree takes place through the acquisition of property—for example, specific clothing, shoes, books, records, vehicles, digital devices, later perhaps land and residential property, etc. The question "Who am I?" cannot be answered in modern society without reference to property. Subjectivity arises from the interplay of relations of disposal and care that define us as subjects and translates into claims or rights and responsibilities.

As a young child learns to distinguish "mine" from "yours," his or her sense of self starts to take shape—and it acquires individual traits in the process of adolescence, when the young person begins to demarcate his or her own material, cultural, and spiritual "realm." Without a doubt, the decision to acquire a certain article of clothing, a particular trainer, book, vehicle, computer game, game controller, tattoo (or whatever else is perceived to be relevant property) proves to be highly relevant for the process of identity formation. *Appropriation* is the process by which a thing becomes property. In the theoretical tradition that runs from Hegel via T.H. Green to contemporary property ethics, we therefore find the conviction that without the right and the practice of freely disposing of certain parts of the world, no subject capable of action can develop because it is the possibilities of experiencing care, planning, and self-efficacy associated with property which provide the chance for "appropriation" (*Anverwandlung*), i.e., for the transformative shaping of the self and the world (cf., for example, Wesche 2014; Brocker 1992).

"Let the individual own nothing but himself, and he will not have a self to own," Henry Jones stated pointedly already in 1910 (Jones 1910, 94).

The "possessive individualism" so harshly criticised by C.B. Macpherson (Macpherson 1962), according to which the modern individual constitutes his or her self-relation as self-*ownership*, is in this sense not only the dominant ideology of political liberalism but the embodied and habitualised *Weltbeziehung* of modernity. For example, the modern individual possesses school degrees ("I *have* A-levels"), offices ("I *hold* the office of second-in-command in the voluntary fire brigade"), professional titles ("I *have* a profession as a doctor") and family titles ("I *have* a husband and three children"), and it is through these relations that his or her self-relation is constituted.

In sum, these three dimensions of modern world-relations, constituted in the form of property, result in a *possessive overall world relation (Weltbeziehung)* that differs from historically or culturally alternative forms of *Weltbeziehung*, not least in that the modern subject even seems to *possess* his or her thoughts and feelings, moods and inclinations, illnesses and abilities. We tend to say: *I have these thoughts, these feelings, these inclinations, these strengths and weaknesses, or even a disease.* And it is difficult to imagine an alternative here. It could well turn out, however, that such qualities were culturally and historically conceived over far longer periods as *participatory states* rather than *possessive ones*. Phenomenologists from Maurice Merleau-Ponty to Herman Schmitz, for example, have repeatedly pointed out that the notion of "feelings" as located inside a person may be a cardinal modern error: they can be more coherently conceptualised as something "extended and shared" between self and world (Schmitz 2019, 2). In this alternative way of thinking, individuals are afflicted, affected, or involved in feelings, moods, or illnesses rather than "having" them. Experts on Japanese and Chinese speech and thought from Heidegger via Rolf Elberfeld (2012) to Francois Jullien (2022) have, moreover, repeatedly discussed the tendency of Asian thought towards participatory *involvement* in a dynamic world, and many varieties of Renaissance thought also portray self and world as mutually interwoven — *dynamically interpenetrated* — in such a way that fixative, attributive relations of possession are hardly conceptualisable (Taylor 2009).

3. The incipient structural change in property in the 21st century

We do not necessarily have to turn, however, to non-European cultural traditions if we want to try to think of alternative forms of *Weltbeziehung*. In fact, according to the thesis put forward in this contribution, a revolution concerning the possessive world relation *(Weltbeziehung)* constituted in this way is currently emerging. The causes behind this can be found in technical, economic, political, and psychological changes that are happening at the same time and affect all three dimensions of relation — relationships to objects, social relations, and the self relation — equally. Property, it could be said, is no longer what it once was, and therefore its structural function and its cultural meaning are changing (Schuppert 2023).

What exactly does this postulate of a structural change in property mean? The thesis is that the habitualized modern forms of property have become questionable and are in flux under the pressure of current technological developments, economic wealth accumulation in the private sector and debt accumulation on the state side, as well as from geostrategic changes in both extensional and intensional as well as temporal and spatial respects. In an *extensional* sense, property structures are changing insofar as things that were not property before are suddenly subject to being owned — such as planets that turn out to be sources of raw materials; the wind, insofar as it is a source of energy; motherhood, insofar as it can be marketed; DNA sequences that can be patented — or, conversely, things lose or at least change their property form. This latter applies to cultural knowledge, for example, when it is no longer collected in expensive encyclopaedias that can be purchased privately, such as the *Brockhaus* or the *Encyclopaedia Britannica*, but can be found in collective, publicly accessible sources such as Wikipedia, which refuses to attribute and market entries as intellectual property because they are of a collective nature.

In general, there is a tendency for the most highly valued cultural goods—the music of Beethoven or Bach, the works of Goethe or Shakespeare, etc.—to become public and freely accessible. That is, they are no longer to be appropriated in the form of private property by buying the books or the recordings, whereas, however, the necessary *infrastructure* (digital devices and streaming services) are expensive.

But this is also obviously changing the intensional meaning of property with respect to social practices as well as for the processes of subjectification. First, it can be noted that, with regard to cultural goods but to some extent even to the material bearers of the *Weltbeziehung* and our processing of the world, a tendency towards a significant change from *property rights* to *rights of use* can be observed: Subjects no longer buy the things by which they subjectify themselves culturally but acquire temporary rights of use for them. This applies, for example, to music as well as films or books which are accessed and used through streaming services; but analogous practices are beginning to establish themselves in other areas as well so that this tendency can now also be observed for clothing and vehicles (from the scooter left on the street corner to the leased or shared automobile and to the evening dress)—not to mention the digital end devices that remain the property of the provider and are regularly exchanged by him.

This has profound consequences for all three dimensions of *Weltbeziehung*—and thus for the late modern way of *being in the world* as a whole: with regard to relations to objects, it means that the relation of care disappears almost completely. The care and provision of "devices" and "products" is the task and responsibility of the manufacturers and providers—while the right of disposal for customers is clearly restricted: only temporary rights of use are acquired which can expire at any time if the service is terminated or payment obligations are not met. But there are no rights of transmission, marketing, alteration, destruction, etc. In fact, in late-modern capitalist societies, the producers of branded products are systematically dependent on the *absence* of close relationships between users and "things" that lead to consumers being so attached to their appliances, vehicles, or clothes that they do not want to get rid of them and replace them with new ones because they formed intense relations of care with them. Instead, customers are now supposed to keep replacing material things at ever shorter intervals, from smartphones to refrigerators to bicycles, while remaining "loyal" to the brands and service infrastructures.

In terms of *social* relations, cultural and knowledge goods in particular are no longer rival or scarce: they can be multiplied and disseminated without restriction and free of charge (this applies to almost all digital products such as audio recordings, books, films, computer games, software), even though their initial development is of course resource-intensive. This means, however, that such things no longer create competitive social relations, unless, of course, rivalry is artificially created through pecuniary or other access restrictions. Exclusive social relations thus shift from the products that carry the cultural meanings to the material and digital infrastructures as *prerequisites* for their use (not everyone can afford Apple products, Amazon

Prime, or Netflix). If property is understood as the connection between the relations of disposal and care, then it seems obvious that we are dealing with a significant change here.

It is true, of course, that this shift concerns only a small part of material reality and thus of the *Weltbeziehung* mediated by objects in late modern societies. Housing, food, clothing, furnishings, etc. are still predominantly acquired, provided for, and used in the form of private property. But there can be no doubt that the transformations occur in an area which is of great importance for the self-relation mediated by objects. The open research question here is: What consequences does it have for subjects, especially young people, when they no longer own the books, the music, the films, and the games (and perhaps even the clothing) through which they develop their self-relation and define their identity but only (temporarily, as long as they care to and their parents pay the providers and streaming services) *read, listen, watch, play (and wear)* them? What does it mean if they no longer have these things materially present in the cupboard or on the shelf? Phenomenologically speaking, it is obvious that the physical relationship to them is already changing: If we leave aside the clothes, they are no longer materially appropriated but enter the home as an immaterial data stream. This can mean that the processes of appropriation, i.e., the processes by which a subject forms, develops, and defines itself through cultural participation, are also changing—but the significance and extent of such transformations are far from clear yet.

In any case, the tendency analysed so far clearly implies a massive dynamisation in the relation to objects and thus also in the ensuing self-relations. Without doubt, the hope and idea of acquiring and establishing a "home of one's own" is of central importance, at least for the bourgeois world relation *(Weltbeziehung)*. Fencing off a plot of land and building a house—this driving motive, which is tremendously strong in modern capitalist society and provides an orientation far beyond the bourgeois life story, was not designed at first for individual ownership but for permanent, intergenerational family structures. The idea and the desire to leave something to the children one day—a flat, a house, a business—was and still is a motive that provides the possessive world relation with its driving energy. It is through home ownership that the bourgeois self expands into the world and literally finds itself interwoven with its structures: It is in the the workshop, the small garden, the kitchen, the living room, etc., where the propensities and features of the world are (or were) literally assimilated *(einverleibt)* and where essential relationships with the social and the material world were created. This is where thing, social and self-relations are (or were) shaped. The literal "growing together" between dwelling, furnishings, and subject (which, of course, could only be a lasting reality for those possessing property), described so vividly by Georg Simmel in his *Philosophy of Money*, experienced a progressive loosening in the course of the 19th and above all the 20th century by the very fact that originally immobile, "built-in" housing components such as a stove, table, settee, and sometimes bed became "movables" (*Möbel*) that could be exchanged at historically shorter intervals and less and less often survived their owners (Simmel 1989, 637).

Of importance to me here, however, is the fact that the property constitutive of the possessive *Weltbeziehung* was, in my view, designed in its basic structure for intergenerational duration. As research has been able to show, even in the cradle of late modern neoliberalism, in Pinochet's Chile, the driving economic motive of the bourgeois classes was not the acquisition of individual property but the accumulation of family property designed for permanence (Basaure i. V.).[10] Such an understanding of property is historically much older and more widespread than the idea of arbitrary individual availability: from Roman law of antiquity to the Chinese tradition of the 19th and 20th centuries, the rights of disposal associated with property were and are rarely individual rights but first and foremost community and above all family rights (Reinhard 2017, especially 27 ff.; Kroker 1959). As Tilo Wesche has mapped out, this intergenerational bridge connects the idea of property with a motif of endurance that points beyond death: property *increases* and solidifies over the life-course of the bourgeois subject while its lifetime simultaneously *decreases* and dwindles (Wesche 2014; 2018).

However, there can hardly be any doubt that this very motivational basic structure of the possessive bourgeois world relation is losing its plausibility and viability in contemporary society. In short, in the late modern stage of "acceleration society" based on the operative mode of dynamic stabilisation, children no longer *want* to have or take over their parents' *things*: not their furniture, not their clothes, not their vehicles and gardens, and quite often not their houses and flats either and certainly not the small businesses or enterprises that they may have built up. And because the son or daughter of a baker couple hardly (and often in no way) wants to be a baker him-

---

10 The strong family inheritance motive is also evident in the pension system, for example, which allows accumulated pension rights to be inherited.

or herself, they distance themselves from the parents' self- and social relations and their relation to objects. Because children often prefer—if they can afford it—to build or acquire residential property near their parents rather than take over the parental home, the idea of building a material world relation for their children (and further generations) is almost obsolete. The idea of permanence now seems to discourage rather than encourage: an inherited house is experienced more as a heavy burden on one's descendants as the spatio-temporal world relation becomes dynamic and as moving remains a constant option, unless of course they *monetise* it. This corresponds to the growing trend to understand home ownership not as a material asset, i.e., in the sense of establishing a material foundation and centre of one's *Weltbeziehung* but as an attractive financial investment and old-age security—and thus as a commodity (Heeg 2013).[11] Interestingly, a somewhat similar development is also evident with regard to the acquisition of a car: for young urban middle classes, owning a car no longer establishes a significant self and object relation because it inhibits rather than promotes (hyper)mobility. They *use* various vehicles to get around quickly; they no longer want *to have* them.

If property is to be understood as a link between the relationships of disposal and care, then a fundamental change can be seen precisely in the transition from the material ownership of things to abstract real estate investment, which can be observed in the real estate market: those who live in their own flat have it at their disposal and care for it. Whoever rents out a flat still has that disposal over and care for it, albeit in a mediated, weakened way: they select tenants, conclude tenancy agreements, and are responsible for refurbishment etc. On the other hand, someone who buys shares in a real estate fund does not even know, as a rule, which properties he or she owns shares in: she has no disposal over it and he does not care, except for the value of the investment. This form of property does not establish any relation to a thing at all and, as Simmel also noted, no substantial self-relation either precisely because it is not connected to any specific "realm of the world." Wherever property ultimately exists as fungible fund shares that are bought and sold by computer algorithms in fractions of a second, this development is taken to the extreme insofar as the two basic relations of property have completely evaporated. Owning shares, being rich, or having a high income is certainly of great importance for the resource endowment of individuals, but it can-

---

11 The SFB's sub-project A07 ("Habitat as collateral: Indebted property and financialisation"), led by Ute Tellmann, is also conducting research on this topic.

not as such form the basis for a sustainable, subjectivising self-relation because it is, as it were, of *no quality*: it does not establish a relation between the self and a qualitatively determined part of the world; it is indifferent to specific life contents and life purposes (Angehrn 1989, 107, following Simmel). As "possessions," the *little house*, the *allotment garden*, the *Mercedes*, or the *Peugeot bicycle*, and the *private library*, the *record collection*, or the *Brockhaus encyclopaedia* all "form" a subject in a qualitative way. Money as "pure potency" does not do that.

According to the argument developed so far, the structural change of property with regard to the relations of self, thing and social relations that it founds and establishes is thus reflected in the fact that the relationships of care and disposal in the realm of things is transformed into a relationship of temporary use without any obligation to care and, precisely because of this, the quality of subjectification of things is at least changed, if not reduced. Self-relations are re-configured as (flexible) user relations. In the social dimension, the competitive form of relationship remains dominant, but the rivalry now relates less to concrete things and sections of the world than to what one could call economic "utilisation potency" or range of disposal. This is determined by the total volume of economic, cultural, social, and physical capital. What does this mean for the transformation of late modern world relations *(Weltbeziehung)*?

4. Conclusion: From a possessive to a participatory Weltbeziehung?

At first glance, it may seem as if the late modern *Weltbeziehung* is being transformed from a basically *possessive* one back into a more *participatory* one: people participate as users in all kinds of services and events, they use buildings, means of transport, infrastructures, and devices without owning them and without having to enter into specific obligations of care for them that go beyond the usual duties of care. And indeed, this shift seems to be mirrored in other areas of life as well: Ideally speaking, late-modern subjects no longer "have" a profession but (temporarily) pursue one; nor do they "have" a spouse but (for the time being) live with someone; perhaps one can even say that they also no longer "have" friends but are friends and such friendship only shows and sustains itself in the execution.

But this impression of a transition from a possessive to a participatory *Weltbeziehung* is deceptive. The relation of use is not participatory in a genuine sense but rests, as it were, on "dead property" *(tote Habe)* (Fromm 1979), namely on economic assets in the form of a shrunken form of property. Because almost all of the participatory and especially material world relations (from living to working to eating and to all expressions of consumption) are "paid," they continue to be based on an encapsulated possessive world relation. People "have" economic assets, and thus a given scope and horizon of possibilities of use in the form of abstract numbers on their accounts. By "using" them, they redeem themselves of any participatory care obligations and secure temporary exclusive rights of use. In short, one has to "have" capital to *buy* participation. In the social dimension, they compete less for concrete goods or "parts of the world" than for the same volume of numbers: the social relation becomes a purely competitive relation, because whenever and wherever the account balance rises in one place, it must fall somewhere else.

My thesis is thus that the currently observable structural change in property undermines the basic structure of property as a combination of a disposal and a care relation, which gave the capitalist development of the last 250 years a robust and more or less solid foundation, and at the same time radicalises the possessive world relation *(Weltbeziehung)* into a shrinking form which exacerbates the competitive relation in the social dimension, reinforces the ecologically problematic side of the relation to things—insofar as it eliminates the relationship of care to things that goes hand in hand with classical ownership—and finally also forfeits, or at least reduces, the ability to create sustainable self-relations.

If we are not to lapse into persistent cultural pessimism about this, the question arises powerfully as to what alternatives to a possessive world relation are even conceivable. As I have already indicated, such alternatives seem to me to lie in the possibility of genuinely participatory *Weltbeziehungen* in which people take care of things and "parts of the world" and participate in them without "having" them. Indigenous traditions and ways of life can certainly provide examples of this: Forests, rivers, and the plants and animals that live in them can be used, for example, and people can care for them without their being considered and experienced as property and without this having to be regulated by corresponding legal claims. And indeed: in late modern contemporary society, microforms of new sharing practices can be observed in many places—sometimes born out of necessity, sometimes out of weariness with the capitalist order, and sometimes emerging as an unintended side effect of technological developments—in which the most diverse actors experiment for the sake of the most diverse interests and in very different ways.[12] Certainly, the habitus, interest and interpretation patterns of possessive relations to thing, self and others will continue to dominate for the time being. But, especially in the field of digital production and consumption, a critical threshold seems to have been crossed in many places that makes it difficult to maintain a possessive world relation: this applies to impressive knowledge structures like Wikipedia, which not only do not "belong" to anyone but also make the concept of intellectual authorship questionable, to new sampling techniques in music, to open source software, to works of art produced by AI, etc.[13] The liquidation of the late-modern *Weltbeziehung* as a result of the structural change in property therefore makes it quite conceivable that a new form of existence one day will emerge from this.

Works cited

Althaber, Agnieszka, Kathrin Leuze and Ramona Künzel (forthcoming 2023). Financial solidarity or autonomy? How gendered wealth and income inequalities influence couples' money management. *Social inclusion*, 11 (1).

Angehrn, Emil (1989). Besitz und Eigentum: Zu einem Problem der Politischen Philosophie, in: *Zeitschrift für Philosophische Forschung*, 43, 94–110.

---

[12] In fact, the empirical research in the SFB sub-project C06 ("Making Things Available. Property as a Specific Form of World Relationship"), led by Jörg Oberthür and myself, was able to show how much sharing practices motivate, sometimes even force, the subjects involved to openly "renegotiate" their relations to things, social relations, and self-relations. In particular, when "couch surfing," i.e. temporarily sharing their own flat with strangers, they experience that "their" coffee cup or even their bathroom are suddenly no longer so readily "theirs," that they suddenly feel like a guest in their own kitchen when the guests are cooking and that the relationship with the "strangers" and "clients" tends to mix with the elements of a friendship and proximity relationship. Equally interesting here seems to be the fact that people who participate in car-sharing practices are not sure whether and to what extent the car they have been driving for a few days is somehow "their" car—and are surprised that they start greeting people they meet in traffic in other cars from the same car-sharing agency as their own kind: Here, too, thing, self, and social relations seem to be in flux in a peculiar way. On car-sharing, see also Henning in the present volume. Cf. also Bhandar et al. 2021 on the uncertainty in all three dimensions of world relations.

[13] This area forms the object of investigation of sub-project C04 ("Intellectual property. Social embedding and functional equivalents") under the direction of Tilman Reitz and Sebastian Sevignani.

Aristotle. Aristotle's Politics.

Bhandar, Brenna, Eva von Redecker, Harrison Lechley, and Hannah Voegele (2021). Unsettling our relationship to things and people. *Interfere*, 2. 24.04.2023 https://cris.brighton.ac.uk/ws/portalfiles/portal/31251444/12._bhandar_et_al._unsettling_our_relationship_to_things_and_people_2.pdf.

Basaure, Mauro (in Vorbereitung). *Die These des temporalen Familismus: Auf dem Weg zu einer kritischen Theorie der Erfahrungshorizonte. Der chilenische Fall.*

Brocker, Manfred (1992). *Arbeit und Eigentum*. Darmstadt: Wissenschaftliche Buchgesellschaft.

Elberfeld, Rolf (2012). *Sprache und Sprachen: Eine philosophische Grundorientierung*, 3rd ed. Freiburg: Karl Alber Verlag.

Fromm, Erich (1979). *Haben oder Sein: Die seelischen Grundlagen einer neuen Gesellschaft*. Munich: dtv.

Habermas, Jürgen (1981). *Theorie des Kommunikativen Handelns*, Band 1. Frankfurt a. M.: Suhrkamp.

Heeg, Susanne (2013). Wohnen als Anlageform: Vom Gebrauchsgut zur Ware. *Emanzipation—Zeitschrift für sozialistische Theorie und Praxis*, 3.2, 5–20.

Hegel, Georg Wilhelm Friedrich (1986a). *Grundlinien der Philosophie des Rechts* [Werke Bd. 7]. Frankfurt a. M.: Suhrkamp.

Hegel, Georg Wilhelm Friedrich (1986b). *Vorlesungen über die Geschichte der Philosophie, Teil II* [Werke Bd. 19]. Frankfurt a. M.: Suhrkamp.

Heidegger, Martin (2022). *Bauen, Wohnen, Denken: Vorträge und Aufsätze*. Stuttgart: Klett-Cotta.

Jones, Henry (1910). *The working faith of the social Reformer*. London: Macmillan & Co.

Jullien, François (2022). *Existierend Leben. Eine neue Ethik*. Berlin: Matthes & Seitz.

Kroker, Edward (1959). The concept of property in Chinese customary law. *The transactions of the Asiatic Society of Japan*, 7, 3rd series, 123–46.

Macpherson, C. B. (1962). *The political theory of possessive individualism: Hobbes to Locke*. Oxford: Clarendon Press.

Peters, Florian (2023). *Von Solidarność zur Schocktherapie: Wie der Kapitalismus nach Polen kam*. Berlin: Ch. Links.

Popper, Karl (1973). *Objektive Erkenntnis: Ein evolutionärer Entwurf*. Hamburg: Hoffmann und Campe.

Reinhard, Wolfgang (2017). *Staatsmacht und Staatskredit. Kulturelle Tradition und politische Moderne*. Heidelberg: Universitätsverlag Winter.

Rosa, Hartmut (forthcoming 2023). Perspektivischer Dualismus: Warum die Kritische Theorie der Phänomenologie bedarf. In Alexis Gros, Jochen Dreher, und Hartmut Rosa, *Phänomenologie und Kritische Theorie*, Berlin: Suhrkamp.

Schmitz, Hermann (2019). *Der Gefühlsraum: System der Philosophie*, Band. III. Freiburg: Karl Alber Verlag.

Schuppert, Gunnar Folke (2023). Wandel des Eigentums: Zu seiner Verortung im Dreieck von Struktur-, Funktions- und Auffassungswandel des Eigentums, in: *Archiv des öffentlichen Rechts*, Vol. 147, 463–517.

Simmel, Georg (1989). *Philosophie des Geldes*. Ed. D. P. Frisby and K. C. Köhnke. Frankfurt a. M.: Suhrkamp.
Taylor, Charles (2009). *Ein säkulares Zeitalter*. Frankfurt a. M.: Suhrkamp.
Wesche, Tilo (2018). Der Wert des Eigentums: Über die Propriation der Zeit. *WestEnd: Neue Zeitschrift für Sozialforschung*, 01, 129–42.
Wesche, Tilo (ed.) (2014). Themenschwerpunkt: Eigentum, *Deutsche Zeitschrift für Philosophie*, 62 (3), 409–14.
Zahavi, Dan (2007). *Phänomenologie für Einsteiger*. Paderborn: Wilhelm Fink Verlag.
Zahavi, Dan (2002). First-Person Thoughts and Embodied Self-Awareness: Some Reflections on the Relation between Recent Analytical Philosophy and Phenomenology. *Phenomenology and the Cognitive Sciences*, 1 (1), 7–26.

Relationship to the Good: On the world-opening and world-connecting power of virtues[1]

Kathi Beier, Dietmar Mieth

1. Introduction

The claim we make in this chapter is that virtues contribute essentially to successful world relations by bringing the virtuous person into a stable relation with the good and the right. To put it in a syllogism: i) A relation with the good is the basis for good *Weltbeziehungen*; ii) virtues establish a stable relation in humans with the good; iii) Therefore, virtues are the basis for good *Weltbeziehungen*. Virtues ensure both a true knowledge of and a good relation to the world, including a good relation to oneself and to others. In what follows, we will explain why this is so.

The good that virtues make possible is meant here in an ethical sense. After all, we humans ask not only whether something is useful, i.e., instrumentally good, or pleasant, i.e., sensually good, but also whether our actions and our lives as a whole are ethically valuable, i.e., whether one should act or live in this way—even if it is unpleasant or useless. The ability to ask about the ethical or moral value of an action and to consider values in one's own actions is an anthropological prerequisite for any assumption of responsibility. Virtues are fundamental value attitudes. In them, our ability to do what is good and right is realised; in this sense, they contribute to a good life. More than good intentions are involved here, for what is required are attitudes that realise what they claim—not only for the individual but also in relations and structures that are necessary to support ethical values. They, too, can be proof of the power of existing virtues.

---

[1] © The author/s 2023, published by Campus Verlag, Open Access: CC BY-SA 4.0
Bettina Hollstein, Hartmut Rosa, Jörg Rüpke (eds.), "Weltbeziehung",
DOI: 10.12907/978-3-593-45587-7_003

The power of virtues has been recognised in almost all ages and by the most diverse cultures. If one understands "world" in a plural sense, i.e., as spatially or temporally sufficiently separated, very different social constellations, then one can also say that the idea of virtue is world-connecting. Alasdair MacIntyre (2007), for example, has traced the history of the concept of virtue in Western thought, beginning with the heroic societies Homer sings about through classical antiquity (Socrates, Plato, Aristotle), the Christian Middle Ages, the Scottish and German Enlightenment thinkers (Adam Smith, David Hume, Immanuel Kant), and the novels of Jane Austen and Henry James. On this conceptual basis, he develops a neo-Aristotelian virtue ethics for the present. Parallel to Greek antiquity, the concept of an excellent character appears in classical Chinese ethics, i.e., in the writings of Kongzi/Confucius and his pupils (Ivanhoe 2013; Tiwald 2018). Contemporary virtue ethicists such as Linda Zagzebski (2017) and Shannon Vallor (2016) incorporate this tradition into their accounts.[2] Vallor and others also refer to comparable teachings in Buddhism (Flanagan 2015; MacKenzie 2018). Furthermore, Zagzebski discusses the ideas of Native Americans, such as the role model function that Plenty Coups (1848–1932), chief of the Crow Nation, is still attributed today—by people both within and outside his tribe.[3]

The basic idea of virtue ethics that runs through all these worlds is as follows: to be able to act and think well as a human being and to lead a successful life, it is not enough to have a somewhat natural sense of (moral) good and bad. This sense can be lost or go astray if it is not rationally reflected upon and socially cultivated. Moreover, knowledge of the (moral) good does not enable us to act according to it as such; passions such as desire, fear, and despair are sometimes stronger than our good intentions. It is only by acquiring stable dispositions of thought and action, i.e., by acquiring virtues that have stood the test of time, that we are able to recognise, understand, and properly respond to the normative demands of the world we live in. The virtues, rightly understood, cause us to aim at what is truly good and to be able to do it.

This idea could also be expressed in terms of a theory of resonance:[4] a person who is virtuous allows herself to be affected, say, by injustice. She finds

---

[2] Zagzebski (2017, 85), for example, states that Confucius "had the same pivotal role in the creation of Chinese philosophy that Socrates had for Western philosophy."
[3] See also Lear (2008), a book that, according to Zagzebski (2017, 89), presents Plenty Coups as an exemplar of Aristotelian virtue.
[4] See the introductory chapter to this book, especially p. 11–12.

an effective answer to the question of what she can do against injustice here and now. By acting justly, she transforms the world and herself, for—through the actions they motivate and control—virtues have a permanent effect on the agent. Whoever acquires virtues and exercises them knows about the uncontrollability of this process, so she can only hope to influence the world and herself—and maybe others who take her as an example—in the search for the good and the right.

In what follows, we will describe the world-opening power of the virtues in more detail. We do this in three steps. In section two, we analyse the concepts of world, relation, and virtue. In section three, we show in general terms how and by what means virtues contribute to good self- and world relations *(Weltbeziehungen)*. In section four, we will focus on three concrete virtues—prudence, charity, and serenity *(Gelassenheit)*—and outline their significance for a good human life on the one hand and the stages in their respective histories of interpretation on the other. We conclude with some brief remarks on the social and institutional preconditions for successful virtue formation and practice.

2. World, relation, virtue: Conceptual reflections

When we speak of relationship, we basically have in mind a form of personal attachment: a person has a relationship with another person. When humans enter into a relationship with each other, this can take various forms: we distinguish, for example, family, friendly, sexual, marital relationships, as well as hostile, dependent, exploitative relationships, and others from one another—always in relation to persons. Relations between persons seem to be paradigmatic for the concept of relationship; such relationships, at least if they are voluntary, imply reciprocity. Therefore, in religion, we can talk of a relationship with God. When we do so, however, it immediately becomes clear that this is a relationship whose correspondences are beyond our control, for God is beyond our control, at least to the extent God cannot or may not be instrumentalised. Other human persons are also beyond our control, i.e., a subject of freedom (Spaemann 1996). If humans were controllable in a neurobiological way, then their personhood would disappear, dissolve into availability. People can have relationships with animals that are sometimes more and sometimes less reciprocal. Can one also enter into a relationship with things, a relationship that meets the requirements of the personal? Talk of a relationship to objects seems to be derived from personal relations. It is metaphorically possible, but it necessarily remains one-sided.

If, for us, the world is the other side of the relation—as in the sense of Martin Heidegger's formula of "being-in-the-world" as a human condition which Rosa (2016, 55) refers to—it would have to be something quasi-personal, i.e., a power beyond our control that can nevertheless be influenced by us, one that changes in and through our relationship with it, just as we are changed by it. In any case, speaking of a "successful" *Weltbeziehung* raises a problem. It is possible to speak of successful human relationships or human-animal relationships: they succeed if the partners care about the relationship and are committed to it. Spiritually, it is possible to speak of a successful relationship with God. But to what extent is the world a partner for human success? What sense of the term "world" is meant here?

In the Latin linguistic tradition, world has many connotations. In the sense of *mundus*, world refers in a comprehensive way to (almost) everything that exists. Immanuel Kant understands it as the "epitome of phenomena" (CpR, B 483) and famously distinguishes between the world of the senses (*mundus sensibilis*) and the world of understanding (*mundus intelligibilis*). In the sense of *saeculum*, world means the earthly time in which one lives, the century or age, sometimes also the spirit of the times. In the sense of *societas*, world refers to the forms of alliances and communities one belongs to. And in the sense of *terra*, world refers, like *globus*, to the earth or globe (as a celestial body) or to the ground or soil (as a substance). Bruno Latour (2018), for example, along with others who use the word in a charged way, speaks of "our earth"—thereby alluding to the care that seems to be an essential component of (personal) relationships. Martin Heidegger, in *The Origin of the Work of Art*, distinguishes the "earth," i.e., the hidden forces or what is concealed, from the "world," understood as existing insofar as it reveals and manifests itself. In classical metaphysics, this is the difference between substance and form. Heidegger's distinction between "environment" (*Umwelt*) and "co-world" (*Mit-welt*) is more familiar, i.e., between things and "stuff" (*Zeug*)—according to Heidegger "the being encountered in concern" (2004, § 15)—on the one hand and being with other people on the other (ibid., § 26). In his view, "environment" and "co-world" make up our everyday existence, whereas there is a "world" beyond and behind it that does not touch us so directly.

If one understands the term "world" not in this latter sense but in terms of the variables of time, nature, and society as everything that immediately surrounds us, then it becomes more understandable that human life essentially takes place in *Weltbeziehungen*. For it is in relation to the people and things around us that we grow and develop, that we build up our understanding of ourselves and the world, that we act and think.

Whether these *Weltbeziehungen* succeed in an objective sense, i.e., whether we can live well together with ourselves and others, with nature and technology, etc., depends not least on ourselves, on the way we are—hence on our attitudes. Virtues and vices are stable attitudes. The Greek philosophers spoke of *hexis*, the Latin philosophers of *habitus*; today we usually speak of character traits.

According to Aristotle's *Categories*, virtues and their opposites, vices, are qualities, that is, they tell us something about what a person is like (Aristotle, Cat. 8). Unlike warmth and cold or health and illness, however, they are, first, not physical but mental or character qualities and, second, not easily changeable constitutions but stable dispositions.[5] Unlike abilities such as sight or hearing, they are not innate but must be acquired. And finally, unlike acquired skills such as cooking or riding a bicycle, they are not ethically neutral; instead, virtues are by definition good and praiseworthy qualities and vices bad and reprehensible ones. For Aristotle, human virtue is therefore a disposition acquired through agency and learning, a disposition by which one becomes a good person or, in other words, through which one becomes good as a person and which thus enables one to do what most constitutes a human being, i.e., to think and act rationally (Aristotle, EN II 5).

In the European Middle Ages, this understanding of virtue was authoritative,[6] even though additions were not excluded. For example, virtues given by divine grace, i.e., so-called "infused virtues" (*virtutes infusae*), were added, as well as the virtues related to God (*virtutes theologicae*), i.e., faith, hope, and love. Moreover, there were completely new understandings of the virtues, such as the one proposed by Meister Eckhart (c. 1260–1328); he conceived of the virtues not as human accidents but as spiritual perfections of God. We will return to this below. As mentioned at the beginning, the idea of acquired attitudes that contribute to our living well as human beings is not lim-

---

5 As Aristotle holds, virtue is a *hexis*, i.e., a state or some kind of habit (Latin: *habitus*). For the claim that virtue in Aristotle primarily means human virtue, see Beier (2019).
6 The following definition from the *Sentences* of Peter Lombard (c. 1100h–1160) was used as a guide: "Virtue is a good quality of mind through which we live rightly and use nothing wrongly." Thomas Aquinas (1224/25–1274), whom we quote more often below, adopts this definition (ST I–II, q. 55, a. 1, arg. 1).

ited to Greek antiquity and medieval Christianity but can be found in almost all times and almost all cultures and worldviews. In the following, we shall illustrate how virtues make a good life possible, first in general terms and systematically, then by looking at three concrete virtues and their respective histories of interpretation.

3. Virtue and the good life

The claim that we as human beings need virtues for a good relation to ourselves and to the world is based on the general concept of virtue, one that transcends time. Aristotle and Thomas Aquinas justify this concept metaphysically (Schockenhoff 1987). The late MacIntyre (1999) places himself partly and explicitly in this tradition (Beier 2020). All three understand virtues as stable character traits whose acquisition is not only possible but absolutely necessary for living well as a human being. This presupposes certain anthropological assumptions about the nature of humans which we shall discuss in more detail in a moment.

By contrast, many proponents of virtue ethics in the 20th and 21st centuries, including the early MacIntyre, are sceptical of Aristotle's "metaphysical biology" (MacIntyre 2007, 148 and 162). That is why they conceptualise virtue differently, often in terms of social theory. MacIntyre, for example, conceives of human beings primarily as agents participating in the practices of their community and therefore defines the concept of virtue by reference to the concept of practice: "A virtue is an acquired human quality the possession and exercise of which tends to enable us to achieve those goods which are internal to practices and the lack of which effectively prevents us from achieving any such goods" (MacIntyre 2007, 191). Others regard virtues as attitudinal models, i.e., models of the good and the right that can be used as a guide in complex situations (Ossowska 1971; Mieth 1984). As such, virtues are above all socially important, for they contribute to moral continuity which in turn is important for the cohesion in the communities we belong to. Without these models, societies disintegrate. In other words, much depends on the appeal of virtues as capacities to act well and rightly. For values are present in societies, and these are the fertile ground for the laws of society: on this soil they sprout and grow, without it, they die.

Neither a metaphysical nor a socio-theoretical understanding of the concept of virtue precludes a historical approach that is sensitive to the variability of virtue catalogues and the changing meaning of individual virtues and vices at different times and in different cultures. So, one should distinguish *concrete access*, i.e., the time- and culture-specific interpretations, versions, or clarifications of general virtue concepts from what one might call *general encroachment*. Maria Ossowska (1971) has provided an overview of socially defined, culturally preferred, and modified virtue schemata in this sense, as has Alasdair MacIntyre (2007). We discuss both approaches in more detail in the next section.

We deem it important to point out that a general understanding of both the concept of virtue as such and the concepts of the individual virtues is needed in order to be able to recognise and describe the historical and cultural variability of the virtues. Without *encroachment* there is no *access* but only bad relativism; consequently, the variability of virtues dissolves into mere variety.

Why do we need virtues? Many virtue ethicists, both old and new, answer this question by referring to the nature of human beings, especially to their complex psychological structure. In Aristotle, for example, the doctrine of virtue is closely linked to his doctrine of the soul. He regards the human being not only as a composite of substance and form, as a psycho-physical entity, but sees very different forces at work in the human soul. Basically, there are two types of forces: rational and non-rational. On the one hand, humans, like other animals, are sensual beings guided by passions or affects, i.e., they experience hunger and thirst, feel pleasure and displeasure, joy, fear, love, sadness, and anger. In the process of human development, these passions appear first; only later do the rational faculties gradually develop. On the other hand, human beings are endowed with reason, i.e., they are capable of reflecting on and controlling their passions, urges, emotions, etc. By virtue of reason and thanks to the reasonable guidance by others, they can learn to place the good that the individual passions directly aim at in a larger context, to recognise other reasons for action besides sensual drives, to weigh reasons, and to act on the basis of a comprehensive judgement. Passions and reason in themselves sometimes drive us to opposing courses of action. The desire for wine, for instance, can be so great that one wants to drink the whole bottle; but the voice of reason warns against that because it knows not only about the pleasure but also about the damage to one's health that it can cause, or simply about the appointment the next morning for which one needs to have a clear head. If what is specific to human beings lies in the ability to reason, then it is important to develop one's rational faculties in order to recognise what is truly good and to be able to lead a good human life. Aristotle speaks of *eudaimonia* (EN I 2), literally: a life on which a good (*eu*) spirit (*daimon*) rests.

Virtues are nothing other than aspects of a reasonable goodness that have become character traits—a reasonableness that does not exclude the passions but guides them. By letting reason reign, the faculties of the soul are ordered such that there is harmony between them. Virtues are expressions of this harmony and hence necessary for a good human life.[7]

The example of wine shows how the virtues which have to do with passions simultaneously ensure a good relation to oneself and to the world. For the virtuous—in this case moderate—wine drinker experiences herself as harmonious (one could also say: as inwardly resonant) insofar as she wills the good she recognises and acts according to her will. Without the virtue of moderation, inner conflicts arise, as Aristotle explains (EN I 13 and VII). Mere controlled or strong-willed people will also not finish the bottle in the situation described, so they ultimately do what they see as good. However, they do not do it willingly but reluctantly; they still have a strong desire to empty the bottle completely, and they have to fight that urge. Uncontrolled or weak-willed people simply give in to their desire to drink and regret their action afterwards since they actually knew better. The dissolute—in this case intemperate—drinker will empty the bottle habitually and without immediate remorse, so she also acts without inner conflict. Her action, however, does not do justice to the situation (it is, as it were, outwardly non-resonant), for she does something bad—which she may realise later.

According to some contemporary virtue ethicists, the metaphysical assumptions Aristotelian moral psychology makes about human nature are too strong. They therefore try to develop a concept of virtue based on contemporary psychological theories, such as the reflections by Erich Fromm, the psychoanalytical studies by D. W. Winnicott or findings in the field of positive psychology (MacIntyre 1999; Swanton 2003; Snow 2010; Kristjánsson 2018).

---

7 An old dispute concerns the question of whether virtues are necessary or sufficient for a good human life. The Stoic tradition that finds many proponents today (Rüther 2022; Whiting and Konstantakos 2021) argues against the Aristotelian tradition for the latter. Other more recent approaches to virtue ethics are no longer eudaemonistic at all, but agent-based, i.e., they explain the value of virtues not in terms of their contribution to a good life but solely in terms of the emotional, motivational, and dispositional qualities of the agent (Slote 2001; Zagzebski 1996 and 2017).

But let us stay a little longer with Aristotle, whose virtue ethics is still influential today. He classifies virtues and vices into two groups, according to the two "parts" of the human soul. Moderation is one of the "ethical virtues." These are the virtues by which our passions are aligned with reason. Someone who is moderate, knows how to deal properly with sensual pleasure and displeasure, i.e., she is neither insensitive nor intemperate. Whoever is courageous can resist fear when it is necessary and muster the right amount of courage, so she is neither cowardly nor foolhardy. Munificence enables the sensible handling of money and wealth on a small scale and is positioned between stinginess and extravagance; generosity refers to the spending of large amounts of money and is the mean between pettiness and ostentation. Gentleness allows us to feel the emotion of anger on the right occasions, in the right measure, and for the right duration, thus preventing irascibility. Kindness preserves the pleasant aspect of the interpersonal sphere and thus prevents us from both aggressiveness and seeking popularity. In short, each of the eleven ethical virtues Aristotle discusses ensures that the person who has it feels the respective passion neither too strongly nor too weakly but precisely in such a way that he or she can act well in the relevant situation. Ethical vices, on the other hand, prevent good actions. Someone who is foolhardy, for instance, does not (any longer) see the existing danger she is in or headed towards; someone who is cowardly cannot overcome her fear despite any possible insight that it is wrong.

The "intellectual virtues" perfect the intrinsically rational "part" of the human soul and thus ensure that we think well in theoretical and practical terms, i.e., that we recognise what is true. In addition to wisdom (*sophia*) and science (*epistēmē*), Aristotle counts prudence (*phronēsis*) among these intellectual virtues. According to him, prudence is crucial for acting well. We will discuss it in more detail in the following section.

In scholasticism, especially through the reflections of Thomas Aquinas, it became common to emphasise four virtues in particular: temperance, courage, justice, and prudence (Keenan 1995). They already occupy a prominent place in Plato's *Politeia*, but it is only Thomas who calls them cardinal virtues (*virtutes cardinales*): "A virtue is called "cardinal," i.e., fundamental, because other virtues are fixed on it like a door on its hinge (*ostium in cardine*)." (*De virt.*, q. 1, a. 12, ad 24)[8] The other virtues are controlled by these

---

8 Thomas' writings are given here according to the scheme: work (e.g. De virt.), volume (if available, for ST, e.g., I–II), question (*quaestio*), and article (*articulus*).

four like a door in its hinge because they are derived from them or can be traced back to them. The number four corresponds to the human soul itself (Thomas Aquinas, ST I–II, q. 61, a. 2). For the rational part of the soul is perfected by the virtue of prudence, the will by justice, the sensual, desiring faculty by temperance, and the sensual, overcoming faculty by courage.[9] Thomas describes more ethical virtues than Aristotle, but makes it clear where they belong. The virtues of devotion to one's parents or fatherland, for example, can be derived from justice, as can gratitude through which one repays one's benefactors (ST I–II, q. 60, a. 3). Patience is part of courage, because it makes us bear evils inflicted on us by others with equanimity (ST II––II, q. 128, a. 1, ad 4 and q. 136, a. 4).[10]

It is interesting to see how the cardinal virtues are considered fundamental even in those approaches that do not metaphysically ground the concept of virtue. MacIntyre, for example, leaves the catalogue of virtues open while considering certain virtues to be fundamental; for him, these are the virtues that define our relationship to other people with whom we share goals and standards that constitute a practice. Justice, he says, helps us recognise what is due to whom; courage prepares us to take whatever self-endangering risks are demanded along the way (MacIntyre 2007, 191). Others adopt MacIntyre's understanding of virtue, including the special importance of the cardinal virtues (Vallor 2017), or at least consider the category of cardinal virtues to be structurally indispensable (Halbig 2013, ch. 2.5; Timpe and Boyd 2014).

Like Aristotle, Thomas believes that virtues are necessary for a good human life. In the Christian Middle Ages, however, Aristotle's *eudaimonia* transforms into *felicitas*, i.e., into earthly or imperfect happiness (*beatitudo imperfecta*). This is so because, as Aristotle (Aristotle, EN I 1) already suggests, we cannot avoid many evils in this life (Thomas Aquinas ST I–II, q. 3, a. 2, ad 4; q. 5, a. 3). From this kind of happiness, Thomas distinguishes the perfect or true happiness promised to man by God (*beatitudo perfecta et vera*); through this kind of happiness a human person becomes a "fellow citizen of the saints and

---

9 Thomas distinguishes more clearly than Aristotle between two forces in the sensual striving part of the soul (ST I, q. 81, a. 2): The power of desire (*vis concupiscibilis*) draws us to simple goods, i.e., to attaining what is beneficial to the senses and fleeing what is harmful; the power of overcoming (*vis irascibilis*) has to do with what is difficult (*arduum*) and always drives us on when obstacles stand in the way of attaining sensual goods. So the latter is, for Thomas, the "champion and defender" of the power of desire.
10 For a more detailed explanation of how Thomas systematises Aristotle's doctrine of the virtues, see Beier (2022a).

member of God's household," as expressed in the Letter to the Ephesians. To recognise that such heavenly happiness is possible for us—and even more to achieve it—is beyond human nature, for it presupposes trust in God and His revelation. Such trust is not given to humans by nature. Therefore, perfect happiness is only possible through God's grace—as are the corresponding virtues. The three so-called theological virtues of faith (*fides*), hope (*spes*), and charity (*caritas*) are crucial insofar as they establish a stable relationship between the human person and God, between this world and the divine world revealed through Him.

We will take a closer look at the virtue of charity in the next section. Apparently, it is important to many virtue ethicists today to understand love/charity as a virtue, not just as a passion. At the same time, it seems difficult for them to do so without abandoning the limits of secular speech (Rohr 2018). Christian thinkers such as Peter Geach (1977) or Josef Pieper (1996), by contrast, have less trouble including the triad of theological virtues into their virtue ethical accounts.

4. Three virtues over the course of time

From a certain, well-founded, point of view, one can say that human nature does not fundamentally change. Humans are and remain living beings consisting of body and soul. For this reason, a human being is, as Kant says, a "citizen of two worlds," for, as a physical being, he is subject to the laws of nature, whereas, as a rational and moral being, he can set laws for himself. A human being is and remains a mortal and social being who strives for a generally good life and asks about the meaning of his life. What changes, not least through human action, is the world in which he lives. This also changes the human being's self-understanding as well as his understanding of the world and, by consequence, the set of virtues and vices. There has never been a fixed set or list. Even those virtues that can be regarded as overarching, i.e., the cardinal virtues, were and still are a constant matter of debate and interpretation. Given that the world is changing, we must always try to understand anew what is really wise, just, courageous and moderate. The virtue concepts are in need of contemporary interpretation because what counts as virtuous in an individual case is an inescapable question that by no means always holds the same answers. Moreover, the list of virtues can be supplemented, as has already become clear with respect to the theological virtues.

Prominent virtue-ethical positions from the 20th century have comprehensively reflected on the historical side of the concept of virtue. Thus, Maria Ossowska's and Alasdair MacIntyre's reflections can be understood as historically informed contributions in the sense of the above-mentioned socio-theoretical understanding of the concept of virtue. According to Ossowska (1971), virtues are moral conventions in the society. They are formed not only in biographies but also in social histories, not only in individual quantities but also in societies. Conventions of this kind have value; they gain attraction from the social environment in which they are conveyed. At the same time, they are not completely arbitrary but solidify into a set or canon of virtues that belong together and appear together. This set is offered and passed on through education and lived experience. Ideologies, religions, and moral teachings aim at making the virtues part of everyday life, for instance by explaining how they can help avoid stressful situations (Mieth 1984). It is often important to know where the virtues come from, who is presenting them and what they are intended for.

Alasdair MacIntyre's study (2007) shows that and how the respective socially enabled, favoured, and enforced virtues are time- and culture-dependent, but he also shows how they, as time-dependent as they are, must be grasped as universally valid and basic ethical qualities, for they are anchored in human social nature. In heroic societies, whether past or present, courage, for example, has a different meaning than in post-heroic ones.[11] Nonetheless, courage is, according to MacIntyre, an indispensable ethical competence for human beings and rightly counted among the cardinal virtues.

We want to illustrate how the meaning of the virtues is subject to different interpretations by focusing on three examples: prudence, charity, and serenity. As it will become clear, these virtues contribute in their own but fundamental way to a successful *Weltbeziehung*.

---

11 For this distinction and its relevance, see Beier (2021). She takes a controversy between two British moral philosophers of the 20th century as a starting point: Richard M. Hare understood the virtue of courage as an ideal that is of use only in war situations; for him, it therefore had had its day. Peter Geach, on the other hand, associated courage with defence and standing one's ground in all kinds of life situations and considered it to be of vital importance even today.

4.1 Prudence: The appropriate practical relation to reality

One can hardly overestimate the importance of the virtue of prudence for a good human life. For Socrates it is so significant that, in Plato's dialogue *Protagoras*, he considers all ethical virtues to be forms of prudence or practical wisdom. In Aristotle, prudence enters into the definition of ethical virtue, for this, according to him, is "a state (*hexis*) that decides, consisting in a mean, the mean relative to us, which is defined by reference to reason (*logos*), that is to say, to the reason by reference to which the prudent person (*phronimos*) would define it" (EN II 6: 1106b36–1107a2). Elsewhere, he even says that prudence, wisdom and ethical excellence in a sense "produce" happiness (*eudaimonia*) insofar as possessing and exercising them makes us happy (EN VI 13: 1144a5). Thomas Aquinas calls prudence the "birthing mother" of all the ethical virtues. What is it that makes prudence so significant?

According to Aristotle, being prudent or wise in a practical sense means being able to think well or, more precisely, to recognise in a concrete situation how to realise the good one wants. Since it primarily concerns thinking, prudence is an intellectual virtue for him. Unlike wisdom and science, however, prudence does not deal with absolute, eternal truths but with contingent ones. In a constantly changing world, it is precisely those truths that are relevant to our everyday life and our practical considerations.[12] So Aristotle defines prudence or practical wisdom as a "state grasping the truth, involving reason, and concerned with action about human goods" (EN VI 5: 1140b21). This places prudence at a crucial interface, for practical deliberation connects the world of thought with the world of action. Considering, judging, deciding—this is the core business of prudence.

Without thinking wisely, one will not be able to act at all or at least not well. Aristotle offers a good example (EN VI 8): If one wants to live in a healthy way and also knows that white meat is easily digestible and healthy, one will not be able to decide which meat to eat until one also knows that poultry meat

---

12 See Aristotle (EN III 5: 1112a22–31):"Now no one deliberates about eternal things—about the universe, for instance, or about the incommensurability of the sides and the diagonal; nor about things that are in movement but always come about the same way [...]; nor about what results from fortune—the finding of a treasure, for instance. For none of these results could be achieved through our agency. We deliberate about what is up to us, that is to say, about the actions we can do [...]. But we do not deliberate about all human affairs; no Spartan, for instance, deliberates about how the Scythians might have the best political system. Rather, each group of human beings deliberates about the actions that they themselves can do."

is white and healthy. The example illuminates important aspects of the virtue of prudence. First, because it is related to action, it does not refer primarily to the general but to the individual. For the same reason it is, second, concerned with the ultimate (*eschaton*), since that is the object of practical consideration. In other words, prudence does not determine ends but what promotes ends.[13] This means, third, that as a virtue, prudence presupposes good ends, for he who finds the means to bad ends is not prudent but merely clever. Whereas cleverness is neutral regarding bad ends, prudence is committed to the good (Müller 1998, 26). This is why both Aristotle (EN VI 13: 1144a8, 1145a5) and Thomas Aquinas (ST I–II, q. 57, aa. 4–5; q. 58, aa. 4–5) emphasise the constitutive connection between prudence and ethical virtue: being ethically virtuous ensures that the goal of action is good, while being prudent ensures that one finds the good means that lead to the goal. Given that prudence is necessary for all ethical virtues—for it determines what it means for a particular person in a concrete situation to act moderately, courageously, kindly, generously, etc.—it is, in a sense, a guiding virtue, "la vertu rectrice qui détermine la tâche des autres vertus" (Aubenque 1963, 65). For Thomas Aquinas, it is the "right reason of action" (*recta ratio agibilium*) since it is only through prudence that we are able to make right judgements about what to do in a specific situation (ST I–II, q. 57, a. 4).

In the history of ethics, both the nature and the significance of prudence have not always been clearly recognised. Thomas Hobbes prominently associated it with self-interest rather than with moral character. Consequentialists and Kantians are focused on commands and prohibitions, not on the context-sensitive judgement and decision-making capacity of the virtue of prudence. For Kant, the "counsels of prudence," along with the "rules of skill," constitute merely hypothetical imperatives and so do not belong to practical philosophy, strictly speaking, but to theoretical philosophy (Kant, CJ: Introduction XIII–XIV).

---

13 Aristotle describes the structure of practical deliberation in the following way (EN III 5: 1112b15–24): "We lay down the end, and then examine the ways and means to achieve it. If it appears that any of several means will reach it, we examine which of them will reach it most easily and most finely; and if only one means reaches it, we examine how that means will reach it, and how the means itself is reached, until we come to the first cause, the last thing to be discovered. [...] And the last thing found in the analysis would seem to be the first that comes into being."

Therefore, more recent virtue ethicists try to take up the Aristotelian tradition. Josef Pieper (2010, 47) describes the relationship that the virtue of prudence establishes between us and the world as follows:

"The development of the moral person takes place in the respective appropriate response to reality, which we did not create ourselves and whose essence is the mutability of becoming and passing away, but not permanent being [...]. Only the virtue of prudence is capable of giving this 'appropriate response'."

Anselm Winfried Müller calls prudence "cultivated practical reason" and emphasises that it is, like all the other virtues, not a mere ability but an irrevocable disposition: "It is not the one who can judge prudently *if* he wants to who is prudent, but the one who, in whatever situation, actually judges prudently *because* he wants to." (Müller 1998, 122). At the same time, it is clear to him: "Prudence not only means well, it also knows how to achieve the good" (ibid., 126). Andreas Luckner, for whom ethics is and can only be a philosophy of prudence, conceives of it as a "self-orientation competence," more precisely, as an attitude that promotes a sensible and life-serving approach to the things of the world; as such, it is "indispensable for an independent conduct in life" (Luckner 2005, 4).

4.2 Charity: The good relationship to the Other

Those who speak of love in ethical terms, i.e., including faithfulness and justice, do not speak inappropriately of feelings, for feelings are underpinned by morally relevant experiences. Contrary to what the world of advertising wants us to believe, feelings are not something purely spontaneous and immediate, coming out of nowhere. Certainly, the feeling of immediate attraction has become present to many of us at first sight, from the palpitation of the heart. But it carries with it our hopes and experiences, that is, our identity which we cannot (or should not) deny. It also carries with it the self-commitments in which Eros' spontaneous goodness can be prolonged. We are responsible for what we have made familiar to us through love. This is not to give way to paternalism or maternalism; rather, it is a truth relevant for every one of us and for the history every one of us has with itself (Mieth 2019).

The diversity of love alluded to here has been perfectly described and analysed in ancient philosophy (Al-Taher et al. 2022). Aristotle, for example, distinguishes between four different forms of love (Beier 2022b). As a sensual passion, love draws us towards things or persons that seem pleasant or pleasurable to us. Rational love takes us towards everything we recognise as good—truth and wisdom as well as useful or virtuous people. As a virtue, love is aimed at the good for the beloved person. And as friendship, love establishes a relation between persons who know of their love and reciprocate it. According to Aristotle, friendship (*philia*) "is a virtue, or involves virtue," and being with friends (*koinōnia*) is "most necessary for our life" (EN VIII 1: 1155a3–5). His conception of the friend as "another self" is widely known (EN IX 9: 1170b7).

In Christianity, the idea of interpersonal friendship is extended to the relationship between humans and God in an almost revolutionary way. In any case, Thomas Aquinas develops his concept of humans' love for God (*caritas*) entirely on the basis of Aristotle, for he is convinced that the three characteristics of Aristotle's concept of friendship can also be found here: *caritas* is a love coupled with benevolence; it is reciprocal; and it does not remain hidden because the friends spend time together, i.e., they form a community. Thus, Thomas concludes,

"Since there really is a commonality of man with God, inasmuch as He communicates His beatitude (*beatitudo*) to us, a friendship (*amicitia*) must be based in this communication (*communicatio*). It states in 1 Corinthians 1:9 about this communication: 'Faithful is God, by whom ye were called unto the fellowship of His Son'. Love (*amor*), however, which is based in this communication, is love of God (*caritas*). Therefore, it is obvious that charity is a kind of friendship of man with God." (ST II–II, q. 23, a. 1)

The particular Christian connotations of love point to the importance of the theological virtues and their unity. Belief in a love that constitutes God's essence and proceeds from Him means something different from love that is just another word for preferences, interests, and forms of desire. Human love out of God is, rather, to use an axiom from Meister Eckhart, a love from a "distinction through indistinction," that is, from a dimension which is radically different from other forms of love but whose difference cannot be easily expressed.[14]

The Judeo-Christian commandment runs as follows: "Love the Lord your God with all your heart and with all your soul and with all your strength and with all your mind, and, love your neighbor as yourself" (Luke 10:27)[15]. Ac-

---

14 Eckhart uses this axiom in his *Expositio Libri Sapientiae*, LW II, 482–91. See also Fischer (1974, 124–28).
15 Bible citations are taken from the New International Version (NIV).

cording to Meister Eckhart (LW IV: Homily XXX, 271–81), Augustine requires that this be understood *ex toto corde* ("with all your heart") in the sense of "loving out of God."[16] He obviously does not mean our love for God but God's love for us. It is God who first loved us (cf. 1 John). His love should grasp us and permeate us. It is ahead of the human being, always already there. God's kingdom is love, and vice versa: where love is, there is God's kingdom. *Ubi caritas et amor, Deus ibi est*: "where charity and love are found, there is God," as the liturgy of the Easter Vigil has it. In Hosea (11:1–9; i.e., in the First Testament), we find this idea again in the following passage:

"When Israel was a child, I loved him, and out of Egypt I called my son. But the more they were called, the more they went away from me. [...] It was I who taught Ephraim to walk, taking them by the arms; but they did not realise it was I who healed them. I led them with cords of human kindness, with ties of love. To them I was like one who lifts a little child to the cheek, and I bent down to feed them. [...] My people are determined to turn from me. Even though they call me God Most High, I will by no means exalt them. [...] My heart is changed within me; all my compassion is aroused. I will not carry out my fierce anger, nor will I devastate Ephraim again. For I am God, and not a man—the Holy One among you."

And further (14:4–8):

"I will heal their waywardness and love them freely, for my anger has turned away from them. I will be like the dew to Israel; he will blossom like a lily. Like a cedar of Lebanon he will send down his roots; his young shoots will grow. His splendor will be like an olive tree, his fragrance like a cedar of Lebanon. People will dwell again in his shade; they will flourish like the grain, they will blossom like the vine—Israel's fame will be like the wine of Lebanon.. [...] I am like a flourishing juniper; your fruitfulness comes from me."

Hosea also shows the angry God who threatens his immoral and ungrateful people with disaster and destruction. God appears here as passionate, as alternately permeated by his feelings. In a similar fashion, parents can become angry out of love. Children who meet their parents with an onslaught of resistance still love them. Love always has the upper hand; it is, as it were, the great "nevertheless." In the First Testament, it already unfolds in images and metaphors of fruitfulness, a state to be achieved through the human continuation of God's action. What would God's love be, the prophet asks, if He were incapable of anger? Why would He be angry if He could not love? On the other hand, how could He be merciful and compassionate if He were not also concerned? Otherwise He would be, as the poet Wolfgang Borchert put

---

16 See also Meister Eckhart in Mieth (2014a, 347–58) and, as an explanation, Mieth (2020a).

it in *Draußen vor der Tür*, a "fairy-tale God of love", i.e., a cuddly toy for the evening. God's love for us, the prophet proclaims, is full of parental care, agitation and conflicting feelings under the rule of love. What would God's love be if it were but an unchanging stream, a warm shower, a mild rain, or a constantly smiling sun?

A look at God's history with human beings thus teaches us to consider God's love for us as a prerequisite for human love. Human beings are permeated by that which they are to permeate the world with. Love has its limits, the prophet knows, and at the same time he teaches: love breaks through these limits. This is both a commonplace and a mystery. It is not surprising that Hosea says at the end of his short work: "Who is wise? Let them realize these things. Who is discerning? Let them understand." (14:9). God cannot, after all, be spoken of in only one way, certainly not in a way that excludes the conflict between feelings. God is not simply one side of feelings; he is the whole of them. Yet this whole is enclosed by love, which also breaks through in God's care for us.

Love in this (theological) sense is a strong virtue. On its own, human love becomes weak, even if it can perhaps be strengthened through practice (Borchers 2018). This is another reason why modern virtue ethicists find it difficult to understand love as a virtue, i.e., as a stable disposition (Swanton 2003), or to associate romantic love or even sex with virtue (Halwani 2003 and 2018). God's love, by contrast, remains: it makes people having the virtue of charity (*caritas*) strong. Filled with this love, they know how to love those who belong to their family or political community as well as strangers and, what is more, even enemies (MacIntyre 2001; Herzberg 2018). Whoever loves in this sense is never alone but has God, the great and passionate lover, at his side. And He is, as the faithful believe, like a well from which people can draw love and a source that never runs dry.

4.3 Serenity: The right attitude to oneself and to the world as such

As Josef Pieper reminds us, Thomas Aquinas says somewhere in the *Summa Theologiae* that on a higher level of perfection, that is, in charity, there is also a higher and extraordinary prudence which decreases the value of all things of this world. Pieper writes:

"Through the superhuman power of graciously bestowed love, one is able to become so much one with God that he receives the ability and the right to see created things, so to speak, from God's perspective and to 'relativise' and 'wrestle' with them from God's perspective—without denying them and contradicting their essence. This is the only legitimate possibility and the only justification of 'contempt for the world' that exists: growth in love." (Pieper 2010, 58)

The Christian understanding of the virtue of charity (*caritas*) thus leads back to prudence, but prudence in a new guise—that of serenity (*Gelassenheit*).

Serenity is an attitude that was as important to Epicureanism as it was to the Stoa; it can be found in Buddhism as well as in Confucianism and Hinduism. The word as such, however, was coined and introduced as a (Christian) virtue by Meister Eckhart, the Thuringian Dominican of the 13th and 14th centuries.[17] With this word, the German Dominican mystics both continued and changed a spiritual tradition of the Church Fathers which is primarily related to the Stoa. Yet for Eckhart, serenity is not a calm immutability but the basic attitude of self-distance and letting go (Mieth 2020b), closely connected with what he calls *Abgeschiedenheit*, i.e., detachment or releasement (Vinzent 2011). In the religious sense *Gelassenheit* originally had, the non-plannability of the future, the awareness of human finitude and their susceptibility to error resonate. In philosophy, reflections on serenity are present in many forms. Plato speaks of *sōphrosynē*, i.e., a form of reasonableness, calmness, or moderation. The Stoics praise *ataraxia* and *apatheia*, i.e., a kind of concentrated, collected mental tranquillity (Latin: *tranquillitas mentis*). Martin Heidegger calls serenity "the basic mood with which humans should relate to Being." Wilhelm Weischedel takes up one of Eckhart's perspectives when he speaks of *Abschiedlichkeit* (farewellness), i.e., a sense of finiteness.

Eckhart is not the first to speak of *Lassen* or letting go.[18] Yet the way he speaks of it shows that he does not mean leaving something behind. What he has in mind, rather, is rethinking or reorienting as becomes particularly clear in his early speeches delivered in Erfurt, written between 1294 and 1298, in which he focuses on the word pair "detachment" (*Abgeschiedenheit*) and "serenity" (*Gelassenheit*) (Panzig 2005, 101 ff.). Central to these speeches is the

---

17 See especially Eckhart's *Reden der Unterweisung* and his German sermons 6, 10, 12, 28, 29, 38 and 43. See also Mieth (2014b).
18 Erik A. Panzig (2005, 56–57) explains how the word, which originally stemmed from the Vulgate *relinquere*, was used earlier.

programmatical saying "Be aware of yourself, and where you find yourself, let yourself go. That is the very best" (RdU 3 / EW 2, 340).[19] Detachment has, it is said, no equivalent in Latin (Panzig 2005, 105). But it seems possible to assume that it comes close to the Latin *abstractio*, for abstraction is the refraining from realities and states of mind that are left behind intentionally. At any rate, Eckhart's description of the processes of approaching the true reality of God, that is, of His being at work in us, represents a process of abstraction. This process is translated by Eckhart from the realm of thinking into the realm of everyday life. In this manner, Eckhart also opposes taking God *"unter einem Felle oder unter einem Kleide"* (DW 1, 123,1), that is, clothed with a coat or a dress, for he is concerned with the "pure" (*lauter*) God, i.e., with the exposure of everything that has been attached to Him. That is why he praises knowledge before love: whereas love imagines, for example, the goodness of God, knowledge abstracts. Detachment, then, is the ability to abstract in thought and in life.

As a stance in life, detachment means an inner distance from everything that moves from the outside and corresponds with wrong inner intentions. Simultaneously, it goes along with an inner looseness and receptivity: not put any obstacles in the way of God's grace—this is what Eckhart teaches. This also includes the instruction to live and to act "without any why or what for" (*âne warumbe*). Niklas Largier puts it as follows:

"Serenity means renouncing all 'why,' that is, all intentionality as well as any specific path that could lead to God. [...] In serenity, man sets himself apart from self-love, the source of the love of the world, and overcomes the human obstruction towards God. [...] Eckhart translates the *abneget semetipsum* of the biblical verse (Luke 9:23) with *sich selben lazen* (Sermon 59, EW 1, 628)." (Meister Eckhart, EW I, 959–62)

But even this interpretation must be contradicted: self-love can no doubt be purified in that, as Augustine and Eckhart say, humans draw love from God, i.e., understand and see themselves from God's unconditional acceptance. Then they can love from within and without any self-interest. So, serenity, detachment, and living "without any why or what for" are, at the same time, forms of crossing out and of receiving inasmuch as there is a *negatio negationis* in the negation. The crossing out leads to a breakthrough, that is, to a purified understanding or attitude in life. In this sense, the realisation of the human being's true serenity is the love of God coming out of Him. Sere-

---

19 We refer to Eckhart's writings as follows: volume, page, and, if necessary, line.

nity is permeability for a love that does not strive for itself as a possession or reward, i.e., for any increasing surplus value but expropriates itself (Mieth 1972). It is not performance but rather some kind of swinging into the self-surrender of God that the human being receives as a gift and grace (Mieth 2015).

Eckhart goes one step further when he states that we should let God go. In his speeches, this reads as follows: "No advice is better for finding God than that of letting God be" (RdU 11 / EW 2, 366). The requirement here is ambiguous. It is meant in the sense of "letting God come," for God is the seeker who finds the human being where he lets himself be found. Hence, a distinction must be made between "letting God go" in the sense of leaving all images of God behind and "letting God go" in the sense of letting Him do His work. The latter is expressed in the beautiful phrase: "God is a God of presence. As he finds you, so he takes and receives you; not what you have been, but what you are now" (DW V, 234,5).

Sermon 12 continues this line of thought:

"The man who stands thus in God's love [...] must have left himself and this whole world behind. If there were a man to whom the whole world belonged, and he, for God's sake, let it be again as it was when he received it, to him our Lord would give again the whole world and eternal life in addition. [...] Yet another man, who had neither bodily nor spiritual things to leave or give, would leave the most. For whoever would leave himself for a moment without reservation, to him everything would be given. [...] The man who has let go and is let go, and never looks back on what he has let go of, and thereby remains constant, unmoved and unchangeable in himself, only this man is serene." (EW 1, 150)

Eckhart also makes use of the biblical motif of leaving behind and receiving anew, especially with reference to Mark 10:28–31. There we can read that the fulfilled life is already granted now, not only in heaven. And so Eckhart writes:

"Once a man came to me, it was not long ago, and he said that he had left great earthly goods so that he might save his soul. Then I thought: Oh, how little you have left! It is blindness and folly if you pay attention to what (goods) you have left. If you have left yourself, you have really left something [Hast du dich selbst gelassen, so hast du gelassen]. The man who leaves himself shines so brightly that the world cannot bear him." (Sermon 28 / EW 1, 318)

This last remark points, perhaps, to the conflicts that can arise from Eckhart's spiritual prioritisation. In any case, real serenity makes everything worldly appear in a different light (Mieth 2003; 2004; 2014b). As popular as Eckhart is today, not least because of his praise of serenity, it seems difficult to secularise this spiritual virtue.

5. Concluding remarks

As we have tried to show, virtues are necessary to living a good human life. For they bring us into a good and stable *Weltbeziehung*, including a good relation with ourselves, to other people, and with God. This can be illustrated by reference to three individual virtues. Prudence combines true thinking with good action; it enables us to find the right answer to the question of how to realise the good here and now through our own actions. Charity ensures that we want and do what is good for the other person; it also works interpersonally as well as between God and humans. Serenity is the basic attitude of proper self-distance and trustful surrender to God.

According to the account of virtue we have proposed, virtues make demands not only on the individual person who strives for them, but also on the institutions in which they arise and in which they are to be lived. Do institutions provide opportunities for virtue? Wise decision-making and action are as important at the political level as they are at the individual level. Autonomy and independent action need encouragement, not suppression. Love and solidarity only arise in cooperation. Law and the laws should also be wise, just, courageously prepared, and moderately designed.

Virtues are bridges between the personal and the social. Like the values we embrace and uphold they do affect our personal as well as our social lives. Therefore, we need space for virtues and for their practice in as many human communities and institutions as possible: in families, schools and universities, businesses and associations. The church is also called upon here. If it is not an end in itself but serves people; it can promote and complement virtues. As a conclusion, then, we should keep in mind the connection between the virtues, practices, and institutions Alasdair MacIntyre reminds us of:

"The integrity of a practice causally requires the exercise of the virtues by at least some of the individuals who embody it in their activities; and conversely the corruption of institutions is always in part at least an effect of the vices." (MacIntyre 2007, 195)[20]

---

20 For helpful comments on an earlier draft of this chapter, we would like to thank Bettina Hollstein and Jana Ilnicka. We also wish to express our gratitude to Henry Jansen who helped translate the text into English.

Works cited

Aubenque, Pierre (1963). *La prudence chez Aristote*. Paris: Presses Universitaires de France.
Al-Taher, Sarah, Vanessa Jansche, and Laura Martena (eds.). (2022). *Was Liebe vermag: Philosophische Liebesdiskurse in der Antike*. Stuttgart: Metzler.
Aristotle (Cat.) (1963). *Categories*. Translated with notes by John L. Ackrill. Oxford: Clarendon Press.
Aristotle (EN). (1999). *Nicomachean ethics*. Translated, with introduction, notes, and glossary, by Terence Irwin. 2nd ed. Indianapolis/Cambridge: Hackett Publishing.
Beier, Kathi (2022a). Ordnung und Anzahl der Tugenden: Thomas von Aquin als Brücke zwischen Aristotelischer und moderner Tugendethik. In Viliam Štefan Dóci and Thomas Prügl (eds.). *Brückenbauer und Wegbereiter: Dominikaner an den Grenzen der katholischen Christenheit*, 39–55. Roma: Angelicum University Press.
Beier, Kathi (2022b). Affekt, Tugend oder Relation? Aristoteles über die Vielfalt menschlicher Liebe. In Sarah Al-Taher, Vanessa Jansche, and Laura Martena (eds.). *Was Liebe vermag: Philosophische Liebesdiskurse in der Antike*, 117–38. Stuttgart: Metzler.
Beier, Kathi (2021). Was ist und wozu brauchen wir die Tugend der Tapferkeit? In Johannes L. Brandl, Daniel Messelken, and Sava Wedman (eds.). *Denken, Reden, Handeln / Thinking, Talking, Acting: Nachträge zum Salzburger Kolloquium mit Georg Meggle*, 661–82. eBook. Open Access: https://eplus.uni-salzburg.at/obvusboa/content/titleinfo/6202655.
Beier, Kathi (2020). Virtue and Tradition: Alasdair MacIntyre's Thomistic-Aristotelian Naturalism. In Martin Hähnel (ed.). *Aristotelian Naturalism: A Research Companion*, 209–22. Dordrecht: Springer.
Beier, Kathi (2019). Why human virtue is the measure of all virtue. In Geert Keil and Nora Kreft (eds.), *Aristotle's Anthropology*, 163–81. Cambridge: Cambridge University Press.
Borchers, Dagmar (2018). Liebe als Haltung: Eine reizvolle Herausforderung für die zeitgenössische Tugendethik? In Winfried Rohr (ed.). *Liebe—eine Tugend? Das Dilemma der modernen Ethik und der verdrängte Status der Liebe*, 293–310. Wiesbaden: Springer VS.
Borchert, Wolfgang (1956). *Draußen vor der Tür*. Reinbek bei Hamburg: Rowohlt.
Fischer, Heribert (1974). *Meister Eckhart*. Freiburg and Munich: Herder.
Flanagan, Owen (2015). It takes a metaphysics: Raising virtuous Buddhists. In Nancy E. Snow (ed.). *Cultivating virtue: Perspectives from philosophy, theology, and psychology*, 171–94. Oxford and New York: Oxford University Press.
Geach, Peter (1977). *The virtues*. Cambridge: Cambridge University Press.
Halbig, Christoph (2013). *Der Begriff der Tugend und die Grenzen der Tugendethik*. Berlin: Suhrkamp.
Halwani, Raja (2003). *Virtuous liaisons: Care, love, sex, and virtue ethics*. Chicago and LaSalle, IL: Open Court.
Halwani, Raja (2018). Sexual ethics. In Nancy E. Snow (ed.). *The Oxford handbook of virtue*, 680–99. Oxford: Oxford University Press.

Heidegger, Martin (2004). *Being and time.* Translated by John Macquarrie and Edward Robinson. Oxford: Blackwell.

Heidegger, Martin (1975). *The Origin of the work of art.* Translated by Albert Hofstadter. New York: Harper and Rowe.

Herzberg, Stephan (2018). Moralität im Licht der *caritas.* Über die Liebe als Höchstform des Wohlwollens. In Winfried Rohr (ed.). *Liebe—eine Tugend? Das Dilemma der modernen Ethik und der verdrängte Status der Liebe*, 169–84. Wiesbaden: Springer VS.

Ivanhoe, Philip J. (2013). Virtue ethics and the Chinese Confucian tradition. In Daniel C. Russell (ed.). *The Cambridge companion to virtue ethics*, 49–69. Cambridge: Cambridge University Press.

Kant, Immanuel (1998). (CpR). *The critique of pure reason.* Translated by Paul Guyer. Cambridge: Cambridge University Press.

Kant, Immanuel (1969). (CJ). *The critique of judgement.* Translated by Meredith James Creed. Oxford: Clarendon Press.

Keenan, James F. (1995). Proposing cardinal virtues. *Theological studies*, 36, 709–29.

Kristjánsson, Kristján (2018). Virtue from the perspective of psychology. In Nancy E. Snow (ed.). *The Oxford handbook of virtue*, 546–68. New York: Oxford University Press.

Latour, Bruno (2018). *Das terrestrische Manifest*, Frankfurt a. M.: Suhrkamp.

Lear, Jonathan (2008). *Radical hope: Ethics in the face of cultural devastation.* Cambridge, MA: Harvard University Press.

Luckner, Andreas (2005). *Klugheit.* Berlin and Boston: De Gruyter.

MacIntyre, Alasdair (2007). *After virtue: A study in moral theory.* 3rd ed. Notre Dame, IN: University of Notre Dame Press.

MacIntyre, Alasdair (1999). *Dependent rational animals: Why human beings need the virtues.* Chicago and La Salle, IL: Open Court.

MacKenzie, Matthew (2018). Buddhism and the virtues. In Nancy E. Snow (ed.). *The Oxford handbook of virtue*, 153–70. New York: Oxford University Press.

Meister Eckhart (EW) (2008). *Werke.* Bd. 1 und 2. Edited by Niklas Largier. Frankfurt a. M.: Deutscher Klassiker Verlag.

Meister Eckhart (DW) (1936 ff.). *Die Deutschen Werke.* Edited by Josef Quint and Georg Steer. Stuttgart: Kohlhammer.

Meister Eckhart (LW) (1964 ff.). *Lateinische Werke.* Edited by Loris Sturlese. Stuttgart: Kohlhammer.

Meister Eckhart (RdU). *Reden der Unterweisung/Unterscheidung.* In EW, Bd. 2, 334–433.

Mieth, Dietmar (1972). *Christus, das Soziale im Menschen: Texterschließungen zu Meister Eckhart.* Düsseldorf: Patmos.

Mieth, Dietmar (1984). *Die neuen Tugenden: Ein ethischer Entwurf.* Düsseldorf: Patmos.

Mieth, Dietmar (2003). Meister Eckhart: The power of inner liberation. In Fernando F. Segoria (ed.). *Toward a new heaven and a new earth*, 314–33. Maryknoll and New York: Orbis Books.

Mieth, Dietmar (2004). *Meister Eckhart: Mystik und Lebenskunst.* Düsseldorf: Patmos.

Mieth, Dietmar (2014a). *Meister Eckhart: Einheit mit Gott. Die bedeutendsten Schriften zur Mystik.* Düsseldorf: Patmos.

Mieth, Dietmar (2014b). *Meister Eckhart*. München: C.H. Beck. (English translation Leuven: Peeters 2023)

Mieth, Dietmar (2015). *The outer and the inner constitution of human dignity in Meister Eckhart*. In Ulrich Schmiedel and James A. Maraazzo Jr. (eds.). *Dynamics of Difference: Christianity and Alterity*. Festschrift for Werner G. Jeanrond, 71–78. London et al.: Bloomsbury.

Mieth, Dietmar (2019). *Sterben und Lieben*. Freiburg: Herder.

Mieth, Dietmar (2020a). "Diligere Deum et proximum": Augustin et Maître Eckhart. In Marie-Anne Vannier (ed.). *Maître Eckhart: Lecteur des Pères Latins*, 145–58. Paris: Beauchesne.

Mieth, Dietmar (2020b): Self-transcendence in Meister Eckhart. In Martin Fuchs, Antje Linkenbach, Martin Mulsow, Bernd-Christian Otto, Rahul Bjørn Parson and Jörg Rüpke (eds.). *Religious individualisation: Historical dimensions and comparative perspectives*, 73–97. New York: de Gruyter.

Müller, Anselm Winfried (1998). *Was taugt die Tugend? Elemente einer Ethik des guten Lebens*. Stuttgart: Kohlhammer.

Ossowska, Maria (1971). *Social determinants of moral ideas*. London: Routledge.

Panzig, Erik A. (2005). *Gelâzenheit und abegescheidenheit: Eine Einführung in das theologische Denken des Meister Eckhart*. Leipzig: EVA.

Pieper, Josef (1996). *Schriften zur Philosophischen Anthropologie und Ethik: Das Menschenbild der Tugendlehre*. Edited by Berthold Wald. Josef Pieper Werke, Band 4. Hamburg: Meiner.

Pieper, Josef (2010). *Über die Tugenden*. Munich: Kösel.

Rosa, Hartmut (2016). *Resonanz: Eine Soziologie der Weltbeziehungen*. Berlin: Suhrkamp.

Rohr, Winfried (ed.) (2018). *Liebe—eine Tugend? Das Dilemma der modernen Ethik und der verdrängte Status der Liebe*. Wiesbaden: Springer VS.

Rüther, Markus (2022). *Als Stoiker leben: Was wir wissen und üben müssen*. Darmstadt: WBG Theiss.

Schockenhoff, Eberhard (1987). *Bonum hominis: Die anthropologischen und theologischen Grundlagen der Tugendethik des Thomas von Aquin*. Mainz: Matthias-Grünewald-Verlag.

Slote, Michael (2001). *Morals from motives*. Oxford and New York: Oxford University Press.

Spaemann, Robert (1996). *Personen: Versuche über den Unterschied zwischen "etwas" und "jemand"*. Stuttgart: Klett-Cotta.

Snow, Nancy E. (2010). *Virtue as social intelligence: An empirically grounded theory*. New York: Routledge.

Swanton, Christine (2003). *Virtue ethics: A pluralistic view*. Oxford: Oxford University Press.

Timpe, Kevin and Craig A. Boyd (eds.) (2014). *Virtues and their vices*. Oxford: Oxford University Press.

Thomas Aquinas (De virt.). *Quaestio disputata De virtutibus*. www.corpusthomisticum.org / *Disputed Questions on the Virtues*. www.aquiansinstitute.org.

Thomas Aquinas (STh). *Summa Theologiae*. www.corpusthomisticum.org / *Theological Sum*. www.aquiansinstitute.org.

Tiwald, Justin (2018). Confucianism and Neo-Confucianism. In Nancy E. Snow (ed.). *The Oxford handbook of virtue*, 171–89. New York: Oxford University Press.

Vallor, Shannon (2016). *Technology and the Virtues: A Philosophical Guide to a Future Worth Wanting*. New York: Oxford University Press.

Vinzent, Markus (2011). *The Art of Detachment*. Eckhart: Texts and Studies, vol. 1. Leuven and Paris: Walpole.

Whiting, Kai and Leonidas Konstantakos (2021). *Being better: Stoicism for a world worth living in*. Novato, CA: New World Library.

Zagzebski, Linda Trinkaus (1996). *Virtues of the mind: An inquiry into the nature of virtue and the ethical foundations of knowledge*. Cambridge: Cambridge University Press.

Zagzebski, Linda Trinkaus (2017). *Exemplarist moral theory*. New York: Oxford University Press 2017.

Three Types of Fatalistic Practice[1]

Andreas Pettenkofer

1. Introduction

Treating our ways of relating to the world as objects for social research offers new perspectives on our presuppositions; it makes it easier to take an empirical look at some taken-for-granted assumptions of current theories of society. A case in point is the widely shared notion that "modern" social practices are sustained by the idea of an open future. This idea can be found in quite different accounts of modernity; its central intuition is that—since many "traditional" institutions have lost much of their cultural power—"modern" structures enable, and compel, those who live in such a society to acknowledge that they can fashion their own world. As this chapter will try to show, such accounts ignore the explanatory importance of fatalistic ways of relating to the world, and the role of practices whose participants project a future about which they have little to choose, because they feel caught in what they (at least implicitly) imagine either as a closed space they cannot leave, or as a stream that sweeps them along.

One reason for discounting such attitudes may lie in the assumption that they must entail a *passive* outlook, and can therefore only sustain prac-

---

[1] I would like to the thank the participants of a panel on "The Power of Powerlessness" organized by Jasmin Siri and Stephan Lessenich, of Gesa Lindemann's Arbeitsgruppe Sozialtheorie, and of a colloquium at the Max-Weber-Kolleg for their comments on earlier versions of these ideas, and Hartmut Rosa for his critical reading of a manuscript of this chapter.

© The author/s 2023, published by Campus Verlag, Open Access: CC BY-SA 4.0
Bettina Hollstein, Hartmut Rosa, Jörg Rüpke (eds.), "Weltbeziehung"
DOI: 10.12907/978-3-593-45587-7_004

tices of avoidance, or "doing nothing."[2] But maintaining such a clear-cut distinction between "doing nothing" and more active versions of fatalism-based practices might be difficult.[3] At any rate, focusing only on cases of "doing nothing" would mean overlooking important other types of fatalistic practice. These practices are fatalistic not because they imply avoiding all activity, but because they are constituted by fatalistic ways of understanding the world. These ways of understanding do not only offer ex-post justifications for these practices; rather, they guide them by selecting a very small set of available options for acting: Alternative ways of acting may remain thinkable in an abstract sense, but they no longer appear as live options (they are understood either to be impossible to perform, or to remain without consequences, or to have disastrous consequences). Hence, the notion that there is no way out selects the elements that make up these practices, generates the energy that drives them, and guarantees their stability. In this sense, these practices are not simply resilient to, or compatible with, fatalistic orientations; rather, they are constituted by them. And while it may seem plausible to assume that fatalism precludes all critical activities, understanding these practices requires acknowledging that this is not the case. Fatalistic ways of relating to the world can generate their own norms and their own modes of critique; they can also adapt and transform existing modes of critique. This is, on the one hand, crucial for the stability of these practices: By creating such options for mutual critique, they enable their participants to identify and correct deviant behaviour. On the other hand, this is part of what enables fatalistic practices to transform their environment. (All three types discussed below have contributed to sustaining radical political movements.) As this chapter will try to show, fatalistic ways of relating to the world are closely tied to activities which are crucial for the dynamics of "modern" society; several puzzling forms of political activity—including some improbable types of collective action—become easier to explain if one recognizes that they are shaped by fatalistic ways of relating to world.

---

2 For an account that focuses on how fatalism can sustain a given social structure by generating passivity, see Pettenkofer (2017). But see Sammet (2014, 73).

3 What taken in isolation may simply appear as "doing nothing" (staying in bed, not going to work, not answering emails, not interacting with others, etc.) can look rather different if its context is taken into account: First, it will be understood by all participants as following *one* line of behaviour rather than another and, in that sense, as performing a choice. Second, in most contexts, such a line of behaviour will be seen as seriously deviant, so following it can require a lot of stamina. Calling such a behaviour "inaction" may therefore be quite misleading.

Why fatalism can have such effects becomes clearer if one recognizes that full-fledged fatalism is a mode of *reflexivity*. Certainly, the firm expectation that change is impossible can also function as a *tacit* preunderstanding. In that mode, however, such a way of relating to the world is easily interrupted: Frictions between an agent's attitude and a given situation can initiate a process of reflection, which may transform existing attitudes and routines. This is what the pragmatist tradition has always emphasized (e.g., Dewey [1922] 1988). Within this tradition, however, the discussion of such processes has mostly focused on a specific version of them, which ends with any blockage being dissolved. Fatalistic practices offer occasions for observing a different type of outcome; in these cases, the process of reflection results in the delineation of a set of actions that, from the point of view of the agent, would be futile to even think about. The solution then consists of learning to take the blockage as given. This does not only imply a renunciation of certain activities, but also a new routine of selectively avoiding reflection, which creates new, self-sustaining forms of selective attention (see Pettenkofer 2017).[4] However, this kind of fatalism does not at all entail a *complete* renunciation of action and reflection. It has social consequences because it produces a specific self-limiting mode of reflexivity which adapts to perceived boundaries of action. As a mode of reflexivity of this kind, fatalism is highly resilient against many possible disruptions: Many objections can now be addressed on the basis of the reflective conviction that "It would be pointless to think about this." It is also because of this particular resilience that norms and modes of critique which emerge from fatalistic attitudes can be so influential. For these reasons, too, taking such attitudes into account offers new explanatory possibilities—including alternatives to current normativist strategies of explanation.

2. The Practice of Process Fatalism

If one looks for empowering types of fatalism that create their own norms and their own forms of critique, the first type that comes to mind may be a practice that, for some decades, has been associated with the Thatcherite

---

4 If pragmatism is meant to work as a general sociological perspective (see Gross et al. 2022) and not just as a partial theory about cases with desirable outcomes, it would profit from systematically addressing cases that deviate from the type of process it has typically focused on.

slogan that "There is no alternative." As has often been pointed out, this practice cannot be reduced to a set of policy proposals; rather, it offers an encompassing way of understanding the world in terms of uncontrollable processes seen as shaping, and constraining, the space available for political action. This type of fatalistic practice is all the more important since it does not only appear within a relatively recent version of free-market conservatism.

2.1 The "Progress" Version of Process Fatalism

As Hannah Arendt has shown in a series of texts published before Thatcher started her political career, this way of talking about politics had already emerged in the 19th century, with its conceptual structure being shared among a set of new competing political positions.[5] Each of them relies on the ontological presupposition that all political action happens within a long-term large-scale process ("History") that is uncontrollable as well as unpredictable (at least as far as its concrete course is concerned), and to which one can only submit. Arendt emphasizes that this presupposition can be found in liberal ideas about progress, in the socialist tradition (particularly in its social-democrat and Leninist strands), and in Social Darwinism. These versions make different assumptions about the character of the assumed process and the type of selection effects it performs (mostly, selection by "the market", by "class struggle", by "race conflict," or by some combination of them), but all are based on the same notion of history.

This type also confirms the pragmatist model sketched above. First, as Arendt underlines, this way of understanding the world results from processes of reflection triggered by profound disappointment about the possibilities of political action, that is, of actively shaping the social world (Arendt [1957] 2012, 100, 108). These reflections had different points of departure—for the "left-wing" version, the feeling that 1848 proved the impossibility of democratic revolution; for the "right-wing" one, the feeling that the French revolution's trajectory proved that political attempts to change the direction of society's development will either be futile or have

---

[5] See, first of all, Arendt ([1954] 2006) and, as an extended version of its second part, Arendt ([1957] 2012); Arendt's starting point was her inquiry into the origins of "totalitarian" political movements (Arendt 1973). For an overview of her account of "process thinking," see Hyvönen (2013).

disastrous consequences.[6] But they converged in a set of very similar ways of understanding the world.

The fatalistic motifs that were crucial for its emergence remain inscribed into the mature versions of this "process" discourse. This concerns, first of all, a general doubt about the ability of humans to act rationally. That doubt even shapes the neoliberal strand of this discourse: Though originating from the discipline of economics, it sacrifices, in the name of an epistemic fatalism, much of the cherished idea of "rational action"—at least in the Hayekian version of neoliberalism, which had a particularly strong political influence (Slobodian 2018). Starting with Hayek (1937), it emphasizes that while agents may try to maximize their utility, their capability of actually doing this is very limited because having the necessary knowledge about the relevant process is mostly impossible. (This view is, again, not so different from the Marxist account which sees agents as capable of a narrow version of local rationality but, due to socially caused distortions of perspective, as incapable of reasonable cognitive generalization.) From this scepticism about action, it also draws the conclusion that political interventions in the assumed process are doomed to fail; according to this view, while economic agents typically have at least some sort of local knowledge, politicians do not even have that. This translates into strong assumptions, often expressed in the language of "complexity," about the limits of political action. In all these versions of process thinking, the idea of the rational agent becomes less important than that of evolutionary selection.—Here, one might object that at least the liberal version of this discourse is linked to a rhetoric of freedom, which seems to imply an accent on the possibilities of (individual) action. There is, however, a semantic shift, as Arendt (2005, 120) shows: Within this mode of description,

"freedom is not localized in either human beings in their action and interaction or in the space that forms between men, but rather is assigned to a process that unfolds behind the backs of those who act and does its work in secret, beyond the visible arena of public affairs. The model for this concept of freedom is a river flowing freely, in which every attempt to block its flow is an arbitrary impediment".

---

6 On uses of the French revolution as a core example in conservative discourses of futility, see Hirschman (1991).

Among the candidates for such subjects of freedom are "the market" (as expressed by terms like "free market" and "freedom of the market") and the unrestrained "class struggle."[7]

And here, too, this fatalistic mode of reflexivity can be empowering. It offers its users new ways of dealing with blockages of action, by making it easier to no longer *reflect* about certain issues. Through its strong claims about indisputable necessities, it liberates its users from diverse ethical considerations, and from the disruptive emotions they might feel if alternative paths of action were seen to be available; they can now rely on the justification that their actions only put into effect what would have to happen anyway.[8] Therefore, even though the "illusion of politics" is a trope that can be shared among the competing strands of this discourse,[9] this kind of process thinking can enable highly ambitious forms of political action, predicated on the idea of doing what is *unavoidable* (rather than merely in line with the agent's preferences). Particularly in the neoliberal version, this can also appear in the guise of a politics of *self-limitation* which makes massive efforts in order to block forms of collective action that, from its point of view, appear to be based on illusory hopes, and thought likely to have disastrous consequences.

2.2 Process Fatalism without Progress

Arendt focuses on a version of this process ontology that sees history as bringing "progress."[10] However, the full action-enabling effect of process thinking can only be grasped if one also considers a version that is not tied to such hopes. The "river" or "stream" metaphor, which communicates such a way of relating to the world, also appears in this other version: Bismarck said, "Man can neither create nor direct the stream of time. He can only travel upon it and steer with more or less skill and experience", adding in

---

7 Concerning the necessity of "liberating" class struggle, Marx ([1848] 1971, 136) writes: "Die beste Staatsform ist die, worin die gesellschaftlichen Gegensätze nicht verwischt [...] werden. Die beste Staatsform ist die, worin sie zum freien Kampf [...] kommen."
8 See Koselleck (1979, 268–270) for a discussion of an early example of this trope.
9 François Furet – a historian whose re-evaluation of the French revolution was essential for the politics of history accompanying the "neoliberal" turn around 1980 – takes up Marx's critique of a bourgeois "political superstition" (in: Engels and Marx [1845] 1962, 128), and translates it into a general statement on *l'illusion de la politique* (Furet 1978, 98).
10 For a different perspective on the concept of "progress" see Kemmerling in this volume.

another context: "if I stick my hand into it, I do so because I believe it to be my duty, not because I hope thereby to change its direction" (quoted in Clark 2019, 118). Here, the "stream of time" is not described as an instance that performs *desirable* selections; nevertheless, one has to adapt to it (an idea that has been crucial, for instance, within international-relations "realism").

Certainly, perceiving the supposed historical process as bringing "progress" offers additional justifications for activities understood as adapting to, and accelerating, such a process. It also offers agents a possibility to *identify* with that process; they may derive a feeling of self-worth from understanding themselves as instruments driving this progress, and as being an "incarnation of the dynamic trend" (Arendt 1973, 215). This mode of understanding enables agents to do things they would otherwise not have been capable of; this can perhaps be seen most clearly by the level of violence that has been performed not only in the name of its Leninist and its Social-Darwinist versions, but also in that of its liberal or neoliberal version.[11] As Arendt has pointed out, this acceptance of violence, too, is encouraged by the view of history-as-progress: The notion that one can only submit to this "historical" necessity makes it easier to think that the presently living should be seen, first of all, as instruments for bringing about a better future (Arendt [1954] 2006, 80), and to consider large parts of a given population as superfluous because they cannot be seen as contributing to that progress.[12]

Nevertheless, the kinds of necessity claims that result from *giving up* a "progress" view of history have their own empowering effects. This concerns, on the one hand, the general problem of legitimating political action. While "Bismarckian" necessity claims offer less in terms of *positive* justifications, they compensate for this by lowering the need for justifications in general. By avoiding claims about progress, they avoid having to rely on the kinds of the evaluative criteria which such claims would require, and which would constitute points of attack for "immanent critique." They also do not have to rely on precarious claims about historical teleology, or suggest what could be understood as utopian promises;[13] they can more fully acknowledge the contingent character of historical processes (without having to draw the self-

---

11 A prominent example is Hayek's much-discussed support for Pinochet's way of introducing "free-market" reforms (see Farrant and McPhail 2014). Like Leninists, Hayekians can have earnest discussions about the uses und problems of "transitional dictatorship."
12 On this motif in Arendt, see Börner (2019).
13 One can assume that for these reasons, Bismarckian process fatalism will gain in importance. In most contexts, the "progress" versions of process fatalism (including neoliberalism) seem to have

undermining conclusion that this element of contingency enhances agents' freedom of action[14]).

On the other hand, this concerns their effects on how agents understand themselves. By making it easier for agents *not* to identify with the acts they perform, these necessity claims permit a version of what Goffman (1961) calls role distance ("This is not who I am, I am just doing what cannot be helped"). Through this, they enable agents to continue participating in activities they would rather not be identified with (and thereby contribute to the stability of these activities). At the same time, these necessity claims can also support role *maintenance*: They make it easier for agents to say that, for the time being, it is simply impossible to do what they would really want to do; with the help of such claims, agents can publicly (and also in their self-understanding) sustain an identity which, under other premises, might be more quickly seen as being contradicted by their activities. By thus offering agents (and organizations) a different way of relating to the norms they publicly identify with, this version of process fatalism empowers them by creating more room for manoeuver. Examples of such empowering effects can be found in climate politics: Central tropes of the current rhetoric of climate-policy delay (Lamb et al. 2020) rely on fatalistic assumptions; this obviously applies to claims that climate action is impossible anyway, but also to claims about inevitable free-rider problems that would make climate action futile ("If we reduce our emissions, others will do nothing"), which is also the premise behind claims like "We are a small country, reducing our emissions will not change anything." The flexibility created by this attitude has been particularly visible in German climate politics, which has combined strong public commitments to sustainability and democracy with continually postponing effective climate action, and has compensated for the postponed energy transformation by establishing long-term business relationships that prop up fossil-fuel-based authoritarian regimes (a policy for which international-relations "realism" has offered helpful justifications); in that context, this fatalistic framework also made it possible for several heads of state to maintain the identity claim of being a "climate chancellor".

---

become minority views. Their power to actually convince has shrunk even if, being entrenched in existing institutions, they continue to shape political action.

14 A radical version of this view has been articulated by the German systems theorist Niklas Luhmann (1971, 44): "Alles könnte anders sein – und fast nichts kann ich ändern."

As these examples show, process fatalism is an important example of a fatalistic way of relating to the world. It also disproves the notion that fatalism can only be found among those who suffer from a relative lack of resources, and not among the elites; a more thorough discussion of fatalistic practices would have to deal with it extensively. Since most versions of this type of fatalism (particularly the "neoliberal" one) have already been widely discussed, this chapter will devote more space to two other types of fatalistic practice, where the enabling effects of fatalism may be less obvious. Before discussing these other types, however, it might be useful to briefly address a methodological question that the practice of process fatalism could be seen to raise.

2.3 Fatalism as Mere Rhetoric?

Like any other structure of meaning, fatalistic ways of interpreting the world can be deployed strategically. Impossibility claims may be quite useful during political conflicts; there can be obvious rhetorical advantages to presenting a course of action as simply being without alternatives, rather than merely corresponding to the preferences of those advocating it. So how can one be sure that fatalistic accounts represent the way in which at least some agents actually relate to their world?

A first answer might be that agents sometimes will not simply find it expedient to claim that there is no alternative; they will find it attractive to look for reasons enabling them to believe that such alternatives indeed do not exist, and to avoid pursuing lines of thought that might lead to a different result. Take again the example of climate-politics inaction: For those who continually decide to postpone climate action while being aware that this will contribute to bringing about large-scale catastrophic results for an enormous number of people, it can be a reassuring thought that attempting another kind of politics would be futile anyway.

A more general answer might be that even committed adherents of *dietrologia*, while firmly convinced that every utterance has to be interpreted in terms of hidden ulterior motives, will probably concede that a rhetorical strategy can only work if there is a public which sees its central claims as credible; so if these fatalistic understandings occur systematically, and those who offer them are politically successful, one should assume that at least parts of the public believe these claims. There is of course at least one important exception: Within uncontestedly asymmetric power constellations, power holders may find it expedient to use justifications which are so evidently implausible that nobody will assume anybody could be convinced by them: By parodying the language game of giving reasons, they signal that truth claims and arguments will not make a difference. Impossibility claims can serve this purpose, too; the more preposterous an impossibility claim, the more useful it is for such a strategy. For instance, statements like "This problem can only be solved by the market" may not function as arguments, but rather as performative gestures conveying that arguments will not be listened to. Still, this is only *one* communicative function of fatalistic utterances, and no general rule for interpreting such utterances can be drawn from it. In this sense, these kinds of objections do not offer good reasons for clinging to the comforting idea that under "modern" conditions, people may talk like fatalists but cannot really mean it.

3. The Practice of Industriousness

While process fatalism is to a large extent an elite practice, the practice of industriousness is particularly visible among those who, within a given division of labour, see themselves as tied to a position they can neither change nor leave. The industrious feel trapped in a constellation of circumstances that is hard to endure, but they no longer think about fighting back or looking for an escape, because they are certain that this would be pointless. (This attitude is quite compatible with fatalism about the course of "history," though it does not require it.) Such a lack of hope, however, does not render them passive; it enables them to perform activities that, under other conditions, might be quite impossible for them.

This way of relating to the world can lead them to no longer adopt a normative perspective: Under these premises, invoking certain norms— even norms that, within a given social order, may appear to be publicly accepted (e.g., ideas about equal dignity)—can seem futile. The industrious may come the conclusion that not only for themselves, but also for all other members of the category to which they belong (including future members of this category), these norms will have no consequences; therefore, they may conclude that these norms cannot even serve as *utopian* points of reference, because viewing one's condition from the vantage point offered by these norms could only create dangerous illusions. The fact that, in East German daily life some decades after the end of the GDR, one continually encounters tropes like "down-to-earth"[15] or "pragmatic" seems to indicate such a loss of plausibility.

This type of practice can also be linked to an explicit rejection of any kind of reflexivity that understands itself as political. Such a rejection can be even easier for those who see themselves as sharing a critical, theory-based awareness of the pressures caused by their own condition, and of the dangers of overburdening themselves. This knowledge enables them to say to themselves: "I can't afford to think like that." A typical example is the answer given by an acquaintance of a journalist at a left-wing Berlin-based daily when asked about outsourcing domestic work: "Do I think it's a good thing someone else does my care work?[16] To be honest, I have thrown all these political questions overboard. Because I simply need it." (Weissenburger 2021)

Nevertheless, this practice can also generate different (mutually compatible) normative articulations, which can also serve as a basis for critique, and for processes of politicization. This is not only essential for the stability of this practice; it also explains why the practice of industriousness can have consequences that reach far beyond the categories of individuals who perform it.

3.1 Normative Articulations of Industriousness (1): Rules of Prudence

The first of these normative articulations takes the form of a rule of prudence: It would be unreasonable not to accept things as they are. The world is what it is, so everybody (at least, the members of one's own category, who will not be able to change this world) should get used to these conditions, avoid irrational hopes (illusions about changing the world), and develop routines enabling them to deal with their situation.[17] This rule of prudence can be linked to norms of emotional display: Complaining or expressing pain can now be seen as pointless, since — according to this view — such emotional expressions will never function as messages that could lead to any kind of positive change. Under these premises, protest can be understood as a manifestation

---

15 See Thériault (2020) on the pervasiveness of this trope in East German everyday life.
16 The interviewee uses the German neologism *Care-Arbeit*, presenting herself as a person who is familiar with the relevant feminist debate.
17 Accordingly, surveys in the rural parts of Eastern Thuringia show huge support for the claim "Workers' interests are being less and less taken into account" *and* for the claim "Criticizing the capitalist system won't help us – these are the rules" (Schmalz et al. 2021, 58).

of weakness, and critique as a mode of losing touch with reality, or (contrary to a common political rhetoric that associates critique with "awakening") as a form of dreaming — as resulting from a state where self-control has been lost.[18]

A key context where such normative articulations are being developed and enforced is a practice of education meant to spare one's children unnecessary suffering. This may be most easy to observe among the underprivileged: Even if they do not accept their position — i.e., do not see the given social order as legitimate, and reject the reasons offered for justifying it — a large part of their socialization work may consist of attempts to help their children get used to the facts of discrimination, in order to protect them against additional avoidable unhappiness, and to "empower" them within the space of the possibilities they were born into. A rather similar activity, however, can be detected among the relatively privileged. In his study of current processes of bureaucratization, Graeber (2018, 77–79) reports that several of his informants — all of them academics or university students — told him how their parents seemed to plead for an early familiarization with meaningless work, pushing them into internships which could only have the value of creating this kind of experience. Graeber concludes that these parents see this as a necessary counterweight to the experience of studying at a university, which they worry might create among their children the expectation that, for them, there could be an alternative to this kind of meaningless work experience, and more generally, create illusory hopes about future possibilities for reflecting, and for enjoying some freedom of action.

3.2 Normative Articulations of Industriousness (2): Distributive Justice and Mutual Respect

The second type of normative articulations takes the form of rules of equal treatment. The starting point for this articulation can be gleaned from statements like "I don't get any help either," or "*Mir hilft auch keiner.*"

On the one hand, this kind of perception can justify a refusal of solidarity that, under these premises, can also be defended by invoking a norm of

---

18 Kamala Markandaya ([1954] 2007, 54) has the narrator of her village novel *Nectar in a Sieve* say: "one gets used to anything [...]; only sometimes when I was weak, or in sleep while my will lay dormant, I found myself rebellious, protesting, rejecting, and no longer calm".

reciprocity. Here, even the awareness that others are suffering from the same problems will not (as optimistic theories about politicization processes tend to assume) make it more likely that a process of solidarization ensues—not even if this kind of suffering appears to be widely shared. On the contrary, it is the very perception of commonality—of shared suffering—that can sustain an avoidance of cooperation: If one's own conditions seems immune to change, it may appear more plausible to say "Everybody has to deal with that", or "*Ich komme damit schließlich auch klar*". This can also become a *collective* statement ("*Wir kommen damit auch klar*"); therefore, this normative articulation can sustain contexts of communication which stabilize this way of relating to the world as well as the practical consensus that builds upon it. This can also reinforce the corresponding rules of emotional display: "We don't complain either." At this point, it can also become plausible to say that there is nothing remarkable, or nothing special, about the suffering of others ("*Mir geht es schließlich auch nicht besser*," "*Das geht allen so, da habe ich kein Mitleid*"), and that, therefore, those who suffer should make no special demands. In a next step, the preunderstanding that "I won't be able to escape my condition either" can make it seem appropriate not to try to understand others' concrete situations in the first place: The impression that there is nothing special about the suffering of others makes it easy to infer that there will be nothing remarkable to understand either. Moreover, for the industrious fatalist, it can seem plausible to say: "Nobody cares about me (about us); why should I (we) try to understand others?" This contributes to stabilizing this practice; it protects the industrious preunderstanding against possible disruptions. This way of thinking does not require a belief that the constraints from which one suffers, or from which others suffer, are *good*—neither in the sense that these constraints are justified in themselves, nor in the sense that they can be expected to have positive consequences (for instance, that they might have disciplinary effects a practitioner of industriousness might find desirable).[19] Therefore, the stability of this kind of practice does not depend on finding justifications for the constraints to which it submits. It also does

---

19 Nevertheless, this attitude can make arguments about the value of discipline seem appealing: The rules of prudence discussed above now can also become attractive because they offer independent justifications for ways of acting that avoid empathy. (Since these rules can help describe a nonempathic activity in a way that makes it socially acceptable, they can also help stabilize this activity.) For example, McCrindle and Rowbotham (1977, 4) recount how, while interviewing workers' daughters in 1970s England, they often were confronted with expressions of hatred against the interviewee's mother: "We were surprised by this hostility until we realized that teaching a daughter

not depend on a possibility to attribute to these constraints the kind of systematic, rule-based character which would be a necessary precondition for most justifications for social restrictions.

On the other hand, the certainty that "I don't get any help either" can promote the emergence of specific criteria of distributive justice: The more attempts at changing their condition seem futile, they more difficult it will seem to react to a structure of inequality either with attempts to rise within that structure, or with expressions of indignation and demands for transforming that structure. Within this fatalistic framework, the participants' main concern can now be that others should not fare better than them: One possible strategy for dealing with their experience of hopelessness, and making their own condition more bearable, is to make sure that they will not have to watch persons with whom they compare themselves end up in positions that seem better than their own. In this sense, fatalism can initiate a turn towards envy—not as a desire to also have a good that the better-off enjoy (after all, this seems hopeless), but as a desire that the goods one cannot enjoy should not be available to others either: the type of envy called *Missgunst* in German.[20]

This type of envy can then be articulated in the guise of new norms (as has been extensively discussed under the label *ressentiment*). Again, this does need to result in a justification of the fatalism-generating constraints as such (e.g., "these constraints are good," "only actions that are subject to these constraints are good"). Such an articulation can also take the form of a rule of distributive justice ("it is only fair if everybody has to submit to the same constraints," *"Warum sollte es ihr besser gehen als uns?"* etc.). In a next step, such a rule can be translated into a norm of solidarity which, for instance, enables the industrious members of a work organization to criticize other members who try to defy the organization's rules (*"Wir ordnen uns auch unter"*). This can be escalated into a norm of mutual respect. Within the kind of normative framework emerging from such a process, only those who submit without complaint can credibly claim that they do not "think that they are special" or "think that they are better than others." Under these premises, any impression of individuality conveyed by a person's behaviour can be understood as

---

her role as a future housewife can all too easily develop a sadistic quality when the mother herself is tired, over-worked and oppressed by her own existence."

20 On the Aristotelian distinction between indignation, emulation, and envy-as-*Missgunst*, as three possible ways of reacting to inequality, see Geuss (2016).

a gesture that devalues others, because it suggests some sort of elbow room that this person uses or tries to use ("Not everything is about you," "*Auch du solltest nicht so viel Aufhebens um dich Machen*").[21]

Those who feel pained by the fact that their own freedom of action seems minimal can then invoke these norms in order to make sure that their equals stay within their bounds. The deeper the fatalism, the more exclusively will this kind of critical attention be directed towards those seen as equal or less privileged: Only they, and not the highly privileged, can still be seen as objects of possible actions. The fatalists' yearning for equality, while mostly felt by them to be illusory, may still take aim at those close to them; there remains the possibility to make sure that their colleagues do not fare better than them. The force of this social mechanism varies according to the degree to which the participants feel that their freedom of action is constrained. As Scheler ([1912] 1978, 7) writes, this experience of powerlessness is particularly intense wherever, in addition to other constraints, there is a strong pressure to avoid even the expression of nonconforming emotions; one current example is the duty to display a permanent smile that applies in large parts of the personal service sector and can also become an obligation that members of certain workplaces impose on each other.

Within everyday cooperation, this practice of industriousness can have strong effects. For instance, in work organizations, envy can create strong commitments to making sure that the current rules are being followed, and to rejecting any criticism directed against these rules ("We have to deal with this, too"). In this sense, envy encourages the self-policing of the less privileged, lowers the costs of centralized control, and facilitates the emergence of stable structures of cooperation. Crucially, this also works where the participants do not see the existing set of rules as justified: This mechanism can sustain *any* kind of norm, and can therefore help free organizations from the demand of having to present themselves as legitimate to all their members. It does not require normative integration according to the official rules of a given structure of cooperation; nor does it require that members can be made to recognize the rationality of these rules. The energy that enables members to conform to these rules and to enforce them also does not depend on the existence of "intrinsic" motivations.

---

21 On the margin of manoeuver that displays of individuality typically require, see Goffman (1961) on "role distance."

For a normativist perspective—a perspective that sees institutions as cooperation structures built on norms—these processes create an observation problem: An observer examining an institution shaped by the practice of industriousness will certainly encounter egalitarian-sounding ideas about justice and mutual respect; however, if this observer always already presupposes that normative attitudes are foundational for the observed cooperation, it will be hard to recognize where such attitudes only emerge as ex-post rationalizations of prior constraints. This does not just amount to an *explanatory weakness*. Often, this kind of analysis is meant to contrast the actual practice of a given institution with the "ideals" or "values" that can be deduced from the norms which operate within that institution; a typical goal of this kind of "immanent critique" is to motivate the members of a given institution to transform their practice in a more universalistic and, for instance, less punitive direction.[22] Those involved in this kind of fatalistic practice, however, will feel that attempts to develop such universalistic rearticulations will be futile. They are also likely, for the reasons described above, to have no interest in making their rules less punitive. Therefore, when confronted with this kind of fatalistic practice, such normativist theories—even if they may understand themselves as adopting a critical point of view—tend to produce descriptions that are highly optimistic.

3.3 Politicizations of Industriousness

Once industrious fatalism has become a normal part of everyday coordination, it also can be politicized (which can, in turn, reinforce its presence within ordinary life). Common fatalistic tropes expressing the experience of being trapped in a constellation of non-cooperation—"I don't get any handouts either," "*Wir kriegen auch nichts geschenkt*"—offer an access to a meaning structure that helps make sense of surprising statistical data about decisions to vote for a "right-wing populist" party.

For understanding how the normative articulations described above come to have political consequences, Tocqueville's ideas about possible transformations of democratic norms remain highly useful (Tocqueville [1840] 1961, 137): At first, democratic institutions may communicate an ideal of equal liberty for all. If, however, some of those to whom this ideal has

---

22 For a prominent statement of this view, see Honneth (2011).

been communicated reach the conclusion that, unlike others, they will never acquire the promised liberty—that they will never enjoy real freedom of action—then this can transform this democratic ideal, with "liberty" and "equality" becoming separate goals. This is how fatalistic ways of relating to the world can change the meaning of egalitarian political norms: They can translate into the demand that the constraints which shape one's daily life should apply to everybody. This can concern the distribution of resources; here, the normative articulations described above can be translated into political statements like "Too much help is given to others," e.g., to refugees, or to other recipients of social benefits. The announcement that the "privileges" of such recipients will be cut is a core topic of what is usually called rightwing populism. (Those who do not believe the promise that these parties will improve the material condition of their voters may still believe in the *negative* goal of ensuring that others, too, "won't be given handouts". Under strictly fatalistic premises, not "The situation will improve for everybody" but "For others, the situation won't improve either" can count as a credible political pledge.) It can also concern the possibility that the members of some social categories might enjoy "special privileges" which might enable them to dodge rules meant to apply to everybody. This kind of worry can focus on the politics of criminal punishment, or on the politics of gender, where transgender issues have become a core topic of "right-wing populist" mobilization; even actors who cannot credibly claim to feel bound to traditionalist gender norms are thus enabled to display indignation over the possibility that "exceptions" would be made for minorities. The central concern within this strand of "right-wing populism," however, still seems to refer to the possibility that others might evade the obligation to *work*.[23]

All these worries are, however, subject to a self-imposed limitation: Here, too, efforts at curtailing "privileges" do not focus on everybody, but only on those seen as equal or less privileged. Since Tocqueville, this has been one of the puzzles of political sociology.[24] This puzzle can be solved by considering the fatalistic element in "right-wing populism," and by retaining the

---

23 This has also enabled a reclassification which is constitutive for a central antisemitic trope: From this point of view, the communist and the banker, far from being polar opposites, belong to the same category, because both try to escape ("real") work, and therefore ought to be seen as "parasites"; see also the related category of the "work-shy".
24 Tocqueville's most explicit statement can be found in an unpublished draft: "Tant que les bourgeois ont été différents des nobles, ils n'ont point été jaloux des nobles, mais entre eux. Et si nous nous examinons de plus près nous-mêmes, ne serons-nous pas tous effrayés d'y voir que l'envie

pragmatist insight that foci of attention and reflection are always shaped by perceived possibilities of action. If, for instance, despite a high willingness to criticize "privileges," almost no demands for downwards economic redistribution can be heard, the reason for this cannot be that supporters of "populist" movements have no idea of the kinds of lives the upper classes lead; news media used by the worse-off are full of depictions of such lives. Rather, what can be observed here is a selection effect produced by a fatalistic mode of reflexivity: Only those motives of critique that still appear to be connected to some credible programme of action are articulated in any serious way; while the conditions of those who, to the "right-wing populist," seem to be on an equal or lower social level might be amenable to change, thinking about reducing the privileges of economic elites will seem pointless. This fatalistic self-limitation also facilitates another transformation process already mentioned by Tocqueville ([1840] 1961, 405): What is, at first, an egalitarian impulse—nobody should be unduly privileged—can translate into a longing for powerful political actors who *guarantee* that this will not happen. In this way, this fatalistic attitude can contribute to institutionalisation of "right-wing populism" also by encouraging the creation of new hierarchies, and by giving plausibility to the ideal of the strongman.

For the ongoing institutionalisation of this type of politics, this envy-as-*Missgunst* scheme is also important because, through the worries and suspicion that it generates itself, it can constantly extend its own scope of application. On the one hand, these worries create a new, affectively grounded form of selective attention that drives a search for cases of unjustified privilege. This enhanced sensitivity makes it possible to apply the core accusation of *laziness* to the populations of whole states ("lazy Greeks") as well as to professional groups with typically long working hours ("lazy politicians"). From this vantage point, even the highly dangerous journey refugees take across the Mediterranean can be depicted as constituting a *touristic* experience, that is, as linked to a practice of laziness.[25] Consequently, within the German "right-wing populist" debate, it has not only become possible to assume that refugees take this kind of journey because they want to avoid hav-

---

s'y fait sentir à l'égard de nos voisins, de nos amis, de nos proches." (Tocqueville 1992, 1170; see Elster 2009, 69)

25 See Hentges (2018, 108–109) for a discussion of two *Alternative für Deutschland* election posters, showing a refugee boat on a calm sea with a sunset in the background, and a group of refugees on a beach, again watching the sunset.

ing to work ("*Einwanderung in die Sozialsysteme*"), but also to talk about *Asyltourismus*. Extending this scope of application also becomes easier because this interpretive scheme makes it possible to feel *downward jealousy* (de Swaan 1989): Being aware of the irreversibility of their own lives, which they experience as having been shaped by a set of inescapable harsh constraints, those who achieved a gruelling social ascent can now feel envy towards the worse-off—if it seems likely that the latter will have to suffer less for improving their economic condition ("*Da mussten wir auch durch*," "*Wir haben uns auch durchgebissen*," etc.). This can be, for instance, a specific envy of the formerly unemployed,[26] but also the general resentment of the old against the young (see Scheler [1912] 1978, 20). This type of envy can also translate into a criterion of recognition which may shape struggles for moral hierarchisation: "For me, everything was hard, so I can only recognize those for whom everything was hard."

Moreover, the concern that "There should be no handouts" can be shared across very different socio-economic positions. Therefore, this fatalistic scheme can sustain new forms of political cooperation—in the German case, particularly between (1) those who have experienced the hopelessness of the post-1989 East German labour market, (2) workers in companies in South-Western Germany who clearly profit from globalization, and (3) small entrepreneurs who may be quite successful economically. As the social structure of those who voted for the "right-wing populist" *Alternative für Deutschland* shows, this vote does not presuppose economic misery (see Lengfeld 2017; Bergmann et al. 2018); industrious fatalists do not have to belong to the "losers of modernization."[27] Surveys suggest it does not require fears about losing one's present economic status, either.[28] What seems nevertheless to be shared by many of these voters is the feeling of being caught in a treadmill from which there is no viable escape. This does not have to be linked to a strong feeling of economic uncertainty; such an uncertainty is only one possible cause of this treadmill experience. What seems forever lost, or has never been available for them, is the hope that they might even-

---

26 At the German federal election in 2017, at least in East Germany, the *AfD* vote correlates with the regional unemployment rate in 2000, but *not* with its rate at the time of the election (Manow 2018, 93–95). If fear of losing one's economic status were the main motive for voting *AfD*, the current unemployment rate should have at least as strong an influence as the former one.
27 On the history of this category, see Ulbricht (2020).
28 For survey data showing that standard explanations of "right-wing populism" seriously overstate the role of such fears of losing one's economic status, see Lübke and Delhey (2019).

tually reach a state of relative ease: Most of those who have been mobilized by "right-wing populism" can understand their (very heterogeneous) work experiences in this way; this also applies to those small entrepreneurs whose working lives can suggest to them that they should give up all hopes about solidarity, and who therefore see no reason to accept that others should be "given handouts." A political rhetoric which articulates these experiences can also create bridges towards those who experience a rural life where already the weak infrastructure can make it plausible to say "We don't get any help either," and who emphasize their pride in having always been "frugal" and "hardworking."[29] Therefore, this political mobilization shows how a fatalistic practice of industriousness can help sustain collective action, even on the level of national politics.

4. The Practice of Vengefulness

Both types of fatalistic practice discussed above imply a strong focus on the future (even if the future they project seems to be without alternatives). To its participants, many elements of the practice of industriousness appear plausible because they promise to make life more bearable (even if the circumstances of this life seem immune to change). The practice of process fatalism is even compatible with the idea of a future that offers improvements over the present (even if, from the point of view afforded by this practice, the set of options for pursuing such improvements is extremely limited).

The third type of fatalistic practice is different. Those who participate in it are convinced that the damages they have experienced cannot be made good. For them, improving their condition, or even maintaining their current position, is no longer an essential consideration. The recurrent experience of blocked action redirects their focus on a past that seems irrevocable. The remaining hope they can see as reasonable is that others will suffer damages, too. This belief can motivate a rejection of *any* kind of activism.[30] It can,

---

29 Searcey (2020) quotes a small entrepreneur in rural Arkansas explaining her vote for Trump: "Out here in rural America, nobody else is going to do it for me. [...] Because life comes so hard here, the Republican ideal is what we have. It's kind of me, myself and I." For an ethnographic account of this rural mode of living in the US, and of the rage it creates, see Wuthnow (2019).

30 To give a brief example: An activist from an NGO which tries to make the Indian state of Madhya Pradesh clean up wells used by Dalits told me that these Dalits often are not enthusiastic about the cleaning of these wells; they expect that once the water of a well is clean again, they will not

however, also lead to an activism for which the revenge motive (which can play a supporting role in the practice of industriousness) becomes dominant. Such an activism does not need to be accompanied by a long-term perspective, or by a weighing of future alternatives. Therefore, this way of relating to the world makes actions possible that, under other circumstances, would be quite unlikely.

While most readers will have encountered the practice of industriousness in their everyday lives, members of the academic middle classes often remain protected from this practice of vengefulness, at least from its more obvious versions. Therefore, this section proceeds differently than the last one: It turns to the debates on two much-discussed protest phenomena which can serve as extreme cases exemplifying two different versions of this fatalistic practice. For both debates, reconstructing the difficulties of some standard explanatory strategies, and the alternative explanations offered by some empirical accounts that contradict these standard approaches, helps identify a fatalistic structure of meaning that is constitutive for these activities.

4.1 Vengeful Activism Embedded in a Context of Future-Oriented Political Cooperation

In the first version of this practice, actions following a fatalistic logic of revenge become integrated into more complex structures of cooperation; only because they are able to make use of this fatalistic way of relating to the world can these structures operate the way they do. A particularly clear example is offered by one type of so-called suicide attacks. Attempts to explain "suicide" bombings often start by emphasizing that they are produced by organizations. This concerns a crucial motive: Some organizations see them as a useful tactic in an asymmetric conflict, and/or as proving the commitment they must demonstrate because they compete with other organizations (Bloom 2004). It also concerns some processes which make it more likely that such attacks actually happen: Organizations create commitment

---

have access to this water any more, since the locally dominant caste will block them. From this point of view, the only thing that, within the given distribution of power, they can aspire to is that the members of the dominant caste will also continue to suffer from this: "We have to drink that dirty water. Our children have to drink that dirty water. They should have to drink that dirty water, too."

devices (like filmed statements of those who agree to blow themselves up), which can bind would-be perpetrators to their promises (Gambetta 2006). But these explanations do not address the question why these organizations have few problems finding persons willing to make that promise.

Here, a common answer says that these perpetrators are deeply embedded into a cooperation structure which strongly values *collective* goals (typically, nationalist and/or religious goals)—to a degree that, for the participants, each individual life becomes much less important. Pape (2006), who elaborates such an explanation, suggests that this kind of activism can be described with Durkheim's concept of altruistic suicide (Durkheim [1897] 2005, chap. II.4).

However, while there may be cases fitting that description, empirical research shows that it is far from generally valid. This also applies to Palestinian "suicide" activism (a case where, given the presence of competing nationalist organizations, one might expect this kind of explanation to work particularly well). Here, the work of Aran (2018), who focuses on the immediate perpetrators and their complicated relationships with their handlers, is highly instructive. He emphasizes that, while these attacks are arranged by organizations which present themselves as nationalist actors, and operate in a context where religious justifications matter, those who carry out the attacks typically do not seem to have undergone a strong process of politicization; they also do not present themselves as having particularly intense religious convictions. There can be a strong disconnect between the programmes of these organizations and these individuals' reasons for participating; these organizations do not try to compensate for this by giving them a long training, either (ibid., 49–51, 58). Many of these perpetrators have lost close relatives, a crucial instance of a damage that cannot be made good — "in the testaments [...], there is always an emphatic expression of the desire for revenge against injuries to the relatives of the suicide terrorist" (ibid., 52) — and many mention experiences of humiliation and violence. But as Aran points out, this is not yet what distinguishes them from the large parts of the population. Beyond this ordinary experience of oppression, those who accept to become "suicide" bombers show what psychologists call an "external locus of control" (ibid., 58)—they understand themselves, to a particularly strong degree, as unable to influence their own condition or, in other words, they react to this constellation of circumstances with a deeper fatalism than others. The importance of this mood of despair is recognized by these organizations; Aran (ibid., 67) mentions a "senior Hamas leader who told his assistants, charged with recruiting suicide terrorists, 'bring me gloomy boys'".

Aran's observations suggest that, for understanding why this kind of attack makes sense to those who carry it out, a different element of Durkheim's theory of suicide could be useful, namely, his concept of fatalistic suicide — "the suicide deriving from excessive regulation, that of persons with futures pitilessly blocked and passions violently choked by oppressive discipline" (Durkheim [1897] 2005, 239). As Durkheim's argument implies, depending on how agents *attribute* their experience, this fatalism can have different affective correlates—among the emotions expressed in a collection of suicide letters, he also finds "anger and all the emotions customarily associated with disappointment"; and this kind of suicide can also take a violent form (ibid., 247–248). It helps make sense of the available biographical information to see one path to becoming a "suicide" bomber as a version of this process. Here, too, an ongoing experience of blocked action leads to a fundamental change in perspective that—by persuading some agents that they no longer should invest any hopes in their own futures (at least, not in their earthly futures), and therefore do not have to think about these futures anymore—enables them to perform actions that, under other conditions, would not have been possible. This enables some militant political organizations to pursue their programme in a new way.

Now, interpreting these "suicide" bombings as *pure* cases of fatalistic suicide may seem problematic: Even if there is a disconnect between the logic of the militant organization and the logic of the immediate perpetrators, these attacks can only happen if the organizational framework makes at least *some* sense to the immediate perpetrators. To that extent, the logic of action guiding this "suicide" activism can be seen as a mixed type, an instance of a category already mentioned by Durkheim: the altruistic-fatalistic suicide,[31] Durkheim's own mythical example being the collective self-annihilation at Masada as told by Flavius Josephus (ibid., 82–83, 252).[32] Still, on the

---

31 An interpretation of "suicide" bombings as cases of altruistic-fatalistic suicide has been proposed by Pedahzur et al. (2003) who loosely build on Durkheim's argument (focusing, however, not on meaning structures underlying these attacks, but on social-structural attributes of the immediate perpetrators).
32 To be exact, Durkheim ([1897] 2005, 252) treats this as a combination between altruistic and what he calls regressive-anomic suicide motives. However, as Besnard (1993, 178–79) has shown, according to the logic of Durkheim's own argument, "regressive-anomic" suicides *are* fatalistic suicides.

backstages of these militant organizations, the dominant emotion concerning the persons who commit to "suicide" bombings is not admiration, but condescension (Aran 2018, 39–40). This seems to indicate that what would count, according to these organizations' standards, as an "altruistic" orientation does not play an essential role for these immediate perpetrators.

The possibility of such disconnects, or loose couplings, is important for the social potentialities of this fatalistic practice: It can fulfil a function within such structures of cooperation without requiring those who perform it to have strong attachments to the norms that sustain this structure. An experience of having no way out, and a revenge motive which becomes more plausible through this experience, can lower the need for elaborate justifications, as well as for the power of justifications to actually convince. Where religious justifications are offered, their details, and their overall believability, can now become less important; those who participate in a genuinely fatalistic practice of revenge do not really need to believe anything.[33] Therefore, this kind of fatalistic practice can make a particular difference in environments where religious or nationalist justifications have lost much of their force, and where strong forms of normative integration have become unlikely. At the same time, this practice does not require a strong attachment to the political *expectations* that sustain the given structure of cooperation. Whether the long-term goal pursued by a political movement organization is likely to be reached ceases to be a vital question for these activists. Consequently, this fatalistic practice offers *one* type of solution for a problem that radical political movements are confronted with: It massively lowers the importance of the question why it would make sense to engage in acts of protest that have very low chances of success; through this, it decouples protest activity from a focus on the given "opportunity structure."[34]

Obviously, the "suicide" attack is a rare, extreme case; one might be tempted to postulate a clear boundary that categorically separates it from other types of protest activities. Here, too, Durkheim's conceptualization remains useful: He describes suicides not as constituting a strictly separate

---

[33] One may choose to call this way of relating to the world "nihilism" (Roy 2016, 123–26), but that term could be misleading: It can be understood as attributing to these perpetrators a new elaborate set of convictions, while the available information suggests that their integration into these organizations' activities depends on their having no systematic convictions at all.

[34] See Pettenkofer (2010) on why this is a fundamental explanatory problem for social movement research.

class of actions, but as resulting from extreme varieties of logics of action that can also be observed in milder versions; therefore, he emphasizes suicide's "unbroken connection [...] with acts, on the one hand, of courage and devotion, on the other of imprudence and clear neglect" (Durkheim [1897] 2005, xliv), which corresponds to a gradual increase in indifference towards one's own future life, and to different degrees of anger towards those seen as responsible for one's condition. This conceptualization helps recognize why the set of mechanisms that can be observed in the case of "suicide" activists not only operates in this kind of extreme case: In other contexts, too, versions of this fatalism can enable self-harming practices that, as elements of larger structures of cooperation, can have social consequences (which include stabilizing these structures of cooperation).

4.2 Pure Vengeful Activism

The practice of vengefulness, however, can also sustain unlikely forms of collective action *without* being embedded in a structure of cooperation focused on future-oriented political goals. A particularly clear example are the protests that happened in a large number of housing projects (*cités*) in many French *banlieues* during three weeks in October/November 2005, with hit-and-run attacks resulting in massive damages to property—among other consequences, 255 damaged school buildings, and ca. 10,000 burned cars, mostly belonging to other inhabitants of the *cités*.[35]

A large part of the debate on these protests opposed two types of accounts: The first describes them as an activity which, for those who performed it, had no political meaning (and ought instead to be seen as, e.g., thrill-seeking, a venting of aggressions resulting from unrelated causes, or a cover for criminal activities). The second type suggests interpreting these events as a version of "normal" goal-oriented political action—a form of bargaining and/or arguing—or at least as a "protopolitical" practice (see, e.g.,

---

35 The protests started, in Clichy-sous-Bois, after three youths – who, as it turned out, had not been implicated in any kind of illegal activity – tried to avoid a police control and, under the eyes of several police agents, climbed into an electricity transformer station; while one member of the police squad explicitly said that the youths were unlikely to survive there, and a phone call to the electricity service could have saved them, the police squad finally chose to simply drive away; after 30 minutes, two of the youths were electrocuted, one survived heavily wounded (Body-Gendrot 2016, 558–59).

Kokoreff 2008; Jobard 2014) which *prepares* future collective action aiming at political change. This interpretation was also taken up by a normativist version of Critical Theory: Using interviews presented by Mucchielli (2009), to which he applies the "reconstructive" strategy suggested by Honneth (1992), Sutterlüty (2014) argues that these protests signal a "demand for equality and equal treatment as citizens" (ibid., 47); if, for example, one of Mucchielli's interviewees says about his interactions with police agents, "All we're asking for is respect" (Mucchielli 2009, 741), it "follows that the demand to be treated before the law and by the guardians of that law in the same way as other French citizens was at the core of what made the police the target of young people's aggression" (Sutterlüty 2014, 47).[36]

Neither of these interpretive strategies seems to grasp the meaning structure underlying these protests. The claim that these acts had no political meaning for the agents has been thoroughly debunked. First, the existing research proves beyond doubt that the category of young men from which the participants came was severely disadvantaged, with many of these disadvantages resulting from political decisions. While these participants were mostly under the age of 19, they could observe the consequences these disadvantages had for their older brothers (Kokoreff 20008, 424–425): They were excluded from large segments of the labour market, which meant that in their twenties, many still had to live with their parents.[37] They had attended, or were still attending, deeply dysfunctional schools unlikely to offer a way out of this. Outside their homes, their daily lives were shaped by a massive police presence linked to recurrent practices of humiliation.[38] (Like the Palestinian "suicide" bombers, these youths felt tied to a specific *physical space* which tends to trap them.) Second, the accounts of the participants as well as their specific activities suggest that it is because of these disadvantages that this type of protest made sense to them: Burning schools is the ultimate gesture of dissatisfaction with this school system (Ott 2007); as one of Muchielli's interviewees says, "what I wanted during the riots was

---

[36] A similar perspective is suggested by Fassin (2009, 1261–63) who, while using a "moral economies" framework, also refers to Honneth's ideas about recognition (ibid., 1244).

[37] See Héran (2021, 213–34) for a brief overview of the relevant research, including the experiments showing that, all other things being equal, having a postal code from these areas makes it much more likely that a job application is rejected, particularly if the applicant has a Muslim-sounding name.

[38] On the practice of identity control and its humiliating effects, see particularly Fassin (2015, 144–52).

to set fire to the high school, because they're the ones who fucked up my future" (Mucchielli 2009, 744). Therefore, these acts can be said to express a political judgment in the sense suggested by Geuss (2010, 16).[39]

The claim that these protests were acts of bargaining or arguing aimed at instigating political change, however, is also hard to sustain. The evidence mobilized for this claim—usually linked to the additional claim that the protests were gestures appealing to a shared normative framework—typically comes from public utterances which were not made during these protest events, but in *other* contexts, for instance, during a peaceful demonstration, in statements by local activists, in the news media, or when participants had to appear in court.[40] Certainly, for activists or public intellectuals who used these protest events as an occasion to emphasize that current policies should be changed, it was rational to portray the protesters as fundamentally sharing the normative assumptions ("values of the Republic," etc.) required for being seen as an acceptable member of the public.[41] But observers were quick to distinguish this intellectual mobilization—the "paper upheavals" (*émeutes de papier*) (Mauger 2006, 7)—from what happened within the *cités* themselves.

Trying to infer from accounts offered in such contexts of public justification why these protests made sense to those who participated in them is quite problematic. The protests in the *cités* do not seem to appeal to an overarching normative framework within which forms of political arguing might happen, or within which the kind of recognition could be fought for that might enable the participants to enter processes of political bargaining. Indeed, from their point of view, the idea of shared norms to which they could appeal in a meaningful way seems hard to reconcile with their own experiences. This becomes clear, for instance, when they talk about local schools. One interviewee says:

"everything that's working class, they're administered by ... schools that ... do nothing. ... In wealthy areas like the 16th arrondissement, for example, school, it's definitely gonna play its role, educating people. [...] And in other areas, school doesn't play the same role at all." (Hartmann 2007, 48)[42]

---

39 See also Scheuerman (2021) on property damage as a political gesture.
40 For an example of the latter, see Sutterlüty (2014, 47).
41 On the ways in which political rhetorics aimed at normalizing protest can shape the perspectives of social movement research, see Pettenkofer (2010, 89–103).
42 The mothers interviewed by Marlière (2007, 80–81) essentially seem to share this view.

They have either come to see these schools as institutions which are not subject to the same norms as schools in other ("better") parts of France, or reached the conclusion that, when dealing with lower-class children of non-European descent, teachers are not bound by the norms that guide their dealings with other categories of children. In their interviews, they seem to be politely implying that only observers who live a relatively comfortable life, and nevertheless generalize from their own experience, could arrive at the conclusion that the norms applying to themselves could also help a *banlieusard*. These interviewees do not seem to think that, between the way these schools operate and the way in which—according to the norms *in fact* applying to these schools—they ought to operate, there really is the kind of tension which could serve as an access point for a critique that might lead to some change.

Moreover, these protest events also do not evoke an *alternative* normative framework *beyond* the dominant discourse of the Fifth Republic. Consisting mostly of hit-and-run attacks, they cannot really be seen as enacting a possible *new* mode of political cooperation. Certainly, the choice of this mode of protest may result from an adaptation to police strategies; as Jobard (2009, 240) writes, the participants' "means of expression were therefore limited [...] by the actions of the police." Still, this mode of protest hardly enables the participants to signal to each other the presence of a political collective that would also be capable of more ambitious and more stable forms of cooperation.[43] Finally, this practice of protest also does not gesture at any kind of future collective action extending beyond the category of the current participants: The massive burning of private cars may have been meant to frustrate the police goal of "maintaining order"; nevertheless, it indicates that the participants did not even think about the possibility of a future cooperation with those inhabitants who owned these cars.[44]

For all these reasons, it is highly credible when participants say that their main aim was to take revenge (Mucchielli 2009, 740–41).[45] In that sense, these

---

43 On the difference that such "prefigurative" protest events can make by giving more plausibility to the idea that articulating critique is not simply futile, see Pettenkofer (2019).
44 As this book goes into print, a very similar type of protest has started after a young man was killed in Nanterre by a policeman for no apparent reason (see, e.g., Chrisafis 2023).
45 Jobard (2009, 240) writes that at least some of these acts of destruction were precisely targeted; for example, a car was burned because its owner was thought to be a racist. However, he offers no reasons for assuming that, rather than pure acts of revenge, these were future-oriented bargaining strategies meant to affect the target's behaviour.

émeutes represent a genuinely fatalistic type of protest: an activity made possible because, among its participants, the set of obstacles that continually interrupt their pursuit of everyday goals had created the shared conviction that thinking about substantially changing their situation would be futile. These protests may react to a tension between a norm of equality and its institutionalisation; this does not mean, however, that they are performed *in the name* of that norm, or driven by a demand to ensure that it will be implemented more fully. The participants do not seem to believe that the promises implied in these norms were ever really addressed to *them*; the idea that they could successfully demand being treated according to these norms seems absurd to them. (While the practice of industriousness is linked to a transformation of existing norms of equality, the practice of vengefulness is based on a loss of trust in such norms.) One may well say that "notions of 'citizenship' [...] played a central role in their motivations" (Sutterlüty 2014, 39); however, the protesters' acts should be understood not as appeals to these notions but as a performance of revenge reacting to the perception that these norms never applied to them in the first place. Hartmann's interviewee describes school as a site of deception that creates illusions about a norm of equality which, in fact, does not exist:

"They're torching schools, but at school, what do you learn? You learn about justice, democracy. We're taught all our lives that we're all equal, that ... that's why ... if we've got a problem, we can go to the police. But when you see that ... in fact, it's not true. But at school ... well, it's no use to us, is it?" (Hartmann 2007, 48)

This attitude is also apparent where they talk about their aim of gaining more respect. Before the statement, already quoted above, that "all we're asking for is respect" (Mucchielli 2009, 741) — which in itself could seem to validate a normativist model of 'recognition struggles' — the interviewee explains *how*, in his opinion, this respect can be gained: "I told the guys, [...] if we're gonna do something, it's gotta be to beat up some cop; that way when they have to come to the neighbourhood, before they get there they'll shit in their pants and they'll be so flipped they won't play the cowboys any more" (ibid., 740–41). Another interviewee says about the police: "We're going to scare them, like that they'll change their behaviour and they'll respect us", adding: "we've got nothing to lose, since they've fucked our lives up" (ibid., 742). So these youths invest their remaining hopes in a bargaining strategy based on issuing threats, and the respect they wish to gain consists of being left alone out of fear — which suggests that their longing for respect is linked to a complete fatalism about the officially accepted norms of equality.[46]

The difficulties of these "protopolitical" explanations are instructive because they reveal some general problems that normativist interpretation strategies—including those proposed by recent versions of Critical Theory—have when dealing with fatalistic practices. These problems are particularly noticeable where this normativist approach tries to preempt the objection that in this empirical case, the presumed normativity does not seem to operate. In a first step, it mobilizes the idea of something that is not being said but *invoked*; Sutterlüty (2014, 46) writes that a "demand for equality" was "invoked, for the most part implicitly but occasionally explicitly" by the protesters; that is, explicit demands articulated at some specific occasions are taken as supporting the conclusion that those who do not voice these demands nevertheless express them implicitly. To spell out this presupposition, this approach uses two different metaphors (their relation to each other is not fully clear): It refers, on the one hand, to a "normative core" (ibid., 39) which though invisible can be inferred from overt behaviour; and, on the other hand, to a "normative grammar concealed in the actions of young people" (ibid., 49). In itself, this would lead back to a familiar problem of social research: Even in cases where it seems certain that what one is observing is rule-following behaviour, there is no easy way to infer, on the basis of an observed behavioural sequence, which *specific* rule is being followed. In order to solve this problem, this approach adds the presupposition that there is one single set of "fundamental values of the political community" (ibid., 50), or one single grammar.[47]

---

46 To the extent that this bargaining strategy is mediated by norms, what seems mostly relevant are norms of masculinity which, to some degree, appear to be shared by these youths and the local police agents: According to Truong (2017, 102–04), the stories told by some youths about their confrontations with the police suggest that they see themselves as engaging in a masculinity contest. (These norms are quite different from the "universalist values of the Republic," however defined; given that they are conceptually linked to notions of hierarchies created by competition, they also cannot produce equal respect for everybody.)

47 The idea of a single latent grammar guiding protest already appears prominently in the subtitle of Honneth's book on recognition struggles (1992): "The Moral Grammar of Social Conflicts". The metaphor of a "normative core" appears already here, too (ibid., 82). (For a different use of the grammar metaphor, see Boltanski and Thévenot (1991), who look for coexisting heterogenous normative grammars, with the hypothesis that different grammars will be activated in different contexts of justification.)

Taken together, these two presuppositions enable their users to extrapolate from an act of protest to an underlying normative structure, and to interpret observed utterances accordingly. This includes the assumption that these meanings can already be inferred from the *words* that the participants use. For instance, having come across the word "respect" in an interview transcript, Sutterlüty (ibid., 47) argues that "Respect is a universalistic category— in contrast to concepts of honour, for example, which always refer to a particular type of status. Respect refers to something that everyone is owed to the same degree and in the same way;" in other words, at least under "modern" conditions, one can safely assume that the word "respect" always has the same meaning. In other aspects too, these assumptions can justify treating available empirical information as irrelevant; particularly, given the presupposition that there is one single grammar of justification, looking for differences between the contexts of justification that elicit a given utterance does not really seem necessary from this point of view.

This interpretive strategy significantly affects how the observed phenomenon is understood: It always confirms the notion that, for the participants, it still makes sense to focus on the officially accepted norms — at least through a type of critique that either emphasizes a disconnect between accepted norms and actual practice, or a need to reform these norms. Should the participants consider the activity of articulating such a critique to be meaningless (for instance, because they see it as a practice of self-deception that would sustain illusory hopes for a situation where articulating such reasons might make a difference), this would be difficult to recognize from the vantage point constituted by these presuppositions.[48] It would also be difficult to recognize whether a given protest expresses a more fundamental dissatisfaction; this normativist vantage point creates a strong focus on those elements that can be seen as positively related to a dominant normative framework. Finally, by always validating the assumption that "modern" institutions communicate a set of norms which can also be used for criticizing these institutions, this vantage point makes it difficult to observe that these institutions can also stabilize themselves by creating the perception

---

48 The assumption that the protesters practice "immanent" critique, roughly in the way academics do, can be a version of what Bourdieu (1990) calls the scholastic fallacy: For many academics, there are contexts – at least within academia – where "immanent critique" seems to prompt meaningful answers, and therefore is experienced as a meaningful activity. For the protesters, the idea of accessing such a context may be simply unthinkable.

that criticizing them would be futile. This is also relevant because the kind of protest that is motivated by such perceptions of futility can contribute to recursively stabilizing the institutions that create these perceptions: If a polity generates, among the members of a given category, a fatalism about all kinds of political action that follow the accepted rules, it encourages them to engage in forms of protest that can easily be labelled as meaningless (for instance, as senseless violence); the spectacle of such protests can be important for the self-affirmation of this polity. This also seems to have been the case with the French protests of 2005: The consequence of these protests did not consist in a mitigation of the circumstances against which they were directed.[49] Rather, their main consequence was to offer French elites enhanced opportunities for treating *banlieue* youths as an incarnation of everything the French republic stood against; these protests came to fulfil the function of a spectacle proving that there is no alternative to an established regime of "progress." In this sense, they also show that the effects of a given fatalistic practice can only be fully recognized if one also looks at its interactions with other types of fatalistic practice.

5. Interactions between Fatalistic Practices

As the example of the French 2005 protests shows, interactions between different types of fatalistic practices can be vital for the stability of each type. The most obvious instances of such interactions are relations of coercion and conflict: By following and re-enacting a process which it assumes to be without alternatives, the practice of process fatalism can construct a social world where many will find it easy to believe that there *really* is no alternative, and that the only options left are industriousness and vengefulness. Whenever this prompts a form of fatalistic protest, a self-sustaining dynamic can start: On both sides of a conflict between process fatalists and the vengeful, ways of acting that only make sense against a background of fatalistic beliefs provoke reactions which confirm these fatalistic beliefs. (In this sense, these practices can complement each other in a way that makes them possible elements of one single order of discourse.)

---

49 On the lack of changes concerning police practice see, among others, Jobard (2015).

These relations are embedded in stabilizing constellations of mutual repulsion, where each of these practices offers to each of the others an opportunity for self-affirmation. From the points of view of the process fatalists and the vengeful, the industrious appear as objects of contempt: If the industrious voice egalitarian demands, their fatalistic preunderstanding leads them to articulate these demands in the mode of envy-as-*Missgunst*. This makes it easy to stigmatize these demands; it also confirms the impression of the vengeful that a large part of those who are dissatisfied with the current state of things nevertheless are impossible to cooperate with. For the process fatalists, those who do not accept that there is no alternative appear as intellectually deficient, so that it would be futile to try to listen to them. The industrious, too, can see the practice of vengefulness as an expression of madness; for them, it can serve as a discouraging spectacle that makes the idea of protesting even less thinkable.

However, the tacit consensus between these different positions, which often gets obscured by such gestures of mutual contempt, also opens possibilities for cooperation. The industrious can feel strongly attracted by the neoliberal promise that from now on, thanks to "the market," *everybody* will continually be disciplined—that is, no longer only themselves, but also the relatively privileged who, from the vantage point of industriousness, appear to "think they're special." The options offered by this overlapping consensus were exploited with particular skill by Margaret Thatcher: By joining the "no-alternative" rhetoric to a public self-presentation as a "grocer's daughter"[50], that is, as linked by birth to the small-entrepreneur practice of industriousness, she managed to appear as embodying a compromise between these two types of fatalistic practice.

For all these reasons, these three types of fatalistic practice can form a self-stabilizing triangle. This can also enable them to form a structural core that does not depend on further external legitimations—so that, at least as a thought experiment, one can imagine a "modern" social order that is entirely sustained by these fatalistic practices.

---

50 For a biographical account that traces the development of this self-presentation strategy, see Campbell (2000).

Works cited

Aran, Gideon (2018). *The Smile of the Human Bomb: New Perspectives on Suicide Terrorism.* Ithaca: Cornell University Press.
Arendt, Hannah (1973). *The Origins of Totalitarianism.* San Diego: Harcourt Brace Janovitch.
Arendt, Hannah (2005). Introduction into Politics. In *The Promise of Politics*, 93–201. New York: Random.
Arendt, Hannah (2006). The Concept of History: Ancient and Modern. In *Between Past and Future*, 41–90. London: Penguin.
Arendt, Hannah (2012). Natur und Geschichte. In *Zwischen Vergangenheit und Zukunft*, 54–79. München: Piper.
Bergmann, Knut, Matthias Diermeier and Judith Niehues (2018). Ein komplexes Gebilde. Eine sozio-ökonomische Analyse des Ergebnisses der AfD bei der Bundestagswahl 2017. *Zeitschrift für Parlamentsfragen*, 49 (2), 243–64.
Besnard, Philippe (1993). Anomie and Fatalism in Durkheim's Theory of Regulation. In Steven Lukes (ed.). *Emile Durkheim: Sociologist and Moralist*, 163–83. London: Routledge.
Bloom, Mia M. (2004). Palestinian Suicide Bombing: Public Support, Market Share, and Outbidding. *Political Science Quarterly*, 119 (1), 61–88.
Body-Gendrot, Sophie (2016). Making Sense of French Urban Disorders in 2005. *European Journal of Criminology*, 13 (5), 556–72.
Börner, Markus (2019). Der "Abfall der Gesellschaft"—Überflüssige Menschen im zweiten Abschnitt der *Elemente und Ursprünge totaler Herrschaft* von Hannah Arendt. In Markus Börner, Anja Jungfer, Jakob Stürmann (eds.). *Judentum und Arbeiterbewegung. Das Ringen um Emanzipation in der ersten Hälfte des 20. Jahrhunderts*, 273–93. Berlin: De Gruyter Oldenbourg.
Boltanski, Luc, and Laurent Thévenot (1991). *De la justification.* Paris: Gallimard.
Bourdieu, Pierre (1990). The Scholastic Point of View. *Cultural Anthropology*, 5 (4), 380–91.
Campbell, John (2000). *Margaret Thatcher, Vol. 1: The Grocer's Daughter.* London: Jonathan Cape.
Chrisafis, Angelique (2023). A Monument to French Rage: Buses Torched in Riots over Police Killing. *The Guardian*, 30.6.2023 [https://www.theguardian.com/world/2023/jun/30/monument-french-rage-buses-torched-riots-police-killing]
Clark, Christopher (2019). *Time and Power: Visions of History in German Politics, from the Thirty Years' War to the Third Reich.* Princeton: Princeton University Press.
Dewey, John (1988). *Human Nature and Conduct.* The Middle Works 14. Carbondale: Southern Illinois University Press.
Elster, Jon (2009). *Alexis de Tocqueville, the First Social Scientist.* Cambridge: Cambridge University Press.
Engels, Friedrich, and Karl Marx (1962). Die heilige Familie oder Kritik der kritischen Kritik. In *Marx-Engels-Werke* 2, 3–223. Ost-Berlin: Dietz.

Farrant, Andrew, and Edward McPhail (2014). Can a Dictator Turn a Constitution Into a Can-opener? F. A. Hayek and the Alchemy of Transitional Dictatorship in Chile. *Review of Political Economy*, 26 (3), 331–48.

Fassin, Didier (2009). Les économies morales revisitées. *Annales. Histoire, Sciences Sociales*, 64, 1237–66.

Fassin, Didier (2015). *La force de l'ordre. Une anthropologie de la police des quartiers. Suivi de La vie publique des livres*. Paris: Seuil.

Furet, François (1978). *Penser la Révolution française*. Paris: Gallimard.

Gambetta, Diego (ed.). (2006). *Making Sense of Suicide Missions*. Oxford: Oxford University Press.

Geuss, Raymond (2010). Political Judgment in Its Historical Context. In *Politics and the Imagination*, 1–16. Princeton: Princeton University Press.

Geuss, Raymond (2016). Identification and the Politics of Envy. In *Reality and Its Dreams*, 163–183. Cambridge MA: Harvard University Press.

Goffman, Erving (1961). Role Distance. In *Encounters*, 73–134. Harmondsworth: Penguin.

Graeber, David (2018). *Bullshit Jobs: A Theory*. London: Allen Lane.

Gross, Neil, Isaac Ariail Reed, and Christopher Winship (eds.). (2022). *The New Pragmatist Sociology: Inquiry, Agency, and Democracy*. New York: Columbia University Press.

Hartmann, Eddie (2017). In the Zone of Spoiled Civil Identity. The Riots in Suburban France in 2005. In Jürgen Mackert, and Bryan S. Turner (eds.). *The Transformation of Citizenship, Vol. 3: Struggle, Resistance, and Violence*, 39–55. London: Routledge.

Hayek, F. A. von (1937). Economics and Knowledge. *Economica*, 4 (13), 33–54.

Hentges, Gudrun (2018). Die populistische Lücke. Flucht, Migration und Neue Rechte. In Karina Becker, Klaus Dörre, and Peter Reif-Spirek (eds.). *Arbeiterbewegung von rechts?*, 101–16. Frankfurt a. M.: Campus.

Héran, François (2021). *Lettre aux professeurs sur la liberté d'expression*. Paris: La Découverte.

Hirschman, Albert O. (1991). *The Rhetoric of Reaction: Perversity, Futility, Jeopardy*. Cambridge MA: Harvard University Press.

Honneth, Axel (1992). *Kampf um Anerkennung. Zur moralischen Grammatik sozialer Konflikte*. Frankfurt a. M.: Suhrkamp.

Honneth, Axel (2011). *Das Recht der Freiheit*. Berlin: Suhrkamp.

Hyvönen, Ari-Elmeri (2013). Invisible Streams: Process-Thinking in Arendt. *European Journal of Social Theory*, 19 (4), 538–55.

Jobard, Fabien (2009). Rioting as a Political Tool: the 2005 Riots in France. *The Howard Journal*, 48 (3), 235–44.

Jobard, Fabien (2014). Riots in France: Political, Proto-political or Anti-political Turmoils? In David Pritchard and Francis Pakes (eds.). *Riot, Unrest and Protest on the Global Stage*, 132–50. Basingstoke: Palgrave Macmillan.

Jobard, Fabien (2015). La police en banlieue après les émeutes de 2005. *Mouvements*, 83, 75–86.

Kokoreff, Michel (2008). La dimension politique des émeutes de 2005 en question. *Swiss journal of sociology* 34, (2), 415–30.

Koselleck, Reinhart (1979). Über die Verfügbarkeit der Geschichte. In *Vergangene Zukunft. Zur Semantik geschichtlicher Zeiten*, 260–78. Frankfurt a. M.: Suhrkamp.

Lamb, William F., et al. (2020). Discourses of climate delay. *Global Sustainability*, 3, e17, 1–5.

Lengfeld, Holger (2017). Die "Alternative für Deutschland": eine Partei für Modernisierungsverlierer? *Kölner Zeitschrift für Soziologie und Sozialpsychologie*, 69 (2), 209–32.

Lübke, Christiane, and Jan Delhey (eds.). (2019). *Diagnose Angstgesellschaft?* Bielefeld: transcript.

Luhmann, Niklas (1971). Komplexität und Demokratie. In. *Politische Planung. Aufsätze zur Soziologie von Politik und Verwaltung*. Opladen, 35–45. Westdeutscher Verlag.

Manow, Philip (2018). *Die Politische Ökonomie des Populismus*. Berlin: Suhrkamp.

Markandaya, Kamala (2007). *Nectar in a Sieve*. New Delhi: Penguin.

Marx, Karl (1971). Die Junirevolution. In *Marx-Engels-Werke* 5, 133–37. Ost-Berlin: Dietz.

Marlière, Eric (2007). Les habitants des quartiers: adversaires ou solidaires des émeutiers? In: Laurent Mucchielli and Véronique Le Goaziou (eds.). *Quand les banlieues brûlent. Retour sur les émeutes de Novembre 2005*, 77–92. Paris: La Découverte.

Mauger, Gérard (2006). *L'émeute de novembre 2005. Une révolte protopolitique*. Broissieux: Éd. du Croquant.

McCrindle, Jean, and Sheila Rowbotham (1977). *Dutiful Daughters*. London: Allen Lane.

Mucchielli, Laurent (2009). Autumn 2005: A Review of the Most Important Riot in the History of French Contemporary Society. *Journal of Ethnic and Migration Studies*, 35 (5), 731–51.

Ott, Laurent (2007). Pourquoi ont-ils brûlé les écoles? In Laurent Mucchielli and Véronique Le Goaziou (eds.). *Quand les banlieues brûlent. Retour sur les émeutes de Novembre 2005*, 126–45. Paris: La Découverte.

Pedahzur, Ami, Arie Perliger, and Leonard Weinberg (2003). Altruism and Fatalism: The Characteristics of Palestinian Suicide Terrorists. *Deviant Behavior*, 24, 405–23.

Pettenkofer, Andreas (2010). *Radikaler Protest. Zur soziologischen Theorie politischer Bewegungen*. Frankfurt a. M.: Campus.

Pettenkofer, Andreas (2017). Fatalismus. Über eine vernachlässigte Stütze sozialer Ordnung. *Berliner Journal für Soziologie*, 27 (1), 123–50.

Pettenkofer, Andreas (2019). Das unhintergehbar Kollektive in der Kritik. In Stefan Joller, and Marija Stanisavljevic (eds.). *Moralische Kollektive*, 49–73. Wiesbaden: Springer VS.

Roy, Olivier (2016). *Le djihad et la mort*. Paris: Seuil.

Sammet, Kornelia (2014). Anomie und Fatalismus. Rekonstruktive Analysen der Weltsichten von Arbeitslosengeld-II-Empfängern. *Zeitschrift für Soziologie*, 43 (1), 70–86.

Scheler, Max (1978). *Das Ressentiment im Aufbau der Moralen*. Frankfurt a. M.: Klostermann.

Scheuerman, William E. (2021). Politically Motivated Property Damage. *The Harvard Review of Philosophy*, 28, 1–58.

Schmalz, Stefan, Sarah Hinz, Ingo Singe, and Anne Hasenohr (2021). *Abgehängt im Aufschwung. Demografie, Arbeit und rechter Protest in Ostdeutschland*. Frankfurt a. M.: Campus.

Searcey, Dionne (2020). A Nation Votes for Joe Biden, and a Red State Shrugs. *The New York Times*, 8.11.2020 [https://www.nytimes.com/2020/11/08/us/politics/nebraska-trump-biden.html]

Slobodian, Quinn (2018). *The Globalists: The End of Empire and the Birth of Neoliberalism*. Cambridge MA: Harvard University Press.

Sutterlüty, Ferdinand (2014). The Hidden Morale of the 2005 French and 2011 English Riots. *Thesis Eleven*, 121 (1), 38–56.

de Swaan, Abram (1989). Jealousy as a Class Phenomenon: The Petite Bourgeoisie and Social Security. *International Sociology*, 4 (3), 259–71.

Thériault, Barbara (2020). *Die Bodenständigen. Erkundungen aus der nüchternen Mitte der Gesellschaft*. Leipzig: Überland.

Tocqueville, Alexis de (1961). *De la démocratie en Amérique II*. Paris: Gallimard.

Tocqueville, Alexis de (1992). De la démocratie en Amérique: Notes et variantes. In *Oeuvres II*, 1084–92. Paris: Gallimard.

Truong, Fabien (2017). *Loyautés radicales. L'islam et les "mauvais garçons" de la nation*. Paris: La Découverte.

Ulbricht, Christian (2020). Modernisierungsverlierer—eine Begriffsgeschichte. *Zeitschrift für Soziologie*, 29 (4), 265–72.

Weissenburger, Peter (2021). Kleine Putz-Umfrage unter Müttern: Dreck, Scham, Politik. *taz*, 10.12.2021 [https://taz.de/Kleine-Putz-Umfrage-unter-Muettern/!5817056/]

Wuthnow, Robert (2019). *The Left Behind: Decline and Rage in Small-Town America*. Princeton: Princeton University Press.

Reconstructing an Impartial and Pluralistic Notion of Progress in Contexts of Diversity

Achim Kemmerling

> "I've tried very hard over these years to avoid recrimination and bitterness," he said. "I just think it's not a good look. One of the ways I've dealt with this whole thing is to look forward and not backwards. What happens tomorrow is more important than what happened yesterday."
> *(Salman Rushdie, Interview in New Yorker Magazine, February 6th, 2023)*

1. Introduction: The paradox of progress as an idea[1]

For many contemporary observers, the idea of progress is either dead or politically unsavoury. Many critics rightfully argue that the notion of progress really took off during the modernisation and industrialisation of the Western world and hence involves a severely Eurocentric and dangerously optimistic bias (Allen 2016; Said 1978; Lyotard 1984). Some scholars would add that this bias helped protect the power and privilege first of colonial and then of capitalist exploitation (Latour 1993; Appadurai 2013). If progress has survived as an idea in some cultural contexts, it is often equated with the left/liberal political spectrum, for instance, in the US American sense of progressivism (Nugent 2010). The apparent demise of progress as a legitimate political idea, however, comes with huge costs, costs that eventually outweigh its benefits.

World relations *(Weltbeziehungen)* are always also political relations, and, in recent years, it seems they are once again at their nadir. Not only do we see

---

1 This chapter is part of a larger book project on progress and diversity. I thank Humberto Beck, Bettina Hollstein, Denis Mäder, and Hartmut Rosa for their invaluable comments. All remaining errors are mine.

© The author/s 2023, published by Campus Verlag, Open Access: CC BY-SA 4.0
Bettina Hollstein, Hartmut Rosa, Jörg Rüpke (eds.), "Weltbeziehung"
DOI: 10.12907/978-3-593-45587-7_005

the political tectonics of West versus East re-erupting in violent conflicts, we also see that the dark side of industrialisation and a modern lifestyle is eventually catching up with humanity in the form of climate change and (hu)man-made "natural" catastrophes. *Weltbeziehungen* are always emotional relationships as well and depend on overarching narratives, and even those grand narratives seem to be in crisis (Beyme 1992; Mills, 1959). When those narratives no longer exist, partial narratives mushroom. Let me give two somewhat notorious examples: development and greatness.

For a long time, *development* was an alternative narrative: industrialisation pushed the envelope of material prosperity, especially in European countries and their offspring. This led to the conclusion that other countries had to emulate the developmental path that those countries had taken (Young 1982). This narrative was eminently lopsided and partial, however, in that it usually equated development with economic growth. Where growth was absent, both governments in developing countries and the international agencies for development assistance failed (Easterly 2001; Escobar 2007; Ferguson 1994; Chakrabarty 2009). Where growth was present, it often led to the over-exploitation of natural and human resources (Sachs 1993; Gowdy 1994; Zaid 2009).

The notion of *increasing national greatness* is an even better example of the fact that the alternatives to progress are even less "palatable" than a notion of progress. While the idea of the *gloria* or *greatness* of one's nation plays an important, and not always negative, role in the history of political thought (Price 1977), it is obvious that such a concept of what a country, and a society, should achieve can lead to very dangerous conclusions. It can lead to ideas of supremacy and of looking down on other peoples or nations. It is not a coincidence that such discourses are on the rise in contexts of crisis and self-doubt (Hagström 2021). The absence of progress as an idea also leads political leaders, such as Donald Trump and Vladimir Putin, to look to an imaginary past—a past which glorifies something that never existed and which justifies discourses and policies of antagonisation and enmity (Reshetnikov 2011; Hopf 2002; Barnett 2017).

Given the alternatives, it might be better to follow the path of those who have attempted to reconstruct a notion of progress (Kitcher 2016; Wagner 2018; Mäder 2014). Otherwise, we easily fall into the spell of highly partial notions of the path towards a common goal focusing on specific aims (e.g., growth) or specific targets (our nation). Whether or not "progress" is the best choice remains to be seen, but it has some advantages over other notions. To name but a few: it does not need to be teleological in the sense of a final state, we can apply it to political decision-making, and it forces people and politicians alike to make normative choices explicitly, rather than hiding them behind some form of technocratic reasoning.

The biggest downside of the idea of progress is, of course, that it does not exist, at least not in a naïve or strong form, such as a Pareto optimal decision rule that would be supported by everyone (Arrow 1951). How can we deal with such a paradox, with progress being both necessary but seemingly impossible (Shabani 2017)? We have to dissect the idea of progress further and see how we can use a plural notion of progress in situations of human diversity.

Diversity, in turn, is arguably the most important fact about humanity. Remarkably, it often leads a surprisingly quiet, unappreciated life for those looking at world history. One example, Charles Fukuyama (2014, 43), defines the human condition in four major dimensions: sociability, cognitive skills for abstract thinking, following norms, and intersubjective recognition. While this list of characteristics is certainly more extensive than simplistic models of human behaviour, it still aims to distil factors that are common to all humanity. One of the defining traits of humanity, however, is that people differ in many respects, e.g., sex/gender, class, and psychological characters. Diversity thus takes many shapes or forms among humans and the ecosystems in which they live. Of course, diversity itself is neither inherently good nor inherently bad. More poignantly, people are diverse in the sense that they do not easily agree on a common notion of progress. Progress can therefore only happen as pluralist decision-making under situations of human diversity and potential disagreement.

This prompts a look at how decision sciences such as economics and hard science have dealt with human diversity, and we find that they have often given diversity short shrift. In order to lead to swift, efficient, and bureaucratically feasible decisions, they have downplayed the role of diversity. Such an efficient version of policymaking has led to accelerating, accumulating, and arguably biased decisions. We thus need to look at the role of decision sciences, and the antidotes that can come from "less rigorous" sciences such as sociology, political science, or anthropology—sciences which usually start with the notion that all humans are different rather than the same.

Once we have understood how progress operates in political decision-making, and once we have peeled from it the cumbersome or even dangerous layers of intellectual history and modern decision science, we will understand that progress as a process requires some form of democratic agreement (Forst 2017). It needs to be pluralist in order to avoid the traps of partiality. This might lead to fewer, slower, truly progressive decisions but hopefully also to less biased ones, and it allows us to focus on the biggest global challenges as a world community, and not fall into the trap of dividing us along lines of partiality.

2. What progress has meant and what it could mean

It would be going too far to recount the history of progress as an idea (see, e.g., Nisbet 1992), yet it is interesting to note that progress in its most optimistic, linear form had its heyday in the eighteenth and nineteenth centuries. Some of its origins go back to Saint Augustine and, indeed, much further back to ancient Rome and Greece. It is also true that only some notions of progress are truly modern (Bury 1920) while others are not (Edelstein 1967; Fulda and Rosa 2011; Kitcher 2016). Notions of progress also differ in connotations and finalities. For Thucydides, for instance, progress was linked to greatness and allowed the Greek nations to go from barbarism to civilisation (Nisbet 1992, 10). In ancient Greece, progress was also linked to blasphemy, a rebellious act against the gods, most famously narrated in the story of Prometheus who steals fire from the gods and is punished eternally for it. Progress has always been ambivalent and contained a notion of resistance.

In the late fourth and early fifth centuries, Saint Augustine looked for ways to reconcile the idea of progress with Christianity. Rather optimistically, he saw (Christian) humanity gradually rising over the centuries (Nisbet 1992, 13; Mommsen 1951). While Augustine's ultimate interest lay in divine providence, his writings reinforced the idea of seeing history as a linear, cumulative process towards reason. The early modern age saw pessimists and optimists debating whether life was in the "state of nature" and how contemporary times related to this. The eighteenth and early nineteenth centuries saw the main rise of optimism in the work of thinkers such as Turgot or Comte (Bury 1920, 75), but it is important to note that even those thinkers always saw progress as something delicate and a product of contention (Mäder 2014). Progress and modernity find their clearest connection in the *Aufklärung*/Enlightenment (Fulda and Rosa 2011; Koselleck 1989), albeit with foreshadowing sinister undertones about some nations or even "races" being more enlightened than others (Barnouw 1994; Eberl 2019; Bernasconi

2002). Even then, however, philosophers disagreed on what progress was eventually about (Harris 1956).

The triumphalism did not last long, and at the end of the nineteenth century, critical voices such as Nietzsche ridiculed the idea of progress: "progress is just a modern idea, i.e. a wrong idea" (Nietzsche 1888, cited in Mäder 2014, 191). The horrors of the twentieth-century world wars struck a fatal blow to strong, almost eschatological notions of progress. The Enlightenment had proved to be perfectly compatible with the horrors of technocratic genocide (Horkheimer et al. 2022). Other ideas of progress, such as the promise of economic prosperity or liberal democracy lived beyond World War II and became instrumental in the post-war renaissance of modernisation theory (Lipset 1959; Wagner 2018), but even their days were numbered.

It did not take long to finally sink the idea of progress. Western colonialism and imperialism had already revealed the enormous level of hypocrisy (Appadurai 2013; Said 1978), preaching universalist values while delivering imperial domination. The atrocities of colonialism suggested that progress was an occidental, Western concept (see also contribution by Fuchs et al. in this volume). It is true that linear, teleological, and strongly optimist notions of progress were closely related to particular Western ideas—although not all Western thinkers shared such an understanding of progress.

Some non-Western cultures had somewhat similar infatuations with progress and civilisation (Young 1982). For example, famous Arab historians like Ibn Khalun wrote about the rise and decline of societies (see also Nakayama 1997). One difference, perhaps, is that there was no clear-cut division between the religious and secular dimensions of progress in the writings of Eastern political thought (Kemmerling and Parida forthcoming). Nonetheless, this should caution us not to take Eurocentrism to its extreme (Graeber and Wengrow 2021) and think that all types of progress are a Western invention. Non-Europeans clearly "thought" about processes similar to progress even when the content and importance differed from context to context.

Nisbet (1992, 31) summarises his tour de force through the history of progress as follows: "So the idea of progress seems a dead end, but we should not write its obituary yet." For progress to survive, however, it needs to shed some of its naïve, outright dangerous partiality (e.g., linking it to greatness or any specific religion). Partiality here always means two things: first, the opposite of impartiality as a fundamental norm of governance

(Rothstein 2011, 6), and, second, partial in the sense of highlighting only one dimension or value of progress while neglecting others (e.g., prosperity over sustainability, freedom/autonomy over security/compliance). There is also little chance of any other type of teleology surviving. Progress then can be merely defined as an event or sequence of events—or, perhaps more practically, decisions—that divide before and after (temporal dimension), better or worse (normative dimension), and an agreement about making such decisions (political or symbolic dimension). Perhaps a parallel can be found in Popper's (1957) idea of "piecemeal engineering" (*Stückwerkstechnologie*) or Kitcher's (2016, 167) local progress, i.e., progress which happens in a narrowly defined temporal and spatial context. In other words, we need to "shrink" the notion to insulate it against any form of hubris.

3. Progress and decision-making under human diversity

Hubris is not the only problem of past notions of progress. A more intricate issue perhaps is that progress happens in the context of human diversity. Arguably, the most remarkable fact about human society and its ecologies is its diversity, be it biodiversity, or social, human diversity. As with all anthropological concepts, there is nothing good or bad about it: it is simply a "fact of life." It can be harnessed to great effect but can also divide people, peoples, and people against nature.

Diversity comes in many shapes and forms. Biodiversity is a good example, and so are people living in biodiverse ecosystems. In a social sense, humans differ in their gender identification, in their psychological traits, and in their access to income and power, to name but a few differences (Diamond 1991; Haidt 2012). These dimensions of diversity do not have immediate moral implications. They also cannot be essentialised. They do not have to exist. Some people do not care about their sexual orientation and would never use it as yardstick against which to judge political proposals, for instance. But diversity implies that people can disagree. They are not ants or any other eusocial insect. While some individual ants might be rebellious, such behaviour occurs rarely and is swiftly punished (Wilson 2012, 19). A worker ant is moulded into the division of labour in its colony. Humans, in contrast, can and do rebel as workers, as citizens, and as family members. Their social positions and roles are elastic and can change. This is what makes eusociality among humans so dynamic (Bowles and Gintis 2011), and with dynamics come new questions for social progress.

While diversity is a fact of life, it constitutes a problem for political decision-making. Some political theorists solve this problem easily by giving all power to one or very few persons, either to a Hobbsian monarch or autocrat, to Plato's philosopher king, or to Leibniz' Panglossian technocrat. Thus, they cut through the Gordian knot of divisiveness.

There is another way to deal with the problem: ignore it. This is the way the science of decision-making often reacts to the nuisance of having to deal with diversity. Unfortunately, the most powerful branches of decision sciences have found ways to achieve this. In economics, for instance, the power of neoclassical thinking lies in assuming away diversity and treating every human being as an identical *homo oeconomicus* (Keen 2010). This has greatly facilitated the computation of rational human behaviour. It allows for decisions but does not often lead to a realistic model of human behaviour. While this is a common critique of neoclassical economics, it also shows why this branch of economics is so successful and hard to expunge. Let me give one example. Gregory Mankiw is perhaps the world's most famous economist. In his textbooks (e.g., Mankiw 2003), he uses stylised macroeconomic models that can explain how, for instance, monetary and fiscal policies affect macroeconomic outcomes such as economic growth or unemployment. But these textbooks rarely and truly engage with diversity. The economic agents that populate the textbook world all look the same. There is no real human diversity when all these books allow for is talking about firms, employees, and governments, for example.

A short scientific paper shows that this is problematic. It contains a simple model with two types of consumers, one "myopic," and one "rational." Here is its conclusion (p. 124):

"A better model would acknowledge the great heterogeneity in consumer behavior that is apparent in the data. The savers-spenders theory sketched here takes a small step toward including this microeconomic heterogeneity in macroeconomic theory, and it yields some new and surprising conclusions about fiscal policy."

The remarkable fact about this paper is its author: Gregory Mankiw (2000). In other words, the author of the scientific article shows that the author of the textbook greatly underestimates the consequences of diversity—or heterogeneity, as economists tend to call it.

As a profession, economics has greatly advanced in recent years, also as a consequence of new sub-disciplines such as behavioural economics and rigorous impact analysis. Yet the crude example of Mankiw's work still highlights an issue: politicians look at decision science to motivate and legitimate their decisions. The clearer, faster, and more powerful such insights are, the better for politicians (and the experts they rely on). There is still a premium for speed and efficiency, even at the cost of realism.

Perhaps the clearest example of bias for action, often with fatalistic undertones (see contribution by Pettenkofer in this volume) comes from management and engineering. In his 2014 book Evgeny Morozov (2014) describes how software engineers and the "tech community" develop a solutionist attitude towards any kind of technical or social problem. Nachtwey and Seidl (2020) show that such a solutionist culture does indeed determine the behaviour of tech elites, but it also trivialises many severe social problems. In the literature on management, it is well known that excessive forms of managerialism create the very problems it supposedly cures (Kuhl 2009; Klikauer 2015).

More ambivalent are legal studies about the role of diversity in human behaviour (and opinions). Perhaps this also makes legal decisions somewhat notorious for being slow and bureaucratic. Nonetheless, modern legal doctrine enshrines the egalitarian concept that people are equal before the law. Of course, there are good reasons why laws should apply universally, and exceptions such as positive discrimination and affirmative action often only serve as exceptions to these rules.

Like behavioural and heterodox forms of economics, recent scholarship in legal studies has emphasised diversity and even plurality, acknowledging the limits of universality (Cubukcu 2017; Glenn 2004; Anghie 2006; Dembour 2012). It is also clear that legal doctrine has a more sophisticated model of individuals, with their freedoms embedded in an organic society (Becker 1996; Hörnle 2015). Legal studies also take more cues from different types of social sciences and humanities (Lüdemann 2006; Funke and Schmolke 2019).

Nonetheless, differences in opinions between legal scholars sit uneasy in the discipline. In many countries there is a *herrschende Lehre/Meinung*, a ruling legal doctrine—to use a somewhat imprecise term (Tuschak 2009; Drosdeck 1989). This is not surprising, given that the legal apparatus has to deal with the pressure and urgency of problems, but this also shows that many legal doctrines not only have a problem with diversity among ordinary people but also among judges and legal experts. Again, this diversity and disagreement is a nuisance rather than a substantive characteristic of (the) discipline (Epstein et al. 2011; Sunstein et al. 2006).

Economics, management, and the hard sciences—and perhaps to a lesser degree legal studies—stand in remarkable contrast to other sciences such as sociology, political science, anthropology, and philosophy, all of which tend to the other extreme. The latter disciplines think of human beings as extremely diverse, leading to all kinds of social and cultural groups, classes, and milieus. Such differences have consequences: unpredictability, misunderstandings, and the potential for conflict. Critics often accuse these social and human sciences of being failures, of not accumulating knowledge, and of being soft or indecisive (Cassell 2002; Elster 2011)—perhaps rightly so. However, the decision sciences could learn from them that "good" political decisions (whatever "good" means) are arguably rarer, slower, and harder to achieve than powerful decision sciences would imply. Decision sciences that ignore human diversity, make the political wheel turn faster, and they accelerate decision-making to cope with ever-new political issues (Rosa 2022), but they rarely solve them.

4. Pluralistic progress in political decision-making

Political decision-making is always pressed for time. In political and policy science, symptoms include complaints that political systems stagnate if they have too many veto players and too many checks and balances (Tsebelis 2002; Immergut 1990). In the European economic context, economists have called this *Eurosclerosis* (Giersch 1985; Siebert 1997), an institutional form of rigidity that (allegedly) makes countries smother the free interplay of market forces, thereby leading to unemployment and a lack of growth. Rather paradoxically, we also find the opposite claim, namely, that there is too much policy volatility, and that decisions are made only to be reversed a few years later (Kemmerling and Makszin 2018; Doyle 2014; Henisz 2004). Other scholars argue that political decisions overreact, inflate, or "bubble up" (Jones et al. 2014; Maor 2012). Again, there is an opposing claim, namely, that political decisions in some areas underreact (Maor 2014; Howlett and Kemmerling 2017), for instance, against truly complex or *wicked* problems such as climate change.

How can all of these claims be true at the same time? I think they only make sense against the background of a notion of progress as decision-making under extreme diversity. Very few political decisions can be rightfully called progress for many, if not most, citizens. In their absence, the decisions accumulate (Adam et al. 2019; Van Engen et al. 2016), making future decisions even more bureaucratic, legalistic, and complicated. They also lead to complaints about politics being deficient in time (Rosa 2022).

What we need, therefore, is, to use a current buzzword, "more mindful" decision-making, taking a step back—a pause—to see what really matters and what does not. This act of stepping back would constitute the kind of *Entschleunigung* or deceleration that Rosa (2021) has argued for. Of course, the legal and political apparatus still needs to churn out urgent decisions. This is not a problem as long as we concede that these are partial solutions and not equivalent to any deeper form of progress. For real progress to occur, people need to accept the basic rationale of a decision. For instance, it is not good enough for a country to adopt liberal political institutions or liberal gender norms if these values are not deeply engrained in a society. Western political thinkers have perhaps counted victory too early (Pinker 2018; Welzel 2013). Some part of the great regression in liberal values and political regimes (V-Dem Institute 2021), has to do with the fact that liberal policies spread rather shallowly, emulating the practices of "Western liberal democracies" rather than really sharing them (Marsh and Sharman 2009; Pritchett et al. 2010).

At first sight, this kind of decelerated decision-making and measuring of progress sounds counterproductive in an age of turbo-charged technological progress and huge impending doomsday scenarios of climate change and nuclear war. In the early twentieth century, Woodrow Wilson had already written: "I am forced to be a progressive, because society itself changes" (Wilson 1913). In this sense, deceleration would mean status quo bias and structural conservatism. It would become partial again, leaning towards a politically conservative side. The contradiction dissolves, however, once we reflect more deeply that non-decisions are also political decisions (Bachrach and Baratz 1963). They are decisions not to make decisions. In this regard, policymakers constantly make (non-)decisions not to regulate the dark space of the internet more heavily or not to fight climate change more thoroughly—to give but two examples. A more reflective and decelerated approach to decision-making also implies taking such non-decisions seriously and weighing their importance against the everyday humdrum of bureaucratic incrementalism (Hayes 2017).

This is where we need to resurrect a notion of impartial progress that is suitable for everyone. *Weltbeziehung* also mean finding a common emotional and rational ground on which to make common decisions. Such common ground can only be achieved by some form of common understanding and a common "democratic" process of deliberation. The common ground is necessary since it needs to mend what is necessarily broken by making a decision. In Niklas Luhmann's ([1994] 2019, 259) words, every decision has a diabolic component: it divides; it forces us to draw a distinction and choose one side of the distinction— government vs. opposition, right vs wrong, good vs bad. However, in the same way that losing a vote in a democracy does not mean losing all political rights, decisions also require a symbolic dimension—something we can all agree on, regardless of whether we disagree on the specific issue at hand or not.

This symbolic dimension thus transcends the decision itself and requires some kind of common interpretation of the context in which the decision arises (Luhmann 2002, 274) and some form of resonance (see introduction to this volume). It allows people to form an understanding of what progress might mean in basic terms in a world society. It would not mean that we construct a common Elysium, Nirvana, or Heaven but that we find a way of interacting with each other that leads to a common understanding about how to come to better and impartial decisions. Impartiality is crucial because it works like an umpire in sports: people come together with diverse, sometimes rival goals. Impartial progress means that the process still leads to fair results. In this way, progress is at least as much about how decisions are generated as it is about desirable outcomes. It is a political concept in the true sense.

Such a worldview would not only contain ideas about a common global governance structure but also some fundamental policy contents, such as the need to achieve a more equitable and sustainable planet. While it would be somewhat self-defeating for me, as a single, potentially partial and thereby biased author, to claim that specific human inventions are clear examples of progress, many people would intuitively agree on some "telltale" achievements across history. The modern welfare state is a good example. One can certainly discuss whether the modern welfare state has grown excessively or whether it devours too much money, but it is also clear that the basic institution of a welfare state has progressively addressed a clear modern problem of risk sharing and social assistance. The symbolic dimension of progress involves appreciating, or even celebrating, such general achievements and how they came about, without forgetting their problems.

Another example of social progress that comes to mind is the peaceful coexistence of religions. For instance, the edicts of toleration from the late sixteenth century onwards symbolise—despite all the backlashes that followed in the Thirty Years' War—a gradual pacification between the Protestant and Catholic religions in Europe. Progress is thus related to another fundamental value: tolerance, and the capacity to endure pain. Decisions always create pain for the decision-maker, but especially for those who do not support the outcome. Toleration is the process of accepting such outcomes without reacting too strongly (e.g., violently) against it (Heywood 1999; Forst 2020). In such a sense, tolerance is also a fundamental value of a functioning democracy if democracy is defined as a system in which governments (can) lose elections peacefully (Przeworski 1999).

But tolerance also works on another level: it is the basic insight that people are different and a basic respect for such differences. In this second sense, tolerance cannot be unilateral, it needs to be mutual in any direction. The toleration of intolerant acts would not work, and neither would an intolerance of tolerant acts. True progress thus only happens if decisions become—at the minimum—tolerable in such a sense for everyone. This would not require agreement but an acceptance of the basic shared insights of progress. This sounds like too little for many observers: we should strive for mutual recognition instead of toleration. To others, even a notion of toleration sounds utopian or naïve. Progress based on minimal notions of toleration, impartiality, and pluralism as a least common denominator, however, might still be preferable to discarding the idea of progress altogether.

Works cited

Adam, Christian, Steffen Hurka, Christoph Knill, and Yves Steinebach (2019). *Policy accumulation and the democratic responsiveness trap*. Cambridge University Press. https://doi.org/10.1017/9781108646888.

Allen, Amy (2016). *The end of progress: Decolonizing the normative foundations of critical theory*. New York: Columbia University Press.

Anghie, Antony (2006). The evolution of international law: Colonial and postcolonial realities. *Third world quarterly*, 27, 5, 739–53.

Appadurai, Arjun, ed. (2013). *The future as cultural fact: Essays on the global condition*. London: Verso Books.

Arrow, K.J. (1951). *Social choice and individual values*. New York: Wiley.

Bachrach, Peter, and Morton S. Baratz. (1963). Decisions and nondecisions: An analytical framework. *American political science review,* 57, 3: 632–42. https://doi.org/10.2307/1952568.

Barnett, Anthony (2017). *The lure of greatness: England's Brexit & America's Trump.* London: Unbound.

Barnouw, Dagmar (1994). Political correctness in the 1780s: Kant, Herder, Forster and the knowledge of diversity. In Wilfried Malsch (ed.). *Herder Jahrbuch/Herder Yearbook 1994,* 51–76. Stuttgart: J.B. Metzler/Springer.

Becker, Ulrich (1996). Das "Menschenbild des Grundrechts." In *Die Rechtsprechung des Bundesverfassungsgerichts.* Berlin: Dunker & Humblot.

Bernasconi, Robert (2002). Kant as an unfamiliar source of racism. In Julie K. Ward and Tommy L. Lott (eds.). *Philosophers on race: Critical essays,* 144–62. Oxford: Blackwell.

Beyme, K. V. (1992). *Theorie der Politik Im 20. Jahrhundert.* Frankfurt a. M.: Suhrkamp.

Bowles, Samuel, and Herbert Gintis (2011). *A cooperative species. Human reciprocity and its evolution.* Princeton: Princeton University Press.

Bury, John Bagnell (1920). *The idea of progress: An inquiry into its origin and growth.* New York: Macmillan and Company.

Cassell, Joan (2002). Perturbing the system: Hard science, soft science and social science. *The anxiety and madness of method: Human organization,* 61, 2, 177–85.

Chakrabarty, Dipesh (2009). *Provincializing Europe: Postcolonial thought and historical difference.* New ed. Princeton: Princeton University Press.

Cubukcu, Ayca (2017). Thinking against humanity. *London review of international law,* 5, 2, 251–67.

Dembour, Marie-Benedicte (2012). Following the movement of a pendulum: Between universalism and relativism. In Jane K. Cowan, Marie-Benedicte Dembour, and Richard A.Wilson. *Culture and rights,* 56–79. Cambridge: Cambridge University Press.

Diamond, Jared (1992). *The third chimpanzee: The evolution and future of the human animal.* New York, NY, HarperCollins.

Doyle, David (2014). The political economy of policy volatility in Latin America. *Latin American politics and society,* 56 (4), 1–22.

Drosdeck, Thomas (1989). *Die Herrschende Meinung: Autorität als Rechtsquelle.* Berlin: Duncker & Humblot.

Easterly, William (2001). *The elusive quest for growth: Economists' adventures and misadventures in the tropics.* Cambridge, MA: MIT Press.

Eberl, Oliver (2019). Kant on race and barbarism: Towards a more complex view on racism and anti-colonialism in Kant. *Kantian review,* 24, 3, 385–413.

Edelstein, Ludwig (1967). *The idea of progress in classical antiquity.* Encore ed. Baltimore: Johns Hopkins University Press.

Elster, Jon (2011). Hard and soft obscurantism in the humanities and social sciences. *Diogenes,* 58, 1–2, 159–70.

Engen, Nadine van, Lars Tummers, Victor Bekkers, and Bram Steijn (2016). Bringing history in: Policy accumulation and general policy alienation. *Public management review,* 18, 7: 1085–1106. https://doi.org/10.1080/14719037.2015.1088568.

Epstein, Lee, William M. Landes, and Richard A. Posner (2011). Why (and when) judges dissent: A theoretical and empirical analysis. *Journal of legal analysis*, 3, 1, 101–37.

Escobar, Arturo (2007). *La invención del Tercer Mundo. Construcción y deconstrucción del desarrollo.* Transl. Diana Ochoa. Caracas: Fundación Editorial el perro y la rana.

Ferguson, J. (1994). The anti-politics machine: Development and bureaucratic power in Lesotho. *The ecologist* 24, 5, 176–81.

Forst, Rainer (2017). The concept of progress. In Rainer Forst (ed.). *Normativity and power: Analyzing social orders of justification*, 69–74. New York: Oxford University Press.

Forst, Rainer (2020). *Toleranz im Konflikt*. Frankfurt a. M. and New York: Suhrkamp.

Fukuyama, F. (2014). *Political order and decay: From the Industrial Revolution to the globalization of democracy*. New York: Farrar, Straus and Giroux.

Fulda, Daniel, and Hartmut Rosa (2011). Die Aufklärung: Ein Vollendetes Projekt? Für einen Dynamischen Begriff der Moderne. *Zeitschrift für Ideengeschichte*, V, 4, 111–18.

Funke, Andreas, and Klaus Ulrich Schmolke (eds.) (2019). *Menschenbilder im Recht*. Tübingen: Mohr Siebeck.

Giersch, Herbert (1985). Eurosclerosis: Working paper 112. *Kieler Diskussionsbeiträge*. https://www.econstor.eu/handle/10419/48070.

Glenn, H. Patrick (2004). *Legal traditions in the world: Sustainable diversity in law*. Oxford: Oxford University Press.

Gowdy, John M. (1994). Progress and environmental sustainability. *Environmental ethics*, 16, 1, 41–55.

Graeber, David, and David Wengrow (2021). *The dawn of everything: A new history of humanity*. New York: Farrar, Straus and Giroux.

Hagström, Linus (2021). Great power narcissism and ontological (in)security: The narrative mediation of greatness and weakness in international politics. *International studies quarterly*, 65, 2, 331–42. https://doi.org/10.1093/isq/sqab011.

Haidt, Jopnathan (2012). *The righteous mind: Why good people are divided by politics and religion*. New York: Pantheon.

Harris, Abram L. (1956). John Stuart Mill's theory of progress. *Ethics*, 66, 3, 157–75.

Hayes, Michael. (2017). Incrementalism and public policy-making. *Oxford research encyclopedia of politics*, (April). https://doi.org/10.1093/acrefore/9780190228637.013.133.

Henisz, Witold J. (2004). Political institutions and policy Volatility. *Economics & politics*, 16, 1, 1–27.

Heywood, Andrew (1999). *Political theory: An introduction*. Palgrave Macmillan.

Hopf, Ted (2002). *Social Construction of International Politics: Identities & Foreign Policies, Moscow, 1955 and 1999*. Ithaca: Cornell University Press.

Horkheimer, Max, T. W. Adorno, and Eva von Redecker (2022). *Dialektik der Aufklärung: Philosophische Fragmente. Sonderausgabe*. Frankfurt a. M.: S. Fischer.

Hörnle, Tatjana (2015). Das Menschenbild des Rechts. In Jan-Christoph Heilinger and Julian Nida-Rümelin (eds.). *Anthropologie und Ethik*, 97–111. Berlin: Walter de Gruyter Verlag.

Howlett, Michael, and Achim Kemmerling (2017). Calibrating climate change policies: The causes and consequences of sustained under-reaction. *Journal of environmental policy & planning*, 19, 6, 625–37. https://doi.org/10.1080/1523908X.2017.1324772.

Immergut, Ellen M. (1990). Institutions, veto points, and policy results: A comparative analysis of health care. *Journal of Public Policy*, 10, 4, 391–416. https://doi.org/10.1017/S0143814X00006061.

Jones, Bryan D., Herschel F. Thomas, and Michelle Wolfe (2014). Policy bubbles. *Policy studies journal*, 42, 1, 146–71. https://doi.org/10.1111/psj.12046.

Keen, Steve (2010). *Debunking economics: The naked emperor of the social sciences*. 5th impression. London: Zed Books.

Kemmerling, Achim, and Kristin Makszin (2018). When does policy diffusion affect policy instability? Cases of excessive policy volatility in welfare policies in East Central Europe. In Agnes Batory, Andrew Cartwright, and Diane Stone (eds.). *Policy Experiments, Failures and Innovations*, 26–44. Cheltenham, UK: Edward Elgar Publishing. https://doi.org/10.4337/9781785367496.00009.

Kemmerling, Achim, and Sushobhan Parida (forthcoming). Conflict and social justice: A global south perspective. In Richter, Solveig and Siddharth Tripath (eds.) *The RLI handbook of peace and conflict studies: Perspectives from the global south(s)*. London and New York: Routledge.

Kitcher, Philip (2016). Über den Fortschritt, *Deutsche Zeitschrift für Philosophie*, 64, 2, 165–92.

Klikauer, Thomas (2015). What is managerialism? *Critical sociology*, 41, 7–8, 1103–19.

Koselleck, Reinhart (1989). *Vergangene Zukunft: Zur Semantik geschichtlicher Zeiten*. Frankfurt a. M.: Suhrkamp.

Kuhl, S. (2009). Capacity development as the model for development aid organizations. *Development and change*, 40, 3, 551–77.

Latour, Bruno (1993). *We have never been modern*. Cambridge, MA: Harvard University Press.

Lipset, Seymour Martin (1959). Some social requisites of democracy: Economic development and political legitimacy. *American political science review*, 53, 1, 69–105. https://doi.org/10.2307/1951731.

Lüdemann, Jörn (2006). *Die Grenzen des Homo Oeconomicus und die Rechtswissenschaft*. Bonn: Max Planck Institute for Research on Collective Goods No 2006, 2.

Luhmann, Niklas (2002). *Die Politik der Gesellschaft*. Frankfurt a. M.: Suhrkamp.

Luhmann, Niklas ([1994] 2019). *Die Wirtschaft der Gesellschaft*. Suhrkamp Taschenbuch Wissenschaft 1152. Frankfurt a. M.: Suhrkamp.

Lyotard, Jean-François (1984). *The postmodern condition: A report on knowledge*. Minneapolis, Minn.: University of Minnesota Press.

Mäder, Denis (2014). Wider die Fortschrittskritik: Mit einem Appendix zum Fortschritt als Human Enhancement. *Momentum quarterly: Zeitschrift für den Sozialen Fortschritt*, 3, 4: 190–205.

Mankiw, N. Gregory (2003). *Principles of economics*. Mason, USA: South-Western.

Mankiw, N. Gregory (2000). The savers–spenders theory of fiscal policy. *American economic review*, 90, 2: 120–25. https://doi.org/10.1257/aer.90.2.120.

Maor, Moshe (2012). Policy overreaction. *Journal of public policy,* 32, 3, 231–59. https://doi.org/10.1017/S0143814X1200013X.

Maor, Moshe (2014). Policy persistence, risk estimation and policy underreaction. *Policy sciences,* 47, 4, 425–43. https://doi.org/10.1007/s11077-014-9203-8.

Marsh, David, and J. C. Sharman (2009). Policy diffusion and policy transfer. *Policy studies,* 30, 3, 269–88.

Mills, C. Wright (1959). *The sociological imagination.* Oxford: Oxford University Press.

Mommsen, Theodor (1951). St. Augustine and the Christian idea of progress: The background of the City of God. *Journal of the history of ideas,* 12, 3, 346–74.

Morozov, Evgeny (2014). *To save everything, click here: Technology, solutionism and the urge to fix problems that don't exist.* New York: Public Affairs.

Nachtwey, Oliver, and Timo Seidl (2020, March 14). The Solutionist Ethic and the Spirit of Digital Capitalism. *SocArXiv.* https://doi.org/10.31235/osf.io/sgjzq.

Nakayama, Shigeru (1997). The Chinese "cyclic" view of history vs. Japanese progress. In Arnold Burgen, Peter McLaughlin, and Jürgen Mittelstraß (eds.). *The idea of progress,* 65–76. Berlin and Boston: De Gruyter.

Nisbet, Robert (1992). *The idea of progress: Literature of liberty.* Bibliographic essay, Liberty Fund. 05.05.2023 https://oll.libertyfund.org/page/idea-of-progress-a-bibliographical-essay-by-robert-nisbet.

Nugent, Walter (2010). *Progressivism: A very short introduction.* Oxford: Oxford University Press.

Pinker, Steven (2018). *Enlightenment now: The case for reason, science, humanism, and progress.* New York: Penguin Books.

Popper, Karl R. (1957). *The poverty of historicism.* Frome and London: Beacon Press.

Price, Russell (1977). The theme of gloria in Machiavelli. *Renaissance quarterly,* 30, 4, 588–631. https://doi.org/10.2307/2859861.

Pritchett, Lant, Michael Woolcock, and Matt Andrews (2010). *Capability traps? The mechanisms of persistent implementation failure.* Washington, D.C.: Center of Global Development Working paper No 234.

Przeworski, Adam (1999). Minimalist conception of democracy: A defense. In Ian Shapiro and Casiano Hacker-Cordon (eds.). *Democracy's value,* 12–17. Cambridge: Cambridge University Press.

Reshetnikov, Anatoly (2011). Great projects' politics in Russia history's hardly victorious end. *Demokratizatsiya,* 19 (2), 151–75.

Rosa, Hartmut (2021). *Beschleunigung und Entfremdung: Entwurf einer kritischen Theorie spätmoderner Zeitlichkeit.* Transl. Robin Celikates. 8. Aufl. Berlin: Suhrkamp.

Rosa, Hartmut (2022). Zur Heuristik des Ausnahmezustandes. In Karl-Rudolf Korte, Gert Scobel, and Taylan Yildiz (eds.). *Heuristiken des politischen Entscheidens,* 263–88. Berlin: Suhrkamp.

Rothstein, Bo (2011). *The quality of government: Corruption, social trust, and inequality in international perspective.* Chicago and London: University of Chicago Press.

Sachs, Wolfgang (ed.) (1993). *Global ecology: A new arena of political conflict.* London; Atlantic Highlands, NJ and Halifax: Zed Books; Fernwood Publishing.

Said, Edward W. (1978). *Orientalism*. New York: Pantheon Books.

Shabani, Omid Payrow (2017). The ineliminability of the idea of progress. *The Journal of Value Inquiry*, 51, 4, 663–80. https://doi.org/10.1007/s10790-017-9617-6.

Siebert, Horst (1997). Labor Market Rigidities: At the Root of Unemployment in Europe. *Journal of Economic Perspectives* 11 (3), 37–54. https://doi.org/10.1257/jep.11.3.37.

Sunstein, Cass R., David Schkade, David, Lisa M. Ellman, and Andres Sawicki (2006). *Are judges political? An empirical analysis*. Washington, DC: Brookings Institution Press.

Tsebelis, George (2002). *Veto players: How political institutions work*. Princeton: Princeton University Press. https://doi.org/10.1515/9781400831456.

Tuschak, Bernadette (2009). *Die Herrschende Meinung als Indikator Europäischer Rechtskultur: Eine Rechtsvergleichende Untersuchung der Bezugsquellen und Produzenten Herrschender Meinung in England und Deutschland am Beispiel des Europarechts*. Hamburg: Dr. Kovac.

V-Dem Institute (2021). *Autocratization turns viral: Democracy Report 2021*. Gothenburg, Sweden: V-Dem Institute, University of Gothenburg.

Wagner, Peter (2018). *Fortschritt: Zur Erneuerung einer Idee*. Frankfurt a. M. and New York: Campus.

Welzel, Christian (2013). *Freedom rising: Human empowerment and the quest for emancipation*. New York: Cambridge University Press.

Wilson, Edward O. (2012). *The Social Conquest of Earth*. New York: Liveright.

Wilson, Woodrow (1913). *What is progress (blog)*. 1913. https://teachingamericanhistory.org/document/what-is-progress/.

Young, Crawford (1982). Ideas of progress in the Third World. In Gabriel A. Almond, Marvin Chodorow, and Roy Harvey Pearce (eds.). *Progress and its discontents*, 83–105. Berkeley: University of California Press. https://doi.org/10.1525/9780520313545-008.

Zaid, Gabriel (2009). *El progreso improductivo*. México: Debolsillo.

II
Comparative Perspectives

How Can Worldviews Be Compared? The pragmatic maxim and intellectual honesty[1]

Hermann Deuser, Markus Kleinert

1. Worldviews

When reference is made to a specific worldview, this presupposes one or more alternatives. Worldviews or *Weltbeziehungen* are spoken of in the plural from the perspective of scientific observation. Accordingly, the research program of the Max-Weber-Kolleg focuses on the cultural pluralism of attractive, repulsive, or indifferent *Weltbeziehungen*. But from which point of view can worldviews be compared at all, if this comparison is supposed to go beyond personal presuppositions and evaluations and makes claims to be methodically controlled and scientific? The complexity of the question is increased by the fact that worldviews are not only theories that can be related to each other in an abstract metalanguage, but that worldviews also and above all concern life practice and are expressed in the respective conduct of life. The difficulty of comparing worldviews is exemplified by the topic of faith and knowledge, in the comparison of religious and secular worldviews—as, e. g., recently in Jürgen Habermas's attempt in *Also a History of Philosophy* (Habermas 2019) to justify from a philosophical perspective the relevance of specific religious traditions for the political discourse of a secular modernity. This chapter will present an American and a European reflection on the problem of referencing and comparing worldviews associated with the names of William James and Max Weber. The fact that in both cases the dimension of space has special significance—on the one hand the metaphor of the hotel corridor and on the other hand the real

---

[1] © The author/s 2023, published by Campus Verlag, Open Access: CC BY-SA 4.0
Bettina Hollstein, Hartmut Rosa, Jörg Rüpke (eds.), "Weltbeziehung"
DOI: 10.12907/978-3-593-45587-7_006

lecture hall—seems a favourable coincidence for the contribution to a book published on the occasion of the Max-Weber-Kolleg's move into the new research building "*Weltbeziehungen*".

2. James' corridor

The claim of pragmatism to be the superior scientific method of modernity was captured by William James in the seductive image of a long hotel corridor that leads on between the individual rooms on the right and left, always in their center: In one room

"you may find a man writing an atheistic volume, in the next someone on his knees praying for faith and strength, in a third a chemist investigating a body's properties. In a fourth, a system of idealistic metaphysics is being excogitated; in a fifth, the impossibility of all metaphysics is being shown. But they all own the corridor, all must pass through it if they want a practicable way of getting into or out of their respective rooms." (James 1995, 21 f.; with reference to Giovanni Papini)

It may then follow from this constellation that pragmatism has "no *fundamental* prejudice against theology" (ibid., 74). The corridor image is perplexing because the methodological middle can be understood as the highest science nevertheless in a hierarchy in relation to all others, while at the same time a complete plurality of all rooms is assumed, which on quasi-neutral terrain no longer form opposites. But is it conceivable that the alternative between atheism and theism is dissolved, while both are convinced of their truth each for itself? (cf. Hingst 2000, 46) The common of the different can probably only be found in the fact that the superiority, the basic understanding or the basic attitude of the sciences, pragmatistically conceived, consists in the fact that there is always the same or at least a comparable basic structure: belief—doubt—(new) behavior, which at the same time compels to the respective truthfulness and consistently recognizes the complete truth as identifiable only in the process of its formation ("in the long run").

Unlike W. James, who does not want to admit abstract objectivism ("metaphysics") for the pragmatic "method," Charles S. Peirce always thematizes the basic structure of the pragmatic maxim also in itself: as logic of research (abduction, deduction, induction), logic as semiotics, threefold category theory, evolutionary metaphysics—thus comprehensively employed in terms of the theory of science and phenomenological life practice, committed to the existential *unavailability* of existence (cf. Rosa 2018, 67) as much as to the law of nature or the *regularity of behaviour*. The "basic reliability" (Ohly 2017, 50) of the world of life and science, which is presupposed in all sciences, is taken up in pragmatism according to its structure, interpreted, and checked in its claim to generalizability. The more attention is paid to the *creative* basic reliability itself, the clearer the access to the religious or theological dimension in the respective case becomes.

In the following, this basic structure (cf. Deuser 2014, 149–72) will be applied in contrast: To clarify the science-theoretical role of the subject in situations of action—by use, "by their fruits you shall know them."

3. The wall of natural sciences

Max Weber's ranking of the competing sciences comes surprisingly close to the corridor image, though this ranking is conceived entirely from the methodological opposition of natural sciences and humanities or cultural sciences. The corridor, to remain in the image, would then be the long demarcation between the natural sciences on one side of the corridor and the cultural sciences on the other, in such a way that when the room doors on the left are opened, those on the right must remain closed—and vice versa. Weber speaks of "incompatibility" and "unacceptability" or also: that *value* judgments (as personal standpoints necessarily at home in the field of culture) have no place in the lecture hall (Weber 1994, 20). But the analysis of this complex relationship, that is, the question of whether the corridor itself has become functionless or whether it needs to be rethought "from its end," becomes even more important now. The founders of (American) pragmatism were natural scientists who were precisely trying to work out the *scientific*, the inner connection between methodologically different disciplines. Weber, on the other hand, is up against the wall of the natural sciences, which now seem to demand the separation of culture as a matter of course. At the same time, however, Weber is working precisely on the independence of a "lecture hall" for cultural studies to thematize cultural values. Theology thereby becomes a special case (ibid., 21), the particularity of which can be proven with examples from the history of religion, while the actual problem, the concept of revelation, takes the functional place of a (religion-)philosophical justification, with which a bridge (instead of a corridor which image no longer fits) could be built. Weber's concept of "disenchantment" limits the validity of theology, which at this point can only be drawn from a—at least respectable—"*quia* absurdum." But then there remains again only an "unbridgeable" opposition, now of the "value sphere of 'science'" and that of "religious salvation" (ibid., 22).

4. Subjectivity and contingency

This description of the situation is inevitable because Weber sees the natural sciences as bound to finding facts, while the values in a cultural community as to how one should "*act*" denote "wholly *heterogeneous* problems." Here, however, it can be observed how Weber, on the one hand, sees the realm of values downgraded to the activities of "prophets" and "demagogues" who speak in the marketplace; but, on the other hand, concedes the inevitability of "errors" and "subjective sympathy," which brings up "one's own conscience" and the "duty to seek the truth". This last, apparently, cannot and must not be absent: that is what "intellectual honesty" (ibid., 15; cf. Harrington 2012, 100), the scholar's probity, dictates. But in which room in the corridor of the sciences can cultural studies (e.g., philosophy of religion), demarcated by the natural sciences, take up residence? Or does it, in the sense of James' pragmatism, stand in the place and function of the corridor? Or at its end, in whose horizon nature and culture integrate? This seems only conceivable if the sense of "subjectivity *and* contingency" (Joas 1999, 40) can be acknowledged by both sides as a condition of understanding and as a task—a much more far-reaching question than the case of conflict referred to by Weber: that a Freemason and a Catholic would not be able to agree on the presuppositions or presuppositionlessness of science; all the more so if one side would refer to miracles and revelation for argumentation (Weber 1994, 16). And would not intellectual honesty consist precisely in the fact that the sciences have the moral duty to enlighten about facts?

5. Religiously musical

What Weber understands by value-commitment in his context has several aspects (cf. Joas 1999, 40):

1. The different "spheres of value" can be empirically-historically discerned and scientifically represented.
2. An objective "value sphere" in the sense of the metaphysical tradition need not and can no longer be assumed. Here, the thesis of "disenchantment" has its philosophical application which results from the authoritative position of natural scientific epistemology.
3. The role of subjectivity (in other theoretical language: the relation to one's own existence) is value-related indispensable, but in its sphere of action it cannot be decided scientifically in cases of conflict and thus it falls outside of public rationality. Moreover, for clarification, the esoteric misconception of prophetic-demonic attitudes must still be excluded from scientific communication, e.g., "Catheder prophecy"—i.e., "surrogates" (Weber 1994, 23) of a powerful religious tradition that has lost its socially immediate power in modernity. Once the genesis of religion is understood, its validity diminishes (cf. Weber 2005, ch. 1).
4. The moral duty and obligation thus results from a twofold value requirement: On the one hand, the scientific-theoretical separation of natural and (empirical-historical) cultural approaches, and on the other hand, the sensitivity for the resulting responsibility for the right to have value commitments, so long as they are preserved from populist deviations.
5. In objective as well as in subjective reference no pre-ordered determinations of being or essence prevail, but the historicity of existence describes the factual situation: contingency. That this applies to subjective experiences as well as to the "pure" natural sciences entails the rediscovery of continuity (in spite of contingency, cf. Deuser 1990), and shows the prospect of a broad plural dialogue situation (W. James' corridor), as it was not yet to be expected in Weber's time in Germany, i.e. the bridge between the separated spheres seems possible (cf. detailed Haudel 2021).
6. But the "final word on life" then remains scientifically inaccessible. What seems possible is a process of interpretation (Weber 1994, 13, 21 f.) or an optional (existential) decisiveness that can be chosen depending on the situation and the level of scientific education, which has its theory-tested, classical model in the Augustinian *quia absurdum*. In Weber's view, however, this is only a "sacrifice of the intellect", which one can make or not. It is a question of individual talent and subjective, aesthetic taste to be "religiously 'musical'" or not. "Revelations" or "sacred states" are in any case excluded by the spirit of the sciences (ibid., 21 f.). By the way, the *quia absurdum* is also found towards the end of Weber's

famous intermediary consideration: "There is by no means *any* unbroken religion, operating as a life-power, which would not have to demand at some point the 'credo non quod, sed *quia* absurdum,'—the 'sacrifice of the intellect'" (Weber 1920, 566).

6. The complicated demand for honesty

If Weber methodologically emphasizes intellectual honesty in this way in his science lecture and also demonstrates it practically in the lecture situation, it remains to be noted, however, that the concept of honesty itself is less unambiguous than his repeated appeal to act with plain and simple honesty suggests. When Nietzsche, to whom Weber refers with his call for intellectual honesty (cf. Bormuth 2018), exhorts the virtue of honesty in the context of his critical genealogy of Christianity, he remains aware of the not least Christian prehistory of this virtue, the demand for unreserved truthfulness. Therefore, a distinction must be made between honesty as an instrument in a concrete situation and honesty as an end in itself (cf. Kleinert 2012; Meier 2023, 95 f., 98). This can also be illustrated by Kierkegaard's newspaper article "What do I want?" which demands honesty with great vehemence as a minimal demand in a time of confusion between Christian heritage, a secularized church, and a religiously indifferent mass society (Kierkegaard 1994). The demand for honesty must not be detached from the historical situation and set absolute, otherwise it develops a dynamic of its own, in which one's own truthfulness can only be proven in the compulsive uncovering of the other's untruthfulness. In contrast, intellectual honesty also and above all shows itself in the disposition for constant self-reflection, for the thematization of one's own world view. Through this processuality, the perspectives only hinted at here, the pragmatism of William James and the theory of science of Max Weber, can be brought closer together. How the disposition for repeated self-reflection can be aptly expressed in the title of an essay has been shown by Ernst Tugendhat (2007): "*Retraktationen zur intellektuellen Redlichkeit*" ("Retractions to intellectual honesty").

Works cited

Bormuth, Matthias (2018). Max Weber im Lichte Nietzsches. In: Matthias Bormuth (ed.). *Max Weber: Wissenschaft als Beruf*. Mit zeitgenössischen Resonanzen und einem Gespräch mit Dieter Henrich, 7–36, Berlin: Matthes & Seitz.

Deuser, Hermann (1990). Kontingenz II. In: *Theologische Realenzyklopädie 19* (1990), 551–59.

Deuser, Hermann (2014). Pragmatische oder pragmatizistische Religionsphilosophie. In Hermann Deuser. *Religion: Kosmologie und Evolution. Sieben religionsphilosophische Essays*, 149–72, Tübingen: Mohr Siebeck.

Habermas, Jürgen (2019). *Auch eine Geschichte der Philosophie*, 2 Bde., Berlin: Suhrkamp.

Harrington, Austin (2012). Von der "intellektuellen Rechtschaffenheit" zur "taghellen Mystik". Aspekte und Differenzen einer Glaubenskonzeption bei Max Weber, Georg Simmel und Robert Musil. In Gerald Hartung and Magnus Schlette (eds.). *Religiosität und intellektuelle Redlichkeit*, 99–123, Tübingen: Mohr Siebeck.

Haudel, Matthias (2021). *Theologie und Naturwissenschaft. Zur Überwindung von Vorurteilen und zu ganzheitlicher Wirklichkeitserkenntnis*, Göttingen: UTB.

Hingst, Kai-Michael (2000). Zur zweiten Vorlesung: James' Transformation der Pragmatischen Maxime von Peirce. In Klaus Oehler (ed.): *William James: Pragmatismus: ein neuer Name für einige alte Wege des Denkens*, 33–67, Berlin: Akademie.

James, William (1995). *Pragmatism*. New York: Dover Thrift Editions.

James, William (2001). *Pragmatismus. Ein neuer Name für einige alte Denkweisen*. Trans. by Klaus Schubert and Axel Spree. Darmstadt: WBG.

Joas, Hans (1999). *Die Entstehung der Werte*. Frankfurt a. M.: Suhrkamp.

Kierkegaard, Sören (1994): Was ich will? (Fædrelandet, 31. März 1855). In Emanuel Hirsch and Hayo Gerdes (eds.). *Sören Kierkegaard: Der Augenblick. Aufsätze und Schriften des letzten Streits*. Trans. by Hayo Gerdes, 48–52, Gütersloh: Gütersloher Verlagshaus.

Kleinert, Markus (2012). Ambivalenz der intellektuellen Redlichkeit am Beispiel von Nietzsches "Antichrist". In Gerald Hartung and Magnus Schlette (eds.). *Religiosität und intellektuelle Redlichkeit*, 71–83, Tübingen: Mohr Siebeck.

Meier, Heinrich (2023). Nietzsches Wille zur Macht. Über die Selbsterkenntnis des Philosophen. In *Zeitschrift für Ideengeschichte* XVII/1, 87–104.

Ohly, Lukas (2017). *Theologie als Wissenschaft. Eine Fundamentaltheologie aus phänomenologischer Leitperspektive*, Frankfurt a. M.: Peter Lang.

Rosa, Hartmut (2018). *Unverfügbarkeit*. Wien/Salzburg: Residenz.

Tugendhat, Ernst (2007). Retraktationen zur intellektuellen Redlichkeit. In Ernst Tugendhat. *Anthropologie statt Metaphysik*, 85–113, München: Beck.

Weber, Max (1920). Zwischenbetrachtung. In Max Weber. *Gesammelte Aufsätze zur Religionssoziologie 1*, 536–73, Tübingen: Mohr Siebeck.

Weber, Max (1994). Wissenschaft als Beruf. In Wolfgang J. Mommsen and Wolfgang Schluchter (eds.). *Max Weber: Wissenschaft als Beruf (1917/1919) / Politik als Beruf (1919), Studienausgabe*, 1–23, Tübingen: Mohr Siebeck.

Weber, Max (2005). *Wirtschaft und Gesellschaft. Teilbd. 2: Religiöse Gemeinschaften.* Ed. by Hans Gerhard Kippenberg. Tübingen: Mohr Siebeck.

"Theorizing Across Traditions": Social science as a polyphonic encounter[1]

Martin Fuchs, Antje Linkenbach, Beatrice Renzi

1. The Problem

Contemporary de-/postcolonial scholarship comprehends colonization as a complex of political, economic, cultural and intellectual exploitation and domination of territories and people by imperial nations. Colonization is conceived as a process, in which various hierarchies intersect and a radical difference between the colonizers and the colonized, between "we" and the "others", or the "West" and the "rest", is being constructed and cemented.[2] De-colonialization as an academic endeavour therefore tries to dissect and explore the mechanisms through which colonial power operates in its different arenas.

Linking up with the decolonization project is urgent for an institution like the Max-Weber-Kolleg whose overarching research focus is the exploration of *Weltbeziehungen*: the culturally different ways human beings relate to and act in the world. In this contribution we engage with decolonization as intellectual project. Scholars in this field address the issue of "epistemic violence" (Spivak 1988) or "epistemicide" (Sousa Santos 2016), that is the devaluation and destruction of non-European, non-modern knowledge (systems) through intellectual regimes of power. Devaluation and ignorance are still deeply engrained in the contemporary global orders of knowledge. We want to focus on one aspect in this broader epistemic field: the still prevalent Eu-

---

[1] © The author/s 2023, published by Campus Verlag, Open Access: CC BY-SA 4.0
Bettina Hollstein, Hartmut Rosa, Jörg Rüpke (eds.), "Weltbeziehung"
DOI: 10.12907/978-3-593-45587-7_007
[2] The matrix of power includes e.g., class, racial, ethnic, gender, sexual, spiritual, epistemic, linguistic hierarchies (Grosfoguel 2010); we have to add caste hierarchies.

rocentrism in the discipline of sociology. In particular, we want to challenge the Eurocentric ways of doing (macro-)sociological/social theory.

According to the geopolitical distribution of scholarly tasks, theoretization has been, and largely still is, the privilege of Western science; guided by questions relevant from a Western perspective, theoretical considerations are mostly based on Western concepts and categories and are pursued by Western (male) academics. The attempt of de-centring and pluralizing sociological discourses and conceptualizations cross-culturally is therefore an important step.

However, in the process of opening up to other cultural concepts one needs to be vigilant and ask whose culture and which concepts are we talking about. Who represents a "culture", and is there actually only "one culture" in a particular societal context? This problem of cultural plurality and its representation affects both sides but is particularly evident in cultural contexts (like India), where historically deeply ingrained social (caste) and patriarchal hierarchies largely silence the voices of certain groups. Consequently, it is paramount to establish an inter- and intra-cultural polyvocality. On this basis the decolonial task itself may get diversified and re-interpreted according to one's positionality.

In the following we will first exemplify how eurocentrically biased research questions influence and direct theories of modernity in such a way that European / Western modernity is exceptionalized and becomes a universal frame of reference. In a second step we plead for doing away with "monological" theorizing and engage in a dialogue between scholars of Western social sciences and those representing thought traditions from other cultural contexts.[3] For this new way of mutual "resonant" reflection we adopt the term "theorizing across traditions", modifying the expression "thinking across traditions" suggested by Nivedita Menon (Nigam 2020, 38; also Banerjee et al. 2016). Thirdly, we illustrate how research at the Max-Weber-Kolleg has attempted to contribute to overcome Eurocentrism. Here, we take examples from research focusing on individualisation and translation. Finally, we reflect on the potential of cross-cultural dialogue for social critique, as well as on the danger of appropriation of decolonial rhetoric by right-wing groups pursuing identity politics.

---

3 We are aware that notions like "other" or "non-Western" continue to reproduce temporal and spatial hierarchies between socio-cultural constellations. However, nobody has so far succeeded in finding an alternative terminology that could replace these.

2. Exceptionality and Dominance of European Modernity

Outlining his new focus on "world-sociology", sociologist Peter Wagner poses what he considers to be the most important question, the discipline of sociology, or rather, sociological theoretization, must answer: "what is the socio-political condition of the world today and how has it become so" (2016, 87)?

For Indian political philosopher Aditya Nigam, who makes a claim for "decolonizing theory", this would be precisely a question, which is problematic to pose, as it can only be answered "by taking Europe and its very 'provincial' experience as primary reference points" (2020, 248). Interestingly, Wagner tells us that those engaged in the critique of Western colonialism and capitalist hegemony, like representatives of postcolonial and decolonial studies, are incapable or unwilling to answer his central question (2016, 87)—a fact, which, he thinks, legitimizes him to refrain from a further engagement with these authors.

Nigam makes us aware of what he considers to be even more explicitly biased questions, such as: Was there feudalism, was there secularism in India? Or: what are the barriers to capital accumulation in India (2020, 248)? Such questions, posed in comparative or historical studies, but also in social theory, provoke answers that confirm the specificity and pioneering role of Europe and, simultaneously, point out what is lacking in "the rest" of the world. This positions the European trajectory as desirable blueprint. Such "Euronormality" has to be rectified, demands Nigam (2020, 21).[4] He proposes that for a decolonial agenda it is crucial to ask different questions, namely those that emerge from and relate to the ways of being, the specific conditions of existence, the choices and aspirations of the (various groups of the) once-colonized. He argues that in the process of reflecting on these questions, one must take up (contemporary or historical) categories and concepts used by members of the respective societies themselves.

A brief look into European sociological and socio-philosophical traditions reveals that many of the leading questions posed by the renowned representatives of the discipline are geared to prove the exceptionality of Europe and the West and its role as reference point for the development

---

4 The term "Euro-normality" was coined by Sudipta Kaviraj (2009).

of humanity. However, it also reveals where these endeavours reach their limits.[5]

Among the "classical" sociologists, Max Weber represents a position that is Western-centred, on the one hand, but also acknowledges achievements of Eastern societies and cultures, on the other. Weber frames his widely read comparative studies on Eurasian "world religions" and "civilizations" (GARS[6]) with a pointed question: Why did modern capitalism and the capitalist "spirit"—or more generally the "ability and disposition of men to adopt certain types of practical rational conduct (*Lebensführung*)" (1972, 12; 2004, 109)—only develop in the Occident, and not in other regions of the world? As is well-known, Weber grounds "the spirit of capitalism" in a particular religious ethic, that of (puritanical) Protestantism. Thus, the model of social action and the idea of the individual, as well as the specific concept of faith that he identifies in the "protestant ethic", become paradigmatic and essential for the development of modern capitalism.

However, in his last text, the *Prefatory Remarks* or *Vorbemerkung* of GARS, Weber qualifies the assumption that only one culture and one religious tradition appears as authentic. He asserts that the cultural phenomena that came to fruition in the Occident possibly define a direction of development of "*universal* significance and validity" only in the eyes of people from the West—in his words: "as at least we like to think" (1972, 1; 2004, 101; emphasis Weber).

Weber had extended his studies to Eastern religions and civilizations (*Kulturkreise*) and initially anchored his comparative approach in a universal theory of rationalization, which included a universal theory of the differentiation and the "autonomous working" (*Eigengesetzlichkeiten*) of "life orders" or "value spheres"—he distinguishes between the spheres of religion, economics, politics, science, aesthetics and erotics (GARS, *Zwischenbetrachtung / Intermediate Reflections*). His intensive engagement with other cultural and social contexts then led Weber to the point where the unity and directionality of rationalization processes began to dissolve; he started recognizing the cultural diversity of rationalizations, even within the very same epoch and cultural region. At the end of his life, Weber emphasized a plurality and

---

5 For a broader critical review of influential positions in social theory and their Eurocentric legacy see the introduction in Randeria et al. 2004.
6 *Gesammelte Aufsätze zur Religionssoziologie* (*Collected Essays on the Sociology of Religion*, GARS), some of which Weber could still edit himself. The volumes were published after his death between 1920 and 1921.

multi-directionality of rationalizations, not only among different cultural regions and religions of salvation or liberation, but also within the same contexts.[7]

Despite his increasing openness towards specific, independent forms of socio-cultural development, ultimately it remains rationalization in its Occidental form that has universal and guiding significance for Weber—as well as in the Weber reception. With the differentiation-theoretical approach to rationalization, he introduces a bundle of process categories which had a lasting effect on the perspective of societal analysis within the discipline.

A more recent attempt to inquire into the processes which led to the development and consolidation of European / Western exceptionalism and supremacy comes from Jürgen Habermas, member of the Frankfurt School of critical theory. He presented with his *Theorie des kommunikativen Handelns* (1981) a rationalization-theoretical conception of society, which he gives a linguistic pragmatic justification. The rationalization of the lifeworld or of communicative action reveals itself as the realization of a rationality potential inherent in language. This is conveyed via learning processes and following a developmental logic. Although language and communication-oriented action always have a rational internal structure (implicit recognition of validity claims and world relations [*Weltbezüge*]), an explicit rationality is only established in the course of the development process, leading to self-reflective reasoning, explicit reference to the objective, subjective and social world and the capability of rational argumentation and discourse (Linkenbach 1986, 34). Drawing inspiration from Jean Piaget, Habermas parallels ontogenetic and phylogenetic development: De-centering the understanding of the world in the process of ego-development corresponds to the development and differentiation of worldviews in the history of humanity. Humanity's implicit claim to reason has finally found its explicit and adequate form in the modern (European, Western) structures of consciousness.

---

7 "It must not be forgotten that one can in fact 'rationalize' life from a vast variety of ultimate vantage points. Moreover, one can do so in very different directions. 'Rationalism' is a historical concept that contains within itself a world of contradictions" (Weber 1972, 62 / 2011, 98). – "[R]ationalizations of the most varied character have existed in various departments of life and in all areas of culture" (Weber 1972, 11 f.; 2004, 109). For a detailed analysis of Weber's sociology of religion and his rationalization theory, see Fuchs 1987; 1988, 224–32; 2017; 2020.

Conceiving of European / Western modernity as a unique phenomenon and ultimate goal for humanity was systematically challenged around the turn of the millennium. Now scholars no longer focus on explaining its singularity but want to explore whether, why, and in which form many modernities exist. Shmuel Eisenstadt is the most prominent protagonist of theorizing of what he coined "multiple modernities". Still guided by an idea of cohesive and separated cultural containers, he argues that axial and non-axial "civilizations" have historically generated independent civilizational patterns. At a certain point these are confronted with Western modernity, which has historical precedence and, due to its expansive dynamics and universalist claims, operates unidirectionally as a constant frame of reference for other cultures or civilizations (Eisenstadt 2000a, 2–3). Multiple modernities, Eisenstadt notes, "developed around the basic antinomies and tensions of the modern civilizational program" (2000b, 17), that is, the different civilizations have to face problems of Western origin and are challenged to solve them independently in their civilisational contexts. Multiple modernities emerge in the process of "creative appropriation" of the cultural programme of modernity as developed in Europe. Multiple modernity approaches mark one of the last lines of defence justifying the centrality of the Western model(s) of modernity.

Influenced by Eisenstadt's concept of multiple modernities, sociologists Johann Arnason and Peter Wagner have developed theories of modernity, which postulate a certain autonomy of social spheres and allow for creative alternative forms of modernity. Both approaches are based on a trans-functionalist, trans-historical distinction of social dimensions and spheres of action, or *problématiques*.[8] Economic, political and epistemic *problématiques* address "the question of how to govern life in common; how to satisfy human needs; and how to establish valid knowledge" (Wagner 2008, 2, see also Arnason 2003, 222). All human societies have (had) to find their own answers to these anthropologically grounded questions, but modernity presents a specific and novel solution. Its vision of an unlimited expansion of rational mastery (based on a new cognitive model, linked to modern science), of autonomy and universality, gives the western (capitalist) model a special status. However, modernity did not develop without the formative impact of other parts of the world. "The most fundamental aspects of Western modernity

---

8 For a more detailed presentation of the approaches to modernity by Arnason and Wagner, as well as their failure to seriously engage with decolonial perspectives, see Linkenbach 2023.

were co-determined by its interaction with the world beyond its original domain", writes Arnason (already 1993, 12), and also Wagner is convinced that from the very beginning modernity is an entangled project. In addition, and like Eisenstadt, both scholars see (developed) modernity as a constant challenge for non-modern contexts. But despite its hegemonic character and the pressure to adopt the western model, modernization is not simply congruent with Westernization. Interaction involves a shaping of modernity by non-western traditions and a re-shaping of these traditions by the modernizing process. Consequently, modernity can appear in different formations, and the alternatives are dependent on the legacies of the respective historical backgrounds.

In order to explore processes of entanglement, and especially identify the agency and impact of non-Western societies on (the development of) modernity, Arnason and Wagner turn to empirical studies: Wagner engages in a project of "World Sociology" that is "necessarily comparative and historical" (2016, 1), while Arnason pursued "civilizational studies" of Japan, the Soviet Union and China. However, European / Western modernity and the political and economic imaginary deriving from it, still remain the main focus and reference point of theoretization of both scholars. This also implies that the often disastrous and highly destructive effects of colonialization are not (adequately) addressed, and other forms of socio-philosophical principles or other possible ways of organizing a life worth living, are disregarded (see Mota's criticism of Wagner, 2018). Finally, dialogues on equal footing with colleagues from the de- or postcolonial camp are rare or almost non-existent.

3. Decolonizing Sociological Theory

3.1 Articulating the Need

Parallel to these macro-sociological deliberations one meanwhile finds a slowly increasing number of German and European sociologists who undertake attempts to reach out beyond the Western-centred views on modernity and, consequently, open up to non-Western perspectives. Several of these have connections to debates in anthropology and global history, which focus on the question of representation. Social science scholars now criticize the "Eurocentric" perspective of sociological research (Conrad and Randeria

2002), make an argument for a cosmopolitan reorientation of the discipline (Randeria et al. 2004; Beck and Sznaider 2006), reflect on postcolonial modernities (Boatcă and Spohn 2010), or plead for democratization and decolonization of sociological methods (Kaltmeier and Berkin 2012).[9] A few scholars have started demanding a systematic dialogue between the Western macro-sociologists, who criticize processual terminologies and inherent deterministic tendencies, and post- and decolonial approaches (Knöbl 2016), with the intention to establish "connected sociologies" (Bhambra 2014). Sociology needs to rethink its own basis "from a perspective that puts histories of dispossession, colonialism, enslavement and appropriation at the heart of historical sociology" (Bhambra 2016, 139), and it needs to accept the provincialization of its viewpoints.

The experience of modernity is different according to one's place and positionality in the world and the relationships one has to particular (totally or partially submerged) traditions or fragments of traditions. Therefore, and despite significant differences, both, post- and decolonial thinkers,[10] have an ambivalent relationship towards modernity: "[G]iven the close complicity between modern knowledges and modern regimes of power, we would for ever remain consumers of universal modernity, never would be taken seriously as its producers" (Chatterjee 1997, 275). Anibal Quijano (2000) evokes "the colonial matrix of power", saying that even after the formal end of colonialism the power relations put in place by colonial knowledge and technologies of colo-

---

9 In 2004, the *Deutsche Gesellschaft für Soziologie* had for the first time a "guest country" at their biannual congress. They had decided for India and scholars from there were invited as panel speakers. The Congress in 2022 had one panel on *Globale Polarisierungen: Postkoloniale Verhältnisse und die Soziologie*.

10 Both, postcolonial and de-colonial thinking thematise the epistemic and socio-political oppression of the colonial subject in Western modernity and are often lumped together as "postcolonialism". However, they have different genealogies and follow different routes (see Mignolo 2011, xxiii ff., Bhambra 2014, 118 f.). Postcolonialism grounds in the experiences of British colonization in Egypt and India, focuses on the 18th/19th century and developed in literature and cultural studies (Said 1978, Spivak 1988); South Asian postcolonial studies (Guha 1983) especially explored the subalternity of the colonial subject. In contrast, de-coloniality is geographically and linguistically localized in the Americas and the Caribbean, focuses on colonialism of Spain and Portugal and looks at the first moments of colonial power in the 16th-18th centuries. De-colonial scholars (Anibal Quijano, Walter Mignolo) see coloniality as foundational for European self-realization, which took shape in the process of differentiation from other cultures; hence they speak of "modernity/coloniality". For Pacific decolonial scholarship see Linda Tuhiwai Smith (1999). We decided to opt for the term decolonial(ity), as it indicates the radical break with the complex modernity/coloniality in all its dimensions.

nial governmentality remain (see Nigam 2020, 7). The "coloniality of being" (Maldonaldo-Torres 2007) not only determines the marginalized position of the once-colonized in many areas of life, but also the way they see themselves politically and intellectually. However, what is not being considered in such statements, are the matrices of power *within* the once-colonized countries and the fact that the traditions of marginalized sections in many societies have often been silenced (Renzi 2015).

Having experienced epistemological violence,[11] decolonial scholars plead for an "epistemological break" (Sousa Santos 2016): they aim to "break the Western code" and "delink" (Mignolo 2010) from Western dominated discourse and the "demands of the global academy" (Nigam 2020, 13 f.). It must then be "us", the critical western scholars, who have to try to link up with the decolonial attempts of delinking! And this means that "we", being part of such scholarship, can no longer argue from a position of pre-eminence and act as gatekeepers deciding on the terms of debate and the terms of theory, on whether and how to let the others in (cf. Nigam 2020, 19).[12] "We" have to prepare ourselves to genuinely listen to other positions, connect to other (philosophical) concepts – including "pre-modern" ones – and start rethinking the ways in which to construct social theory under conditions of collaboration. A new "we", if it were to be accomplished, would be one of debate and critique, dialogue and exchange. Shared views cannot be assumed, shared views might be an outcome, but what we possibly can accomplish at this stage are shared platforms of equal discussion.

3.2 The Decolonial Project

Decoloniality is likewise a theoretical and a normative project, which intends to critically illuminate and overcome the "coloniality of being". It has three basic premises: first, a decolonial perspective understands the historical emergence of modernity in its cognitive and practical (political,

---

11 Epistemic violence includes "eliminating knowledge, damaging a given group's ability to speak, being listened to and being heard, and unequally distributing intelligibility" (Brunner 2021, 202, with reference to Spivak 1988, and Dotson 2011; 2014).
12 We also have to take into account the functioning of academic hierarchies within western critical scholarship. Positionality here too defines who can act as gatekeeper, hampering or blocking access for example for junior researchers or those who bring in alternative theories (e.g., queer scholarship).

economic and socio-cultural) dimensions as an interactive process from the very beginning — therefore we have to think of coloniality — modernity in an hyphenated form; second, decoloniality recognizes non-western forms of life (with their particular relationships to the world, imaginations of their futures and ontological conceptualizations) as equal options of human existence. Hence, decoloniality postulates a "pluriverse".[13] This, finally, means that interpreting the world, also in its special(*ist*) form of socio-philosophical (sociological) theoretization, has to become a polyphonic encounter on the basis of the co-presence and equal recognition of non-western (intellectual, knowledge) traditions and forms of argumentation. Mutual respect and understanding not only helps Western scholars to gain access to, and explicate the world of others, but also to multiply their own worlds (Castro 2015, 85).

In the following we can only highlight a few steps regarding how to criticize and overcome the "coloniality of being" in the context of the social sciences. First of all, one has to shed light on the Cartesian break between the modern and premodern epochs from plural perspectives and traditions, and analyse the categories that signify this break, like object-subject-relation, autonomy, individual, rationality. It might be the case that this break is overemphasized in some areas (e.g., individualisation; see below), while in others it truly marks a profound change in *Weltbeziehungen* (e.g., objectification of nature). Second, the multiple forms of entanglement have to be reconstructed. The epistemic entanglement, which is of interest here, can be explored in a twofold way.

Anibal Quijano (2010) was interested in the *global context and the particular conditions* that made it possible for Europeans to think in the ways they did, and he takes up the example of the construction of the modern subject-object-dualism. In the dominant European philosophy, the individual, knowledgeable and rational subject stands in opposition to the "object", considered as nature, and positioned exterior to the subject. Quijano argues that, while the concept of the atomic individual could be explained by referring to the liberation of the subject from restrictive social structures, the second component in the dualism cannot be grasped with reference to the internal context of Europe alone. For him the key lies in the special position of the "other"

---

[13] The concept of "pluriverse", by now a keyword in the decolonial debate, is framed as counter-term to "universe" and "universality". For Mignolo (2011, 230), pluriversality should be "a universal project"; it relates to the Zapatista demand for "one world in which many worlds fit". See also Reiter 2018; Kothari et al. 2019.

under colonial conditions. He remarks: "the 'other' is totally absent; or when present, can be present only in an 'objectivised' mode" (2010, 27). The subject-object-dualism mirrors the relationship to the non-European subject, which was objectified, declared as nature and thus doomed to exteriority: possibilities of communication, interaction and interchange of knowledge with other cultures were blocked.

Decolonial scholars also try to reconstruct the *mutual influences and, thus, mixtures of thought traditions*, which are constitutive of modern knowledge systems. This seems to be possible, and partly has been done, with regard to contributions from the so-called great civilizations like China, India, the Arab world. The encompassing work of Joseph Needham and his main Chinese collaborators Wang Li, historian and Sinologist, and Lu-Gwei-djen, biochemist and historian, on the Chinese innovations in the field of science and technology is recognized as sustainably stimulating the discourse on the multicultural roots of modern science. Moreover, innovations from India in the fields of mathematics, astronomy, medicine and language theory are well acknowledged (Joseph 2000; Arnold 2004). Similarly, the importance and influence of Arabian scholars and philosophers, who were important transmitters of Greek philosophy, receives recognition (e.g., al-Farabi / Alpharabius; Ibn Sina / Avicenna; Ibn-Ruschd / Averroes; Ibn al-Shatir; Al-Kharizmi).

These examples should not allow us to lose sight of all those knowledge traditions that have been destroyed and were irretrievably lost in the process of violent colonial conquest, especially those in the American and Carribean regions. There are also those that are not considered relevant and have become historized and marginalized, like knowledges of indigenous groups around the world, or certain Indian schools of philosophy. Even despite selected contemporary attempts to retrieve, collect and revive non-western ways of knowing, they are mostly (de-)valued as "local" or "historical" forms of knowledge, emphasizing their only partial and limited relevance (Reiter 2018). This stands in contrast to the undisputed universality of Western cognitive systems. Well-known African philosophers like Paulin Hountondji and Kwame Wiredu are labeled "ethnophilosophers", and African sociologist Akinsola Akiwowo is seen as doing "indigenous sociology" (see Mignolo 2010; Bhambra 2014).

Decolonial authors argue that such different forms of "ethnic cleansing of philosophy" (Nigam 2020, 67) are a key condition for establishing European exceptionality and intellectual leadership. Therefore, it seems paramount to join the decolonial project of constituting a world in which multiple relationships to, and ways of, interpreting the world are allowed to thrive. Only under conditions of pluriversality and contemporaneity of life worlds and intellectual traditions, monological ways of theorizing can be countered.

Engaging in the decolonial project of polyvocal intellectual dialogue calls for certain conditions to be met. First of all, an epistemic revival (or "re-emergence" in the words of Jonardon Ganeri, 2016) of partially lost and marginalized traditions is needed and those who can represent these traditions must be ready to share their knowledge and enter into a discourse; second, scholars of Western social sciences (and humanities) must show uncompromised openness towards other epistemologies and ontologies as well as willingness to seriously engage with categories and concepts inherent in non-western thought traditions. Third, both sides must engage in a process of mutual categorial translation, and show a readiness to learn, unlearn and explore new ways of relating to the world.[14]

Taking these demands seriously, Aditya Nigam declares the search for "a pure, unspoilt indigenous knowledge tradition" or for some "pristine source of authentic knowledge" a "cul de sac" (2020, 3 f.). Like other contemporary "non-Western" intellectuals, he feels compelled to acknowledge how deeply marked his thinking is by Western education and Western theories. However, in so far as "non-Western" intellectuals can still connect to systems of knowledge that originate in their own cultural contexts they might be able to act as mediators and translators to relegated or forgotten traditions of thought.

4. Max-Weber-Kolleg: Attempts of Theorizing Across Borders

4.1 Challenging Process Categories: Individualisation on Trial

One of the standard narratives of sociological discourse tells us that *individualization*—the detachment of the human being from social constraints and ties—is a core feature of the process of modernization. Individualisation can take different forms in the multiple arenas of social life. In economics it is

---

14 Such reorientation through educational and translational process has been described for the interaction of Zapatistas and indigenous groups (Mignolo 2011, 222; Linkenbach 2023).

seen as co-constitutive of private property (possessive individualism); in the legal realm it goes along with the assignment of individual (human) rights; regarding religion it refers to the freedom of worship and conscience, and the ability to establish a personal relationship to god. With individualisation, modernity is set apart from all preceding societies, which are said to be essentially collective or collectivist (with the exception of a few "great individuals") and are lumped together as "pre-modern".

The Kollegforschungsgruppe of the Max-Weber-Kolleg on *Religious Individualisation in Historical Perspective*[15] has taken this highly problematic standard narrative as its starting point and challenged it in a twofold way. The Kollegforschungsgruppe argued that assuming collectivity as the essence of the "pre-modern", did not allow, firstly, to search for the different modes of (religious) individualisation in so-called pre-modern societies and times; secondly, to identify social embeddedness and relationality in modern constellations. Using religious individualisation as a heuristic category and "lens", researchers from all over the world explored and compared the multiplicity of processes of religious individualisation and its institutionalisation in Western and (South-)Asian ancient, medieval and modern religious contexts. This required a critical approach to translation and terminology, a broadening and rethinking of concepts by including other experiences, narratives, and other forms and trajectories of individualisation. The results of the project are available in a two-volume open access publication (Fuchs et al. 2019).

The dimensions of religious individualisation, which the researchers could identify across times, religions and geographical spaces include: increases of *religious self-determination* leading to an enhanced range of individual options or choices; *creativity and awareness of selfhood*, encompassing independent thinking on religion and religious identity, developing concepts, norms, practices, laying an enhanced focus on individual salvation and religious self-reflection; forms of religious *deviance and critique*, like liberation from social and religious constraints and authorities; *individual, experience-based spirituality*, leading to forms of inwardness (*Innerlichkeit*)

---

15 The Kollegforschungsgruppe *Religious Individualisation in Historical Perspective*, initiated by Hans Joas and Jörg Rüpke, was funded by the German Research Foundation (DFG). Working for more than ten years between 2008 and 2018, it hosted altogether 120 Fellows from a wide range of academic disciplines (including History, Theology, Religious studies, Sociology, Social anthropology, European classics, Indology, Buddhist studies, Archaeology).

in several cases. However, given that many processes of religious individualisation are closely connected to the formation of institutions and the creation of traditions and conventions, such processes can have the paradoxical effect of limiting the scope of individualisation once again. Therefore, individualisation and de-individualisation are in many cases intertwined.

Inspired by the idea of "entangled history", which has become a core approach in historical scholarship in recent decades, the research group also focused on investigating the relationship between religious individualisation and cultural entanglement. The researchers asked whether, or how far, diverse cultural interactions, connections and transfers of ideas and practices between persons, regions and religions, had an influence on individualisation processes. They were able to identify such influences in the field of religion—not only in modern times and in Europe, not only at the time of major breaks in European tradition since the 18th century, but also in non-European regions and in various earlier epochs.

The critical perspective on process categories also allowed for the development of an alternative or complementary account to the aforementioned master narrative of "individualisation". Here, the concept of "dividuality" comes into play, not only with regard to non-Western contexts but also when looking at the development and forms of Western modernity. Various authors with an anthropological background, such as Edward LiPuma (1998; 2001) and Alfred Gell (1999; 2013), but also Charles Taylor (2007), the philosopher of the modern self, have started pointing out (two) different coexisting dimensions of personhood found across time and space, including the modern West. Of these, one is more individual and the other more dividual. The research group understands dividuality in two different ways: on the one hand, as an ontological dimension complementary to the concept of the individual, that is as a *conditio humana* that refers to relationality, porousness, and vulnerability of the human subject in general. On the other hand, it addresses the lived realities (ideas, practices) of divisibility, of closeness and connectedness of actors, from a socio-historical perspective, as they occur in particular societal constellations. Human beings are across times and geographies constituted by both dividual and individual qualities (Linkenbach and Mulsow 2019).

The trajectory of the work initiated by the Kollegforschungsgruppe proves the necessity and the fruitfulness of a non-Eurocentric and polyvocal engagement with people, concepts, terms and paradigms from non-Western, as well as Western religions, regions and epochs. The rich outcome of research and publications should be seen as a stimulus to further take up and elaborate on ideas and concepts that attend to the manifold phenomena and historical processes beyond the early modern period and Europe.

4.2 Translation as De-colonializing Practice

Research agendas like the one concerning (religious) individualisation involve comparisons, and the comparative dimension is in fact constitutive of the interdisciplinary approach pursued by the Max-Weber-Kolleg and its focus on *Weltbeziehungen*. However, what is required today is a novel approach towards comparison, one that rethinks the hermeneutics of difference and the requisite methodologies.

For a long time, one-directional approaches of comparison prevailed in Western Social Sciences and Humanities (especially in History). These approaches subsumed cultural differences (differences between forms of life, concepts and perspectives) under a pre-conceived conceptual frame, deriving from one's own conceptual language and super-imposing categorizations onto unruly realities. Many of the terminologies employed carry the ballast of modern "Western" modes of sociality, associated with societal tensions and structural features typical of modernity in its Western shapes, and of modern ideas and ideologies of selfhood. Other thought traditions were put into boxes: typified cultures, societies, civilizations (exemplary are Weber's civilisational comparisons). Categorizations tended to follow a binary logic, objectifying "the other", talking *about* the other (the issue of representation), instead of conversing *between* and *across* different thought traditions. Modern functional and conceptual differentiations—at its core the differentiation between religion, the political and economics—were universalized. While these modern Western differentiations had a deep impact on the other parts of the world, it has increasingly become clear that structural and conceptual configurations in non-Western contexts (pre-modern as well as modern) differ in several respects from those in the prototypical West. Regarding "religion" this has meanwhile been widely acknowledged. Similarly, discussions have started concerning the multiplicity of secularities (Bhargava 2013; Kleine and Wohlrab-Sahr 2020) and, most recently, regarding the contextual differences of notions and materialities of "the political" (Banerjee 2020).

We argue that comparison has to be undertaken from both ends, accounting for the problematics, experiences, and perspectives of all the sides concerned. Comparison must be undertaken interculturally and has to be reconceived as an ongoing dialogical process of (reciprocal) interpretation, in which comparables are being constructed, deconstructed, and then again changed (Ricœur 2006, 36; Srubar et al. 2005; Fuchs 2005). Of key importance, thus, are the ways of translating between different conceptual worlds, idioms or paradigms—of continuously correcting and broadening our conceptual languages and analytical approaches. Theoretical reasoning itself already means translation (from the everyday into an abstract idiom). What is now required is that we draw upon additional conceptual traditions (resources) and supplementary life worlds and social arrangements and bring these into dialogue. Theory has to transcend the boundaries between contexts. Here, the current debates in the field of Translation Studies, in which scholars from the Max-Weber-Kolleg participate, provide important impulses.

Translation of concepts into another conceptual language does not insinuate equivalence of meaning. Stepping outside a system of reference and translating between different conceptual worlds means being open to new ideas, new meanings and different architectures of argumentation. Translations (into the so-called "target" language) "echo" the configuration of meanings (concepts, articulations etc.) of the so-called "source" language they are referring to.[16] Being refracted through the translation, the other meanings and concepts still shine through in the new articulation—at the same time, established thought tradition gets ruptured, and hence broadened, by the "alien" ideas.[17] Real understanding (in an always limited way), and appropriately including new or different perspectives, might however need time.

The demand for intellectual exchange across thought traditions, forms of life and reference frames gets ever more urgent today in view of the global challenges of planetary survival and intensified inter- and transcultural interactions and conflicts. Insights concerning the conditions of cross-contextual and cross-categorial exchange are the result of various rounds of reflec-

---

[16] For Walter Benjamin the task of the translator "consists in finding that intention toward the language into which [a work] is being translated which awakens in it the echo of the original" (Benjamin 1977, 57; transl. by the authors; compare Steven Rendall's translation: Benjamin 1997, 157).

[17] Rudolf Pannwitz, as quoted by Benjamin, demanded to be led by "awe" for an "alien" work, allow oneself to be moved and challenged by the "alien" language, and let one's own language be "broadened and deepened" by it (Benjamin 1977, 61; 1997, 163 f.).

tion which, starting from the relativist-inclusionary ideas of "culture" and "life forms" have got us to a position in which differences as well as ambivalences and multiplicities of references are accepted as the basic condition of social existence in a deeply entangled world. "Nobody exists in one context only" (Fuchs 2009), nor are thought traditions relative to only one context. Translation becomes visible as an existential process, we all live "in translation".

People move between contexts and between reference systems, within a "society" as well as interculturally, people are involved in multiple ways. Positionalities and contexts are not fixed nor are they necessarily exclusive. Important is the recognition of the basic fact that someone's identity and the thought traditions and reference systems someone relates to, need not be identical; one can step across interpretive and epistemic boundaries and get involved, even immersed, into other traditions of thought and practice.[18]

Acknowledging the *differences* between thought traditions or reference systems requires to look for *interconnections* and not, straightforwardly, for a "common conceptual world" (as Sarukkai suggests, 2013, 321), if we want to initiate or strengthen thinking across traditions. The denial of such engagement and reciprocal translation between traditions of thought means a refusal of recognition.

To underline a point previously made in passing: thinking across traditions is not just about connecting to the perspectives of contemporaries elsewhere; it is as much about connecting to, and taking *relevant* concepts from earlier non-Western traditions of thought as "resources" (similar to how European thinkers relate, for example, to those from Greek antiquity). This entails attentiveness to other ways of doing theory. Recent examples include philosophical exchanges on notions of "self", tapping into Buddhist, Jaina, Vedantist and Western phenomenological as well as analytical traditions (Siderits, Thompson, and Zahavi 2011; Ganeri 2012). Pathbreaking is also Ganeri's discussion of the Theravāda philosopher Buddhaghosa's observations on "attention", pre-intentional awareness, and the human mind's structure and functioning, in dialogue with contemporary cognitive psychology and contemporary philosophy of mind (Ganeri 2017). Already before, Indian scholar Daya Krishna pursued dialogues (*saṃvāda*) between Western, Indian as well as other Asian (social) philosophies that included

---

18 It is majority sections of western scholarship as much as parts of post- and decolonial scholarship in non-western countries that enshrine debates and discourses in cultural containers.

sharp criticisms of assumptions and stratagems at both ends (Mayaram 2014; Raveh 2021). Other concepts that could be of interest for Sociology include *syādvāda* and *anekāntavāda* (the concept of manifold perspectives, the multi-layered nature of reality) (Parson 2019; Banerjee, Nigam and Pandey 2016, 43 f; Nigam 2020, 112). Sociology has to open to neighbouring disciplines, especially reflexive forms of Cultural Anthropology, Comparative Philosophy and self-aware parts of the Humanities. But equally important for sociologists would be to engage with subdued and marginalized traditions and perspectives in other as well as one's own cultural worlds.

5. The Ambivalent Potential of Decolonial Critique

5.1 Decolonial Perspectives, Dialogue and the Possibilities of Social Critique

Focusing on the "coloniality of being"—the continued existence of uneven power relations between the former colonizers and the "once-colonized"—, decolonial approaches assume, at first glance, a two-tiered structure of economic, political and epistemological hierarchies. However, the "once-colonized" are not a homogenous group but exhibit significant internal stratification and diversity, including epistemic diversity. Decolonial approaches, therefore, must take care not to ignore the differences and hierarchies *within*—the caste/class, gender and other differences that characterize social constellations (states, nations)—and thus themselves sideline the perspectives of entire sections of society.

Historically, in the Indian case, the critique of Brahmanocentrism and alternative social visions found expression in several *bhakti* religious formations, most powerfully with Kabir (15th century) and the *varkaris* (Keune 2021). In the first half of the 20th century, Bhimrao Ambedkar undertook a vigorous attack on social hierarchy and its legitimations, employing a sociological perspective developed in close conversation with concepts of John Dewey and grounding himself in a new appropriation of Buddhist ethics (Ambedkar 1979–2006; Fuchs 2019). Today, the number of Dalit scholars has grown considerably.[19] Separate from this, postcolonial Indian historians,

---

19 This sets them apart from Adivasi, who are still extremely underrepresented in academia – even though academic literature representing Adivasis and Adivasi struggles has increased. If at all, Adivasi voice themselves as activists in public media and as literati.

inspired by Gramscian and postmodernist approaches, started in the 1980s to study so-called *subaltern* groups, especially peasants and Adivasis (but, until a late stage, not Dalits), as autonomous socio-political and cultural agents (*Subaltern Studies*, 12 volumes, 1982–2005). Engaging in "history from below", various contributions focused on rebellious actions and crowd politics, but tended to regard the relation between "subalterns" and ruling classes within the networks of capitalism, colonialism, and nationalism, as a "binary relationship" and to portray subalterns from a communitarian angle. Quickly gaining prominence, this endeavour was accompanied by critique (exemplary that of Sumit Sarkar 1997), which revolved around the subaltern-colonizer-divide, the reification of community identities, the neglect of internal dimensions of power, and generalizations about Enlightenment rationalism. While the *Subaltern Studies* project has continued to expand and transform itself over the decades (Ludden 2001), a radical critique (e.g., Natrajan 2011; 2008; Aloysius 1997) has highlighted how the project failed to explore the implications of the cultural basis of Indian nationalism (which they see centered on "Brahmanism") not only for tribal and Dalit identity formation and politics, but also for Indian modernity and national identification.[20]

Dalit intellectuals have adamantly rejected not only what they perceive as "patronising or posterior epistemology" (Guru 2002; 5009). They also condemn how language, canons and protocols are used systematically to exclude Dalits from entering into the high grounds of scholarly establishments and from questioning received knowledge through alternative approaches, especially those that threaten to erode the current "cultural hierarchies that tend to divide social science practice into theoretical brahmans and empirical shudras" (Guru 2002, 5009; Sukumar 2008). More broadly, it is on questions of "voice" and representation, as well as on the understanding of Dalit/anti-caste epistemology and the nation, that the two sides greatly diverge (Renzi 2015, 82).

The demand for dialogical theorizing across traditions has thus not only an inter-, but also an intra-cultural dimension. "Cultures" and "civilizations", and even nations today, have not been as integrated and united as many Western sociologists as well as many decolonial critiques assume;

---

20 Especially in the modern context the situation of minorities (above all Muslims) and the increasingly violent attitude of the Hindu majority towards minorities deserves high attention. However, this cannot be done here.

cultural constellations instead encompass hegemonic as well as alternative and counter-traditions. The task therefore is to systematically integrate social critique into decolonial approaches. Only if one establishes a polyvocal encounter and dialogue, in which multiple traditions and critiques gain a voice through genuine representatives, power differentials in all arenas of social life can be addressed, conceptions of the human being, of dignity, of nature etc. confronted, and, in a more practical way, alternative futures imagined, and strategies of transformation mapped out.

In this process, values and universalist validity claims from different cultural backgrounds are on trial and will be negotiated — possibly resulting in the fact that some decolonial positions get modified and re-interpreted. Delinking from Western epistemologies and value systems is one option, but in a dialogical encounter on eyelevel, and in a process of confrontation and comparison, a variety of "Western" norms and values, like human dignity, will remain valid. Bhimrao Ambedkar, the main drafter of the Indian Constitution and himself a Dalit, was convinced that caste undermines India's culture and morality (enshrined in the Constitution), as it embodies the principle of separation, and therefore is opposed to the idea and praxis of general cooperation, communication and critique. Caste prevents the formation of a self that has the ability for abstraction and dissociation and thus does not allow to each person to be socially perceived as a human being, first and foremost (Mehta 2010; see also Renzi forthcoming 2023). The value of humanness and human dignity is not only a Western one but can be found also in Buddhism—the religion which Ambedkar finally embraced.

5.2 Decolonial Rhetoric and the Political Right: Identity Politics in Hindu-nationalist India

Post- and decolonial critique can easily fall into the trap of identity politics, and even does not necessarily represent a social emancipatory agenda. The aim in this final section is to draw attention to the need for a contextual understanding of globally influential theoretical constructs, which highlights the multiple (sometimes problematic) possibilities of their appropriation. In the Indian context, decolonial rhetoric has become a major tool in Hindutva identity politics, invoking indigeneity and historical depth of Indic (de facto: high-caste or Brahmanical) culture and religion as mark of national identification. On the flipside, Hindu nationalists also attack postcolonial social critique as Western imported instruments to discredit the greatness of Indian culture.

Self-proclaimed ideologues of India's "modern right" have mounted an all-out attack on postcolonial *subalternism* (a label that includes a variety of critical voices and extends beyond the Subaltern Studies group), which they discredit as a Western theory imported into India by its own Marxist intellectuals and as "the divisive foundation of Breaking India forces" (Malhotra and Viswanathan 2022, xxiv; see also Malhotra and Neelakandan 2011). In particular, they consider the subalternist blaming of the Brahminical uppercastes, oppressors of Dalits, Muslims and others, as having created the ideological basis for present-day Indianized versions of Critical Race Theories morphed into Critical Caste Theories. Rajiv Malhotra (2011) argues that postcolonial scholars have served the interests of Western states and churches in supporting separatist movements among Dalits, Dravidians and minority religions by constructing distinct histories, religions, linguistic and political identities on their behalf. To him, subalternists have championed cultural differences "from below" on Indian soil, to be taken over by power holders abroad under a refashioned "remote-controlled colonialism". At the same time, postcolonial theory is also seen by India's Right as beneficial in unifying "Indians". Malhotra's own essentialist identitarian categories around Indic civilizational terms are purportedly used to counter the "separatist" movements and what he considers to be their neo-colonial masters in the West. To Malhotra, it is arguments disputing the uniqueness and distinctiveness of Indian civilization that allow for it to be made vulnerable and destroyed.

Proponents of decolonial approaches are aware of the danger of essentializing difference and using decolonial critique against emancipatory projects. Nigam warns of the "nativism" of many intellectuals aligned to the Hindu right and demands to steer clear of "the dead-end of indigenism" (2020, 9, 38). He also underlines its "derivative" character, both with regard to the fact that propositions about Hinduism and nationalism were drawn from Orientalist Indological scholarship and for drawing in elements from monotheism (2020, 7–9). The plea to "think across" traditions is also meant to forestall such tendencies (Banerjee/Nigam/Pandey 2016, 46).

6. A Brief and Final Remark

This contribution calls for a decolonialization of social theory, that is its reorientation towards cross-contextual dialogue and cross-categorial reflection, which includes a comparative angle and requires de-familiarizing our own pre-understandings.

A genuine re-orientation of social theory has two basic dimensions: On the one hand, it means reconsidering the idea of modernity by focusing the view on, and listening to, the once-colonized—and this category includes those who have been the victims of "progress" and were overrun by externally determined developments, as well as all those who got involved in "modernizing developments" in ways not reflected in Western-centric theories. Some of them might even have profited from processes of "progress", without necessarily being able to determine its directions. On the other hand, it means to become aware of the loss and devaluation of thought of certain traditions and cultural practices, of the fact that they were ignored, cut off, or even suppressed during histories of domination and colonization.

Concerning Western-based theorists, a decolonial agenda requests acknowledging epistemic and ontological plurality. This involves exploring concepts and ideas from other backgrounds seriously and in a collaborative manner, and to integrate them into sociological frameworks of theorization.[21] Such broader and richer frameworks may allow to see unheeded dimensions of *Weltbeziehungen* and, in certain respects, help to address the limitations and weaknesses of Western modernity and amend the one-sidedness of accustomed concepts. However, showing uncompromising openness also means keeping a critical perspective on forms of exclusion and constraining categorization, including such that are carried over from the past or get newly legitimized by reference to their ancestral origins (usually in combination with new power dynamics and forms of subjugation). It is not abstract values per se—like the values of equality or liberty—which are the way out and provide the key and solution for contemporary predicaments; it is the contextual significance of such values that matters as well as

---

21 An attempt in that direction is the *M.S. Merian – R. Tagore International Centre of Advanced Studies "Metamorphoses of the Political"* (ICAS:MP) that has its hub in Delhi and started in 2015, funded by the German Federal Ministry of Education and Research. The center is run by more than seventy scholars of Indian and German background, including some from third countries, and is supported by four German and two Indian academic institutions, including the Max-Weber-Kolleg,

their relationship to the "non-modernist" values of solidarity, commonality, care, and others.

The points we made in this contribution concern forms of sociality and social domination, but the plea for decolonizing theory also relates to the other dimensions of human world-relations, especially the relation to what we embrace by the concept of "nature." Pluriversality most strikingly shows alternative ways in which the human-nature relationship is conceived, the Cartesian human-nature-divide is challenged, and multiple subjectivities and agencies are postulated. This topic cannot be expanded upon in this article, but it is part of the work done at the Max-Weber-Kolleg.

"Theorizing across traditions" is a call. It sets out a broad agenda, but it does not determine the directions theoretical debates may take or the outcome dialogues may have. It means opening deadlocked discussions.

Works cited

Aloysius, G. (1997). *Nationalism without a nation in India*. New Delhi: Oxford University Press.

Ambedkar, Bhimrao Ramji (1979–2006). *Dr. Babaseb Ambedkar writings and speeches*, Vols. 1–21. Ed. Vasant Moon and others. Bombay: Education Department, Government of Maharashtra.

Arnason, Johann P. (1993). *The Future that failed: Origins and destinies of the Soviet model*. London and New York: Routledge.

Arnason, Johann P. (2003). *Civilisations in dispute: Historical questions and theoretical traditions*. Leiden and Boston: Brill.

Arnold, David (2004). The New Cambridge History of India: *Science, technology and medicine in colonial India*, Cambridge: Cambridge University Press.

Banerjee, Prathama (2020). *Elementary aspects of the political: Histories from the Global South*. Durham: Duke University Press.

Banerjee, Prathama, Aditya Nigam, and Rakesh Pandey (2016). The work of theory: Thinking across traditions. *Economic and Political Weekly*, 51 (37), 42–50.

Beck, Ulrich, and Natan Sznaider (2006). Unpacking cosmopolitanism for the social sciences: a research agenda. *The British Journal of Sociolog*, 57 (1), 1–23.

Benjamin, Walter (1977). Die Aufgabe des Übersetzers. In Walter Benjamin. *Illuminationen, Ausgewählte Schriften*, 50—62. Frankfurt a. M.: Suhrkamp.

Benjamin, Walter (1997). The translator's task, Walter Benjamin, translated by Steven Rendall. *Traduction, Terminologie, Rédaction*, 10 (2): 151–65.

Bhambra, Gurminder K. (2014). *Connected sociologies*. London: Bloomsbury.

Bhambra, Gurminder K. (2016). A connected sociologies' approach to global sociology. In Markus S. Schulz (ed.). *The futures we want: Global sociology and the struggles for a better world. Selected writings from the webforum*, 138–41. Berlin et al.: International Sociological Association.

Bhargava, Rajeev (2013). Multiple secularisms and multiple secular states. In Anders Berg-Sørensen (ed.) *Contesting secularism*, 17–42. Farnham: Ashgate.

Boatcă, Manuela, and Wilfried Spohn (eds.). (2010). *Globale, multiple und postkoloniale Modernen*. München und Mering: Rainer Hampp Verlag.

Brunner, Claudia (2021). Conceptualizing epistemic violence: an interdisciplinary assemblage for IR. *International Politics Reviews*, 9, 193–212.

Castro, Eduardo Viveiros de (2015). *The relative native: essays on indigenous conceptual worlds*. Chicago: Hau Books.

Chatterjee, Partha (1997). Talking about our modernity in two languages. In Partha Chatterjee. *A possible India. Essays in political criticism*, 263–85. Delhi: Oxford University Press.

Conrad, Sebastian, and Randeria, Shalini (eds.). (2002). *Jenseits des Eurozentrismus: Postkoloniale Perspektiven in den Geschichts- und Kulturwissenschaften*. Frankfurt a. M.: Campus Verlag.

Dotson, Kristie (2011). Tracking epistemic violence, tracking practices of silencing. *Hypatia*, 26 (2), 236–57.

Dotson, Kristie (2014). Conceptualizing epistemic oppression. *Social Epistemology*, 28 (2), 115–38.

Eisenstadt, Shmuel N. (2000a). Multiple modernities. *Daedalus*, 129 (1), 1–29.

Eisenstadt, Shmuel N. (2000b). The civilizational dimension in sociological analysis. *Thesis Eleven*, 62, 1–22.

Fuchs, Martin (1987). Fremde Kultur und soziales Handeln. Max Webers Analyse der indischen Zivilisation. *Kölner Zeitschrift für Soziologie und Sozialpsychologie*, 39 (4), 669–92.

Fuchs, Martin (1988). *Theorie und Verfremdung. Max Weber, Louis Dumont und die Analyse der indischen Gesellschaft*. Frankfurt a. M.: Peter Lang.

Fuchs, Martin (2005). Interkulturelle Hermeneutik statt Kulturvergleich. Zur sozialen Reflexivität der Deutungsperspektiven. In Ilja Srubar, Joachim Renn and Ulrich Wenzel (eds.). *Kulturen vergleichen. Sozial- und kulturwissenschaftliche Grundlagen und Kontroversen*, 112–50. Wiesbaden: VS Verlag für Sozialwissenschaften.

Fuchs, Martin (2009). Reaching out; or, nobody exists in one context only: society as translation. *Translation Studies*, 2 (1): 21–40.

Fuchs, Martin (2017). India in comparison: Max Weber's analytical agenda. In Thomas C. Ertman (ed.). *Max Weber's economic ethic of the world religions. An analysis*, 223–66. Cambridge: Cambridge University Press.

Fuchs, Martin (2019). Dhamma and the common good: Religion as problem and answer—Ambedkar's critical theory of social relationality. In Martin Fuchs and Vasudha Dalmia (eds.). *Religious interactions in modern India*, 364–413. New Delhi: Oxford University Press.

Fuchs, Martin (2020). Weltreligionen, Welteinstellungen, Zivilisationen: Max Webers vergleichende Religionssoziologie und die Analytik indischer Religiosität. In Volkhard Krech and Hartmann Tyrell (eds.). *Religionssoziologie um 1900. Eine Fortsetzung (Religion in der Gesellschaft, Bd. 48)*, 595–629. Baden-Baden: Ergon.

Fuchs, Martin, Antje Linkenbach, Martin Mulsow, Bernd-Christian Otto, Rahul Parson and Jörg Rüpke (eds.). (2019). *Religious individualisation: Historical dimensions and comparative perspectives*. 2 vols. Berlin: de Gruyter.

Ganeri, Jonardon (2012). *The Self: Naturalism, consciousness, and the first-person stance*. Oxford: Oxford University Press.

Ganeri, Jonardon (2016). Why philosophy must go global. A manifesto (Comprised of the text of "Manifesto for a re:emergent philosophy", and "Reflections on re:emergent philosophy"). *Confluence. Online Journal of World Philosophies*, 4, 134–41 and 164–86.

Ganeri, Jonardon (2017). *Attention, not self*. Oxford: Oxford University Press.

Gell, Alfred (1999). *The art of anthropology: Essays and diagrams*. London and New Brunswick, NJ: The Athlone Press.

Gell, Alfred (2013). *Art and agency: An anthropological theory*, reprint. Oxford: Clarendon Press.

Grosfoguel, Ramón (2010). Die Dekolonisation polit-ökonomischer und postkolonialer Studien: Transmoderne, Grenzdenken und Postkolonialität. In Manuela Boatca and Wilfried Spohn (eds.). *Globale, multiple und postkoloniale Modernen*, 309–338. München und Mering: Rainer Hampp Verlag.

Guha, Ranajit (1983). *Elementary aspects of peasant insurgency in colonial India*. Delhi: Oxford University Press.

Guru, Gopal (2002). How egalitarian are the social sciences in India? *Economic and Political Weekly*, 37 (50), 5003–09.

Habermas, Jürgen (1981). *Theorie des kommunikativen Handelns*, 2 Bde. Frankfurt a.M.: Suhrkamp.

Joseph, Gorge G. (2000). *The crest of the peacock: The non-European roots of mathematics*. Princeton, NJ: Princeton University Press.

Kaltmeier, Olaf, and Sarah Corona Berkin (eds.). (2012). *Methoden dekolonisieren: eine Werkzeugkiste zur Demokratisierung der Sozial- und Kulturwissenschaften*. Münster: Westfälisches Dampfboot.

Kaviraj, Sudipta (2009). Marxism in translation: Critical reflections on Indian radical thought. In Richard Bourke and Raymond Geuss (eds.). *Political judgement. Essays for John Dunn*, 172–99. Cambridge: Cambridge University Press.

Keune, Jon (2021). *Shared devotion, shared food: Equality and the Bhakti-caste question in Western India*. New York: Oxford University Press.

Kleine, Christoph, and Monika Wohlrab-Sahr (2020). Comparative secularities: tracing social and epistemic structures beyond the modern West. *Method & Theory in the Study of Religion*, 32 (4), 1–30.

Kothari, Ashish, Ariel Salleh, Arturo Escobar, Frederico Demaria, and Alberto Acosta (eds.). (2019). *Pluriverse: A post-development dictionary*. New Delhi: Tulika.

Knöbl, Wolfgang (2016). On the future convergence between postcolonial thought and mainstream macrosociology. In Markus S. Schulz (ed.). *The futures we want: Global sociology and the struggles for a better world. Selected writings from the webforum*, 151–53. Berlin et al.: International Sociological Association.

Linkenbach, Antje (2023). Ambiguity, contingency, and dominance: Decolonizing theories of modernity. *International Journal of Social Imaginaries*, 2, 47–76.

Linkenbach, Antje (1986). *Opake Gestalten des Denkens: Jürgen Habermas und die Rationalität fremder Lebensformen*. München: Fink Verlag.

Linkenbach, Antje, and Martin Mulsow (2019). Introduction: The dividual self. In Martin Fuchs et al. (eds.). *Religious individualisation: Historical dimensions and comparative perspectives*, Part II, 323–43. Berlin: de Gruyter.

LiPuma, Edward (1998). Modernity and forms of personhood in Melanesia. In Michael Lambek, and Andrew Strathern (eds.). *Bodies and persons: Comparative perspectives from Africa and Melanesia*, 53–79. Cambridge: Cambridge University Press.

LiPuma, Edward (2001). *Encompassing others: The magic of modernity in Melanesia*. Ann Arbor: The University of Michigan Press.

Ludden, David (2001). A brief history of subalternity. In David Ludden (ed.). *Reading subaltern studies*, 1–39. Delhi: Permanent Black.

Maldonado-Torres, Nelson (2007). On the coloniality of being. *Cultural Studies*, 21 (2–3), 240–70.

Malhotra, Rajiv (2011). *Being different: An Indian challenge to western universalism*. Uttar Pradesh: HarperCollins Pubisher.

Malhotra, Rajiv. and Aravindan Neelakandan (2011). *Breaking India: Western interventions in Dravidian and Dalit faultlines*. New Delhi: Amaryllis.

Malhotra, Rajiv, and Vijaya Viswanathan (2022). *Snakes in the Ganga: Breaking India 2.0*. New Delhi: Occam.

Mayaram, Shail (ed.) (2014). *Saṃvāda and svarāj. Dialogical meditations on Daya Krishna and Ramchandra Gandhi*. New Delhi: Sage.

Mehta, Pratap Bhanu (2010). What is constitutional morality? *Seminar*, 615. http://www.india-seminar.com/2010/615.htm.

Mignolo, Walter D. (2010). Delinking: The rhetoric of modernity, the logic of coloniality, and the grammar of de-coloniality. In Walter D. Mignolo, and Arturo Escobar (eds.). *Globalization and the decolonial option*, 330–68. London and New York: Routledge.

Mignolo, Walter D. (2011). *The darker side of western modernity: Global futures, decolonial options*. Durham and London: Duke University Press.

Mota, Aurea (2018). World-Sociology beyond eurocentrism: Considerations on Peter Wagner's theory of modernity. In Gerard Rosich and Angelos Mouzakitis (guest eds.). Special issue: The struggle over world-interpretation(s) and progress revisited. Festschrift for Peter Wagner. *Social Imaginaries*, 4 (1), 71–86.

Natrajan, Balmurli (2008). Cultural values. In Vincent N. Parrillo (ed.). *Encyclopedia of social problems*, 193–96. New Delhi: Sage.

Natrajan, Balmurli (2011). *Culturalization of caste in India: Identity and inequality in a multicultural age*. London: Routledge.

Nigam, Aditya (2020). *Decolonizing theory: Thinking across traditions*. New Delhi: Bloomsbury.
Parson, Rahul (2019). Individualisation and democratisation of knowledge in Banārasīdās' Samayasāra Nāṭika. In Martin Fuchs et al. (eds.). *Religious individualisation: Historical dimensions and comparative perspectives*, 865–93. Berlin: de Gruyter.
Quijano, Anibal (2000). Coloniality of power, eurocentrism, and Latin America. *Nepantla: Views from the South*, 1 (3), 533–80.
Quijano, Anibal (2010). Coloniality and modernity/rationality. In Walter D. Mignolo, and Arturo Escobar (eds.), *Globalization and the decolonial option*, 22–32. London and New York: Routledge.
Randeria, Shalini, Martin Fuchs, and Antje Linkenbach (eds.). (2004). *Konfigurationen der Moderne: Diskurse zu Indien*. Baden-Baden: Nomos.
Raveh, Daniel (2021). *Daya Krishna and twentieth-century Indian philosophy*. London: Bloomsbury.
Reiter, Bernd (ed.) (2018). *Constructing the pluriverse: The geopolitics of knowledge*. Durham: Duke University Press.
Renzi, Beatrice (2015). Anti-caste Radicalism, Dalit Movements and the many critiques of secular nationalism in India. In Marian Burchardt, Monika Wohlrab-Sahr, and Matthias Middell (eds.). *Multiple secularities beyond the West: Religion and modernity in the global age*, 63–94. Berlin, München, Boston: De Gruyter.
Renzi, Beatrice (forthcoming 2023). Intersectional perspectives on Dalit women and justice: Exploring the systemic interlinkages between patriarchy, caste and class. In Antje Linkenbach, and Aditya Malik (eds.). *Realizing justice? Normative orders and the realities of justice in India*. Delhi: Manohar.
Ricoeur, Paul (2006). *On translation*, with an introduction by Richard Kearney. London: Routledge.
Said, Edward (1978). *Orientalism*. London: Routledge and Kegan Paul.
Sarkar, Sumit (1997). The decline of the subaltern in Subaltern Studies. In Sumit Sarkar, *Writing social history*, 82–108. Delhi: Oxford University Press.
Sarukkai, Sundar (2013). Translation as method. Implications for history of science. In Bernard Lightman, Gordon McOuat, and Larry Stewart (eds.). *The Circulation of knowledge between Britain, India and China. The early-modern world to the twentieth century*, 309–29. Leiden: Brill.
Siderits, Mark, Evan Thompson, and Dan Zahavi (2011). *Self, no self? Perspectives from analytical, phenomenological, and Indian traditions*. Oxford: Oxford University Press.
Smith, Linda Tuhiwai (1999). *Decolonizing methodologies: Research and indigenous peoples*. London: Zed Books Ltd.
Sousa Santos, Boaventura de (2016). *Epistemologies of the south. Justice against epistemicide*. London: Routledge.
Spivak, Gayatri Chakravorty (1988). Can the subaltern speak? In Cary Nelson and Lawrence Grossberg (eds.). *Marxism and the interpretation of culture*, 271–313. Urbana, IL: University of Illinois Press.

Srubar, Ilja, Ulrich Wenzel, and Joachim Renn (2005). *Kulturen vergleichen. Sozial- und kulturwissenschaftliche Grundlagen und Kontroversen*. Wiesbaden: VS Verlag für Sozialwissenschaften.

Sukumar, Narayana (2008). Living a concept: semiotics of everyday exclusion. *Economic and Political Weekly*, 43 (46), 14–17.

Taylor, Charles (2007). *A secular age*. Cambridge Mass.: Belknap Press of Harvard Univ. Press.

Wagner, Peter (2008). *Modernity as experience and interpretation: A new sociology of modernity*, Cambridge: Polity Press.

Wagner, Peter (2016). World-sociology: An outline. *Social Imaginaries*, 2 (2), 87–104.

Weber, Max (1972 [1920]). *Gesammelte Aufsätze zur Religionssoziologie, Vol. I.*, 6th ed. Tübingen: Mohr.

Weber, Max (1978 [1921]). *Gesammelte Aufsätze zur Religionssoziologie*, Vol. 2: Hinduismus und Buddhismus. Tübingen: Mohr.

Weber, Max (2004). Prefatory remarks to the collected essays in the sociology of religion. In Sam Whimster (ed.). *The essential Weber. A reader*, 101–12. London: Routledge.

Weber, Max (2011). *The protestant ethic and the spirit of capitalism*. The revised 1920 edition, translated and introduced by Stephen Kalberg. New York: Oxford University Press.

The Cultural Meaning of "Market" in China and the Western tradition: Worlds apart?[1]

Carsten Herrmann-Pillath, Qian Zhao

1. Introduction

China's economic policy has been often characterized as "pragmatic." Hence, Western observers were caught by surprise when under the leadership of Xi Jinping government intervention into the economy was strengthened, sometimes with immense economic costs, such as the catastrophic losses in the stock market valuation of the leading Chinese tech companies when the government reined in their marvellous growth. In this contribution, we argue that these policies do not reflect fundamental changes in Chinese worldviews and conceptions of the nexus between government and economy (Leutert and Eaton 2021). On the contrary, this does not only stand in line with Chinese Communist Party (CCP) policies since 1978, but also reflects a historically deep tradition in economic thinking about the economy since earliest times. In this sense, we claim that Chinese views on the market root in deeper ways of *Weltbeziehungen*, in this case the world seen as object of economic actions, and as being constituted of economic entities, such as resources or entrepreneurs. In a nutshell, markets are also institutionalized forms of cognitively constructing and performing the economy (Herrmann-Pillath and Hederer 2023, 31 ff).

Our argument begins with characterizing the CCP understanding of the "market," which defines the crucial difference to Western ways to conceptualise the economic world, which are also maintained by leading international institutions like the International Monetary Fund (IMF). We then proceed

---

[1] © The author/s 2023, published by Campus Verlag, Open Access: CC BY-SA 4.0
Bettina Hollstein, Hartmut Rosa, Jörg Rüpke (eds.), "Weltbeziehung"
DOI: 10.12907/978-3-593-45587-7_008

with a brief account of historical roles of the market and Chinese economic thinking, which reveals the continuities over millennia. One example of this continuity is the persistent weakness of economic liberalism as a doctrine in China, as is also evident in the precarious role of liberal economists today that we discuss in section 4. However, in our conclusion we ponder whether there is room for reconciling Chinese mainstream views with intellectual traditions of liberalism in the West that depart from the key notions of mainstream economics, in particular the assumption of a functional autonomy of the market and hence of the duality of market versus government.

A problematic fault line in the contemporary economic logic of the market as an autonomous functional system in society is its reliance on the explicit analogy to Western historical experience, while claiming universality.[2] In fact, conceptualizing the market in a specific way is itself a cultural and historical construct. When we think of Chinese market economy from a Western perspective, we tend to note that Chinese policymakers did not do what they should have done, given various challenges in economic policy. However, contemporary Western ideas and language about the market deviate from Chinese stances towards the market. Questions must be asked about how culturally specific forms of market understanding shape the policy references and preferences. The following thoughts on culturally determined understanding and perceptions of markets in China offer a brief sketch of how concepts and institutions relate to history and cultural context.

The word "economy" (*jingji* 经济) first appears in the *Book of Changes (Zhou Yi)* (Rutt transl. 1996) compiled in the first millennium BCE. "*Jing*" is the longitudinal yarn or silk thread in textiles, alluding to the "management" and "governance" of the country and society; the original meaning of "*ji*" is to cross a river, as in the same boat, implying to help others through difficulties. By extension, "*ji*" means to benefit others. In this word, the object of "*ji*" is not an individual or a group of individuals, but the "people," i.e., the general public. Hence, the word "*jingji*" (经济) as used by the ancients meant better ruling the country and benefiting the people. The phrase "*Jing shi ji min*" (经世济民), with the characters "*jing*" and "*ji*", means to govern well and to provide a good livelihood to the people. A causal relationship is implied when the word "*jing shi*" is before "*ji min*," so that the aim is to benefit the people in

---

2 This is another instance of the colonizing epistemologies discussed by Fuchs, Linkenbach and Renzi in this book.

general through good governance of the state and management of society. The word "economics study" also means a statecraft discipline of study that state officials need to pursue, and those who are proficient in this discipline are called "economics talents." The first use of the word "economy" in this context is found in the chapter "Rites and Music" in Wang Tong's *Zhong Shuo* (also known as *Wen Zhong Zi*) of the Sui Dynasty (581–618) and meant "the way of statecraft."

From the second half of the 19th century onwards, Japanese scholars borrowed the ancient Chinese word *"jingji"* when translating the English word "economy," but its meaning changed fundamentally and became a term that referred exclusively to the material production activities of society. After the *Xinhai* Revolution (10/1911–2/1912), on the advice of Sun Yat-sen, pioneer of the Kuomintang who had close ties with Japan, Chinese scholars unanimously followed the Japanese translation of the English word "economy." However, if we look at the modern conceptions of economic policy that evolved since Reform and Opening-up in 1978, the family resemblances with the original meaning loom large.

2. What is a "socialist market"?

China's market is often referred to as a "socialist market" due to its unique combination of elements of the so-called socialism and capitalism. In the "socialist" aspect, the Chinese government maintains a significant degree of control over the economy through state-owned enterprises (SOEs) and strategic industries such as energy, banking, and telecommunications. The government also uses macroeconomic policies, such as interest rate adjustments, to manage economic growth and stability. At the same time, the government has implemented free-market-oriented policies such as price liberalization, deregulation, and the creation of special economic zones (SEZs) to attract foreign investment since the 1990s. Overall, China's socialist market economy is considered different from a free market economy because it highlights certain elements that do not prevail in the free capitalist market, such as maintaining state ownership in certain industries and tight control of the financial sector, and also has a unique set of policies that promote domestic innovation and protect domestic industries.

This socialist market system evolved through four decades. After the Cultural Revolution's chaos, political leaders realized the urgent need of revitalizing the economy. After several years of fumbling and struggling, CCP leaders became committed to building a new socialist market based neither on state-run planning nor on a capitalist market economy, but rather on a middle path, which they defined as a "socialist market economy with Chinese characteristics" (Ding 2009; Boer 2021). The initial phase of economic reform (1978–1984) was carried out under Deng Xiaoping, who set the country on a path of economic reform and modernization. Deng was the key player in the CCP's inner circle of power holders after Mao Zedong.

On 26 November 1979, when meeting with the deputy editor-in-chief of the Encyclopaedia Britannica of the United States, Deng Xiaoping (1993a, 148) said: "It is certainly incorrect to say that market economy is confined to capitalist societies and capitalist market economies. Why can't socialism have a market economy?" In October 1985, in response to a question from Gronwald, head of an American entrepreneurial delegation, on the relationship between socialism and market economy, he said:

"The question is what approach is more conducive to the development of the productive forces of society. In the past we had a planned economy, which was certainly a good approach, but years of experience have shown that using this approach alone will fetter the development of the productive forces, and that we should combine." (ibid., 332–33)

When visiting Shanghai in December 1991 and during the South China tour in early 1992, Deng pointed out a target in economic reform:

"Don't think that a market economy is the road to capitalism, there is no such thing. A planned economy is not the same as socialism, capitalism also has plans; a market economy is not the same as capitalism, socialism also has markets. Both planning and the market are economic means (*shouduan* 手段). Whether there is more market or more planning is not the essential difference between socialism and capitalism." (ibid., 373)

According to Deng, "[p]lanning and market forces are both means of controlling economic activity. The essence of socialism is liberation and development of the productive forces, elimination of exploitation and polarization, and the ultimate achievement of prosperity for all" (ibid.).

Deng's understanding of the market and economy is that the production and exchange of commodities on the market are necessary for the development of human social civilisation and material progress. The pursuit of wealth that results from the exchange of commodities is also a natural part of human civilisation. Deng believes that market forces encourage social progress, advanced technology, efficient production, and rational use of resources. Chen Yun, who was in charge of the economy in the Standing Committee of the Central Politburo, argued that the socialist economy must have both a planned economy and a market economy, and that their coexistence was both necessary and essential (Chen 1984, 245, 247). He later borrowed Huang Kecheng's reference to "the relationship between the cage and the bird" to summarise the relationship between planning and the market.[3]

The moral concerns that arise in economic and exchange relations are another aspect that Chinese leaders have always debated and struggled with. The promotion of a "socialist spiritual civilization," launched by Deng in the early 1980s, was an attempt to counteract moral challenges to the emphasis on economic growth and reform (Dai 2010). The idea of "two civilizations," and a campaign to promote it, were formally inaugurated beginning in 1982.[4] The "Communist spiritual civilization" ideology became ubiquitous and formidable on an institutional scale. Deng's ideological concern for moral civilization was best manifested in his famous saying "one hand is tough while the other is soft", meaning that material civilization was being emphasized, whereas spiritual values were neglected (ibid.). In September 1986, the Sixth Plenum of the Twelfth Party Central Committee (CPCC) approved the adoption of Deng's maxim, "In grasping with two hands, both hands must be firm", as party guideline (Deng 1993). Both hands being firm actually means socialist spiritual civilization should be paid more attention. The idea of the two civilizations provided a new ideological framework to cope with the moral concerns among Party members who sought to control the balance between social order and economic liberalization.

Based on the joint promotion and active exploration by Deng and Chen Yun as reformists, the "Decision on Economic System Reform" was adopted at the Third Plenary Session of the Twelfth CPCC of China in 1984. According to Deng Xiaoping, the *Decision* was "the first draft of a political economy

---

[3] Chen Yun described that this "cage", as big as it should be, is not necessarily limited to one province or one region but can also be cross-provincial and cross-regional. It is not necessarily confined to one province or one region, but can also span provinces and regions, and is not even necessarily confined to the country, but can also span countries and continents. See also Chen Yun, *People's Daily*, Dec. 03, 1982.

[4] In September 1982, the Twelfth Party Congress adopted a report entitled "Pioneering a New Situation in Socialist Modernization", which further emphasized the significance of building a socialist spiritual civilization. The Congress made a decision to vigorously promote the building of socialist material and spiritual civilizations and set "building a high level of socialist material civilization while striving to build a high level of socialist spiritual civilization" as a strategic policy for China's socialist modernization.

that combines the basic principles of Marxism and the practice of Chinese socialism" (Deng 1993, 364).

In October 1992, the 14th National Congress of the Communist Party of China (NPC) set the goal of "reforming the establishment of a socialist market economy" (Jiang n.d.). In November 1993, the Third Plenary Session of the 14th CPCC inaugurated the "Decision on Several Issues Concerning the Establishment of a Socialist Market Economic System". This *Decision* clearly put forward a new reform strategy of "integral promotion and key breakthroughs", formulated specific plans for promoting market in all aspects of the economic system, and required the establishment of a market economic system by the end of the 20th century (CPCC n.d.). The documents issued in these meetings are commonly regarded as cornerstones of the Chinese market reform.[5] Meanwhile, these state documents do imply that a "comprehensive" market has inherent deficiencies. To avoid it, government adjustments and control mechanisms must be built into the market system. The Party should not allow "capitalist market forces," which produce income disparity and class struggle, to dominate the market system (ibid.).

Spanning forty-four years, when looking at the guidelines and party policy statements on the economy and market, the continuity of certain principles over the reform period is salient. The 12th CPCC in 1984 proposed that a planned economy should be the mainstay and a market economy should be the supplement, and the Third Plenary Session of the 12th CPCC (October 1984) proposed a "planned commodity economy". The 13th CPCC (October 1987) put forward the operational mechanism of "the state regulating the market and the market guiding enterprises", and the 14th CPCC (October 1992) clearly put forward the target model of establishing a socialist market

---

5 Documents include: "Decision of the Third Plenum of the 14th Central Committee of the Communist Party of China on Certain Questions in the Economic and Social Development" (October 1993), which sets out the main principles and guidelines for the establishment of a socialist market economy; "The Decision of the Central Committee of the Communist Party of China on Reform of the Economic Structure" (December 1993), which provided more detailed policy measures for the establishment of a socialist market economy, including the reform of state-owned enterprises, the establishment of a legal framework for a market economy, and the development of a social safety net; later, "The Program for the Development of a Socialist Market Economy", which outlined the government's plans for economic reform and development, including the establishment of a socialist market economy, the development of a legal and regulatory framework for a market economy, and the promotion of private enterprise and foreign investment. These documents were the foundation for the development of a socialist market economy in China and provided the basis for the implementation of market-oriented economic policies over the following years.

economy system. The Third Plenary Session of the 16th CPCC (October 2003) proposed to further improve the socialist market economy system, and the Third Plenary Session of the 18th CPCC (November 2012) proposed to enable the market to play a decisive role in the allocation of resources, and to enhance the role of the government.

During the 19th CPCC (October 2017), the "Decision of the Central Committee of the Communist Party of China on Several Major Issues of Comprehensively Deepening Reform" was issued. Regarding the market and the government, it comments,

"[o]n making the market play a decisive role in the allocation of resources and giving better play to the role of the government. This is a major theoretical viewpoint put forward in the decision of this plenary session. This is because the reform of the economic system is still the focus of the comprehensive deepening reform, and the core issue of the reform of the economic system is still to deal with the relationship between the government and the market [...] The market plays a decisive role, in the overall sense, but one cannot blindly speak of the market playing a decisive role. There are areas, such as defence construction, where the government is expected to play the leading role. There are strategic energy resources that the government should have a firm grip on, but this can be realized through market mechanisms." (CPCC, n.d.-a)

When referring to "socialist market economy", Xi Jinping argued: "We are developing a market economy under the leadership of the Communist Party of China and the premise of a socialist system, and at no time should we forget the definitive term 'socialism.' The reason why we say socialist market economy is to uphold the superiority of our system and effectively prevent the drawbacks of capitalist market economy. We need both an 'effective market' and a 'proactive government,' and we are striving to solve this worldwide problem in economics in practice" (Xi n.d.).

The Fourth Plenary Session of the 19th CPCC (October 2019) clearly pointed out that "with public ownership as the mainstay and a variety of ownership systems developing together, distribution according to labour as the mainstay and a variety of distribution methods co-existing, he socialist market economy system is the basic socialist economic system" (Editorial n.d.). To note, for the very first time since 1978, the "socialist market economy system" is included in the basic socialist economic system.

In his report to the most recent 20th CPCC (October 2022), Xi stressed that "Chinese-style modernization is a modernization in which material and spiritual civilization are in harmony"; "The realization of the Chinese dream is the result of the balanced development and mutual promotion of material and spiritual civilization." (Xi 2022) He points out that material abundance and spiritual wealth are the fundamental requirements of socialist modernization. To promote Chinese-style modernization, it is necessary not only to continuously build up the material foundation of modernization, but also to better construct the Chinese spirit, Chinese values, and Chinese power (ibid.).

In sum, we recognize that since the founding of the country, the leaders of the Chinese Communist Party have not seen the economy and the market as autonomous. On the contrary, their way of thinking and practice seems to hark back to their historical predecessors, where the market was a necessary means of governing the country. At the same time, they were always wary of the moral corruption of the ruling class due to the economic benefits of market exchange relations. In the next section, we show that these themes have been shaping the Chinese economic discourse since ancient times.

3. Markets as statecraft in Imperial China

The economist Sheng Hong (2010) points out that Western liberalism in economic thought has been inspired by Chinese thinking about economy and society. This thesis is well recognized in Western scholarship on the early enlightenment, when European scholars such as François Quesnay and Christian Wolff avidly read the Jesuit reports about China and praised the "enlightened" rule of the Emperors (Mungello 1999; Hobson 2004). Evidently, this praise of China was also a critical mirror of the Ancien Regime, but the scholars were also referring to many details about institutions and conditions of the Chinese empire, including about economic life. One idea where such inspiration is salient concerns the primacy of agriculture as the root of economic prosperity, an idea which has been maintained in China for two millennia and which became a key notion in physiocracy. More fundamentally, some authors argue that the specific relationship between government and the market as envisaged in the emerging European liberalism is an intellectual import from China (Gerlach 2005). This is the conception of the economy and the market as a kind of "natural" phenomenon where economic forces interplay and balance, and which should not be disturbed by government action: This is the famous *"wu wei"* (无为) (not-act) doctrine in classical Chinese thought.

However, this picture seems to distort Chinese thinking about the market. Whereas the European liberal thinkers juxtaposed the government and the market as an emerging realm of freedom, in China, from early times on, the market was seen as an important lever of statecraft. This approach was rooted in a long literary tradition of conceptualizing the market, which precedes Europe roughly 1500 years. The core sources are the *Guanzi*, an apocryphal text with different temporal layers from between the 7th and 1st centuries BCE, and the "Discourse on Salt and Iron" (*Yantie lun*), that took place at the Han Imperial court in the 2nd century BCE.[6] These formative discourses are placed in the Han dynasty, thus reflecting an intellectual consolidation after the disruption of the Empire-founding Qin dynasty. The former text may be seen as an early theory about market mechanisms, and the latter is a systematic view on economic policy.

The *Guanzi* contains a comprehensive account of price movements and a quantity theory of money. As such, it seems to state the autonomy of the market in the sense of the recognition of its specific regularities. At the same time, however, the text also defines the role of government as the provider of the currency and the conductor of market operations via monetary policy. The author(s) had already discovered basic mechanisms such as balance of payments and inflation, which endorsed the case for government regulation of money. Indeed, from that time onwards Chinese Imperial governments always pursued the goal of enforcing a government monopoly of money production. Yet, in practice this was often undermined during times of weak or collapsing Imperial authority, and, most importantly, in late Empire when Mexican silver dollars became a secondary currency alongside government-minted copper coins, flowing into the country via the current account surplus with Europe, especially Britain, and the vast trade networks linking the Americas, the Pacific and Europe.

Hence, from early times onwards Chinese thinking emphasized the close relationship between government and market. The book *Guanzi* repeatedly stresses that the state must first encourage the people to develop production, reduce taxes and levies so that the people can live in relative stability and prosperity, and then will be able to "order the source of flowing water", i.e., orders can be enforced. Otherwise, "orders that do not work" will only re-

---

6 Space is limited, so we cannot add more detail on the history and background of the texts. On the *Guanzi*, see von Glahn (2016, 64, 120) and the penetrating analysis of Chin (2014) On the *Yantie lun*, see Zanasi (2020).

sult in the subversion of the regime. The most famous of *Guanzi's* words are "[w]hen the granary becomes filled, people observe etiquette; when people become well-fed and clothed, they know honour and shame" (Rickett transl. 2021, 292).[7] Remarkably, this phrase has been repeatedly quoted by Chinese emperors and political officials. Xi Jinping first cited it as early as 1989.[8] His most recent citation is in the speech, "High Level Dialogue on Global Development", in 2022 (Xi, n.d.-a).

In this larger cultural setting, the two opposing views that clashed at the Imperial court in the *Yantie lun* defined the discourse about markets that is continuing today. In simplest terms, this is the view on government control and intervention in the market versus the morality of markets, while in both views a shared reference was the idea of the primacy of people's livelihood and the stability and sustainability of the commonwealth ("*tianxia*" 天下). The latter topic also included a notion of political economy, and even of the distribution of power in that commonwealth.

Let us begin with the last point, since this directly touches on the comparison with Western liberalism. One key concern of Chinese rulers was (and is, *mutatis mutandis*) the unity of the Chinese body politic, ritually represented by the emperor. The economy was seen as a key guarantor, but also as a threat. The threat results from the inherent forces of inequality in the market, epitomized in the potential accumulation of land as the key productive asset in the hands of a few landholders. Two dangers lurk here: The first is that the accumulating riches leave an increasing number of people landless and mired in poverty, which may trigger unrest and even revolt; the other is that the rich will undermine the tax base of the government, thus eroding its capacity to conduct public policy. Accordingly, the government must contain such forces. This does not mean that markets would be suppressed.

This idea of the primacy of people's livelihood and the stability and sustainability of the commonwealth was rooted in the notion of the "Mandate of Heaven." Since the overthrow of the Shang by the Western Zhou (1050 BC), the rulers of the Western Zhou claimed that their overthrow of the Shang dynasty was just: the Shang king had lost the "Mandate of Heaven" through his tyrannical rule, and the Zhou dynasty, which was able to protect its people, was the successor to the Mandate of Heaven. The idea of the Mandate

---

7 *Guanzi*, chapter *mu min*, "仓廪实而知礼节，衣食足而知荣辱".

8 Xi Jinping made a speech titled "Building a good spirituality in poor areas [建设好贫困地区的精神文明]" and quoted this sentence. (Xi 2014).

of Heaven was gradually sanctified and eventually became the basis for the legitimacy of dynastic rule in imperial China (Loewe 1972). It is the core part of long-standing tradition of governing and among some principled themes that have a clear continuity through centuries.

Mandate of Heaven contains two clusters of meaning. "Mandate" means government is obliged to have effective measures as a mission to secure adequate revenues to support state making and state running; meanwhile state officials must devote efforts to promote and regulate the economy for the benefit of people's lives ("*min sheng*" 民生). In traditional Chinese religion and culture, the nature of "Heaven" is a moral and relational universe ("*Weltverhältnis*"). It rewards and punishes humans through moral judgement. Heaven here indicates the authorization of ruling power stemming from a moralized natural power. The Confucian classics *Zhongyong* and *Da Xue* (*Daxue and Zhongyong: A Bilingual Edition* 2012) emphasise that the ideal ruler and his governing must fulfil these two fundamental mandates of ruling and gain the support of Heaven by virtue of the fulfilment of its mandates with morality, so that his rule will have the legitimacy of Heaven's mandate, while governments that fail to fulfil mandates or are not moral will also lose the legitimacy of ruling.

Mandate of Heaven as the legitimization of governing has been the foundation of Chinese state formation since the Xi [Western] Zhou dynasty (1045 BC—771 BC) and the Spring-Autumn period (771 BC—476 BC). During this time, China's state political power and ideology gradually merged into one, and there was a close interdependence between China's imperial legalist state government and Confucianism as ideological orthodoxy (Henderson 1998; Zhao 2015). Later, the Han dynasty's governance underwent a significant transformation following the adoption of the ideas espoused by Dong Zhongshu, a proponent of the benevolent political philosophy of Confucianism. As a result, literati began to be appointed to state positions, which constituted a radical departure from the early Han dynasty's practice of exclusively elevating individuals of military origin to key government posts based on their military prowess. The new selection system for state officials superseded the military ranking system that had been in place since the Qin dynasty. This system incorporated elements of both Legalism and Confucianism, with the latter being represented by the ritual, benevolence, and righteousness teachings found in the Confucian classics, such as the *Spring and Autumn Annals* and the *Analects*. The examination and education of officials in the Han dynasty were primarily based on Confucianism's social order and moral norms, such as respect for monarchs, upholding righteousness, filial piety, brotherhood, loyalty, and faithfulness. The imperial government used Confucianism as the official ideology to stress its legitimacy. State power was to some extent monitored and controlled by a Confucian-dominated ideological hierarchy; the Confucian community continued to stably supply the imperial bureaucracy with administrative officials through various merit-based selective means such as the *chaju* system during the Han dynasties and the *Keju* imperial examination during the Sui and Tang dynasties. This is the basic structure of Chinese imperial centralized bureaucracy government (Elman 2000; Liu 2018).

However, this apparent synthesis was not yet achieved in Han times and was manifest in the clash of doctrines in the *Yantie lun*. In most conceptualizations of Chinese cultural heritage, Confucianism is emphasized, perhaps alongside of Taoism and Buddhism.[9] Yet, when it comes to the issue of economy and the public good, the philosophical school of legalism is of prime importance, which opposed the Confucians at the Han court (Huan Kuan n.d.). Legalists were the proponents of absolute Imperial power and argued that the market must be contained via establishing government control and even monopoly in key sectors (salt and iron). This would also guarantee sufficient state access to resources. A strong Imperial government would also be able to rein in the power of landholding elites. But there is a surprising shift of perspectives on the market, compared to the Western discourse. This is salient in the fact that the *Guanzi* is a legalist text: that means, recognizing the autonomy of the market forces combines with an emphasis on government hegemony.

The main feature in Legalist economic thought is "*wu wei*" (non-act) as first principle, thus clearly showing the misunderstanding in the narratives about the import of "liberalism" from China to the West.[10] It asserts that individuals have full autonomy in their economic activities and, due to the tendency of self-interest, will not need the intervention of the state at all: "where profit lies, although a thousand-foot mountain, people will go up; into the deepest well, people will enter; therefore, those who are skilled in government control the presence of wealth so that the people are naturally content. Without pushing them, they go; without pulling them, they come. Without

---

9 The locus classicus remains Max Weber (Weber 1968), even until today. In the context of economics, Hofstede's view on Confucianism is influential, see (Hofstede et al. 2010).
10 More details see *Guanzi*, chapter *jin cang*.

trouble or worry, the people enrich themselves. The state should treat market development like a bird hatching an egg, invisible and silent, left to its own devices, there is neither shape nor sound, but the young suddenly appear quite complete".[11] The government's role is to "be skilled in government control of the presence of wealth" and not interfering. In the history of Chinese economic thought, this understanding of economic activity as a technique of governance was first proposed by the Legalists and became the ideological basis for the economic policy of "rest with the people" in the early Han Dynasty.

The Legalists first advocated the idea of "affairs of the market" (*wu shi shi* 务市事) as state affairs, that is, government regulation of the market. They considered commerce and industry to be a national necessity and were the first in Chinese history to refer to the scholar-officials, the farmers, the artisans, and the merchants as "the pillars of the state" (*guo zhi shi min* 国之石民). Bringing together people from the same occupations facilitates the exchange of skills and the improvement of techniques. For example, merchants gathering in the market is conducive to the exchange of information on commodities, supply and demand, effectively stabilising prices, optimising the allocation of resources and effectively promoting the production and circulation of commodities.

Against this background, the *Yantie lun* shows another surprising turn, namely that the Confucians adopted a "liberal" position vis-à-vis the government. The reason is twofold. One is that throughout Imperial history Confucians systematically favoured a low-tax regime, coupled with the notion that only agriculture is productive: low taxes manifest the benevolence of the ruler vis-à-vis the populace.[12] The emphasis on agriculture means that the state cannot tax commerce, thus, perhaps unintendedly, resulting in a pro-commerce policy which was only given up in the 19th century when the government desperately searched for revenue sources in the face of Imperialist aggression against China. The other "liberal" idea is that government should keep a distance to the economy because officials will be corrupted by the wealth close to their fingertips.

---

11 *Guanzi*, chapter *jin cang*, "故利之所在，虽千仞之山，无所不上；深源之下，无所不入焉 故善者势利之在，而民自美安，不推而往，不引而来，不烦不扰， 而民自富。如鸟之覆卵，无形无声，而唯见其成" (Rickett 2021, 220).

12 This low-tax regime is a unique feature of Imperial China compared to other empires in Europe, Russia and the Middle East (Brandt et al. 2014).

The latter opinion is one important aspect of the morality of markets emphasized by the Confucians, against the autonomy claims of the *Guanzi*. The notion of government corruption also played an important role in European thinking about absolutist rule, for sure. In China, this must be seen against the background of a fundamentally different conception of social structure. Whereas European enlightenment still struggled for the recognition of the main actors of the commercial economy in the frame of the medieval estates of nobility, clergy and peasants, the fourfold conception in China reflected the role of market society in distinguishing scholar-officials, farmers, artisans, and merchants already in the first millennium BCE. China finally overcame feudalism with the establishment of Empire in 221 BCE, whereas Europe still battled against it in the 18th century. There was in China neither the duality of kingdom and church, nor the identification of rulers with the sword. Against this background, the often-cited moral disqualification of commerce must be put into context, as this referred to the corrupting impact of commerce on officials idealized as Confucian "gentlemen" ("*junzi*" 君子) (Gassmann 2007; Pines 2017). For ordinary people, the daily concern for prosperity is fully legitimate and even praiseworthy in maintaining the economic life of the Empire. This gradually became mainstream opinion in Late Imperial China (Yü 2021). In fact, Imperial officials and policies directly endorsed markets in many respects, such as fighting against fraud and deception, both via criminal law and organizational measures such as a governmental system of licensed brokers (von Glahn 2016, 296, 312).

The morality of markets was also reflected in the perennial concerns about luxury, a theme that is also familiar from Europe. European liberalism often expressed the opinion that luxury is benefitting the entire society as it creates jobs and income for workers. In China, this view was also expressed in Late Imperial China, but always stood in tension with concerns about sustainability (Zanasi 2020). In this major new study, Margherita Zanasi argues that basic notions of a free market economy emerged in China a century and half earlier than in Europe. In response to the commercial revolutions of the late 1500s, Chinese intellectuals and officials called for the end of state intervention in the market, recognizing its power to self-regulate. They also noted the elasticity of domestic demand and production, arguing in favour of ending long-standing rules against luxury consumption, an idea that emerged in Europe in the late seventeenth and early nineteenth centuries. Zanasi challenges Eurocentric theories of economic modernization as well as the assumption that European Enlightenment thought was unique in its ability to produce innovative economic ideas. She instead establishes a direct connection between observations of local economic conditions and the formulation of new theories, revealing the unexpected flexibility of the Confucian tradition and its accommodation of seemingly unorthodox ideas. This points to a fundamental difference between European liberalism and Chinese Confucian liberalism: The former was wedded to colonial expansion and was thus combining with the vision of a literally endless world, especially in North America. In China, thinkers and officials perceived the world in terms of the borders of the Empire, and hence were keenly aware of the limitations of resources. European industrialization reinforced these divergent views, which can be conceived as two fundamentally different forms of *Weltbeziehungen*.

We conclude that the discourse about markets in Imperial China was already as sophisticated as economic thinking in Europe at the eve of industrialization, yet defined the fundamental issues in an entirely different way. In Europe, the market was seen as one of the social domains that liberates society from the fetters of political domination, hence is idealized as a domain of freedom. This went hand in hand with the emergence of economics as a science of the autonomous workings of the market. In China, the idea of autonomous market forces emerged much earlier, even combined with an incipient mathematization of economic knowledge. But this converged with the legalist view that markets are a tool for government to enhance the economic power of the Imperial body politic. The opposing view is the Confucian which accepts markets only as embedded into a moral order, hence denying the autonomy of markets, while at the same time maintaining a distance between government and markets, for moral reasons. The government must keep its hands off the market not to protect individual freedom, but to safeguard its own moral excellence.

In sum, China has a long and sophisticated tradition of thinking about markets and the common weal. This tradition lives forth in the present, yet it is not explicitly debated beyond narrow scholarly circles. In these circles, the issue of free markets is a key theme.

4. Why are liberal economists so rare in China?

Liberal economic thought began to enter China in the late 19th and early 20th centuries, primarily through the opening of ports of commerce to foreigners and the translated writings of Western economists. In a fascinating episode of Chinese intellectual history, in the time of transition between 1911 and 1949, important, though today neglected debates over the market and its conceptualization took place. One leading translator of Western economics, Wang Yanan, explicitly criticized the "metaphysical" view of the market in the Austrian School (Menger) and championed a historical approach, informed by the German historical school, and developed scientifically in Marxism (Karl 2017). Liberal economic thinking remained weakly represented in Chinese debates, even though the precursors in Imperial times were also recognized (Borokh 2016). It was not until the late 1970s and early 1980s, following the end of the Cultural Revolution, that the Chinese Communist Party began to adopt more liberal economic policies. It was expected that Western liberal economic thoughts would play an essential role in China's market reform, like in the post-socialist countries after the cold war era.

In the face of growing economic collapse in the 1970s, this opened a door to the engagement of intellectuals and technocracy in theoretical quarrels over re-designing the planned economy (Weber 2021). The increased visibility and influence of intellectual actors and institutions associated with the market idea and the intellectual revival of the market concept in reforms created the conditions of the surge of a new realm of economics discourses. Since the late-1970s, several institutions groomed a staff of specialist economic professionals, including local policy research offices, professional newspapers, and universities. The discourse of economics could rely on three particularly important institutional vehicles: think tanks, economic research institutes, and the Chinese government economic reform administration.

The rise of the think tanks and research institutes is an especially important development to consider in any explanation of the ascent of new ideas (Hall 1993; Cockett 1994). Market economy think tanks in China originally emerged as a reaction to the pro-government, anti-market communism and against the highly interventionist policies of the government. This movement for an introduction of Western economic theories crystallized in the liberalization of markets when top ranking members of the Communist Party, together with local provincial leaders, paved a theoretical path for marketization. The new economic institutes, "libertarian" think tanks and economic press were devoted to the promotion of Western economic views.

In many ways, the emergence of liberal think tanks on the public scene would not have been possible without a broader transformation in the political mechanism. Since the Reform and Opening up, with economic recovery and construction becoming the overriding central task, the powerful movement to revive almost dying economics created another high tide of study in Europe and America (the first wave was at the beginning of the 20th century as part of "national salvation")—the scale, scope, and impact of which greatly exceeded that of the first one. According to the statistics of the Ministry of Education, from 1978 to 2004, a total of 815,000 students went abroad and 198,000 returned home after their studies, of which (114,700 and 25,000 respectively in 2004), economists accounted for a considerable number (Sheng 1996). With the return of this large number of international students, the economics paradigm shifted from Marxist economics to a combination of domestic economic research and Western liberal and neoliberal economics. The previous mainstream Marxist economics was marginalized. The impact of mainstream Western economics, epitomized by American neoliberal economic thought, on China's economic reforms post-1979 is indisputable. Neoliberalism, exemplified by Milton Friedman, emerged as one of the most prominent mainstream Western economic theories since China commenced its reform era. Friedman himself received an invitation to China as early as 1980, coinciding with the inception of the nation's Reform and Opening up, to deliver a lecture on global economic trends, inflation, and the incorporation of markets within planned economies. In 1988, CCP General Secretary Zhao Ziyang even granted Friedman an audience. The Chinese Academy of Social Sciences' invitation to a delegation of distinguished American economists for an economic exchange marked the onset of a pivotal legitimization of mainstream Western economics in China. The delegation's report showed that Chinese scholars exhibited particular interest in econometric methodologies, public economics, microeconomic aspects related to enhancing firm efficiency, and the theoretical underpinnings of trade and economic planning (Warner 2017). Initially, the mathematical modelling language inherent in neoliberal economics projected a "scientific" and "neutral" image, which significantly contributed to its popularity among Chinese economists.

From the onset of 1979 until around 2010, organizations such as the American Economic Association (AEA), Ford Foundation, Center for International Private Enterprise (CIPE), Cato Institute, National Bureau of Economic Research (NBER), World Bank, International Monetary Fund, and the Federal Reserve System vigorously promoted the initial dissemination of neoclassical and neoliberal economic theories in China. This was accomplished through various means, including organizing Sino-American economic exchanges and visits, economic workshops, lecture tours, doctoral programs in the United States, graduate training centres, visiting scholar scholarship programs, joint conferences between Chinese and American economists, the establishment of research institutes, the creation of libraries, the provision of conditional loans, and the sponsorship of textbook publication and translation projects (Cohn 2017).

Examining the channels of ideological dissemination, American neoliberal economists and their affiliated institutions played a crucial role in this historical process. For instance, the Ford Foundation allocated annual funding exceeding 1–1.5 million dollars for "deliberately promoting the development of areas vital to China's economic success" (ibid., 138). These organizations established the first cohort of specialized economic research institutions within China's top-tier universities, such as the China Center for Economic Research (CCER) at Peking University.

This research centre mobilized a substantial number of economic researchers, designed economics courses and graduate programs modelled after the University of Chicago, organized international seminars, developed core textbooks, published journals, and maintained digital networks. Initially, the centre was perceived to reflect the significant influence of Chinese liberal economists, Justin Yifu Lin and Zhang Weiying, who were then considered the foremost advocates of economic liberalization and free markets in China. However, intriguingly, Lin Justin Yifu has since become the dean of Peking University's New Structural Economics Research Institute, no longer adhering to his original liberal economic ideology. Lin's transition will be discussed in subsequent sections. Since 2008, the CCER has been rebranded as the National School of Development (NSD).

Reform economics contends that an economic system predicated on private property rights, corporate legal entities, and the promotion of free-market development fosters a free, democratic, and civilized modern culture and society. Consequently, during the early stages of reform, several Chinese liberal economists emerged, exhibiting a resolute and persistent determination to advance China's economic reforms toward laissez-faire. The robust support for new classical and neoliberal economic thoughts also originated from the pressures induced by China's economic difficulties at the time.

Faced with the urgency of economic reform, some economists began advocating for a renewed understanding of value laws, emphasizing economic outcomes, granting enterprises greater autonomy, and reducing central planning control, while opposing market economies (with Sun Yefang as a representative figure). In essence, this call to action stemmed from a focus on micro-level economic efficiency concerns. In May 1979, Liu Guoguang and Zhao Renwei co-authored an article entitled "On the Relationship between Planning and Market in Socialist Economy," which was regarded as the harbinger of economists propelling reform initiatives (Liu and Zhao n.d.). Marxist economists Yu Guangyuan and Xue Muqiao contended that a socialist economy embodies both market and commodity economies. Some Marxist economists, such as Jiang Yiwei, began focusing on worker autonomy and industrial democracy to stimulate enterprise vitality (Zhang 2018; Herrmann-Pillath 1987; 1991).

Economists represented by Dong Fureng examined ownership issues in the market and argued that only under the existence and development of non-public ownership economies, along with market development and the establishment of market economic systems, can a public ownership economy be integrated into the market. Thus, China's market system must undergo property rights and ownership reforms (Zhang 2018). Hua Sheng advocated for a wholesale market transition centred on clearly defined property rights. Reform economists represented by Li Yining emphasized enterprise shareholding system transformations. Li has advocated for the privatization of state-owned enterprises, ownership reform, the establishment of a legal framework to protect property rights in the market, and the introduction of stock markets (Zhang 2018). Another liberal icon, Wu Jinglian, defined market economy and economic system reform from the perspective of resource allocation, advocating market-oriented reforms centred on price deregulation, and recommended a complete shock therapy script. He also called for the strategic reorganization of state-owned enterprises and corporatization reform (Naughton, 1995).

In comparison, Mao Yushi and the Tianze Institute (English name: Unirule Institute of Economics) represent a unique case among liberal economists. Established in 1993, the Tianze Institute has become a prominent advocate for an independent liberal market economy in China. Over a 25-year existence, the think tank played a crucial role in developing and promoting liberal market discourse. The *New York Times* referred to it as one of China's last remaining bastions of liberal thought. However, in July 2018, its Beijing office was forcibly closed.

The 25-year trajectory of the Tianze Institute reflects the recent history of Chinese economic thought. At its inception, numerous liberal scholars eagerly participated in the Institute's discussions and conferences. A plethora of articles endorsing free markets were published under the auspices of Tianze seminars during this period. Nevertheless, as the concept of the free market became increasingly linked with moral failures and governance incompetence in the public's perception, the Tianze Institute's previous arguments and publications attracted mounting criticism. Mao Yushi, seen as a leading proponent of liberal economic thought, has faced continuous attacks since then. In a series of public gatherings in Shenyang and Changsha in 2013, enraged audience members denounced him as a traitor and an "American jackal."

It is evident that property rights and ownership transformation have been the most widely discussed topics in the discourse on economic reforms. Compared to the swift market price reforms, market mechanism reforms, introduction of foreign investment, and the establishment of special economic zones, property rights and ownership reform (including land and other factors of production) has been the longest-lasting, slowest, and most challenging aspect of China's market economy transformation. This is also evident when observing the actions of high-level policymakers.

As seen previously in more detail, as early as the Third Plenary Session of the 11th CPCC in 1978, market-oriented reforms were proposed. The 1984 Party plenary decision redefined the socialist economy as "a planned commodity economy based on public ownership." From October 12th to 18th, 1992, the 14th NPC was held, clarifying that the goal of China's economic system reform was to establish a socialist market economic system. It was not until 35 years later, in 2013, that the Third Plenary Session of the 18th CPCC's "Decision" finally stated that "both public and non-public ownership economies are essential components of the socialist market economy and are crucial foundations for our country's economic and social development" (*Communiqué of the Third Plenary Session of the 18th Central Committee of the Communist Party of China- China* n.d.). This was the first time that non-public ownership economies were placed on an equal footing with public ownership economies.

If we extend the timeline of our examination to the most recent decade, we find that the differences between pre-reform Marxist economists and the second generation of economists influenced by mainstream Western economics have persisted but have never been reconciled. This fundamental disagreement also lies at the heart of the recent divide between the New Left and neoliberal economists. On the one hand, the reform of economic theory paradigms has freed itself from the Marxist economic framework, and instead began to consider and propose ideas within the efficiency and utility-based neoliberal paradigm. On the other hand, it may come as a surprise to those involved in this two-to-three-decades-long "implantation movement" of neoliberal economic thought that the "socialist" elements in economic reforms have never been downplayed by policymakers, aside from the objective of "achieving economic growth."

In other words, throughout the tenure of four generations of leadership since Deng Xiaoping, China's economic and market policies have increasingly diverged from the neoliberal model, which advocates for an economic and social system built on private property rights, corporate legal entities, and the promotion of free market development. In this light, the commitment to "state governing the market" as a socialist fundamental by top political leaders has been upheld.

The three major debates among Chinese economists were not purely academic in nature; instead, they carried quite strong policy-oriented implications. These economic debates were also characterized by a significant amount of ideological factionalism, wherein economic theories were divided along ideological lines (Liu 2021). This suggests that for Chinese economists, the discussions surrounding certain economic theories were not solely focused on "economic" issues but also carried a strong "state governance" aspect.

This reflects a *longue durée* of *Weltbeziehungen* across the revolutionary divide between the Chinese empire and the People's Republic. Relating back to the "Salt and Iron Debate" mentioned earlier, a Chinese ideological tradition is that "state governance" issues possess a "moral" dimension. Consequently, these economic discussions among Chinese economists took on a highly moral debate characteristic. Confucians believe that the moral attribute of a "good" economic policy stems from its ability to "benefit the people" and "nurture the livelihood of people," as the people's well-being is the legitimation source of the "Mandate of Heaven." Legalists, on the other hand, argue that the moral attribute of a "good" economic policy comes from "enriching the nation" and "strengthening the military," as a wealthy and powerful nation is the legitimation source. The essence of the "Mandate of Heaven" concept is a moral one: if a ruler and their policies are moral, Heaven, as the arbiter of ethics, can grant them legitimacy in governance. Therefore, governing policies possess moral attributes. This necessitates evaluating the morality or immorality of a particular economic policy based on different moral backgrounds. The fundamental differences in these moral backgrounds determine whether an economic policy is considered moral or not.

When socialism and public ownership are considered moral due to their societal design intentions of overthrowing class differences and implementing social equity, their attributes in economic policies are deemed moral and must be preserved. When the market system is regarded as good because it can promote the well-being of the people—the fundamental source of legitimacy in governance—the market should be retained. However, market policies can lead to liberalization, such as uncontrolled widening of wealth disparities and rapid accumulation of private capital. Such outcomes are deemed immoral because they are detrimental to social equity, warranting strict government control. This, in turn, reflects the basic stance of Legalist morality, grounded in the "state governing market" approach.

Now, the question "Why should socialism and public ownership matter in the market reform?" has an answer. If the holistic ontology of neoliberal economics regards free-market capitalism as a social form with "beautiful" and "virtuous" value implications, we should not merely view socialism and public ownership as functional tools for achieving modernization in the modern Chinese context. In this sense, they matter. As Lin Chun commented on Weber's (2021) analysis of reform economic intellectuals,

"[Weber] stops short of recognizing the significance of this parallel intellectual (under) current corrective to the (hidden) ideological impulse of radicalizing the reform. The pressing question for the 1980s, after all, was whether market mechanisms could be mastered for the socialist end." (Lin 2023, 12)

We certainly cannot regard this understanding of the state, market, economy, and their respective relationships as part of the Marxist economic paradigm. Efforts to institutionalize Western mainstream economics (neoclassical and neoliberal) in China, which began in the mid-1980s, have effectively failed in the past fifteen years, and even the Chinese intellectual community has become increasingly sceptical of Western neoliberal economics. This scepticism stems from anger over corruption during the marketization and privatization processes, growing income and wealth inequality, and a reassessment of consumerism.

Starting around 2010, neoliberalism faced extensive criticism. The "Washington Consensus" was regarded as a manifestation of the international monopoly capital's attempt to dominate the global will (中国社会科学院 "新自由主义研究" 课题组 [Research Group on "Neoliberalism", Chinese Academy of Social Sciences] 2003). The failures of economic transitions in Russia, Eastern Europe, and Latin America were attributed to the adverse effects of neoliberal radical transformation. This shift in thought has been accompanied by the rise of New Left economists and government economists. These New Left economists advocate a more balanced approach between the market and state intervention, prioritizing social equity and sustainability. They draw on Marxist and state-oriented ideas, critiquing the negative social consequences of market reforms in areas such as income inequality and environmental degradation. Well-known figures associated with the Chinese New Left include Wang Hui, Hu Angang, and Cui Zhiyuan. While some have become influential, others, like Cui Zhiyuan, have been shunned by the party due to their radical leftist views, even verging on a Maoist revival.

In 1993, Wang Shaoguang and Hu Angang published "A Study of China's State Capacity", arguing that a strong state is necessary for Chinese market reform. Wang and Hu's report is said to have helped prompt the taxation reform of January 1994, which divided revenues and responsibilities between the central and provincial authorities (Li 2015). Many New Left economists in the 2000s contended that the efficiency principle in the market should no longer be "prioritized," as it would perpetuate the widening gap between the rich and the poor, leading to a substantial erosion of the interests of the socially disadvantaged (Editoral n.d.-b). Wu Zhan, former advisor to the Development Research Centre of the State Council, emphasized that for reform to serve as the driving force of economic and social development, it must first adhere to a fundamental premise: the orientation and nature of such reform must be socialist.

Between liberal economics and the New Left, a group of scholars currently wields significant influence in shaping government policies. These scholars advocate a strong interventionist role for the government while still assigning a key role to markets, thus aligning with the Chinese Communist Party's conception of a "socialist market economy." The leaders of this group boast an impressive record of international activities, with Justin Yifu Lin[13] being particularly prominent as a former World Bank Chief Economist and Vice-President. In 2009, Justin Yifu Lin introduced the concept of "New Structural Economics" (Lin et al. 2011), and in 2012, he published the book *New Structural Economics: A Theoretical Framework for Rethinking Economic Development and Policy*. This book is recognized as a potent critique of neoliberalism and the Washington Consensus. According to Lin, both New Structural Economics and the Washington Consensus acknowledge that market prices form the basis for resource allocation, but New Structural Economics places greater emphasis on the role of government in economic development.[14] The New Structural Economics is now lauded as the "Chinese school" of economics (ibid.). Lin serves as the dean of the Institute of New Structural Economics at Peking University, which evolved from the aforementioned neoliberal centre CCSR.

Another economist gaining prominence is David Daokui Li[15] and the Academic Centre for Chinese Economic Practice and Thinking (ACCEPT) at Tsinghua University. Li serves as the dean and Chief Economist of the New Development Bank, often considered the "Chinese response" to the World Bank. This newly established think tank's mission is "to promote the study of government and market economics worldwide, to analyse the incentive behaviour and role of government in modern market economies, and to contribute new knowledge in the field of government and market economics to the world" (Tsinghua University Website n.d.). Li advocates a genre of "government-market economics," which encompasses more than public finance. This approach emphasizes that "the role of government must be highlighted as a focal point in all modern economic analyses... Firstly, the government is an extremely important direct player in the modern market economy; secondly, government behaviour directly influences the performance of the market economy; and thirdly, a mechanism must be put in place to incentivize government to nurture and regulate the development of the market economy, so that the roles of government and the market work in

---

13 https://www.nse.pku.edu.cn/en/people/professor/245722.htm
14 BiMBA, National School of Development, Peking University, "The 'New Structural Economics' and the 'Chinese School of Economics'," official website of Peking University. https://www.bimba.pku.edu.cn/wm/xwzx/htly/zzzd/409478.htm. Last access: 26.01.2023. Translated by the author.
15 https://www.sem.tsinghua.edu.cn/en/info/1216/7510.htm

the same direction" (Li n.d.). ACCEPT has launched a new international and peer-reviewed economics journal, *The Journal of Government and Economics*.[16] Consequently, both the New Left and these scholars concur on the necessity for a stronger and more competent government. However, the New Left remains considerably more critical of the market. Concerning the understanding of the market, Yang Yao, Dean of the National School of Development at Peking University, argued,

"[i]n a complex modern society, markets are far from being the markets of Adam Smith's time but are heavily influenced by public goals. Markets have the advantage of encouraging individual innovation but are not adept at solving the problems of collaboration, which are increasingly prevalent in modern societies; they are highly responsive, but also often cause excessive economic volatility; and finally, they naturally bring about social differentiation, but society cannot help but be concerned with issues such as equality and fairness. The question of how to balance the role of the market and government remains an unresolved issue in modern society." (Yao n.d.)

Thus, these leading Chinese economists are highly suspicious of the "free self-regulating market" and view government regulation and moral claims of people's livelihood as priorities in economics.

The Institute of New Structural Economics, the National School of Development at Peking University, and ACCEPT at Tsinghua University are the current leading economic think tanks. Notably, all of them have strong international ties, particularly with the United States. Both Justin Lin and David Li received their PhDs from the University of Chicago, a bastion of Friedmanite thought. The current top-level thinking on market reform in China is closely connected to them. The government adapts and improves governance in line with the ideas and suggestions found in their intellectual discourse. Contemporary mainstream Chinese economists generally regard the market as a means of statecraft.

However, there is a remarkable convergence among liberal, New Left, and government economists. They do not disagree on the morality of the market. Although neoliberal economists have diverged in their academic views, with some becoming neo-institutionalist scholars and others becoming leaders of the Neo-Confucian school, almost all of them have written influential books about morality in the market.[17] We should consider the profound influence of

---

16 https://www.sciencedirect.com/journal/journal-of-government-and-economics.
17 Mao Yushi published The Moral Prospect of the Chinese; Shuguang Zhang published How Do Economics Discuss Morality; Li Yining published Ethical Issues in Economics, Beyond the Market

intellectual traditions on conceptual thinking, as the attitude or advocacy for addressing economic issues from a moral perspective likely originates from the Chinese traditional understanding of the concepts of economy and market. These traditions provide and enable indigenous sources for the modern market idea and its creation. More importantly, these intellectual traditions have already foregrounded the target model of economic transition and market setting in a moral context.

The moral commitment of state power in taking care of people's livelihood should be highlighted as a resilient cultural background in Chinese economics study. We used to think of modern liberal economics as a global paradigm. However, it is precisely the development of the Chinese market, unlike any other market, that urges us to think about the importance of different understandings of market.

5. Conclusion: Is there room for convergence between Western and Chinese views?

In the current global political polarization, the alleged contrast between "Western" and "Chinese" views seems starkly confirmed, while in fact Western governments, foremostly the USA, are starting to follow Chinese precedent in industrial policy and economic nationalism.[18] There is a deeper issue, though, namely that in the context of the economy, "Western" often means a peculiar brand of market thinking in the English-speaking world. This is salient when considering Fukuyama's much misunderstood book "*The End of History.*" Fukuyama is commonly understood in terms of the universal acceptance or at least "victory" of capitalism and democracy as defined by the Western mainstream. Most citations outrightly ignore the theoretical pivot of his reasoning: He refutes the Anglo-Saxon tradition of liberalism and claims that what has been reinstated is the Hegelian view of liberalism which approaches freedom as manifesting mutual recognition of people as persons, and which views the market as being embedded in structures of ethical and political life.

---

and Government: The Influence of Ethical Factors and Economy; Sheng Hong published Morality, Utilitarianism and the others; Fan Gang published "Immoral" Economics.
18 *The Economist*, January 14th–20th, 2023.

This is important because there are strong affinities between Hegelian thinking and Chinese views on the economy.[19] Sure, the law does not play such a decisive role in China as in Hegel. But there are important points of convergence even in this respect, most importantly, seeing rights always in conjunction to obligations. The differences mainly loom large in the specific treatment of the civil society as market society based on property and contract. Hegel clearly asserts that the law enables and empowers individual freedom, and that property — he even coined the term "private property" — is the medium by which individual freedom is actualized (Ritter 2004). The Chinese tradition is clearly different, as property is seen as the root of prosperity of the commonwealth, grounding in the labour of peasant families. This is still true today: The constitutional recognition of private property is justified by its contribution to the common prosperity (Long 2009).

Yet, despite this fundamental difference there are important points of convergence: This is because Hegel went beyond the analysis of civil society in recognizing the potentially negative social effects of unbridled market action. Therefore, he approached the market as being embedded in an overarching institutional framework of ethical life, based on the pillars of family, associations, and the state. Here, the similarities with Confucian views clearly abound, and the shared differences to the Anglo-Saxon tradition. Even though the market rests on the foundation of civil law, this remains merely abstract, and the actualized life of the market must be ethically and politically bounded.

Hegel's thinking deeply shaped German conceptions of the social welfare state. When the *Verein für Socialpolitik* was founded, which is today the "German Economic Association," the role of government in regulating the market was a key concern. Indeed, economics was even seen as "*Staatswissenschaft*" ("science of the state"), and even today at several German universities, such as the University of Bonn, the department of economics is part of the "*Rechts- und Staatswissenschaftliche Fakultät*" (officially translated as "Faculty of Law and Economics"). Chinese liberals strongly favoured the Hayekian brand of liberalism, often unaware that German liberals early criticized Hayek as "stone age liberalism" and favoured the "*Ordo*" view of markets as being even "performed" by law and with strong government supervision and regulation. Indeed, the notion of "order" (*zhixu* 秩序) even has assumed a key role in Chinese political discourse about the market.

---

19 For more detail, see (Herrmann-Pillath 2015).

To summarize, beyond the clash of worldviews based on different forms of *Weltbeziehung* there is a huge potential in recognizing the factual diversity of ideas about the market in both the West and China, and eventually paving the way for productive dialogue.

Works cited

Boer, Roland (2021). China's Socialist Market Economy and Planned Economy. In Roland Boer (ed.), *Socialism with Chinese Characteristics: A Guide for Foreigners*, 115–37, Heidelberg: Springer.

Brandt, Loren, Debin Ma, and Thomas G. Rawski (2014). From Divergence to Convergence: Reevaluating the History behind China's Economic Boom. *Journal of Economic Literature*, 52 (1), 45–123.

Borokh, Olga (2016). Liberal Economic Thought in Republican China. In Gilles Campagnolo (ed.). *Liberalism and Chinese Economic Development: Perspectives from Europe and Asia*, 63–85. London: Routledge.

Chen, Yuan (1984). *Chen Yun wen xuan* (Di 1 ban). Ren min chu ban she: Xin hua shu dian fa xing.

Chin, Tamara T. (2014). *Savage Exchange: Han Imperialism, Chinese Literary Style, and the Economic Imagination*. Harvard: Harvard University Press.

Cockett, Richard (1994). *Thinking the Unthinkable: Think-Tanks and the Economic Counter-Revolution, 1931–1983* (First Edition). London: Harpercollins Publishers LTD.

Cohn, Steven (2017). 西方新古典经济学如何主导了中国的经济学教育?(一) [How can the Western New Classical Economics Dominate China's Economic Education? Part 1]. *Journal of Economics of Shanghai School*, 15 (1), 121–44.

China.org.cn (2014) *Communiqué of the Third Plenary Session of the 18th Central Committee of the Communist Party of China*. 27.03.2023 http://www.china.org.cn/china/third_plenary_session/2014-01/15/content_31203056.htm.

CPCC. (n.d.-a). *Communiqué of the Sixth Plenary Session of the 19th Central Committee of the Communist Party of China*. 27.03.2023 http://zw.china-embassy.gov.cn/eng/zgjj/202112/t20211216_10470615.htm.

CPCC. (n.d.-b). *Decision of the CPC Central Committee on Some Issues Concerning the Establishment of a Socialist Market Economic Structure—Beijing Review*. 27.03.2023 http://www.bjreview.com.cn/special/2013-10/23/content_574000_2.htm.

Dai, Anlin (2010). 邓小平的社会主义精神文明建设思想 [Deng Xiaoping de shehuizhuyi jingshen wenming jianshe sixiang/Deng Xiaoping's Socialist Civilization Construction Thoughts]. 重庆社会科学 [*Chongqing Shehui Kexue/Chongqing Social Science*], 8.

Deng, Xiaoping (1993). *Deng Xiaoping Wen Xuan: Di san juan [The collected works of Deng Xiaoping, vol.3]*. Zhonggong Zhongyang Dangxiao Chubanshe.

Ding, Xiaoqin (2009). The Socialist Market Economy: China and the World. *Science & Society*, 73 (2), 235–41.

Editoral (n.d.). 我国基本经济制度的重大创新 *[A major innovation in our basic economic system]*. 27.03.2023 http://www.qstheory.cn/wp/2019-12/17/c_1125354961.htm.

Editoral. (2005, November 21). 改革的分歧与共识 [Divergence and consensus on reform]. *Business Weekly*. 27.03.2023 https://business.sohu.com/20051121/n240765751.shtml.

Elman, Benjamin A. (2000). *A Cultural History of Civil Examinations in Late Imperial China*. Berkeley: University of California Press.

Gassmann, Robert H. (2007). Die Bezeichnung jun-zi. Ansätze zur Chun-qiu-zeitlichen Kontextualisierung und zur Bedeutungsbestimmung im Lun Yu. 27.03.2023 https://doi.org/10.5167/UZH-97971.

Gerlach, Christian (2005). Wu-Wei in Europe. A Study of Eurasian Economic Thought. *London School of Economics*, Working Paper 12 (5).

Hall, Peter A. (1993). Policy Paradigms, Social Learning, and the State: The Case of Economic Policymaking in Britain. *Comparative Politics*, 25 (3), 275–96.

Henderson, John B. (1998). *The Construction of Orthodoxy and Heresy: Neo-Confucian, Islamic, Jewish, and Early Christian Patterns*. Albany: SUNY Press.

Herrmann-Pillath, Carsten (1987). Die Wechselwirkung zwischen Reformtheorie und Reformpolitik in der Volksrepublik China. *Zeitschrift für Wirtschaftspolitik*, 36 (1), 69–100.

Herrmann-Pillath, Carsten (1991). *Institutioneller Wandel, Macht und Inflation in China: Ordnungstheoretische Analysen zur Politischen Ökonomie eines Transformationsprozesses*. Baden-Baden: Nomos.

Herrmann-Pillath, Carsten (2011). A "Third Culture" in Economics? An Essay on Smith, Confucius and the Rise of China. *SSRN Electronic Journal*. https://doi.org/10.2139/ssrn.1757833.

Herrmann-Pillath, Carsten (2015). *Wachstum, Macht und Ordnung*. Weimar (Lahn): Metropolis.

Herrmann-Pillath, Carsten, and Christian Hederer (2012). *A New Principles of Economics: The Science of Markets*, Abingdon and New York: Routledge.

Hobson, John M. (2004). *The Eastern Origins of Western Civilisation*. Cambridge: Cambridge University.

Hofstede, Geert H., Geret J. Hofstede and Michael Minkov (2010). *Cultures and organizations: Software of the mind: intercultural cooperation and its importance for survival* (3rd ed). New York: McGraw-Hill.

Huan, Kuan (n.d.). Yantie Lun: Die Debatte über Salz und Eisen—Perlentaucher. 27.03.2023 https://www.perlentaucher.de/buch/huan-kuan/yantie-lun-die-debatte-ueber-salz-und-eisen.html.

Jiang, Zemin (n.d.). Full Text of Jiang Zemin's Report at 14th Party Congress. Beijing: Beijing Review. 27.03.2023 http://www.bjreview.com/document/txt/2011-03/29/content_363504.htm.

Johnston, Ina, and Wang Ping (2012). *Daxue and Zhongyong* (A Bilingual Edition). Hong Kong: The Chinese University of Hong Kong Press.

Karl, Rebecca E. (2017). *The Magic of Concepts: History and the Economic in Twentieth-Century China*. Durham: Duke University Press.

Leutert, Wendy, and Sarah Eaton (2021). Deepening Not Departure: Xi Jinping's Governance of China's State-owned Economy. *The China Quarterly*, 248 (S1), 200–21.

Li, Daokui (n.d.). 修好政府与市场经济学 [Fixing the Economics of Government and Markets]. Peking: Tsinghua University Press. 27.03.2023 https://www.tsinghua.edu.cn/info/1662/94406.htm.

Li, He (2015). China's New Left. In He Li (ed.). *Political Thought and China's Transformation: Ideas Shaping Reform in Post-Mao China*, 46–59. Basingstoke: Palgrave Macmillan UK.

Lin, Chun (2023). China's Market Reform Debate / Review on Isabella M.Weber, How China Escaped Shock Therapy: The Market Reform Debate. *Development and Change*, 54 (2), 422–41.

Lin, Justin Y. Anne Krueger and Dani Rodrik (2011). New Structural Economics: A Framework for Rethinking Development [with Comments]. *The World Bank Research Observer*, 26 (2), 193–229.

Liu, Guoguang, and Renwei Zhao (n.d.). 论社会主义经济中计划与市场的关系 [On the Relationship between Planning and Market in Socialist Economy]. 21.03.2023 http://www.reformdata.org/1979/0531/11876.shtml.

Liu, Haifeng (2018). *The Examination Culture in Imperial China*. Chicago: Paths International Limited.

Liu, Wei (2021). 中国经济学的探索历程、构建原则与发展方向 [The history of exploration, principles of construction and directions of development of Chinese economics]. 中国科学基金 [China Science Foundation], 35 (3), 361–67.

Loewe, Michael (1972). Herrlee G. Creel: The origins of statecraft in China. Vol. one. The Western Ghou empire, xiv, 559 pp., 2 maps. Chicago and London: University of Chicago Press, 1970. $ 17.50, £7 18s. *Bulletin of the School of Oriental and African Studies*, 35 (2), 395–400.

Long, Qinglan (2009). Reinterpreting Chinese Property. *Southern California Interdisciplinary Law Journal*, 19, 55–71.

Mungello, David E. (1999). *The Great Encounter of China and the West, 1500–1800*. Lanham: Rowman & Littlefield.

Naughton, Barry (1995). *Growing Out of the Plan: Chinese Economic Reform, 1978–1993*. Cambridge: Cambridge University Press.

Pines, Yuri (2017). Confucius' Elitism: The Concepts of junzi and xiaoren Revisited. In Paul R. Goldin (ed.), *A Concise Companion to Confucius*, 164–84. Hoboken: John Wiley & Sons, Ltd.

Rickett, W. Allyn (2021). *Guanzi: Political, Economic, and Philosophical Essays from Early China*. Princeton: Princeton University Press.

Ritter, Joachim (2004). Person and Property in Hegel's Philosophy of Right (§§ 34–81). In Robert B. Pippin and Otfried Höffe (eds.) and Nicholas Walker (trans.). *Hegel on Ethics and Politics* (1st ed.), 101–23. Cambridge: Cambridge University Press.

Rutt, Richard (1996). *Zhouyi: The Book of Changes a New Translation With Commentary* (Annotated edition). London: Routledge.

Sheng, Hong (1996). 关于中国市场化改革的过渡过程的研究 [A study on the transition process of market-oriented reforms in China]. 经济研究 *[Jingji Yanjiu / Economic Reaserch Journal]*, 1.

Sheng, Hong (2010). *Wei wan shi kai taiping [Creating Peace Forever]: Yi ge jingji xuejia dui wenming wenti de sikao [An economist's thoughts on civilisation]*. Zhongguo fazhan chubanshe.

Tsinghua University Website. (n.d.). 政府与市场经济学国际学会成立大会暨首届政府与市场经济学国际年会 *[Inaugural Conference of the Society for the Analysis of Government and Economics and the First Annual International Conference on Government and Market Economics]*. 27.03.2023, https://www.tsinghua.edu.cn/info/1181/35206.htm.

Von Glahn, Richard (2016). *The Economic History of China: From Antiquity to the Nineteenth Century*. Cambridge: Cambridge University Press.

Warner, Malcolm (2017). *The Diffusion of Western Economic Ideas in East Asia*. London: Routledge/Taylor & Francis Group.

Weber, Isabella (2021). *How China Escaped Shock Therapy: the Market Reform Debate*. Abingdon, Oxon; New York, N.Y: Routledge.

Weber, Max (1968). *The Religion of China: Confucianism and Taoism*. Los Angeles: The Free Press.

Xi, Jinping (n.d.-a). *Chair's Statement of the High-level Dialogue on Global Development*. 27.03.2023 https://language.chinadaily.com.cn/a/202206/28/WS62babbdca310fd2b29e6913d.html.

Xi, Jinping (n.d.-b). 习近平主持中央政治局第二十八次集体学习并讲话 *[Speech at the Twenty-eighth Group Study of the Political Bureau of the 18th Central Committee]*. 27.03.2023 http://www.gov.cn/xinwen/2021-02/27/content_5589187.htm.

Xi, Jinping (2014). 摆脱贫困 *[Baituo pinkun]*. 福州:福建人民出版社 [Fuzhou: fujian renmin chubanshe].

Xi Jinping (2022). Full Text of Xi Jinping's Speech at China's Party Congress. (2022, October 18). *Bloomberg.Com*. 27.03.2023 https://www.bloomberg.com/news/articles/2022-10-18/full-text-of-xi-jinping-s-speech-at-china-20th-party-congress-2022.

Yao, Yang (2018, August 16). 准确把握现代化经济体系的内涵 [An accurate grasp of the meaning of a modernised economic system]. 经济日报 *[Economic Daily]*. 27.03.2023 http://views.ce.cn/view/ent/201808/16/t20180816_30042061.shtml

Yü, Ying-shih (2021). *The Religious Ethic and Mercantile Spirit in Early Modern China*. Ed. Hoyt C. Tillman (Yim-tze Kwong, trans.). New York: Columbia University Press.

Zanasi, Margherta (2020). *Economic Thought in Modern China: Market and Consumption, c.1500–1937*. Cambridge: Cambridge University Press.

Zhang, Shuguang (2018). 中国经济学风云史: 经济研究所60年 *[A History of Chinese Economics: 60 Years of the Institute of Economic Research]*. Singapore: Ba fang wen hua chuang zuo shi.

Zhao, Dingxin (2015). *The Confucian-Legalist State: A New Theory of Chinese History*. Oxford: Oxford University Press.

中国社会科学院"新自由主义研究"课题组 [Research Group on Neoliberalism, Chinese Academy of Social Sciences] (2003). 新自由主义研究 [Research on Neo-Liberalism /

xin ziyou zhuyi yanjiu]. 马克思主义研究 [*Studies on Marxism / Makesi Zhuyi Yanjiu*], 6, 18–31.

Triumphant Utopia—Shabby Bourgeois World—Totalitarianism: Transmuting visions of real existing socialism in Eastern interpretations of Walter Benjamin's Marxism[1]

Gábor Gángó

1. Introduction

This chapter deals with different interpretations of Walter Benjamin's Marxism in the early 1970s in two countries of the Soviet Bloc: East Germany and Hungary. Both were a polemical consequence of the rediscovery of Walter Benjamin in West Germany from the 1950s onwards, with the re-edition and simultaneous interpretation of his life's work according to the interests of the Frankfurt School. The whole enterprise—editorial work on his texts and his correspondence (Benjamin 1955; 1966), a (re-)situating of Benjamin's biography as part of the hagiography of the Frankfurt School (*Über Walter Benjamin* 1968), and, last but not least, a general evaluation of his thought—revolved around a central, highly controversial issue: Benjamin's approach to Marxism in the 1920s. What was the extent, depth, and scope of this turn? What causes led to this decision? What consequences did this shift have in terms of the unity of Benjamin's thought? These questions, and the Frankfurt School's original response to them, triggered an internal West German debate in the late 1960s to which scholars east of the Iron Curtain also made their own contributions. Possessing manuscripts unknown to the Frankfurt School, East German literary historians advocated Benjamin's fully accomplished Marxist turn. This position, although in a state of de-contextualised sterility, was

---

1 © The author/s 2023, published by Campus Verlag, Open Access: CC BY-SA 4.0
Bettina Hollstein, Hartmut Rosa, Jörg Rüpke (eds.), "Weltbeziehung"
DOI: 10.12907/978-3-593-45587-7_009

adopted by the "official" Marxist reception in Hungary in the text edition by Dénes Zoltai (Benjamin 1969) and Éva Ancsel's short book (1982). But that was not all. A Hungarian aesthetician and philosopher belonging to the Budapest School, Sándor Radnóti, also contributed to the debate between the Frankfurt School and the review *alternative* with a book *Credo and resignation: An aesthetical-political study of Walter Benjamin* (in Hungarian) in 1974, trying to find a third way between the appropriation efforts of the Frankfurt School and the orthodox Marxist-Leninist interpretation of official cultural politics in Hungary and the GDR and arguing for a pluralist-revisionist, democratic socialist agenda with Benjamin at hand.[2] The publication of the manuscript in its entirety proved impossible in the Hungary of the 1970s. Some of its chapters were published in English in various forums of the New Left between 1975 and 1983 (Radnóti 1975; 1977; 1978 republished in 2005 (quoted here); 1981a; 1981b; 1983–84, republished in 1989). The complete manuscript, with the author's retrospective remarks, came out in Hungarian as late as 1999 (Radnóti 1999a and 1999b).

This hitherto unanalysed position invites a comparative study between different interpretations of Walter Benjamin's Marxism in the Soviet Bloc. By establishing the similarities between the East German reception and Radnóti's, such as the enumeration of a (different) set of motives leading to Benjamin's Marxist conversion and laying emphasis on the texts written after the Marxist turn, I highlight the causes of the differences between them. The first cause is Radnóti's culturally conditioned relations to his world (*Weltbeziehungen*[3]), seeing it neither as an imposed totalitarianism from outside nor as a triumphantly incarnate Marxist utopia. Rather, he saw it as a bourgeois world, though a "shabbier" one than the one in the West. Second, unlike in the GDR, Marxism had another function in Hungary. Besides serving as the official ideological superstructure of the political system, it also undertook (at least from the young Georg Lukács' time on) the function of a non-existent bourgeois critique of capitalist modernity. This function was cross-class and not necessarily interlinked with communist implications. Radnóti's intellectual constellation was soon blurred by the anti-communist turn of the émigré

---

2 For the term revisionism as "the restoration of a measure (optimistically a full system) of pluralism," see Fehér and Heller 1987b, 40. I thank Sándor Radnóti for his remarks and suggestions on the first draft of this chapter.
3 In the sense of Hartmut Rosa's theory (Rosa 2012).

members of the Budapest School and their adherence to the New Left, which also resulted in the "Frankfurtisation" of their interpretation of Benjamin. As a contribution to the inner dialogues of Marxism and a case study for "comparative reception history" *(vergleichende Rezeptionsgeschichte)*, my contribution highlights the different circumstances and hermeneutical strategies that determined the diverging interpretations of the same segment of Benjamin's work (Dornheim 1987; Curtis 1997). The polemical or confraternal cross-views among the protagonists of this story had already been established in the secondary literature: the attacks of the West German New Left review *alternative* of the Frankfurt School; the alliance between East German literary scholars—above all, Rosemarie Heise—and the editor of the *alternative*, Hildegard Brunner, in this polemic; and the reiteration of the accusations by East German editors of Benjamin's Marxist works in the early 1970s (Bathrick 1979; Garber 1987, 121–93; Albrecht et al. 2000, 349–67; Neuffer 2021, especially 134 ff.; 182 ff.).

In this chapter, I first offer a reconstruction of Radnóti's position between what he considered the two "extremes" of dealing with Benjamin's Marxism: the strategies of the Frankfurt School and the review *alternative*.[4] Second, and perhaps more importantly, I provide a comparative analysis of those two remaining interpretations which were not connected by cross-views: that of East German scholarship and Radnóti. My critical comparison emphasises the context-dependent differences between two positions that had a number of similar circumstantial elements. I shall prove that the similarities derive from their shared genealogy (Griffiths 2017, 2), i.e., their dialogue position with the internal West German debate. The similarities of the orthodox Marxist interpretation in Hungary and East Germany show the common patterns of Marxism as a state ideology. The specific difference in Radnóti's approach that opens up new interpretive vistas is his interpretation of Marxism as a substitute for the bourgeois critique of modernity. These differences invite the revision of some generalisations in theory building related to the cultures in the "totalitarian" states of the Soviet Bloc, first and foremost, seeing these countries as thoroughly totalitarian.

---

4 As Radnóti wrote in a passage in chapter 3 (Benjamin's politics) omitted in the English version: "Beyond the philological polemic with the editions of Benjamin by Adorno, Scholem, and Tiedemann, the complete neglect of the so-called 'theological-speculative' early works is to be found as another extreme of Benjamin's evaluations (cf. the special issues of the review *alternative* on Benjamin: no I (October–December 1967), and no II (April–June 1968)" (Radnóti 1999a, 207, n. 155).

Third, my contribution reconstructs the dissemination and reception of Radnóti's work in English-speaking scholarship. This analysis also addresses an apparent categorical tension in the comparative research. While other protagonists are seen as institutionalised actors behind the positions to be compared (the Frankfurt School, the review *alternative*, and East German Benjamin scholarship), Radnóti's interpretation is presented as an individual strategy. In this part, I explain why there was no uniform pattern of dealing with Benjamin's Marxism in the Budapest School. Radnóti's interpretation coincided with the internal crisis of the Budapest School in Hungary and testifies to his personal efforts to find his own revisionist Marxist position. The émigré members of the Budapest School reconfigured themselves not as a Marxist but as a "Marxisant" group, and they directed their efforts at demolishing East European "totalitarianism." Given this basis, their interpretation of Benjamin was in harmony with that of the Frankfurt School and, accordingly, at odds with Radnóti's original intentions. The presentation of some isolated chapters from Radnóti's original manuscript a decade or so later as creations of an institutional agent (the Budapest School) required their radical re-contextualisation. While taking the categorical differences of agency into consideration, the causes for differences of the dependent variable (i.e., the interpretations of Benjamin's Marxism) are indicated in this transnational comparison not as subjective, individual motives but objectively existing structural preconditions. In the conclusion, I formulate some critical suggestions with regard to generalisations and theory building in comparative historical research in post-World War II Eastern Europe.[5]

The cases analysed here seem to comprise the complete set of relevant instances. Benjamin's reception in Eastern Europe before and after 1989 was wide-ranging and "tumultuous." His works inspired scholarly and artistic works outside the official sphere of cultural politics in the most varied ways. Still, it seems that the polemics with the Frankfurt School about Benjamin's Marxism during the early 1970s in the Soviet Bloc is characteristic of East Germany and Hungary exclusively. Parallel tendencies in revisionist thought and a simultaneous translation and edition practice can be found in connec-

---

5 Regarding the methodology, I draw on Mahorney and Rueschemeyer 2003a, especially Mahorney and Rueschemeyer 2003b, and, following their lead, Skocpol and Somers 1980; Skocpol 1984; Schutt 2006.

tion with the Praxis Group in Yugoslavia, i.e., within the "socialist world" but outside the Soviet Bloc.[6]

2. Walter Benjamin's reception in Germany, West and East

Adorno's interpretation of Benjamin "as a philosopher of culture within the theoretical framework of the Frankfurt school" (Bathrick 1979, 247) posed a challenge in West Germany. The most controversial element in Adorno's appropriation of Benjamin touched upon Benjamin's Marxism and its relations to the *Institut für Sozialforschung*. Helmut Heißenbüttel and Hannah Arendt formulated their criticism in connection with them: Adorno cancelled the Marxist-materialist side of Benjamin's thought, marginalising his later oeuvre and relativising his friendship with Brecht. This was followed by the attack from the left, based on the co-operation between the editor of *alternative*, Hildegard Brenner, and Benjamin's editor in East Germany, Rosemarie Heise. On the basis of the Potsdam manuscripts, they accused Adorno of altering Benjamin's texts in order to modify the latter's Marxism (Albrecht et al. 2000, 351–53; Pursche n. d.).

In the East, the claim for Benjamin's appropriation was based on the exclusively East German source base of Benjamin scholarship, i.e., his manuscript on Baudelaire, and other documents which, as is well known, were taken by the Gestapo in Paris, then brought from Upper Silesia to the Soviet Union by the Red Army and given back to the GDR in 1957 (Heise 1971, 10). Both editions of Benjamin's works in the GDR, *Lesezeichen* (1970) and *Das Paris des Second Empire bei Baudelaire* (1971), supported the polemic stance against Adorno and advocated Benjamin's close intellectual and ideological affinities with Bertolt Brecht. The position attributed to Benjamin in the GDR was, in Rosemarie Heise's (1971, 10) formulation, that both he and Brecht argued for the "necessary social revolution [...] the decisive role of

---

6 According to a first overview made by the international conference *Walter Benjamin in the East: Networks, conflicts, and reception* (Leibniz-Zentrum für Kultur- und Literaturforschung, 7–9 July 2022, organised by Caroline Adler and Sophia Buck). See the report by Caroline Adler and Sophia Buck in the blog of the *Journal of the history of ideas* (Adler and Buck 2022). For Benjamin's editions in Yugoslavia (and some other East European countries), see https://monoskop.org/Walter_Benjamin 23.12.2022. The present paper is a fully revised and extended version of my lecture "Walter Benjamin and the Budapest School" at this conference.

the proletariat as the subject of history [...] and the historic meaning of the October revolution." This political position was supported by the selection from Benjamin's writings: besides texts on Bertold Brecht, the *Lesezeichen* contains the article entitled "Work of art in the age of mechanical reproduction," in which Benjamin comes close to a Marxist aesthetics (Bathrick 1979, 249–50).

The East German Brecht scholar Gerhard Seidel (1970b, 7) claimed in the preface to the *Lesezeichen* that the only available centre for Benjamin's philology was in East Germany. Rosemarie Heise's preface to the Baudelaire work put into relief the differences between Benjamin and the Frankfurt School, as well as the personal tensions between Adorno and Benjamin. She pushed those texts into the foreground, which made these contrasts apparent. According to her reconstruction, Benjamin was inclined towards Marxism, while Adorno wanted to discourage and distract him. Letters in the Potsdam *Nachlass* should make this super-ego relationship manifest, as if Adorno knew Benjamin's real intentions better than Benjamin himself did (Heise 1971, 18; cf. Wiggershaus and Robertson 1994, 191)[7] and the Institute for Social Research in Frankfurt was Benjamin's superior and therefore his attachment to Marxism was the outcome of an emancipation process from this abusive relationship. Hence, the retrospective appropriation is nothing less than the continuation of the pressure on his worldview exerted by the Frankfurt School. Adorno was accused by Heise of falsifying Benjamin's words and eliminating the differences between him and Benjamin. These claims were based on editorial modifications on Benjamin's texts. For example, the edition of the correspondence omitted passages referring to Benjamin's Marxism and the contemporary discussions of his changing perspective (Albrecht et al. 2000, 361). In this sense, the archive in Frankfurt is, according to Seidel (1970b, 7–8), the continuator of Adorno's falsifications. Based on these modified texts, the Frankfurt interpretation of Benjamin's thought was manipulative, aiming at the dissimulation of its "progressive development" (Seidel 1970a, 427).

This was the debate to which Radnóti wanted to contribute. In the footnotes to the introductory passages to his article "Benjamin's politics," Radnóti makes it clear that the polemics between the Frankfurt School and the circle of the review *alternative* constitute the context of his approach: "Such a

---

7 For Benjamin's influence on Adorno, see Davis 1975, and, above all, Lunn 1982, Part three: Benjamin and Adorno, with a comprehensive bibliography on pages 302–03.

conclusion [i.e., Scholem's position] is as unacceptable as the view that, after his turn, Benjamin cannot be considered a philosopher" (Radnóti 2005, 337). He added in footnotes:

"Hannah Arendt raised this possibility in her essay on Benjamin. [...] Hildegard Brenner embraces this notion and stresses the historical as against the philosophical character of Benjamin's work. [...] The *sole* common ground between the two interpretations is in the sharply critical assessment of the Frankfurt School's picture of Benjamin." (Radnóti 2005, 352, n. 1)

From this perspective, the book *Zur Aktualität Walter Benjamins* (Unseld 1972) can be seen as reinforcing the positions of the Frankfurt School after the polemic. The book on Benjamin's "timeliness" was centred around Jürgen Habermas' study, to which the others provided a pregnant context (Habermas 1972; republished in English in 2005). But this undertone conveyed a strong message. Its contributors did not discuss the rival interpretations: on the linguistic level, they stigmatised and discredited the opposite side and denied Benjamin, with reference to his life, the autonomy or authenticity of what he had written. Witnesses to his life reported on Benjamin's Marxist "error" (Kraft, 1972, 68-69), with emphases on his awkward position as a "Marxist rabbi" (Scholem 1972, 88). Even the appraisal of Habermas as an "unbiased" interpreter (ibid., 129) communicated the message that Benjamin was constantly being judged and that the verdict concentrated on the evaluation of his Marxist turn.

As to Radnóti's other contexts, there was a socio-political context around 1974 for the Hungarian manuscript (of which a chapter or two were published at that time) and a scholarly context for the chapters scattered in forums of Benjamin scholarship with a considerable delay but still before the collapse of the Soviet world. This latter was channelled into the anti-totalitarian and anti-communist worldview which determined how the Budapest School viewed Benjamin. The contextual field of Radnóti's manuscript in Hungary includes events such as Georg Lukács' death in 1971 and the dissolution of the original community of his disciples' intention and action (the Budapest School) and their re-orientation both philosophically and politically. In political terms, these years saw the crackdown on dissidents and revisionists in Eastern Europe, in Hungary as well, after the left-wing movements in 1968 in the West and the East. In 1973, the process against the philosophers dispersed the Budapest School (Pickle and Rundell 2018; Beilharz 2018). Finally,

Radnóti's book is inseparable from the early history of the edition of some of Walter Benjamin's writings in Hungary.

As Radnóti writes in his recollections about the genesis of the manuscript: "At the end of the 1960s and the beginning of the 1970s, each member of this circle [i.e., the Budapest School] privately saw the common intellectual structure wobble" (Radnóti 1999b, 193). Lukács' late aesthetics turned Radnóti's attention directly to Benjamin:

"I learned Walter Benjamin's name from Lukács' aesthetics, where it is cited in a polemical context. [...] Perhaps it was Benjamin's *voice* that impressed me first; a voice that was so different from that of the old Lukács and so close to the young one." (Ibid., 195)

The Budapest School cultivated a continuous internal dialogue, the community saw itself as a closed interpretive community. Radnóti was also keen on documenting that he wrote his book on Benjamin to his "friends" (Radnóti 1999a, 5). His political objectives were specifically East European: the establishment of democratic socialism with an emphasis on the word "democratic." This objective should be seen against the backdrop of the recurrent thesis in the writings of the Budapest School that they borrowed from the dissident intellectual György Konrád, namely, that the transition to democratic capitalism (i.e., bourgeois democracy) from communism seemed impossible in Hungary. In other words, the basic dilemma touched upon the possible alternative to communism. Due to the consolidation of János Kádár's system after the political crackdown following the 1956 revolution, the intellectuals' default position was that the existing system had no alternative. The year 1968, however, saw events both in the West and in Czechoslovakia which indicated that time had not frozen for the countries of the Soviet Bloc either. Because bourgeois democracy, built upon and managed on the economic basis of capitalism, was anything but a trivial alternative for intellectuals who were critical of the existing regime, seeking alternatives became not only possible for leftist intellectuals but also necessary.

Dénes Zoltai's 1969 selection, *Commentary and prophecy* (Benjamin 1969), is similar to the editions in the GDR, although it preceded its East German counterparts by a year or two. Based on Benjamin's writings on Brecht and his study on the work of art in the age of technical reproducibility, Zoltai offered a reading of the leftist revolutionary Benjamin. In his opinion, Benjamin's study of the reproducibility of works of art reveals that the author belonged to the "Anti-Fascist Left" (Zoltai 1969, 20). He added: "True, he [Benjamin] stayed outside the Party until the end of his life. But it was also true that, as a freelance intellectual, he advocated the cause of communism and remained faithful to his decision until the very end" (ibid., 8).

As the editor, Dénes Zoltai, was himself one of Lukács' disciples, the edition can be seen as the Lukács school's own initiative to start a dialogue with Benjamin. Therefore, Benjamin's fate in Hungary, from the revolutionary leftist interpretation through Sándor Radnóti's attempt at an exposition of his work in the theoretical context of a democratic socialist alternative to approaches to Benjamin in conformity with the Frankfurt School, appears to be an internal debate or development within the Budapest School. This shift was accomplished within a decade. In the 1980 edition of Benjamin's works in Hungarian, *Angelus novus*, edited by Radnóti, the accompanying study penned by the sociologist Zsolt Papp did situate Benjamin in the context of the Frankfurt School (Benjamin 1980).

An answer to this challenge that conformed to the system arrived from outside the Budapest School in 1982 in the form of Éva Ancsel's essay, *Polemic with history: An essay on Walter Benjamin*. In this book published by the official publisher of the communist party, she portrayed Benjamin as a left-wing writer whose thought aligned with real existing socialism. According to Ancsel, "the attraction of Marxism prevailed most in Benjamin's thought" (Ancsel 1982, 24), who was connected to Marxism "by his political conviction, his left-wing orientation without quotation marks. In his left-wing position, he was incorruptible. He regarded history clearly as a class struggle between oppressors and oppressed" (ibid., 33). Ancsel's reading aimed to demonstrate this thesis across the entirety of Benjamin's work.

3. Walter Benjamin's contrasting interpretations in the Soviet Bloc: A comparison

The strategy of both the East German Benjamin scholars and Radnóti was the same: to reclaim Benjamin from the Frankfurt School. According to the Eastern reading, Benjamin's accomplished Marxist turn was beyond question. Hence, the task of the interpreter consisted in the reconstruction of "the process of this left bourgeois thinker's approach to Marxism" (Seidel 1970b, 8). The Marxist turn went hand in hand with overall intellectual progress in Benjamin: his prose improved as he approached the workers' movement in the 1920s (Seidel 1970a, 421). Discussion is fruitful only in relation to its motivation: meeting with "actual communism" (Heise 1971, 7; Seidel 1970a, 421) in the person of Asja Lacis, Brecht's influence, Benjamin's journey to the Soviet Union, and his own proletarification. Tellingly, Lukács is not mentioned as he was anathema in the GDR.[8]

Radnóti's interpretation offered a coherent solution to the puzzle. Unlike East German scholarship, he did not turn Benjamin into an orthodox Marxist. According to Radnóti, Benjamin followed Lukács' Marxist shift but did so in a "better" way insofar as he did not take up what had by then become a discredited political practice.[9] Benjamin diagnosed the error of modernity in the idiom of Marxism. Real existing socialism was, as Radnóti held, not an answer to this error, a going beyond it, or a totalitarian strike against it. It was the very consequence, symptom, and petrification of this error.

The differences reveal that the readings were in the service of divergent political visions. Scholars in East Germany advocated the perspective of existing socialism, and Radnóti the alternative of democratic socialism. Radnóti did not build a utopian image of Benjamin but a critical one based on Eastern sources and categories. In East Germany, only the later texts from Benjamin's oeuvre were examined, whereas Radnóti relied on Benjamin's entire life's work. The main cause of East German resentment consisted in the falsification of the "bourgeois leftist" Benjamin by the Frankfurt School; Radnóti's resentment was nourished by its neglect of Lukács. He considered it as his task "to unveil Lukács' fundamental impact on Benjamin, and, on a given occasion, on the Frankfurt School as well" (Radnóti 1999b, 195). On another occasion, he lamented that "[t]his student of Adorno [i.e., Rolf Tiedemann] is so loyal to that dubious tradition of the Frankfurt School that he does not even mention the theoretical foundation of his critique: Lukács' study of reification" (Radnóti 2005, 353, n. 3). To prove the opposite, he cites Benjamin's letter to Gershom Scholem on 16 September 1924 from Capri, emphasising praxis from his reading of *History and class consciousness* (Radnóti 2005, 338).

Benjamin's separation from the Frankfurt School seemed necessary, just due to their different attitudes towards action:

"The ought, by contrast, is either filled with religious elements, or else it is preserved within a solitary ethos as no longer realizable values. The path of the Frankfurt School leads in this

---

8 On revisionist philosophy in the GDR, see Kapferer 1990, Introduction, and Maffeis 2007, 105–11.
9 For Benjamin's "independence from party politics," see Müller-Doohm 2009, 137.

second direction. Benjamin, popular opinion to the contrary, does not belong with them." (Ibid., 348)

It follows from this that the difference is not a theoretical one. The fact that the Frankfurt School modified Benjamin's texts proves, in Radnóti's eyes, no more and no less than their diverging positions:

"It is evident from the editorial refinements which Horkheimer performed on Benjamin's *Reproduction* essay before its publication that his standpoint was not in agreement with the Frankfurt School. The whole first chapter fell victim to this refinement; fascism was everywhere replaced with the category of totalitarianism, etc." (Ibid., 349, with reference to Gallas 1968, 76 ff.)

Radnóti drew a parallel between his own historical situation and that of Benjamin's, whose Marxist moment was characterised by the search for alternatives in the wake of the "renaissance" of Marxism in the 1920s, when the established Marxism-Leninism robbed the alternatives of "proof of the existing movement" (Radnóti 1999a, 8). His moment is the political crackdown after the 1968 Marxist renaissance when an aesthetic alternative had to be advocated without the support of ongoing political movements. For Radnóti, it was clear that the Frankfurt School's interpretation of Benjamin denied this alternative, both retrospectively and in reference to its own period. His reading of Benjamin's Marxism goes against Adorno's (and is in line with Habermas') interpretation, seeing it not as a "deficient" Marxism but as a critique of Marx. In other words, it codes the revisionism in Benjamin's approach:

"The emancipatory turn to a critique of society, the choice in values favoring communal culture, the turning away from the purely theoretical sphere, and the insight into the necessity of social activism led Benjamin to Marx; but in such a way that his position is sometimes called a deficient Marx-reception (this was the aim of Adorno's critique), and sometimes a Marx-critique. The decisive point where Benjamin's philosophy of history deviates from the Marxian one is the problem of communities. In Benjamin's view, the bourgeois world is not a society without communities, but a world of the open, plural communities embedded in many different traditions (pluralism is coded in communal culture, even from Marxist point of view); a world which is not transcended but depraved by the tendency of commodity production to universalize the market, to atomize the individual and to destroy tradition." (Radnóti 1983–84, 182–83)

He recast Benjamin's political objectives in the "democratic revolutionary transformation"—i.e., Benjamin was driven to Marxism by political goals—it was a motivation from within, not a decision triggered by external circumstances. While accepting Adorno's judgment that this turn was not beneficial for the coherence of his work, he rejected Gershom Scholem's accusation that Benjamin "was forcing an alien language on himself" (Radnóti 2005, 337).

Radnóti reused Benjamin's texts published in East Germany, which were thought to endorse an orthodox Marxist-Leninist position, in the interest of the revision of this very position. He held the communal culture to be the vehicle of revision, change, or alternatives. In connection with this, his regard focused not on the lack of pluralism in the political system but on the more stratified complex of the communal culture, which preserved its (pluralistic) bourgeois characteristics in many respects. The existing socialism does not create the communal culture but leaves latitude for action aiming at the development of these pluralistic structures (Radnóti 1999a, 69).

As Eugene Lunn wrote, the Marxist turn in Benjamin (and Adorno) was preceded by an *"aesthetic* revolt against bourgeois society and traditional cultural life" (Lunn 1982, 178). That aspect of Benjamin's philosophy proved to be particularly inspiring to Radnóti:

"As is known, Benjamin transferred liberation to messianic perspectives. That is, because he regarded every community of the bourgeois era as depraved and in a state of *rigor mortis*—just as, on the other hand, because of messianic hope with holds every existing thing in existential insecurity, he considered everything to be provisional—these communities are only evidence derivable from the truth content of cultural products, of works of art. From the point of view of aesthetics this meant the transcendence of the strict distance between art and life." (Radnóti 1983–84, 183)

In his essay on Ferenc Fehér, Radnóti did claim that it seemed possible to transcend the bourgeois world in the field of aesthetics:

"Aesthetics had a special place within 20th-century Marxism, and many of its most significant figures were aesthetics, including Lukács but also Ernst Bloch, Theodor Adorno, and Walter Benjamin. There may have been structural reasons for this as well. As opposed to the particularism of class struggle, whose promised fruits were all in the distant future, the idea of high culture promised riches that were already tangible in the arts, which had been accumulating since the distant past: man's inheritance to make his own." (Radnóti 2018, 55)

Communal culture denies total subordination and may contribute to its suppression:

"All politics are based on power and interest structures and bring such structures into existence. Yet, politics embodies certain moments, e.g., movement, action, community and publicity which may be subordinated to the previously-mentioned structures but their total subordination is not necessary and they may hope to gradually put an end to that subordination." (Radnóti 2005, 342)

Radnóti intended to base his reading on the impact that Ernst Bloch and Lukács made on Benjamin—the religious experience through Bloch and the praxis-based reading of *History and class consciousness* (Radnóti 1999a, 13–14). In fact, the result was rather something of the opposite: reading the young Lukács from the perspectives opened up by Benjamin, that is, retrieving the possible alternatives in the young Lukács, beyond Lukács' orthodox dialectical materialism after his communist turn. And it was to seek a common philosophical ground for the young and the mature Lukács: "A common ultimate foundation for both philosophies is the rejection of the existing world, not a rejection in an indirect and apologetic way, and the necessity of transcending this world" (ibid., 25).

With reference to Paul Nizan's novel *The conspiracy*, Radnóti argues for a resonance scenario borrowed from humanist communism: "Within that integration, the sacrifice to party discipline is experienced as liberation from the 'freedom' of bourgeois isolation" (Radnóti 2005, 349–50). As he quotes from the novel: "[The communist's] ambition is to be a whole man. [...] Because we are not living for occasional little truths but for a complete, all-embracing relationship with other human beings" (ibid., 350).

According to Radnóti's observation, the inspiring sources of Benjamin's Marxist turn were closely connected to praxis and therefore determined Benjamin's approach as well:

"The ethical bases of Benjamin's turn to Marxism are symbolized in the two encounters that initiated the chain reaction: Lacisz Aszja, a Bolshevik woman, and Lukács' *History and Class Consciousness*. Both are examples of political action." (Ibid., 338)

With this claim, Radnóti not only offered a more plausible motivation for Benjamin's Marxist turn than the proletarisation of the biographical Benjamin but also deduced speculative consequences from a chronological argument. Benjamin, so Radnóti, became Marxist when it became definitive that the world revolution would not take place: "The question is: why does Benjamin's engagement come so late and, if there is no longer a revolutionary alternative, then why politics?" (ibid., 340).

Sándor Radnóti's fundamental insight was nothing less than that the consolidated regime of János Kádár, which was in fact a one-party political dictatorship, was experienced by people living in it not as totalitarianism but as a distorted bourgeois culture and way of life. When Radnóti put the communal culture in the foreground, it manifested itself as a shabby bourgeois way of life. As his postscript to the 1999 edition recollected:

"My work belonged to the modest rear-guard actions of the renaissance and revision of Marxism. My perspective was anti-capitalist, directed at the—so we said it at that time—transcending of the bourgeois world condition, to a new societal community, democratic socialism. To this, I found or sought no starting point whatsoever in the 'real existing' socialism that I believed to be a more disagreeable and shabby bourgeois system than bourgeois democracies. The radical denial of the existing socialism concerned, theoretically, both of them." (Radnóti 1999b, 196)

In this sense, Benjamin can contribute to an alternative. In contrast to totalitarian regimes, the distorted bourgeois way of life and culture does have, at least as a thought experiment, an alternative. In other words, while communism, at least on the level of intention, was supposed to be a new beginning erasing the past and as such a "uniform" experiment, when alternatives open up in post-communist Eastern Europe, each country, as a distinct national culture, stands alone confronted with its past. This is how Radnóti understands Benjamin's study on German tragic drama:

"It is a vision of future full of resignation which drives Benjamin to the interpretation of German tragic drama. The result of the interpretation is a great revision of what *is*, i.e., the bourgeois life. Later, as his left-wing turn matches the 'is' with the 'ought,' [...] the programme remains the same: the bourgeois life has to be scrutinized, the history of the present in order to understand the present; whatever this history is, the future becomes only from it." (Radnóti 1999a, 55–56)

The concept of an alternative is anchored in that of the worldview *(Weltanschauung)*, whereas the worldview in turn is anchored in the undeletable and inalienable historical facticity of art works. This entails the paramount role of aesthetics in philosophical investigations into political alternatives. The artwork provokes or creates a worldview. This is fundamental for the community and for a communicable aesthetic judgment and, hence, for action—consequently, for alternative political action as well.

According to the underlying assumptions of Radnóti's theory, the cultural superstructure in real existing socialism is not merely a more broadly conceived state propaganda that provokes "dissident thought" as its opposite. Bourgeois culture has always been present as the residue of the old bourgeois system. One of Lukács' basic insights in 1919, which prompted him to analyse the proletarian consciousness, was that the culture of the Hungarian Soviet Republic basically remained a bourgeois one. Radnóti's account of Hungarian poets who shaped his thought confirms this truth in the post-World War II context. His "gods" in Hungarian literature were thoroughly *bürgerlich* figures: János Pilinszky, Sándor Weöres, Dezső Tandori, and György Petri (Radnóti 1999b, 194). All this was compatible with Marxism, thanks to the other preliminary assumption of Radnóti's revisionist reading. Besides functioning as the official *dialmat*, Marxism was also present in Hungary, as well as in some other countries of the Soviet Bloc, as a critical theory (of culture). This bifurcation resulted from the non-existence of an autochtonous bourgeois critique of modernity. In East-Central Europe, Marxism was, in this sense, the only way to grasp modernity intellectually beyond the unqualified affirmation of "progress."[10] Lukács and his Sunday circle was, before his communist conversion, virtually the only representative of the bourgeois critique of culture as a marginalised counter-current which vanished after 1919 due to political repression and the emigration of its members. Lukács' communist turn accomplished this process through a theoretical self-elimination of this alternative.

Hence, for those with Marxism as their intellectual native language (as Radnóti confessed of himself), Marxist categories and its vocabulary offered the natural and mostly only way of reasoning about society and politics. The nature, depth, or authenticity of Benjamin's Marxism could be a matter of discussion: the essential thing was the *idiom* used by Benjamin which provided access to his whole life's work. This was exactly what West German interpreters denied or tried to prove the invalidity of. This was not possible in the GDR, where a definitive break with the bourgeois tradition provided one of the ideological mainstays of its very existence.[11]

4. Walter Benjamin and the Budapest School

On the international scene, Radnóti was seen as "the youngest member of the Budapest School" (Smith 1983–84, viii). This institutionalisation of his interpretation of Benjamin resulted in its radical re-contextualisation.

The fate of the texts of the Budapest School was different in the West and in the East (in Hungary), in English and in Hungarian respectively. In

---

10 For this notion, see Achim Kemmerling's chapter in this volume.
11 Recent research shows, however, the presence of bourgeois tradition, especially in the life projections of aesthetic forms. See, for example, Max 2018.

the West, they mirror a consequently cultivated image of a community of friendship and solidarity manifested in, among other things, the fact that the School's members who had emigrated to the West provided publication opportunities also for the members of the so-called Lukács kindergarten who did not leave Hungary. The émigrés were integrated into the discourse of the New Left. In emigration, they identified themselves as political dissidents, and a considerable part of their work consisted in the critique of the East European communist political systems which they viewed as dictatorship and totalitarianism. Totalitarianism, according to Fehér and Heller, is "a state in which pluralism is outlawed" (Fehér and Heller 1987a, 49). Heller (1987), though she differentiated between totalitarian systems in a fictive foreword to Hannah Arendt, left the crucial point of Arendt's theory considering East European regimes as a kind of totalitarianism untouched.[12]

By the time their Western works were published in Hungarian after the fall of the Berlin Wall, the context of their texts was their own work in its entirety rather than the original political and intellectual context which had ceased to exist. To this new context belonged the language and political position of their early, orthodox Marxist-Leninist, period, invisible in the West on the one hand and the individual creative periods after 1989 on the other. This simultaneous appearance of the different chronological layers of their career generated tensions in the big picture, which provoked retrospective, autobiographical, and self-interpretative texts subservient to the self-documentation of the history of the Budapest School. As an element of this post-1989 constellation, Radnóti's book on Walter Benjamin, written in the early 1970s, was published in its entirety in the Hungarian language in 1999.

Radnóti's orientation towards democratic socialism was, of course, not unique in the Budapest School. In *Dictatorship over needs* (Fehér, Heller, and Márkus 1983), Ágnes Heller, Ferenc Fehér, and György Márkus also advocated the prospect of democratic socialism and the impossibility of the democratic capitalist restoration. What is unique was the connections to Walter Benjamin in theorising about the possibilities of democratic socialism in connection with the initial position from which they wanted to arrive at democratic socialism. The difference between Radnóti and the authors of *Dictatorship over needs* lies in their position concerning the real nature of "existing" socialism. Consulting US-American literature on Kremlinology and focusing on the Soviet Union, they defined the system through its oppressive,

---

12 For Hannah Arendt, see Andreas Pettenkofer's chapter in this volume, pp. 66–70.

terrorist measures against society. For Heller and Fehér, the intellectual programme which was derived from the overall theory of communist totalitarianism was the critique of the "system of Yalta" that defined Eastern Europe as the playground of the Great Powers and resulted in its incorporation into the Russian sphere of interest. Their critique was consistent with the international anti-communist propaganda. According to Fehér and Heller's (1987b, 5) politically shaped interpretation, the real existing socialism was a beginning from nothing after a threefold rupture: the "tyranny" of Hitlerism, the pact of the Great Powers in Yalta, and the destruction of the transitory "new democracies" in the East-Central European region between 1945 and 1948. The fourth core member of the Budapest School, Mihály Vajda, who did not participate in this comprehensive analysis of communist systems, made an important, corrective addition in his *Russian socialism in Central Europe*. Vajda (1991) maintained that the only authentic form of existing socialism was its Soviet Russian version. In the other East European countries, however, the system was imposed from above (and from outside); therefore, scrutiny of the communist political system cannot provide any full description of their historical identity.

As for Radnóti's publications on Benjamin in English, there was one single context: that of the Frankfurt School which East European dissident thought aligned with as another intellectual antagonist of East European totalitarianism. This reading was promoted by the Budapest School, whose position no longer allowed a *transition* to democratic socialism—only its establishment from scratch on the ruins of "totalitarianism."

György Márkus' article "Walter Benjamin or the commodity as phantasmagoria" (2001; cf. Ahmadi 2002), which sometimes represents the Budapest School's account of Walter Benjamin, is a debate with a de-Marxised Benjamin on consumer culture and as such belongs with the interpretive trends of the Frankfurt School insofar as the problem of the artwork as commodity was first thematised by Brecht and Adorno. Márkus held that Benjamin had situated himself on a no-man's-land between Brecht, Adorno, and Gershom Scholem (i.e., Márkus denied the plausibility of Benjamin's intellectual decision). Behind Benjamin's attraction to Brecht, Márkus detected fundamental differences between Benjamin and the German dramatist. According to György Márkus' further remarks in his *Language and production: A critique of the paradigms* (1986, 146–47), Benjamin was an "ambiguous" or "warm" (i.e., Western or cultural) Marxist. According to Heller (2011, 11), Benjamin did not consistently follow either the road of messianism or Marxism. In her article on the Frankfurt School, she took an agnostic stance with respect to Walter Benjamin's relations with the Frankfurt School. She held that the changes made by the Frankfurt School were permissible as necessary measures for the "cause" (Heller 2002; 2003, 278)—i.e., hindering any appropriation of Benjamin in the interest of anything which seeks alternatives to the existing political order in Eastern Europe instead of its eradication. The chapter on Benjamin in her *Concept of the beautiful* ("The fragmentation of the concept of the beautiful") (Heller 2012), which begins with a quote from Adorno, is heavily indebted to his theory of the "crisis" of the beautiful (cf. Bathrick 1979, 247–48) during the production (and reproduction) process of high art in modernity. In his study in the volume *Reconstructing aesthetics: Writings of the Budapest School*, published in 1986, Ferenc Fehér (1986, 72) rejected Benjamin's unconditional affirmation of the technological age in his study of reproduction. In the same volume, Sándor Radnóti (1986), with his chapter called "Mass culture" placed Benjamin close to Adorno's circle. Radnóti's (1983) article on Lukács and Bloch also appeared in a volume in which the four core members of the Budapest School published their only joint text, their breakup with Lukács' Marxism (Fehér, Heller, Márkus, and Vajda 1983). His article, "Benjamin's dialectic of art and society" was published in the Benjamin issue of the *Philosophical Forum* in 1983–84, re-issued later as the volume *Benjamin: Philosophy, aesthetics, history* by The University of Chicago Press in 1989, with Gary Smith as editor. Other authors in this volume included Gary Smith, Theodor W. Adorno, Jennifer Todd, Rolf Tiedemann, Richard Wolin, Stéphane Moses, and Leo Löwenthal.

As indicated above, the intervention of the Frankfurt School in Benjamin's texts resulting in the substitution of the word "fascism" by "totalitarianism" is mentioned by Radnóti only in a cursory remark. The fact that this crucial moment went unobserved below his radar shows that it was beyond his imagination to consider East European reality as totalitarianism. As a matter of fact, by this change, the Frankfurt School denied the theoretical possibility of Benjamin's revisionist East European Marxist interpretation. As the émigré members of the Budapest School did start to label East-Central European countries totalitarian states or dictatorships, the revisionist interpretation of Benjamin in the East European context became indeed practically impossible. Scholarship at the Budapest School was more than happy to accept this self-reconfiguration and comfortably situated the whole activity of the Budapest School as a response to an original experience of "totalitarianism." As Jonathan Pickle and John Rundell asserted in their volume on the School: "the Budapest School was [...] framed by their experience of a further *sui generis* Central-East European totalitarianism: soviet communism" (Pickle and Rundell 2018, 1). As Adorno himself viewed National Socialist Germany and the Soviet Union (together with the Soviet bloc) (Lunn 1982, 287) from the same theoretical platform, the adoption of the totalitarianism theory provided the common denominator for the Frankfurt School and the Budapest School to interpret Benjamin's Marxism.

5. Conclusion

My comparison of contexts pointed out the limitations of generalising about the non-pluralistic lifeworld of the countries embracing "real existing socialism." The very existence of Radnóti's manuscript shows the plurality of Benjamin's reception within the Soviet Bloc, and, consequently, it is also indicative of the plurality of the perceptions of this world and the relations to it (*Weltbeziehungen*). My case study invites a reconsideration of the widely accepted thesis in comparative historical analyses of post-World War II Eastern Europe advocating the non-pluralistic uniformity of the countries of the Eastern Bloc and evaluating Marxism as their pure ideological mainstay (Heller and Fehér 1990; Ekiert 1996, 11). In theory building about the extensibility of resonant *Weltbeziehungen* beyond the sphere of value-neutral liberal democracies, the description of the world of real existing socialism as a place of forced or compulsory resonance (Rosa 2019, 457) should be complemented by other forms of *Weltbeziehung* that challenge its existence, not by aiming at its destruction but by "loosening" it by preserved or created forms of pluralism in aesthetically-culturally projected, resonant lifeworlds.

What did it mean to grasp the reality of existing socialism? As the case of the Budapest School shows, the adoption of the perspective of the Frankfurt School eliminated (the possibility of) the internal perspective, thereby marking the beginning of "the transition to capitalism." The adoption of the position of the Frankfurt School in Walter Benjamin's Hungarian reception was a recognition of the fact that there was an alternative, but only one: the transition to capitalism—at the end of an argument whose starting point was just the impossibility of this very transition. This theoretical impasse urges the consideration of other forms of alternative thinking.

Viewed as resistance against totalitarianism, East European history may well prove to be the political weakness of totalitarianism, but it also proves to be the conceptual power of totalitarianism theory in the explanation of historical processes in post-World War II Eastern Europe. According to this explanation model, revolutions and any forms of violence show that there is no alternative but the violent annihilation of the system. But for those who wanted to transcend the world of real existing socialism, (violent) opposition (i.e., the various forms of political resistance, including, first and foremost, the sequence of armed uprisings against the regime) was not the only way. From the perspective of communal culture, there were considerable efforts to seek resonant *Weltbeziehungen*. As this case study shows, the Budapest School contributed significantly to the marginalisation of the latter alternative in intellectual discourse by adopting the totalitarianism theory in historical research on East-Central Europe, with the 1945 Yalta agreement on the future of East-Central Europe, i.e., an externally and violently imposed political system, as the never-changing starting point of their approaches. In contrast, an aesthetic approach enables us to detect culture in East European countries as a variant of bourgeois consciousness through the mediality of literature.

In this alternative, reconciliatory approach to post-World War II East-Central Europe, relationships to the world (*Weltbeziehungen*) should be regarded as horizontally and vertically stratified and distinguished from one another. There is no such thing as total submission: there remained areas, where resonance could be established. Such an area was culture in the Hungary of real existing socialism, which remained distortedly bourgeois. Radnóti developed his alternative from the interpretation of Benjamin's Marxist turn. The latter's East German reception fits into the theory of forced resonance, but Radnóti's does not. Forced resonance, which gives ontological priority to the (even if incomplete) totalitarian systems in the explanation of East European *Weltbeziehungen* in the era of "real existing socialism," understands these *Weltbeziehungen* as false, inauthentic, imposed from above. As this case study suggests, it might be fruitful to ask for the manifestations of authentic resonance displaced from the here and now of the political system: spatially, as inner emigration, exile, smaller communities from families to religious groups; temporally, as nostalgia or utopia; "ontologically," as life projections or possible alternative worlds; and discursively, as irony, allegory, and parable. They are modes of existence, which made it possible to live a resonant, even if a not fully successful life according to Western conceptions—in a displaced sense. East European discourse and practice of displaced resonance made a perhaps stronger and surely more lasting impact on collective consciousness than the compulsorily resonant cultural superstructure of the party state.

Methodologically, this analysis invites the extension of the theory of the human being's relations to the world (*Weltbeziehungen*), to aesthetics and literature and other creative expressions, especially outside the Western World where political conditions are not (fully) favourable for a successful life. Literature and other forms of aesthetic expression as (pluralistic) life projections provide opportunities to discuss resonant *Weltbeziehungen* even in political systems with no latitude for plurality in choice or action. They challenge the evaluation of the world of real existing socialism as a world of forced resonance and urge a further deconstruction of the blanket theory of East European totalitarianism. These formations made the consciousness of the bourgeois way of life continuous and contributed to the shapes of the cultural formations of the present. They relativised (even if they did not counterbalance) the lack of political pluralism without postulating the equivalence of displaced East-Central European resonance with West European patterns.

Works cited

Adler, Caroline, and Sophia Buck (2022). *Walter Benjamin in the East: Networks, conflicts, and reception*. Conference report / Intellectual history. 23.12.2022 https://jhiblog.org/2022/12/05/walter-benjamin-in-the-east-networks-conflicts-and-reception/.

Ahmadi, Amir (2002). Intellectual dandyism: The perils of form. In John Grumley, Paul Crittenden, and Pauline Johnson (eds.). *Culture and enlightenment. Essays for György Márkus*, 305–29. Burlington, VT: Ashgate.

Albrecht, Clemens et al. (2000). *Die intellektuelle Gründung der Bundesrepublik: Eine Wirkungsgeschichte der Frankfurter Schule*. Frankfurt a. M. and New York: Campus.

Ancsel, Éva (1982). *Polémia a történelemmel. Esszé Walter Benjaminról*. Budapest: Kossuth Könyvkiadó.

Bathrick, David (1979). Reading Walter Benjamin from West to East. *Colloquia Germanica* 12, 246–55.

Beilharz, Peter (2018). The Budapest School—travelling theory? In Jonathan Pickle and John Rundell (eds.). *Critical theories and the Budapest School: Politics, culture, modernity*, 15–33. London and New York: Routledge.

Benjamin, Walter (1955). *Schriften*. 2 Vols. Frankfurt a. M.: Suhrkamp.

Benjamin, Walter (1966). *Briefe*. Ed., with annotations by Gershom Scholem and Theodor W. Adorno. 2 Vols. Frankfurt a. M.: Suhrkamp.

Benjamin, Walter (1969). *Kommentár és prófécia*. Introduction Dénes Zoltai, transl. László Barlay et al. Budapest: Gondolat.

Benjamin, Walter (1980). *Angelus novus: Értekezések, kísérletek, bírálatok*. Ed. Sándor Radnóti, transl. György Bence et al. Budapest: Helikon.

Curtis, Michael (ed.) (1997). *Marxism. The Inner Dialogues*. 2nd ed. London and New York: Routledge.

Davis, Devra Lee (1975). Theodor W. Adorno: Theoretician through negations. *Theory and society* 2/3 (Autumn), 389–400.

Dornheim, Liane (1987). *Vergleichende Rezeptionsgeschichte: Das literarische Frühwerk Ernst Jüngers in Deutschland, England und Frankreich*. Frankfurt a. M. etc.: Peter Lang.

Ekiert, Grzegorz (1996). *The state against society: Political crises and their aftermath in East Central Europe*. Princeton: Princeton University Press.

Fehér, Ferenc (1986). What is beyond art? On the theories of post-modernity. In Agnes Heller and Ferenc Fehér (eds.). *Reconstructing aesthetics: Writings of the Budapest School*, 60–76. Oxford and New York: Blackwell.

Fehér, Ferenc, and Ágnes Heller (1987a). Are there prospects for change in the Soviet Union and Eastern Europe? In Ferenc Fehér and Ágnes Heller. *Eastern left, Western left: Totalitarianism, freedom and democracy*, 48–60. Cambridge: Polity Press.

Fehér, Ferenc, and Ágnes Heller (1987b). Introduction. In Ferenc Fehér and Ágnes Heller. *Eastern left, Western left: Totalitarianism, freedom and democracy*, 1–47. Cambridge: Polity Press.

Fehér, Ferenc, Ágnes Heller, and György Márkus (1983). *Dictatorship over needs*. Oxford: Blackwell.

Fehér, Ferenc, Agnes Heller, György Márkus, and Mihály Vajda (1983). Notes on Lukács' Ontology. In Ágnes Heller (ed.). *Lukács revalued*, 125–53. Oxford: Blackwell.

Gallas, Helga (1968). Wie es zu den Eingriffen in Benjamins Texte kam oder Über die Herstellbarkeit von Einverständnis im Hinblick auf die "Kritische Ausgabe", *alternative*, 59–60, 76 ff.

Garber, Klaus (1987). *Rezeption und Rettung: Drei Studien zu Walter Benjamin*. Tübingen: M. Niemeyer Verlag.

Griffiths, Devin (2017). The comparative method and the history of the modern humanities. *History of humanities* 2/2, 473–505.

Habermas, Jürgen (1972). Bewußtmachende oder rettende Kritik—die Aktualität Walter Benjamins. In Siegfried Unseld (ed.). *Zur Aktualität Walter Benjamins*, 173–223. Frankfurt a. M.: Suhrkamp.

Habermas, Jürgen (2005). Walter Benjamin: consciousness-raising or rescuing critique. In Peter Osborne (ed.). *Walter Benjamin: Critical evaluations in cultural theory*. Vol 1: Philosophy, 107–36. London and New York: Routledge.

Heise, Rosemarie (1971). Vorwort. In Walter Benjamin. *Das Paris des Second Empire bei Baudelaire*, 5–21. Berlin and Weimar: Aufbau-Verlag.

Heller, Agnes (1987). An imaginary preface to the 1984 edition of Hannah Arendt's *The origins of totalitarianism*. In Ferenc Fehér and Ágnes Heller. *Eastern left, Western left: Totalitarianism, freedom and democracy*, 243–59. Cambridge: Polity Press.

Heller, Agnes (2002). The Frankfurt School. In Jeffrey T. Nealon and Caren Irr (eds.). *Rethinking the Frankfurt School: Alternative legacies of Cultural Critique*, 207 ff. Albany: State University of New York Press.

Heller, Ágnes (2003). A Frankfurti Iskola. Transl. János László Farkas. In *Filozófiai labdajátékok*, 274–302. Budapest: Gond-Cura Alapítvány—Palatinus.

Heller, Ágnes (2011). Messiás és három angyal: Tordai Zádor Walter Benjamin-tanulmánya elé. *Múlt és Jövő* 1, 10–13.

Heller, Agnes (2012). *The concept of the beautiful*. Lanham etc.: Lexington Books.

Heller, Agnes, and Ferenc Feher (1990). *From Yalta to glasnost: The dismantling of Stalin's empire*. Oxford: Basil Blackwell.

Kapferer, Norbert (1990). *Das Feindbild der marxistisch-leninistischen Philosophie in der DDR 1945–1988*, Darmstadt: Wissenschaftliche Buchgesellschaft.

Kraft, Werner (1972). Über Benjamin. In Siegfried Unseld (ed.). *Zur Aktualität Walter Benjamins*, 59–69. Frankfurt a. M.: Suhrkamp.

Lunn, Eugene (1982). *Marxism and modernism: An historical study of Lukács, Brecht, Benjamin, and Adorno*. Berkeley: University of California Press.

Maffeis, Stefania (2007). *Zwischen Wissenschaft und Politik: Transformationen der DDR-Philosophie 1945–1993*. Frankfurt a. M. and New York: Campus.

Mahorney, James, and Dietrich Rueschemeyer (eds.) (2003a). *Comparative historical analysis in the social sciences*. Cambridge: Cambridge University Press.

Mahoney, James, and Dietrich Rueschemeyer (2003b). Comparative historical analysis: Achievements and agendas. In James Mahorney and Dietrich Rueschemeyer (eds.). *Comparative historical analysis in the social sciences*, 3–38. Cambridge: Cambridge University Press.

Markus, Gyorgy (1986). *Language and production: A critique of the paradigms*. Dordrecht etc.: D. Reidel Publishing Company.

Márkus, György (2001). Walter Benjamin or the commodity as phantasmagoria. *New German critique* 83 (Summer–Spring), 3–42.

Max, Katrin (2018). *Bürgerlichkeit und bürgerliche Kultur in der Literatur der DDR*. Paderborn: Fink.

Müller-Doohm, Stefan (2009). Der Intellektuelle, seine Kritik und die Öffentlichkeit: Benjamin, Adorno, Habermas. In Sylke Bartmann, Axel Fehlhaber, Sandra Kirsch, and Wiebke Lohfeld (eds.). *"Natürlich stört das Leben ständig": Perspektiven auf Entwicklung und Erziehung*, 137–43. Wiesbaden: Verlag für Sozialwissenschaften.

Neuffer, Moritz (2021). *Die journalistische Form der Theorie: Die Zeitschrift* alternative *1958–1982*. Göttingen: Wallstein Verlag.

Pickle, Jonathan, and John Rundell (2018). Introduction: The Budapest School and its legacies: Migration, modernity, philosophy. In Jonathan Pickle and John Rundell (eds.). *Critical theories and the Budapest School: Politics, culture, modernity*, 1–11. London and New York: Routledge.

Pursche, Robert (n. d.). Walter Benjamin zwischen Ost und West. 26.12.2022 https://www.literaturarchiv1968.de/content/walter-benjamin-zwischen-ost-und-west/.

Radnoti, Sandor (1975). Bloch and Lukács: Two radical critics in a "God-Forsaken World". Transl. by David J. Parent. *Telos* 25 (Fall), 155-64.

Radnóti, Sándor (1977). The Early Aesthetics of Walter Benjamin. *International Journal of Sociology* 7, 77-123.

Radnóti, Sándor (1978). Benjamin's politics. *Telos* 36 (Summer), 63-81.

Radnóti, Sándor (1981a). Mass culture. *Telos* 48 (Summer), 27-47.

Radnóti, Sándor (1981b). The effective power of art: On Benjamin's aesthetics. Transl. John Fekete. *Telos* 49 (Fall), 61-82.

Radnóti, Sándor (1983). Lukács and Bloch. In Ágnes Heller (ed.). *Lukács revalued*, 63-74. Oxford: Blackwell.

Radnóti, Sándor (1983-84). Benjamin's dialectic of art and society. *The Philosophical Forum* 15/1-2 (Fall-Winter), 158-87.

Radnóti, Sándor (1986). Mass culture. In Agnes Heller and Ferenc Fehér (eds.). *Reconstructing aesthetics: Writings of the Budapest School*, 77-102. Oxford and New York: Basil Blackwell.

Radnóti, Sándor (1989). Benjamin's dialectic of art and society. In Gary Smith (ed.). *Benjamin. Philosophy, Aesthetics, History*, 126-57. Chicago and London: The University of Chicago Press.

Radnóti, Sándor (1999a). *Krédó és rezignáció. Esztétikai-politikai tanulmány Walter Benjaminról*. Budapest: Argumentum Kiadó—Lukács Archívum.

Radnóti, Sándor (1999b). A szerző magamentsége. In *Krédó és rezignáció. Esztétikai-politikai tanulmány Walter Benjaminról*, 193-98. Budapest: Argumentum Kiadó—Lukács Archívum.

Radnóti, Sándor (2005). Benjamin's politics. In Peter Osborne (ed.). *Walter Benjamin: Critical evaluations in cultural theory*. Vol 1: Philosophy, 337-56. London and New York: Routledge.

Radnóti, Sándor (2018). Criticism and aesthetics: Ferenc Fehér's views on art. In Jonathan Pickle and John Rundell (eds.). *Critical theories and the Budapest School: Politics, culture, modernity*, 49-62. London and New York: Routledge.

Rosa, Hartmut (2012). *Weltbeziehungen im Zeitalter der Beschleunigung. Umrisse einer Gesellschaftskritik*. Frankfurt a. M.: Suhrkamp.

Rosa, Hartmut (2019). *Resonance: A sociology of our relationship to the world*. Transl. by James C. Wagner. Cambridge: Polity Press.

Scholem, Gershom (1972). Walter Benjamin und sein Engel. In Siegfried Unseld (ed.). *Zur Aktualität Walter Benjamins*, 87-138. Frankfurt a. M.: Suhrkamp.

Schutt, Russell K. (2006). *Investigating the social world: The process and practice of research*. London: SAGE Publications, Inc.

Seidel, Gerhard (1970a). Im Passat der Kritik. In Walter Benjamin. *Lesezeichen: Schriften zur deutschsprachigen Literatur*, 417-30. Leipzig: Philipp Reclam jun.

Seidel, Gerhard (1970b). Zur vorliegenden Ausgabe. In Walter Benjamin. *Lesezeichen: Schriften zur deutschsprachigen Literatur*, 5-8. Leipzig: Philipp Reclam jun.

Skocpol, Theda (1984). *Vision and method in historical sociology*. Cambridge: Cambridge University Press.

Skocpol, Theda, and Margaret Somers (1980). *The uses of comparative history in macrosocial inquiry*. Comparative studies in society and history, 22/2, 174–97.

Smith, F. Gary (1983–84). The images of philosophy: Editor's introduction. *The Philosophical Forum* 15/1–2 (Fall–Winter), i–ix.

Über Walter Benjamin (1968). Mit Beiträgen von Theodor W. Adorno, Ernst Bloch, Max Rychner, Gershom Scholem, Jean Selz, Hans Heinz Holz und Ernst Fischer. Frankfurt a. M.: Suhrkamp.

Unseld, Siegfried (ed.) (1972). *Zur Aktualität Walter Benjamins*. Frankfurt a. M.: Suhrkamp.

Vajda, Mihály (1991). *Russischer Sozialismus in Mitteleuropa*. Transl. Maria A. Dessewffy. Vienna: Passagen Verlag.

Wiggershaus, Rolf, and Michael Robertson (1994). *The Frankfurt School: Its history, theories, and political significance*. Cambridge, MA: The MIT Press.

Zoltai, Dénes (1969). Előszó. In Walter Benjamin: *Kommentár és prófécia*, 5–28. Budapest: Gondolat.

Relating to Other Worlds: Religious spatiality and the beyond of the city in ancient cities' dealing with the dead[1]

Jörg Rüpke

1. Introduction

The aim of this contribution is to analyse how religious practices shape world relations in urban contexts. This will help to further develop the concept of urban religion, which is becoming popular in current, but also in historical religious research (Garbin and Strhan 2017; Lanz 2018; 2019; Rau and Rüpke 2020; Rüpke 2020b),[2] in a relational framework. To this end, it is central to examine the character of religious practices in relation to space. In this way, we can understand the *specific* roles of religion in its relationship to urban space and urban life. This will then need to be discussed in more detail in view of the decision—in cultural comparison by no means self-evident and in the end only a temporary decision—of many variants of ancient Mediterranean urbanity to spatially and conceptually exclude the dead from the city, unless they are attributed the status of a god. Gods were welcome to urban space and even fixed to specific locations in numbers unseen in villages by means of architecture and high investments, combining material world relations to objects with vertical world relations to the sacred or the divine.[3]

I will start by briefly reflecting on religion as a spatial practice (1). Secondly, how is such religion interwoven with urbanization, and not with the "city" or even the "urban space"? (2) In order to unravel the two analytically,

---

[1] © The author/s 2023, published by Campus Verlag, Open Access: CC BY-SA 4.0
Bettina Hollstein, Hartmut Rosa, Jörg Rüpke (eds.), "Weltbeziehung"
DOI: 10.12907/978-3-593-45587-7_010
[2] The chapter has been elaborated in the context of the Kolleg-Forschungsgruppe (KFG) "Religion and urbanity: Reciprocal formations," financed by the German Science Foundation (DFG, FOR 2779).
[3] For the notion of spatial fix, Urciuoli 2022.

a two-pronged approach is needed. First, I will briefly discuss the role of religious practices and ideas in processes of urbanization. Then I will discuss the effects of urbanization on the religion and urbanity of city dwellers when they transform settlements into "cities" by producing "urbanity"—shaping world relations in material, horizontal (between citizens) and vertical dimensions. Against that background, I will turn to my case study, religion and urbanity beyond the limits of the urban space.

2. Religion as a spatial practice

What is the "religion" the spatial properties of which I am interested in? For a start, I use religion as an umbrella term for those forms of human action and experience that differ from other cultural forms in that they consist of or are based on communication with special actors.[4] These actors have characteristics that differ from those of ordinary people: They can be dead (ancestors) or unborn (angels) beings, slightly (demons) or completely superhuman (gods); their conceptualisation can range from human-like to objects. It is not the characteristics of these addressees that distinguish this kind of communication, but the way in which the addressees are approached. It is not undeniably plausible to give them room for manoeuvre, that is, to accord agency to them in the specific situation. In routine situations, the risk of not finding applause by bystanders and observers might be reduced to an unexpected lack of responsivity; in other situations, predefined by strong hierarchies or fixed non-religious procedures, to unexpectedly introduce religious communication might be daring, and as such a successful innovation or be quickly subdued. In other words, communication with or through such "divine" addressees could enhance or diminish human agency, create or change social relationships and alter power relations. The religious agency is a medal with two sides: the agency ascribed to non-human or even superhuman actors, and the agency thus arrogated or attributed to the human actor who enters into such communication. Such a speaker can thus not only ascribe the agency to the "Divine." Frequently, she or he also claims to receive from these addressees an agency of his or her own, becoming an agent of the di-

---

4 Fundamental for the following is Rüpke 2015. For the concept of "special" see Taves 2009; Taves 2010.

vine actor. In such a way, religion can enter into negotiating power relations and shape the image and self-experience of the human instigator.

Like any other cultural practice, religious communication is a spatiotemporal practice. Basic spatial phenomena figure prominently in descriptions of religious practices and "data" from ancient times onwards, whether in East Asian or ancient Mediterranean texts, as "sacred places" and "sanctuaries," zones of taboo or routinised ritual action (Rüpke 2013a; Rüpke 2013b; cf. Rüpke 2016). There was even a tendency in modern research to stress the givenness of such places (Eliade 1954, widely taken up). Only as part of the spatial turn in other disciplines, scholars of religion have started to more intensively deal with the spatial dimension of religious action, the production and appropriation of space.[5] This has led to a necessary and welcome series of ethnographic and historical studies on the micro-level, not least to the concept of urban religion as referred to at the very beginning. Yet, the definition of religion introduced in the following implies that there is a specific spatial character of religious communication, a conceptual relationship that is not comparatively valid for other cultural practices.

The use of religious communication is preceded by a selection. It recognises and accepts the character of spaces as defined by prior, shared or prescribed use, but it also changes the space through performance, thus altering the *future* memory of the place. I have introduced the term "sacralization" to describe this change in space (Rüpke 2021). Even religious "traditions" are not simply given. On the contrary, they require constant reproduction and are altered by the microscopic (and sometimes revolutionary) changes of their users.

This kind of appropriation refers to space as well as to time, because the use of both can be flexible or, to use a temporal metaphor, ephemeral. The use of space can also be rhythmic or permanent. Given the problem that religious communication is facing in dealing with what is not unquestionably given, i.e., the problem of transforming the unavailable transcendent or a diffused immanent into something available, that is graspable and addressable, religious communication tends to use media on a large scale that go beyond sounds and gestures. These include gifts, architecture, inscriptions and tools such as knives and books. In other words, religious communication

---

5 Fundamental Knott 2015; Knott 2010; Knott 2008; Knott 2005; see Urciuoli, and Rüpke 2018. For the concept of appropriation see Certeau 2007; Certeau 1984; developed for History of Religion in Raja, and Rüpke 2015b; Raja, and Rüpke 2015a; Albrecht et al. 2018; Gasparini et al. 2020.

tends to be "material religion."[6] The media of this religious communication, i.e., the tools used for or in communication, may be more or less, temporarily or permanently connected to it and thus "sacred" through the connection with the particular addressees. As such, spaces can be challenged by various religious or non-religious actors, visibly or invisibly, legally or illegally occupied. Open, accessible spaces (not always centrally managed or in "public" ownership) can be contested or occasionally ceded.

Place-making offers a different perspective on such processes (e. g. Bielo 2013; Creekmore and Fisher 2014; Ferri 2021), and we could also think metaphorically of something like "calendar-making" as similarly organized and differently qualifying time. This perspective emphasizes the mental maps, living and actual patterns of use that correlate with the experience of a certain atmosphere, as well as the emotional relationships to places, which are primarily conceived as a *connection* to places. Identifiable relationships, clear markings or even ownership are central to such an analysis.

If site design can be equated with "dwelling," i.e. identifying with a place, and is often achieved through religious practices, then religious communication is also inherently a practice of "crossing," of transcending that place—to use the terminology used by Thomas Tweed to illustrate this tension (Tweed 2006; 2011). Religion, to repeat the definition developed above, is *defined* as a human action that transcends (in a very simple sense) the immediate and undoubtedly given situation and establishes a relationship with the divine. There is no sharp dividing line between "immanent" and "transcendental" religion.[7] Even the sacralization of contemporary objects and institutions, whether in the domestic or public sphere (Jonathan Zittel Smith's *here* and *there* in the site-specific nature of his classification of religion) (Smith 2003), not only deals with spatial presence, but also contains a reference to an afterlife; even sacral kingship contains elements of risk, whether empirically, like droughts, or in ritual competitions (see for example Assmann 2006; Hooke 1958; Nygaard 2016; Weinfurter 1992; Alexander et al. 2006; King 1999; Wengrow 2013). This is the basis for a meaningful application of the conceptualization as "religion." The translocal references inherent in religious communication about its claims to action need not wait for a radicalized transcendence in the axial age-style, which is opposed to a heavenly order to the norms and power relations of the contemporary society in which these re-

---

6 For the concept, Droogan 2013; Rüpke 2020a; Promey 2014; Chidester 2018; Meyer et al. 2010.
7 See Strathern 2019, despite his interest in differentiating between the two.

ligious activities are located. Such translocal references and the weakness of their claims have been the basis for long-standing debates on icons, representation, and presence, on anthropomorphic or non-anthropomorphic forms, on images or no image.[8] The ritual can be miniaturized or virtualized; the prayer in the heart can *take place anywhere*. Urban control techniques through representation in the form of maps, numbers or texts were used to escape the place by transforming religious practices into intellectual debates and confrontations with Scripture, into commentaries *on* rituals rather than rituals. If we want to understand the complexity of the interweaving of religion and urbanization, this aspect must also be taken into account.

If urbanization is about the densification and differentiation of space, inclusion (or even trapping) and exclusion on a larger scale, then religion is uniquely beneficial and uniquely collides with urbanization—or at least it held such a unique status until the advent of efficient telecommunications. From this perspective, religious places would also be places in an eminent, super-empirical sense.

Religious practices and signs can serve as tools for such "site design," but equally relevant are grouping processes, such as the formation of networks or the creation of even closer organizations. The closing of a passage through neighbours to create a space for a shrine, or the erection of small shrines on street corners that are important for the neighbourhood alone, while the latter has the potential to be more visible, are examples of such place design (e. g. Steuernagel 2002; 2001). The subsequent results are sometimes permanent and sometimes not. Here we are increasingly concerned with the specifics of practices that were explicitly considered religion by contemporary or later observers, and subsequently with sacralized places. But even these places could be taken over by others or expropriated by an authority that might declare the place the "heritage" of another or larger group (such as the nation) (Narayanan 2015). This latter trend, for instance in ancient centres of walled cities in India, has had a major impact at the national level since the 1980s, but it can also be triggered by a simple influx of tourists who cancel out the localized appropriation of a place (Stausberg 2010).

---

8 The bibliography is endless within and between religious traditions.

3. Religion and urbanity

It has become a frequently emphasized truism among religious scholars that religion is not simply given. The fact that it is a scientific construct must be made explicit in order to allow an open discussion about the limits and usefulness of the term. As I have argued elsewhere (Rüpke 2015), an agent-centred version of religion, such as the one briefly outlined above, avoids many of the pitfalls identified by the standard critique of the concept of religion as a Christian-biased or inherently Western concept, because the agent-centred approach allows us to model religion interculturally as a spatial practice. The conceptual status of the "city" and even of "towns" is no different. Despite the pre-reflexive overwhelming evidence of the proliferation of cities and urban growth, these concepts need to be more clearly delineated. Even if such details may seem unnecessary in view of the current reality of urban growth, we need to be aware that an unknown but certainly significant part of recent urban growth is the result of reclassifying settlements in order to classify them as part of urban settlements, thus reflecting administrative approaches and notions of cities rather than changing settlement patterns (Robinson, et al. 2016, 18). Cities such as (Greater) London show how such conceptualizations can change within a few decades and sometimes in even shorter periods of time.

As a result of such variations over time and certainly, between places, I take the term "city" as an expression of object language, a term used by the people I study. This term implies a self-differentiation from the non-city, regardless of whether its counterpart is described as "rural," "wilderness," "uncivilized," or, in a less derogatory way (at least sometimes), as villages and landscapes. Thus, "city" is only an invitation to look for the classification operations used by people to distinguish and often evaluate settlement forms (including nomadic lifestyles or transhumance).

In the following, I will use the term urban as a part of a metalanguage. It designates on the one hand, dense settlement patterns of a large number of people (far beyond the upper limit of the number of inhabitants of a community in which all members could maintain personal contacts with all others), which are characterized by a corresponding density of interaction. On the other hand, it also assumes external connections to other settlements, which are also regarded as cities in the above-mentioned culturally and historically variable sense.[9] The second element has two important consequences: Urban settlements do not appear individually but in networks — even if these only have very distant corresponding nodes. And urban diversity goes beyond the mere effect of numbers, but is rather enhanced by intercultural contacts and migration — even if this is limited to more regional variants and distances.

On this basis, I follow Susanne Rau in her distinction between urbanization and urbanity. Urbanization, or more precisely urbanizations, are different and reversible processes of growing and spreading settlements as urban settlements (the history of constitution, perception and appropriation of urban spaces). Urbanity, on the other hand, is the specific way of life in such cities, defined by the fact that the inhabitants realize that they live *in a city* (again, however they define city) (Rau 2014, 405 f.). And even more, it is an image, or better: imagination of what a city and what urban life should be, a normative concept that can be lived outside of cities, too (Rüpke and Urciuoli 2023). It is urbanization as a larger historical process that offers us a lens through which we can see the religious change here. It is not a matter of closing our ears to the claim of a comprehensive "planetary urbanization" as diagnosed, for example, by Christian Schmid[10]. Part of the unequal, hegemonic character of urbanity is that elements of urban lifestyles in far-flung areas have been acknowledged and sometimes copied. After all, it is precisely such a widespread notion of the superiority of urban life that has produced urban aspirations and immigration to cities. And yet the city has also produced, or continues to produce, violent or violent rejections of such a way of life, as can be seen in the emigration from cities to places where alternative models of living and settlement can be pursued, be they out-of-town monasteries, garden cities with an emphasis on "back to nature" or remote islands. The relationality of urbanity to cities is complex and needs sensitive analysis. Whether the agents are urban dwellers who leave in order to realize urbanity outside of urban space, or temporary inhabitants of cities who refuse to accept urbanity, is an important question, not least for the history of religion. That the global city today is the solution to all problems relating to climate change, demography and sustainability is an assertion by urban scientists that may well be correct, but must nevertheless be tested on the possibility that it is merely an ideologically cultivated position that belongs to the hegemonic urban ideology. My own enterprise here must therefore remain self-

---

9 Cf. the definition by Robinson et al. 2016, 5.
10 For example, Brenner, and Schmid 2014.

reflexive when it comes to claims to the urban as well as to religion. I will now test these conceptual and methodological reflections on a very specific case of relationship, on the urban dead.

4. The beyond of the city

A widespread part of ancient Mediterranean urbanity was a deliberate stance on where to place urbanites after their death. Corpses had to be removed from the city, the cremation or any burial of the body had to take place outside the city. At Rome, this was certainly already the case in the fifth century BCE; in some Campanian cities this was regulated by law in the early imperial period.[11] Everything else was optional. In principle, dealing with deceased relatives allowed all those possibilities of distinction, self-location and self-assertion to be exploited that were already evident in the early Iron Age. Splendid funerary ceremonies and visible or even extravagant tombs offered the possibility to assert one's status after death and were often planned and architecturally realised already during a lifetime, otherwise in a last will. These opportunities were coupled with social pressures and the expectations of religious institutions to fulfill "obligations" towards the dead. To this end, standards had been established in the upper and middle classes, which in family-like group structures were also appropriated by better-off slaves, but above all by freedmen. Which percentage of the population was covered by these standards and how many deceased ended up in what Varro described in the second half of the first century BCE as *puticuli*, "little holes," for which the Esquiline hill offered itself,[12] we do not know. But in the case of an epidemic or catastrophe with many deaths, even for members of the elite, a mass grave was standard, as demonstrated by the incidence of a plague around two hundred CE.[13]

A crematorium *(ustrinum) was* one of the typical service facilities of a city; in the Campanian town of Puteoli, for example, it was part of a complete package offered by a monopolistic leaseholder, which included the rental of

---

11 Rome: Cicero, *On Laws* 2.58: Twelve Tables. Campanian laws (especially Puteoli): *AE* 1971, 88; Libitina 2004; Castagnetti 2012; Schrumpf 2006; for the burial of children see Varro, fr. 109 Riposati; Servius, *In Aeneidem* 12.142 f.
12 Varro, *Latin Language* 5.25. On the problem: Hope 2009, 158.
13 As a funeral in precious robes: Blanchard et al. 2007.

an altar and premises *(chalcidium)*. If there was a grave, then — regardless of whether it was a new, family, or club grave — the relation to this extra-urban place was publicly updated by the relatives moving with the deceased from the home to the cremation or burial site. In the case of children, for example, the removal could take place at night or, in the case of executed slaves, in a dishonourable form on a hook. Usually, this was the most visible part of a procedure, which was strongly ritualized and thus easily recognizable in terms of content for observers and participants. In the case of members — in the first century BC also female members — of Rome's political elite, the funeral procession even included a stop and a funeral speech at the forum.[14] The family also had living statues carried along, i.e., actors with masks of important ancestors who had been honoured with public statues. By these means, families and their place in society were made visible and public by their descendants until the early imperial period (Rüpke 2006; different: Flower 1996; see also Flaig 1995).

But how did the survivors mark the exceptional situation of a death? How did they negotiate their relationship to the dead *and* the urban society? They did it by ostentatiously neglecting their own appearance, leaving their hair unkempt (or at least without hair decoration), wearing tattered, "dirty" (or at least dark) clothes, in short, by giving up everything that distinguished them — if they came from the upper classes — from the lower urban classes (Degelmann 2016). At the same time, they did not want to give up the opportunity to use the publicity given by the rituals of mourning to represent their own position and the prestige of their own family or group. Therefore, those who were to be buried became the projection screen. The use of more than three cloaks *(ricinia)* and a small purple tunic — probably for the deceased — had already been forbidden in the Twelve Tables, Rome's supposedly oldest collection of laws, which was attributed to the fifth century BCE.[15] But mourning was also a way of showing off. During this time, the praise of the dead from the senatorial class was not to be sung by young male voices from the peer group (as in continuous historical commemoration), but rather by women in a plaintive voice. And this, too, could be qualitatively enhanced by professional singers (and possibly the funeral speech). Here, too, the *peers* had already attempted to limit family ostentation in funerals with the Twelve

---

14 For the *laudatio funebris* s. Kierdorf 1980; Mommsen 1905; Vollmer 1892. On the reconstruction of the procession passing the Forum: Favro, and Johanson 2010.
15 *Twelve Tables Act* 10.3; Cicero, *Act* 2.59 with Dyck 2004; Crawford 1996, 2, 705 f.

Tables Act by setting an upper limit of ten flute players.[16] This created a constant interplay between control and circumvention of this very control.

The attempt to visibly mark the special situation of the death of an important family member through well-rehearsed traditional actions and at the same time to transcend these traditions within a highly competitive elite resulted in constant innovations, even in waves of fashion. In the late republic and the earliest imperial period, members of the Roman upper class mostly relied on the cremation of their dead. In the second century CE, they gradually replaced this with burials, whereas the signs and practices used remained overall in line with the procedures of ritual communication with gods, for instance, through the depositing or burning of objects (Porter and Boutin 2014; in the provinces: Pearce 2011). Similar changes could also be observed elsewhere and led to great differences both between geographical areas and at individual burial sites.[17]

The cremation was a multi-stage process of laying out, cremation lasting several hours, collecting the bones, and their burial (a portion of the undistinguishable ashes included). Possibly cremation offered a particularly attractive framework for family self-presentation on a stage that could be arranged quite freely. The Republican leadership as a whole reacted to this with luxury laws that thematized the burning ritual. Norms of the first century BCE thus regulated the use of certain types of wood, the scattering of perfumes, the use of oversized wreaths for the dead, as well as the use of special incense or scented altars.[18] Cypresses were used to reduce the odor nuisance of cremation (Varro, vita p.R. fr. 111 Riposati). In addition to ornate deathbeds, other objects or sacrificial animals were visibly thrown into the fire on the most splendid of these occasions (Tacitus, Annals 3,2,2; Buccellato, et al. 2008, 86). Contemporary authors suggested to connoisseurs of Greek literature that these practices should also be seen as a connection to Homeric burial rituals (Vergil, *Aeneid* 11, 201).

The burning ritual of the Augusti had to compete with these practices. Indeed, it had to outdo them. This had already begun with individual and monumentalized crematoria. The successors then had to compete with the

---

16 *XIItab.*, ibid.
17 See for Rome for example Grossi, and Mellace 2007, for the provinces the further contributions in Faber et al. 2007 and Scheid 2008; Palmyra: Henning 2013; Heyn 2010.
18 Bodel 2004, 157. s.a. Cicero, *Laws* 2,60: *sumptuosa respersio; longae coronae; acerrae* with Dyck ad loc. Lucian, *Grief* 12, emphasizes the contrast.

memories of earlier rituals in the design of the next burial ritual, and only then could they come to terms with the current practice of the elite. In this way, they often lagged far behind socially widespread changes. When, for example, sarcophagi for more intimate placement in the context of bodily burials spread throughout the city of Rome in the second century CE, the Augusti initially went away empty-handed.

But establishing intimate relations with the deceased was also possible in the older rituals. For the step following the burning procedure, the removal of the bones not incinerated at normal temperatures, an Augustan poet could imagine a high level of emotionality in collecting and touching the remains, although this was precisely what was pushed back by prohibitions.[19] In fact, the cremated corpses collected in the urns often contained only minimal amounts, down to less than a hundred grams in some areas and especially in the early imperial period (Bel 2010). However, the personality of the deceased was not made dependent on certain physical remains[20] but resulted from the gradual change in the way they were handled (Scheid 1993).

Especially child burials seem to have given an important impetus to the creation of elaborate and, at the same time more intimate forms of corporeal burial at Rome at the end of the first century CE.[21] The first stone sarcophagi commissioned in Rome were intended to receive children to a greater extent than later (Mielsch 2009). Whoever wanted to use sarcophagi for burials could fall back on a supra-regional market for them from the middle of the second and until the end of the third century throughout the *Imperium Romanum*. This led to an enormous diversity in the interaction between importers, local suppliers, and buyers. The most momentous developments, however, were not changes in decor. Space, the focus of this chapter, was more critical. Beginning in first century CE, the empire's elite no longer erected elaborate tomb buildings in the immediate surroundings of Rome, probably primarily so that these projects would not be seen as competing with the Augusti (Borg 2011). When the richest moved their residences from

---

19 Cf. Properz 4,7 with Cicero, *Laws* 2,60 *(XIItab)*. On this materiality of memory see Graham 2011b. *Ossifragus* was a separate occupational or functional designation: it was someone who broke larger bones in such a way that they fitted into the urn; see also *AE* 2007, 260, A21-24 as an underworld imagination in an escape tablet in the necropolis on via Ostiense before Rome.
20 Accordingly, the handling of the *os resectum*, a small bone that appears in antiquarian literature as a minimal object of earth covering, seems inconsistent (see Graham 2011a, 92–103).
21 The following is summarizing my analysis in Rüpke 2018.

the cities of the western part of the *Imperium Romanum* to palatial country estates ("villas"), especially from the third century CE onwards, this resulted in a further factor in the choice of location for grave projects. In terms of architectural design, these builders usually dispensed with the building ideas that had characterized the first century BCE. Consuls of the second half of the second century CE built tombs in the form of rectangular temples like others of their class. Unlike some of the freedmen, they avoided a direct claim to be understood as gods. But with the form and the precious execution of their tombs, they, too formulated a position in the intensive debate about divinization, which was conducted in the Senate about deceased members of the imperial family.

Anyone who wanted to visit their family's tomb regularly had to stay within a perimeter of a few kilometres. Around Rome (and in other places), since the end of the second century CE, space in this area had become scarce (Borg 2013). Intensive use of existing graves, for example by placing urns or using multi-layered burials, was, therefore, the method of choice. In addition, even the smallest gaps between existing graves were now used. In the third century CE, free-standing sarcophagi were then also designed as miniature mausoleums. New terraced tombs also provided for small, partitioned plots. Investors could now also cut the grave area: A market had emerged that was dominated by property developers who increasingly operated underground facilities. In this way, they satisfied the demand for single graves as well as for family vaults or grave complexes for associations. Until well into the fourth century CE, religious organisations, associations, synagogues or churches played no role in this. For burials, boundaries between religious identities were unimportant (Rebillard 2003; Rüpke 2005; Borg 2013, 274). Churchyard cemeteries, even around inner-city churches were not yet the standard, as it was established for long periods of later European history down into the Early Modern Age and beyond. Urbanity still demanded both, to exclude the dead members and the ritual demonstration of the religious and even divine dimensions of family relations from urban space, but also to allow a viable upkeeping of that relationship on the part of the urbanites.

5. Conclusion

In an attempt to overcome a presentism bias in many, if not all, cases where the term "urban religion" is used, I have argued that we need to understand the spatial character of religious practices more precisely and that we should replace the timeless pairing of "religion in the city" or "religion and the city", focusing instead on the intertwining of religious change and notions of urbanity. Religion offers a toolbox for establishing a complex web of relations, to spaces, to people, to a beyond that is conceptually combining distance and contiguity. The brief analysis of burial practices and funerary rites has shown in detail the working of such relations within the framework of an urbanity that amply employs the continuous membership of dead family for claiming social positions and, at the same time, conceptually excludes them from urban space proper. Relational analysis of world relations, particularly the inquiry into the quality of such relationships in all their variety—from attraction to rejection and resonant qualities—offers tools to start from here.

Works cited

Albrecht, Janico et al. (2018). Religion in the Making: The Lived Ancient Religion Approach, *Religion*, 48 (4), 568–93. doi: 10.1080/0048721X.2018.1450305.
Alexander, Jeffrey C. et al. (eds.) (2006). *Social Performance: Symbolic Action, Cultural Pragmatics, and Ritual*. Cambridge Cultural Social Studies. Cambridge: Cambridge University Press.
Assmann, Jan (2006). Kulte und Religionen: Merkmale primärer und sekundärer Religion(serfahrung) im Alten Ägypten. In Andreas. Wagner (ed.). *Primäre und sekundäre Religion als Kategorie der Religionsgeschichte des Alten Testaments*. Beihefte zur Zeitschrift für die alttestamentliche Wissenschaft 364, 269–80. Berlin: De Gruyter.
Bel, Valérie (2010). Evolution des pratiques funéraires à Nîmes entre le IIe siècle av. J.-C. et le IIIe siècle ap. J.-C. In Jörg Rüpke and John Scheid (eds.). *Bestattungsrituale und Totenkult in der römischen Kaiserzeit/Rites funéraires et culte des morts aux temps impériales*, Potsdamer altertumswissenschaftliche Beiträge 27, 93–112. Stuttgart: Steiner.
Bielo, James S. (2013). Urban Christianities: place-making in late modernity. *Religion*, 43 (3), 301–11. doi: 10.1080/0048721x.2013.798160.
Blanchard, Philippe et al. (2007). A mass grave from the catacomb of Saints Peter and Marcellinus in Rome, second-third century AD, *Antiquity* 81 (314), 989–98. doi: doi:10.1017/S0003598X0009606X.

Bodel, John (2004). *The Organization of the Funerary Trade at Puteoli and Cumae*. In *Libitina e dintorni: Libitina e luci sepolcrali; le leges libitinariae campane; Iura sepulcrorum; vecchie e nuove iscrizioni; atti dell'XI Rencontre Franco-Italienne sur l'Epigraphie*. Libitina 3, 147–72. Roma: Quasar.

Borg, Barbara E. (2011). What's in a Tomb: Roman death public and private. In Javier Andreu, David Espinosa and Simone Pastor (eds.). *Mors omnibus instat: Aspectos arqueológicos, epigráficos y rituale de la muerte en el Occidente Romano*, 51–78. Madrid: Liceus.

Borg, Barbara E. (2013). *Crisis and Ambition: Tombs and Burial Customs on the Third-Century CE Rome*. Oxford Studies in Ancient Culture and Representation. Oxford: Oxford University Press.

Brenner, Neil, and Christian Schmid (2014). The "Urban Age" in Question. *International Journal of Urban and Regional Research*, 38 (3), 731–55. doi: 10.1111/1468-2427.12115.

Buccellato, Anna; Paola Catalano, and Stefano Musco (2008). Alcuni aspetti rituali evidenziati nel corso dello scavo della necropoli Collatina (Roma). In John Scheid (ed.). *Pour une archéologie du rite: nouvelles perspectives de l'archéologie funéraire*. Collection de l'École francaise de Rome 407, 59–88. Rome: École francaise de Rome.

Castagnetti, Sergio (2012). *Le "Leges Libitinariae" flegree: Edizione e commento*. Pubblicazioni del dipartimento di diritto Romano, storia e teoria del diritto "F. de Martino" dell'università degli studi di Napoli "Federico II" 34. Napoli: Satura editrice.

Certeau, Michel de (1984). *The practice of everyday life*. Berkeley: University of California Press.

Certeau, Michel de (2007). *Arts de faire*. Paris: Gallimard.

Chidester, David (2018). *Religion: Material Dynamics*. Berkeley: University of California Press.

Crawford, Michael H. (ed.) (1996). *Roman Statutes*. Bulletin of the Institute of Classical Studies, Suppl. 64. London: Institute of Classical Studies.

Creekmore, Andrew T. III and Kevin D. Fisher (eds.) (2014). *Making Ancient Cities: Space and Place in Early Urban Societies*. Cambridge: Cambridge University Press.

Degelmann, Christoph (2016). *Prekäres Handeln: Trauerszenen im republikanischen und frühkaiserzeitlichen Rom*. Unpubl. Diss. Erfurt.

Droogan, Julian (2013). *Religion, material culture and archaeology*. Bloomsbury advances in religious studies. London: Bloomsbury.

Dyck, Andrew R. (2004). *A commentary on Cicero, De legibus*. Ann Arbor: University of Michigan Press.

Eliade, Mircea (1954). *Die Religionen und das Heilige: Elemente einer Religionsgeschichte*. Salzburg: Müller.

Faber, Andrea et al. (2007). *Körpergräber des 1.-3. Jahrhunderts in der römischen Welt: Internationales Kolloquium Frankfurt am Main 19.–20. November 2004*. Schriften des Archäologischen Museums Frankfurt 21. Frankfurt a. M.: Archäologisches Museum Frankfurt.

Favro, Diane, and Christopher Johanson (2010). Death in Motion: Funeral Processions in the Roman Forum, *Journal of the Society of Architectural Historians* 69 (1), 12–37. doi: 10.1525/jsah.2010.69.1.12.

Ferri, Giorgio (2021). *The Place-making Function of Ritual Movement at Rome: from the Salians to Our Lady of Mount Carmel, Mythos* 15. doi: 10.4000/mythos. 3300.

Flaig, Egon (1995). Die Pompa Funebris: Adlige Konkurrenz und annalistische Erinnerung in der Römischen Republik. In Otto Gerhard Oexle (ed.) *Memoria als Kultur,* 115–48. Göttingen: Vandenhoeck & Ruprecht.

Flower, Harriet I. (1996). *Ancestor Masks and Aristocratic Power in Roman Culture.* Oxford: Clarendon Press.

Garbin, David, and Anna Strhan (eds.) (2017). *Religion and the Global City.* Bloomsbury Studies in Religion, Space and Place. New York: Bloomsbury.

Gasparini, Valentino et al. (eds.) (2020). *Lived Religion in the Ancient Mediterranean World: Approaching Religious Transformations from Archaeology, History and Classics.* Berlin: De Gruyter.

Graham, Emma-Jayne (2011a). From fragments to ancestors: Re-defining the role of *os resectum* in rituals of purification and commemoration in Republic Rome. In M. Carroll (ed.). *Living through the dead: burial and commemoration in the classical world.* Studies in funerary archaeology 5, 91–109. Oxford [u.a.]: Oxbow Books.

Graham, Emma-Jayne (2011b). Memory and Materiality: Re-embody in the Roman Funeral. In Valerie M. Hope and John Huskinson (eds.). *Memory and Mourning: Studies on Roman Death,* 21–39. Oxford: Oxbow Books.

Grossi, Maria Cristina, and Valeria Silvia Mellace (2007). Roma, Via Portuense: la necropoli di vigna pia. In Andrea Faber (ed.). *Körpergräber des 1.-3. Jahrhunderts in der römischen Welt.* Schriften des Archäologischen Museums Frankfurt 21, 185–200. Frankfurt a. M.: Archäologisches Museum.

Henning, Agnes (2013). *Die Turmgräber von Palmyra: Eine lokale Bauform im kaiserzeitlichen Syrien als Ausdruck kultureller Identität.* Orient-Archäologie 29. Rahden: Leidorf.

Heyn, Maura K. (2010). Gesture and Identity in the Funerary Art of Palmyra, *American Journal of Archaeology,* 114, 631–61.

Hooke, Samuel Henry (ed.) (1958). *Myth, Ritual, and Kingship: Essays on the Theory and Practice of Kingship in the Ancient Near East and Israel.* Oxford: Oxford University Press.

Hope, Valerie M. (2009). *Roman death: The dying and the dead in ancient Rome.* London: Continuum.

Kierdorf, Wilhelm (1980). *Laudatio funebris: Interpretationen und Untersuchungen zur Entwicklung der römischen Leichenrede.* Beiträge zur Klassischen Philologie 106. Meisenheim a. Glan: Hain.

King, Richard (1999). *Orientalism and Religion. Postcolonial Theory, India and "The Mystic East".* London and New York: Routledge.

Knott, Kim (2005). *The location of religion: A spatial analysis.* London: Equinox.

Knott, Kim (2008). Spatial Theory and the Study of Religion, *Religion Compass,* 2 (6), 1102–16.

Knott, Kim (2010). Cutting Through the Postsecular City: A Spatial Interrogation. In Arie Molendijk, Justin Beaumont and Christopher Jedan (eds.), *Exploring the Postsecular: The Religious, the Political, and the Urban,* 19–38. Leiden: Brill.

Knott, Kim (2015). Walls and Other Unremarkable Boundaries in South London: Impenetrable Infrastructure or Portals of Time, Space and Cultural Difference? *New Diversities*, 17 (2), 15–34.

Lanz, Stephan (2018). Religion of the City: Urban-Religious Configurations on a Global Scale. In Helmuth Berking, Silke Steets, and Jochen Schwenk (eds.). *Religious Pluralism and the City: Inquiries into Postsecular Urbanism*, 65–80. London: Bloomsbury.

Lanz, Stephan (2019). Urbane Religion—religiöse Urbanität: Zum Boom neuer religiöser Gemeinschaften und Bewegungen in den Städten. In Christopher Zarnow, Birgit Klostermeier, and Rüdiger Sachau (eds.). *Religion in der Stadt: Räumliche Konfigurationen und theologische Deutungen*. Theologisches Labor Berlin 1, 119–43. Berlin: eb-Verlag.

Libitina (2004). *Libitina e dintorni : Libitina e luci sepolcrali; le leges libitinariae campane; Iura sepulcrorum; vecchie e nuove iscrizioni; atti dell'XI Rencontre Franco-Italienne sur l'Epigraphie*. Libitina 3. Roma: Quasar.

Meyer, Birgit et al. (2010). The Origin and Mission of Material Religion, *Religion* 40 (3), 207–11. doi: 10.1016/j.religion.2010.01.010.

Mielsch, Harald (2009). *Überlegungen zum Wandel der Bestattungsformen in der römischen Kaiserzeit*. Paderborn: Schöningh.

Mommsen, Theodor (1905). Zwei Sepulcralreden aus der Zeit Augusts und Hadrians. In Theodor Mommsen (ed.). *Gesammelte Schriften 1: Juristische Schriften I*, 194–240. Berlin: Weidmann.

Narayanan, Yamini (2015). *Religion, heritage and the sustainable city: Hinduism and urbanisation in Jaipur*. Routledge research in religion and development. Abingdon: Routledge.

Nygaard, Simon (2016). Sacral rulers in pre-Christian Scandinavia: The possibilities of typological comparisons within the paradigm of cultural evolution. *Temenos*, 52 (1), 9–35.

Pearce, John (2011). Marking the dead: Tombs and topography in the Roman provinces In Maureen Carroll (ed.). *Living through the dead: burial and commemoration in the classical world*. Studies in funerary archaeology 5, 121–53. Oxford: Oxbow Books.

Porter, Benjamin W., and Alexis T. Boutin (eds.) (2014). *Remembering the dead in the ancient Near East*. Boulder, CO: University of Colorado Press.

Promey, Sally M. (2014). Religion, Sensation, and Materiality. An Introduction. In Sally M. Promey (ed.). *Sensational Religion. Sensory Cultures in Material Practice*, 1–21. New Haven: Yale University Press.

Raja, Rubina, and Jörg Rüpke (2015a). Appropriating Religion: Methodological Issues in Testing the "Lived Ancient Religion" Approach. *Religion in the Roman Empire*, 1 (1), 11–19. doi: 10.1628/219944615X14234960199632.

Raja, Rubina, and Jörg Rüpke (2015b). Archaeology of Religion, Material Religion, and the Ancient World. In Rubina Raja and Jörg Rüpke (eds.). *A Companion to the Archaeology of Religion in the Ancient World*, 1–25. Malden: Wiley.

Rau, Susanne (2014). *Räume der Stadt. Eine Geschichte Lyons 1300–1800*. Frankfurt a. M.: Campus.

Rau, Susanne, and Jörg Rüpke (2020). Religion und Urbanität: Wechselseitige Formierungen. *Historische Zeitschrift*, 310 (3), 654–80. doi: 10.1515/hzhz-2020-0021.

Rebillard, Éric (2003). Groupes religieux et élection de sépulture dans l'Antiquité tardive. In Nicole Belayche and Simon C. Mimouni (eds.). *Les communautés religieuses dans le monde gréco-romain: Essais de définition*, 259–77. Turnhout: Brepols.

Robinson, Jennifer et al. (eds.) (2016). *Working, Housing, Urbanizing: The International Year of Global Understanding – IYGU*. SpringerBriefs in Global Understanding. Berlin: Springer.

Rüpke, Jörg (2005). Bilderwelten und Religionswechsel. In Raban v. Haehling (ed.). *Griechische Mythologie und frühes Christentum*, 359–76. Darmstadt: Wissenschaftliche Buchgesellschaft.

Rüpke, Jörg (2006). Triumphator and ancestor rituals between symbolic anthropology and magic. *Numen*, 53, 251–289.

Rüpke, Jörg (2015). Religious Agency, Identity, and Communication: Reflecting on History and Theory of Religion. *Religion*, 45 (3), 344–66. doi: DOI:10.1080/0048721X.2015.1024040.

Rüpke, Jörg (2016). Individual Appropriation of Sacred Space. In Yves Lafond, and Vincent Michel (eds.). *Espaces sacrés dans la Méditerranée antique: Actes du colloque des 13 et 14 octobre 2011, Université de Poitiers*, 69–80. Rennes: Presses universitaires de Rennes.

Rüpke, Jörg (2018). *Pantheon: A New History of Roman Religion*. Princeton: Princeton University Press.

Rüpke, Jörg (2020a). Urban Religion at the Neighbourhood Level Across the Mediterranean. *Religion in the Roman Empire*, 6, 125–37. DOI 10.1628/rre-2020-0010.

Rüpke, Jörg (2020). *Urban Religion: A Historical Approach to Urban Growth and Religious Change*. Berlin: De Gruyter.

Rüpke, Jörg (2021). *Ritual als Resonanzerfahrung*. Religionswissenschaft heute 15. Stuttgart: Kohlhammer.

Rüpke, Jörg, and Emiliano Rubens Urciuoli (2023). Urban Religion Beyond the City: Theory and Practice of a Specific Constellation of Religious Geography-Making. *Religion*, 53, 1–25. doi: 10.1080/0048721X.2174913.

Scheid, John (1993). Die Parentalien für die verstorbenen Caesaren als Modell für den römischen Totenkult. *Klio*, 75, 188–201.

Scheid, John (ed.) (2008). *Pour une archéologie du rite : nouvelles perspectives de l'archéologie funéraire*. Collection de l'École française de Rome 407. Rome: École française.

Schrumpf, Stefan (2006). *Bestattung und Bestattungswesen im Römischen Reich: Ablauf, soziale Dimension und ökonomische Bedeutung der Totenfürsorge im lateinischen Westen*. Bonn: V & R unipress.

Smith, Jonathan Z. (2003). Here, There, and Anywhere. In S. B. Noegel, J. T. Walker, and B. M. Wheeler (eds.). *Prayer, magic, and the stars in the ancient and late antique world. Magic in history*, 21–36. University Park, PA: Pennsylvania State Univ. Press.

Stausberg, Michael (2010). *Religion and tourism: Crossroads, destinations, and encounters*. London: Routledge.

Steuernagel, Dirk (2001). Kult und Community—Sacella in den Insulae von Ostia. *Mitteilungen des Deutschen Archäologischen Instituts Römische Abteilung*, Bd. 108, 41–56.

Steuernagel, Dirk (2004). *Kult und Alltag in römischen Hafenstädten: soziale Prozesse in archäologischer Perspektive*. PawB 11. Stuttgart: Steiner.

Strathern, Alan (2019). *Unearthly Powers: Religious and Political Change in World History*. Cambridge: Cambridge University Press.

Taves, Ann (2009). *Religious experience reconsidered: A building block approach to the study of religion and other special things*. Princeton, NJ: Princeton University Press.

Taves, Ann (2010). Experience as site of contested meaning and value: The attributional dog and its special tail. *Religion*, 40 (4), 317–23. doi: 10.1016/j.religion.2010.09.012.

Tweed, Thomas A. (2006). *Crossing and dwelling: A theory of religion*. Cambridge, Mass.: Harvard University Press.

Tweed, Thomas A. (2011). Space. *Material Religion*, 7, 116–23.

Urciuoli, Emiliano Rubens (2022). Jumping Among the Temples: Early Christian Critique of Polytheism's "Spatial Fix". In Corinne Bonnet et al. (eds.). *Naming and Mapping the Gods in the Ancient Mediterranean*, 989–1009. Berlin and Boston: De Gruyter.

Urciuoli, Emiliano, and Jörg Rüpke (2018). Urban Religion in Mediterranean Antiquity: Relocating Religious Change. *Mythos*, 12, 117–35. doi: 10.4000/mythos. 341.

Vollmer, Friedrich (1892). Laudationum funebrium Romanorum historia et reliquiarum editio. *Jahrbücher für classische Philologie*, Suppl. 18, 445–528.

Weinfurter, Stefan (1992). Idee und Funktion des Sakralkönigtums bei den ottonischen und salischen Herrschern (10. und 11. Jahrhundert). In Rolf Gundlach, and Hermann Weber (eds.). *Legitimation und Funktion des Herrschers: Vom ägyptischen Pharao zum neuzeitlichen Diktator*, 99–127. Stuttgart: Steiner.

Wengrow, David (2013). "Fleshpots of Egypt": rethinking temple economy in the ancient Near East. In Elizabeth Frood, and A. McDonald (eds.). *Decorum and experience: Essays in ancient culture for John Baines*, 291–98. Oxford: Griffith Institute.

III
Practical Perspectives

Values of Exchange, Values of Sharing: The ambivalence of economic *Weltbeziehungen*, explained for the example of carsharing[1]

Christoph Henning

My contribution will introduce the ambivalences of exchange and its counterpart, sharing, as it has recently been discussed in the context of "sharing economies". We share many things and places: as children perhaps toys, a bedroom and our parents, as pupils the classroom and the attention of the teacher, as students the shared flat, as old people the sick room. So, it sounds rather normal. What is actually revolutionary about sharing only becomes visible through its classification in terms of social philosophy. As a part of practical philosophy, social philosophy aims to understand what holds the social world together. Eighty-three million people do not simply live side by side (that's how many we are in Germany by now), as if everyone lived for themselves—although the automobile society sometimes gives exactly this impression. Rather, together we form a social texture or society—one, not two or five. But which kinds of activity really bind us together?

This question searches for the glue that binds people together, for the social cement that Georg Simmel called "social interaction" (*Wechselwirkung*, Simmel 1908, 17). To find it we may look in thick books, but what you find there went over a thousand desks, it is heavily filtered through all sorts of preconceived doctrines and paradigms. Therefore, there is not one answer, but hundreds. Alternatively, we could also look at everyday experiences for a change, and ask simple questions. When in the day do we actually start meeting others? One meets for breakfast with parents and siblings or with roommates, talks, drinks coffee together—an elementary experience, perhaps in a relationship. But it is not yet the centre of society; first and foremost, there we find individuals.

---

[1] © The author/s 2023, published by Campus Verlag, Open Access: CC BY-SA 4.0
Bettina Hollstein, Hartmut Rosa, Jörg Rüpke (eds.), "Weltbeziehung"
DOI: 10.12907/978-3-593-45587-7_011

Traditionally, individual relationships are dealt with in ethics (what duties do parents have towards children, the healthy towards sick people; what duties do you have in a shared flat when someone has to go into quarantine, etc.). These are important questions, in everyday life as well as in philosophy, but for our topic they are a bit too small-scale. Sometimes it is not even socially visible what happens at home (hence the large fences and investments in private security). Conversely, one starts oversized when asking about crystallized meta-structures that surround us all: for example, adults vote every few years (or should do so); they pay taxes (or should do so); and they are protected (or monitored, as the case may be) by the police. This takes us one level too high now, into political philosophy. The fact that we all vote or pay taxes doesn't really bring us together. Individuals work it out with their own tax slips or their tax office; people rarely come into contact with each other (except perhaps at a tax assistant's office). This relations remain abstract, which is why the young Marx characterised it as political "alienation" (MEW 1, 367): in modern states people no longer get together, except maybe in large protests. Social philosophy, however, wants to know what happens in the normal, everyday practices of togetherness, for example at breakfast, and how this binds a society together. Not infrequently, therefore, researchers like Erving Goffman or Arlie Hochschild have actually sat down at people's breakfast tables and listened.

What distinction is touched upon here, by this talk of smale-scale and large-scale? One can roughly separate social spheres from each other in a social ontology: Family, State, and Society. This has been quite common since G.W.F. Hegel's *Elements of the Philosophy of Right* (from 1821), and I am using it here by distinguishing the social dimension from political (state-centered) and ethical (family- or group-centered) concerns.

1. The Texture of the Social in Modernity: Exchange Relations

So what *is* the practice that weaves the social tapestry in the traditional view of social philosophy then? Let's stay with the everyday situation at breakfast. What is the most important thing? Bread and butter, of course! Jam, coffee, or optionally organic muesli with soy milk. One could object that these are things, they are not "social." But that misfires, because these things are deeply embedded in social practices (Henning 2022). Where do they come from? I've been to the bakery around the corner, or to the supermarket with an SUV. And precisely this is the central intersection of social circles in modern societies, where people meet every day: *exchange*. People have to get their food, clothes, and tools this way, because you can't produce everything yourself anymore, even if you try hard. We usually exchange money for goods, and to get this money, we exchange something else—usually our labour time, for which we get wages or salary. We get it from an employer, and thus numerous acts of exchange intersect. People do this not only in our country, but all over the world; thus the toaster comes from China, the apple from Italy etc. Exchange relations span a worldwide web, a world society or system (Wallerstein 1974). Only with the recent rise of populism and neo-nationalism, with Brexit, the pandemic, and the Russian imperial war, borders have started to be closed and guarded again.

If this is true, then exchange is not a day-to-day triviality, but a pattern of many of our smaller and larger *Weltbeziehungen*, both in theory and in practice. Our dealings with things, with nature, with others and with ourselves are deeply shaped by it (Henning 2021c). From the standpoint of market exchange, they are preconceived as potential raw material, tradeable goods, trade partners or competitors. It begins with the fact that the exchange is not over yet after I went shopping for ten minutes. After all, where do students go after breakfast? If not back to bed, they go to school or to university—and why? To qualify for a job. Many of them want to get a well-paying one, hence there is a shortage of social workers and care workers, who are not well paid. This is how many people understand the good life, and thus themselves: possessing and consuming a lot, and hence working a job that pays for all that. Everything should become more and more, bigger, faster, and more expensive. In order to participate in this, we endure school and training, work, uncertainty, and stressful colleagues. All this cannot be done without exchange, and therefore modern states have done a lot to create trade reliabilities: logistical infrastructures, internal legal security, and international treaties. *Weltbeziehungen* are thus shaped by the exchange paradigm even in a literal sense—globalisation first and foremost is a globalisation of trade (Henning 2023).

Exchanges also affect close social relations: children grow up in milieus that are strongly influenced by their parents' neighbourhood, which in turn often depends on their type of work. Most of our friends we know through school and work, so habitual class differences are passed on. Social philosophy looks at the social consequences and meanings these practices have for people and their communities. Because they matter a lot, exchange became a central pattern of thought to interpret sociality in theory, from Rousseau, Adam Smith, and David Ricardo to Georg Simmel, Adorno and modern rational choice or game theory. To see what is at stake in these framings, we must distinguish the pro and contra of the exchange paradigm.

2. The Social Imaginary of the Good Exchange

Let's start with the good news. Adorno once said: "Exchange is [...] key to society".[2] Which values are in the foreground when an entire society is imagined to be based on processes of market exchange?[3] For social philosophy, the most important effect of exchange relations, and the implied notion of private property of goods bought on the market, is individual freedom from traditional restraints (Simmel 1900). Anyone who has bought something for the first time with self-earned money will know the feeling, even if it is only a piece of cake: no one can talk you out of this. It's my money, I can buy cake and eat it when and where I want. It is my property now. How wonderful! What an emancipation! I don't have to beg, I don't have to wait. Each one can do as they please, at least with their own money. In the store or on the market, that's all that counts—provided I have the wherewithal. Where I come from, what I look like, none of that matters. (At least it shouldn't.) One will not sell things to friends and neighbours; with them one rather exchanges gifts or inherits things without any money involved. In gift giving there is no need for immediate countervalues and social relationships play a central role. The gift therefore leads further *into* social relations, while the exchange mediated by money leads *out* of them and can thus liberate (Henning 2021a). If a contract ends, the parties go their separate ways. You only barter with strangers (since time immemorial, merchants have come from the outside, bringing things from foreign lands and people). Exchange presupposes distance and thus can break up constricting bonds in the family, village, and milieu.

The second value is equality: where barriers of status lose their grip, everyone can try to make the most of themselves. Today famous singers, actors, athletes have all sorts of genders, ethnic backgrounds, or religions. Maybe not everyone is equally lucky, but the ideal of equal opportunity allows for

---

2 This is how Ritsert (2017, 21) cites Adorno's seminar from 1962 (as reported by H.G. Backhaus).
3 Of course, this is an idealization, which is only applicable for modernity. I do not assume this myself, but examine how this idea is treated in social theory.

continued attempts, and thus reduces stigma related to origin. This does not eliminate every factual inequality, but at least many *perceived* injustices: if everyone has their turn, the playing field seems levelled. Exchange relations, where everyone is the architect of their own fortune, appear to bring justice and equality of opportunity. In the end, everyone has what they deserve: the rich their wealth, the poor their poverty (MEW 23, 742).

The third positive feature is said to be wealth: societies based on market exchange create more of it than previous modes of socialization, since there are more incentives and possibilities to increase productivity. Division of labour and competition (Adam Smith's "invisible hand") ensure that everything becomes more, better, faster, and more colourful. As long as some wealth reaches them, this makes even the relatively poor in a society "better off," as Rawls phrased it, following John Locke and Adam Smith. Thus, at least in theory, our societies become richer and more just. A practice that appears to bring freedom, equal opportunity, justice, and prosperity to all seems to create "the best of all possible worlds" (Leibniz, see Marx's remarks on the "very Eden of the Innate Rights of Man," MEW 23, 85). Hence, exchange found strong advocates in social theory, from neoclassical economics (where everything looks just "perfect") to rational choice or postmodernist "progressive neoliberalism" (Fraser 2019).

3. The Social Imaginary of the Evil Exchange

So much for the good news! But from the perspective of critical social philosophy, the balance looks significantly less rosy. Individual freedom, for example, may come at a high cost and can even go too far: the distancing through exchange mediation can also lead to isolation and loneliness—the consequence would be atomization or "anomie." Ties become looser, families smaller, villages and cities more anonymous, divorces more frequent, friendships more difficult, individuals more oddball, cities and villages unsafe, social relations more hostile and competitive, the meaning of life permanently questionable. In consequence, people go "bowling alone" (Putnam 2000), or take refuge in the so-called "social" media, where one is often "alone together," as Sherry Turkle (2011) described. England has already introduced a Loneliness Minister in 2018. Communication among present persons erodes, relationships become non-committal, attention spans shorter, and the apparent protective zone of the social media bubble is subject to merciless attention, commercialisation and surveillance from the outside (Zuboff 2019).[4] Since market exchanges are about maximizing one's own advantage, it becomes rational to spy on others (i.e., on potential exchange "partners") and collect data about them. Exchange-mediated freedom can tip over into loneliness, restlessness, and depression.

Exchange-mediated equality is double-edged as well. Its appearance is rooted in the fact that certain things are invisibilized: exchange value abstracts from qualitative abundance and looks only at saleability, a strategic presumption about how others might perceive the thing and how much money they are willing to spend on it.[5] Participants in the social exchange of goods and services are equal only in the fact of offering some *thing* (or commodity). Who they are, where they belong, what they want—all of this is blanked out. This does not eliminate existing inequalities, for example between social classes or genders. It covers them up. This rosy surface can seduce us into a marketplace-mentality, inducing an understanding of self and world as comparable things, as something "reified": one defines oneself by the thing one has or wants to have, and soon also misunderstands society as a complex of things.[6] Solving the remaining social problems via a "technofix,", i.e., by mechanical means, as the Silicon Valley ideology wants, is then an obvious consequence (Barbrock and Cameron 1995).

If, contrary to the social promises of this imaginary, one experiences real inequality in everyday life, one is easily tricked into trying to compensate for it by consuming even more (which fights fire with fire): if a neighbour has a big car, I want to buy an even bigger one. A spiral of status consumption sets in, leaving everyone dissatisfied and putting a strain on resources. But all effort is in vain because no-one will accept the belittling, everyone will constantly come up with even bigger things (hence the tendency of private cars of getting monstrously large, against any functionality, see Henning 2021b). Exchange-equality conceals existing structural inequalities, which can intensify as a result. Rousseau subtly described the resulting alienation of people from each other and from themselves (Henning 2020).

---

[4] Surveillance did not start in social media; conventional stores also monitor customers and employees; cameras and facial recognition are even installed in public places today.

[5] Th. W. Adorno has compared this exchange-abstraction – in a sweeping identification that runs against his own philosophy of non-identity – to generalization in the natural sciences and has thus encouraged a peculiar scepticism of science within critical theory.

[6] It "is a definite social relation between men, that assumes [...] the fantastic form of a relation between things" (MEW 23, 86).

Thirdly, this also poisons prosperity and our relation to things: there is an accumulation of goods no one really needs (except to impress others), which clutter up the environment, destroy natural spaces, squander resources, poison the atmosphere and heat up the climate. It is as if a peak has long been passed, after which *more things* become rather toxic and only translate into more trash and poison.[7] Meanwhile, the things we have and do are no longer appreciated. According to Rousseau, when we only need them to signify status, we lose the sense for their inner depth. So, the theory of alienation in the spirit of Rousseau also implies an *ethics of things*.

And finally, this also has effects on the social *Weltbeziehung*. Contrary to the ideological textbook-wisdom, market-mediated exchange thinking makes us antisocial.[8] If it would not, nobody could become rich by trade—there is a transfer of wealth from one side to the other. One has not the good of the other, but one's own advantage in mind (that is the point in Adam Smith).[9] For Aristotle and many Christian philosophers in his lineage, trade, and even more so money trade, had a problematic status in the community. Later liberal theories therefore located the justice of exchange no longer in terms of content (they do not explain how one can become rich through exchange), but procedurally: it is enough that the exchange partners have entered into the exchange willingly, regardless of who gets what (in the end, white colonizers traded glass pearls, hard liquors or even infected blankets).[10] Whether this strengthens or loosens the bonds between them is not an issue. Following the conservative and romantic critique of capitalism, critical social philosophy has pointed out that the marketization of life erodes social relations.[11] Taken together, we must conclude that for every benefit of exchange (freedom, equality, wealth), a counter-story can be told.

---

7 Henning 2022. According to the Genuine Progress Indicator, development towards a good life turned negative in the late 1970s due to the increased social and ecological cost of the many goods produced.
8 Peukert 2018; Gerlach 2017.
9 "It is not from the benevolence of the Butcher, the Brewer or the Baker that we expect our dinner, but from their regard to their own interest" (Smith 1776 I.2).
10 This voluntariness can be stretched quite far, as was seen with John Locke: according to his liberal reading, indigenous people of North America, for example, presumably have consented to their own displacement by entering into the use of money, which he conceives as an implicit contract. Indeed, colonialism proceeded with legal means, it was a dispossession by treaty (see Banner 2007; Greer 2018; or Pistor 2019).
11 Starting with Karl Polanyi; today we may think of Satz 2010 or Sandel 2012.

Positive view	Negative view
Liberty	Loneliness
Equality of opportunity	Social inequality and reification of social relations
Wealth	Waste, ecological disaster

Table 1: Ambivalence of exchange (source: by the author)

Despite this ambivalence, the exchange paradigm was a success story in social theory: not only did it withstand conservative, romantic, and socialist criticism, it has even expanded into areas that basically have little to do with it. This applies to the theoretical coverage of these areas, but also to their practice. The contract for example, which actually originates from acts of sale, has migrated as "contractualism" into the heart of the political theory of liberalism. On the other hand, families now also know marriage contracts, marriage dissolution contracts, inheritance contracts, custody agreements and so on. Thus, the exchange paradigm is also at work in family and politics. In theory, this is reflected in rational choice, which models every action as a calculating decision that maximizes utility, even in the family or in politics. Individuals look to their own advantage and only come out of cover when they spot one. In this mindset of exchange people appear, as Hobbes inimitably put it, as solitary predators.[12]

Let's return to the imaginary where practices and theories are neatly pigeonholed. De facto, they are not so clearly limited to certain areas, hence exchange can also spill over into the other areas of politics and the family. But this spillover to other spheres potentiates the problems of the exchange paradigm.[13] So, might the expansion of another sphere be a solution? State-socialism could be interpreted as the reverse extension of *political* mechanisms to *social* provision. But the answer is negative: the centrally administered economy from above brought many restrictions on freedom, because the inherent logic of society, namely the unleashing of individuals, their right to self-determination, was no longer preserved in most communist coun-

---

[12] By the way: "homo homini lupus" is actually doing injustice to wolves, which are highly social animals.
[13] For Michael Walzer, justice demands that social logic stay within its own "for spheres".

tries.[14] But in the trinitarian picture of family, state, and society which we used so far, one possibility remains: designing the overarching concept from below, from families or smaller *communities*. And as we will see in a minute, it is from such small communities indeed that sharing originates. Could it be the sought-after solution to frequently diagnosed "pathologies of modernity" that can result from both market-radical precarization of everything and statist overregulation? That depends on the version of the story told. For in the case of sharing, too, there is an ambivalence between (at least) two perspectives, two sides of the coin. Let's start with the good news again!

4. The Social Imaginary of Good Sharing

Sharing keeps us warm. Everyday life indicates that we share above all with people close to us—we share the blanket. Or consider the family breakfast: bread and butter or rent for the room are not charged to the children, they are shared. This is also known from festivities or from camping, where everything is shared. Marshal Sahlins (1972) used this to create a model of reciprocity norms that depend on social proximity: in the inner social circle, one shares everything and does not think about reciprocation (he calls it "generalized reciprocity"). Rather, what we find is "pooling:" resources are assembled in a central place and handed out to members later on. In the middle circle, one still gives generously, but here one expects reciprocation—though it is not specified when, how, and how much. We already touched on this in the neighbourhood example. Or think of the pub crawl—if you buy a round of drinks, that is a gift exchange: you give something to others. Eventually you might get something back, but what and when remains open, and maybe you won't. You can also experience this when traveling—you may be unexpectedly hosted by strangers and can't reciprocate anything. Yet eventually you may get into the opposite situation and give something back. Only those who are considered outsiders, strangers, and potential enemies experience "negative reciprocity": one then tries to exploit or even rob them (lat. privare). This corresponds to market exchange, where one puts profit over people, and the lan-

---

14 Of course, not every economic "interference" of politics has to be a command economy – there are other models. Yet "regulations" do not have a good reputation in today's politics; one tries to leave as much as possible to the decisions of individuals and therefore prefers to rely on "incentives" and self-organization.

guage used there is amazingly close to military events. Words like "battle for customers" or "cut throat competition" are common, and Marx picked this up when he spoke of "armies" of labour.[15]

Sahlins' influential model ties the alternative of sharing vs. exchange to the degree of social proximity. While this is plausible, it leads to a problem: in this imaginary, sharing cannot be an *alternative* to exchange on a larger scale, so it cannot be a cement of modern society, exactly because it originates in smaller groups with high levels of trust (tribal societies, brotherhoods e.g.). Max Weber spoke of "fraternity ethics" (1922, 366). How could we translate this into larger contexts?

A first answer to this question is historical. The commons, which existed and still exist all over the world (but have been plundered for centuries now), did not always presuppose kinship; nevertheless, overuse did not occur for long periods of time. The communal property was shared between local people in a sustainable way.[16] As Ostrom and others have shown, in many cases social coordination mechanisms have been in place locally, but these can quickly be thrown out of balance by well-meaning outside interventions that misread or ignore local contexts. Today private property and market exchange have become the dominant social forms. As sharing seems to presuppose close social bonds and a shared ownership, how is it possible in a world dominated by private property? Here the "sharing economy" comes in, because it has decisively modernized sharing practices; it reintroduced them into the realm of private property and expanded them beyond the limits of intimate groups. What exactly has changed here?

In the positive version of the sharing-economy-narrative, the decisive change occurred with the Internet: more precisely, with the interactive Web 2.0 and the platform economy.[17] Before that, resource-sharing practices indeed had a coordination problem when things were shared beyond a smaller group: if someone had things to spare, it wasn't easy to find people to invite and share with. In every shared flat, there are arguments about who was the last to shop or clean. A privately-owned car stood idle for a long time, but when you needed it (during vacations, e.g.), the neighbours needed one as well. So, both families had their own cars, even if they were

---

15 Marx spoke of the "reserve army of labour" (MEW 23, 657), Lenin of "commanding heights" etc.
16 For the commons see Ostrom 2015; Dardot and Laval 2019; Standing 2019; or Helfrich and Bollier 2020.
17 Botsman and Rogers 2010; Sundararajan 2017.

not used most of the time. But here are the glad tidings: this problem has been solved today! Now there are digital platforms that help us coordinate perfectly. If I need a car now and my neighbours do too, I can borrow one from the neighbours one street over, because they're going on vacation by train. If a bakery now has leftover bread, they put it on the platform, and collectors are found immediately. It's all a question of perfect information! In this way, unused resources can be shared: they are now consumed jointly (hence the term "collaborative consumption"; Botsman and Rogers 2010), not alone, thus avoiding waste. Thanks to the digital work from home, we can even work from a vacation and don't have to stick to other people's plans when traveling, thus using off-seasons and weekdays to relax.

Which *values* are associated with this? First, users retain their freedom through the use of helpful things, but in addition they are now free from the responsibility and care for the things and the costs involved. Even without owning a car myself, I can drive to the hardware store in a car-sharing car and bring home the wanted stuff—if I still need to buy it, that is. I could also use a drill without buying it (this is a standard example): if it is not simply borrowed from the neighbour next door, it is freely available in the local "library of things" (Ameli 2020). Second, this freedom avoids the loneliness and reification that consumer freedom can bring, as sharing often happens in some form of community: "sharing is caring!" They who have too many cherries in the garden and offer that others fetch them finally get to know the long-time neighbours whom they often see but with whom they have never spoken. If you want to earn some extra money by subletting a room at short notice, you can establish contact with a wide variety of people. This can counteract the modern tendency toward isolation.

Nature also benefits: things no longer spoil, but are consumed by others; this saves waste and avoids buying new things. Those who use drills, cars, apartments, or office space together consume fewer resources than those who constantly buy or hire everything for themselves but rarely use it. And finally, this also seems to enable a more equal access to many things: you no longer have to be rich to drive a car. In the interviews we conducted in our research project on the sharing economy, many users reported that now they only care about the use value, no longer about the status signal or "fetish" of things. In other words, they no longer need to brag about them or outdo others. Being an early user of sharing practices may bring some prestige of its own kind, but this is no longer exclusionary, but open to all.

Now, isn't *that* the best of all worlds? On the one hand, you retain the advantages of exchange: freedom, equality, and prosperity. On the other hand, you avoid the disadvantages: there are "communities" instead of isolation, less objectification and more equal access to things than in exclusive private ownership. We even save resources: e.g., one shared car can save up to 20 private cars, which would leave more space for life in inner cities.[18] Since 2010, therefore, there has been a real hype about sharing.[19] So much for the good version.

5. The Social Imaginary of Bad Sharing

Critical social philosophy, however, sees a dark underside here as well. This criticism does not want to belittle anything, but rather aims to provide a more complete picture, on the basis of which one can form one's own judgment. The goal is maturity, not bickering. For this more complete picture, let us stay with the advantages of exchange: market mediation works through money, which creates distance and a sense of freedom by abstracting from details. Money is also involved in sharing in many cases, otherwise it would not be called a sharing *economy*.[20] A certain distance to others and a small price to pay for services rendered by a third party is welcomed by many users we spoke to, because this way one saves a lot of time and trouble that would otherwise be wasted on planning, discussing, and arguing. This is the first *negative* image of sharing: sharing between a group of peers or co-owners may lead to time-consuming discussions and social conflict (anyone who has lived in a shared flat will have experienced this). So, the sharing economies introduce one advantage of exchange—freedom by monetary mediation—to outsource one disadvantage of sharing: social conflict. Once money is in the game, however, it brings unintended effects. But how does money actually get in? Here are some examples.

- *Exchange without owning:* Even without money involved one can gain access to services by opening a gift exchange: e.g., I mow your lawn and get

---

18 There are different estimates: the BCS (2016) mention a rate of 1 to 15, the city of Bremen a rate of 1 to 16, (one shared car saving 16 private cars, cf. Schreier et al. 2018). The numbers are lower for free-floating (Share 2018; Rid 2018, 22, 33).
19 For an overview, see Ravenelle 2019; Ameli 2020; Schor 2020; Cesnuityte et al. 2021.
20 Schreyer 2020 therefor writes: "Sharing ≠ Sharing Economy".

a haircut in return; or: I offer my sofa for free to travellers, in return I can sleep on sofas of others in other places. This was the basic idea of couchsurfing.com, and there were also webpages where simple services could be exchanged (easyswap.org, Diensttausch.com, taskrabbit.de etc.). But even if you no longer have to pay for an exchange, you may have to pay a fee to access the platform.

- *Renting without owning:* Thanks to digital sharing platforms you can now easily rent out things out for money without owning them; for example, rental apartments via *Airbnb*. This creates additional income—in this case not for the owners, who already receive one, but for the tenants. This promises more equality: the money potentially spreads more widely if both owners and tenants get an income from the same object. One even expected a job miracle from this: if thanks to digitalized "sharing" one can sell services without having to own a company or rent an office, unemployment becomes technically impossible: every person with an internet connection can offer something—a car, a flat, some time, or a couch. One can become a self-employed entrepreneur without owning any capital in the literal sense. Access to simple commodities is enough (one's car, tools etc.) to make some money with it.
- *Data trade and advertising:* Once money is involved, it can also be earned from other sources. It is no coincidence that the first sharing platforms like Uber were financed by venture capital early on. One of the first investors in those start-ups was the right-wing-extremist Peter Thiel. What do venture capitalists expect from the sharing economy? Platform providers profit in two ways: one source of profit is the sale of data for personalized advertising, another the sale of advertising space on their websites, which made companies like Facebook, Instagram, and Google very rich.[21]
- *Tariffs and fees through artificial scarcity:* Crucial for the aspired high profits is a critical size of the platform; there is therefore a tendency towards monopolization (as could be observed with Amazon, Microsoft, Google, Facebook, etc.). Once you control a monopoly (or are near to it), a

---

21 In digital platforms, private property has not disappeared, it just moved upwards and became transcendental, as an unavoidable framework. Even to lend to neighbours, I have to deposit data online and sometimes pay. Therefore, platform owners (like Amazon, Alibaba, Microsoft, Zoom, Google, Facebook, TikTok, etc.) have been able to multiply wealth and influence especially during the recent Coronavirus pandemic.

third stream of earnings opens up: now you can charge fees. Couchsurfing.com, Spotify, or Amazon Prime, for example, all do that. Airbnb made an astonishing $ 350 million profit this way in 2021, without owning real estate! But it changes this market as well: real estate companies are buying up hundreds of apartments to rent them to tourists via Airbnb. This is much more profitable than renting out regular apartments long-term. In the long run, this displaces the "normal" living space for normal people. Here the ecological promise dissolves: an extra demand is created that calls for an additional supply. The sharing economy thus fuels a kind of gentrification 2.0: a permanent and growing influx of wealthy people who never stay for long but are ever changing and therefore cannot establish any ties. The profit principle of these digital platforms is reminiscent of robber baron waylaying: "You want to get through here, so pay." It's like a return of the repressed: only recently, in global free trade, public institutions lost the opportunity to earn from trade through levies (though those institutions often helped local producers). Now private platforms have filled the void. They earn from brokering access to things that do not belong to them and spend labour that they do not pay for.

- *Disruptive deregulation*: In addition to these direct effects there is another, more indirect, but highly political effect. To the extent that sharing generates access to income for short term work units, it undermines achievements that were once fought for in regular labour markets: minimum wage, health, pension and accident insurance, a right to vacation, to participation in work councils and protection against sexual harassment. It is a radicalization of neoliberal deregulation, an almost complete loss of labour rights. Peter Thiel calls this "disruptive," Naomi Klein "shock therapy:" the change is so radical that resistance is paralysed.[22] Likewise, social work is outsourced from communal budgets to the people affected—as "self-help" was always popular with market radicals (Bendix 1960). From this perspective, the success of the sharing economy around 2010 was no incision by new internet tools, but by the financial crisis that made many people poor, particularly in the USA and Greece. This forced many to somehow make money out of their private things (cars, beds, tools), driving the "commodity frontier" much deeper into intimate life (Hochschild 2003, 30 ff.).

---

22 Klein 2007. "Airbnb and Lyft [...] were projects designed to reshape labor markets, removing the protections that workers had enjoyed since the New Deal" (Chafkin 2021, 190).

Alexandrina Ravenelle (2019) and Juliet Schor (2020) have shown how this increases inequality instead of reducing it: among the work providers on sharing platforms, only those who do not need additional income really benefit—wealthier people who put their second homes on Airbnb. People who depend on income from Uber, task-rabbit, etc. for lack of alternatives can barely make ends meet and bear all the risks and costs themselves. Instead of reducing unemployment, this further displaces regular jobs and replaces them with precarious ones, while on the other hand big players expand their market power.

There is one last point: The lack of regulations and the display of user photos on the platform profiles, which are supposed to bring people together, also bring back social prejudices: while a hotel is not allowed to reject anyone based on their appearance, sharing platforms allow discrimination based on colour or gender (Edelman 2017). At the same time, this fuels superficial self-optimization, because you have to constantly show yourself in the best light and collect recommendations and "likes" (as on Facebook etc.). Users need to reify and advertise themselves like a commodity on the market. We are thus faced with a great contradiction: as with exchange, also with sharing. Important and by no means "false" values are opposed by great disadvantages these same values bring as side-effects.

Positive interpretation of sharing	Negative interpretation of sharing
Freedom through things, but in community	Exclusion by communities Extensive coordination & discussions
Equalized access to things and income streams	Precarization of labour Superprofits for platform owners
Decreasing resource consumption	Additional markets, more consumption

Table 2: The Impacts of Sharing (source: by the author)

6. The Explanatory Power of Ownership Structures

Now what are we to do with all this? How do we deal with this contradictory complexity? Neither can we simply cross out a page and cut the analysis in half, seeing only the good sides of one practice and the bad of the other, or vice versa. Nor can we leave it at these ambivalences. But how can we explain that practices of exchange and sharing turn out one way in one case and differently in another? I propose that the distribution of ascribed positive and negative effects of both practices is not at random, but follows a certain pattern that is based on *structures of ownership* and their effects on the resulting practices.

Evidently, exchange presupposes a certain ownership: merchants need to own the goods they aim to sell (at least at one point in time, as in the case of "futures"); hence the pattern to perceive the world as a bundle of marketable things. But ethically speaking, property itself is ambiguous. On the one hand, positive values such as freedom and security are associated with it: owners may feel independent of short-term events or from the influence of others (as long, that is, as their titles are recognized, which again is a social affair). On the other hand, there clearly are disadvantages. Owners bear responsibility: maintenance and repair work or taxes are incurred; capital needs utilization and profitable sales channels. Above all, one is tied to the *thing* (we may call this "thing-care," to distinguish it from person-care). If you own a house or a car, you are not exempt from ongoing consumer spending. On the contrary, roofs and pipes have to be replaced regularly, heating and renovations are necessary, etc. To own a car, you need licences, parking space, tires, fuel, repairs, you pay taxes and insurance, not to mention the occasional legal disputes. Ownership *encourages* rather than relieves permanent spending on consumption. It can become quite a nuisance. From the perspective of non-owners, there are even more disadvantages of property—just to mention capitalist exploitation: profit is legally appropriated by whoever owns the means of production (entrepreneurs, banks, shareholders), not by the ones who do the work or have to bear the negative effects.

In view of these downsides, for many *sharing* represents the good side of overcoming private property, hence the slogan "sharing instead of owning": sharing something saves resources, it conserves household budgets as well as the environment. Giving away and using things together even promises to make us more fraternal. This egalitarian nimbus of sharing stems from a long and early phase of humanity, when captured food was not stored but consumed together (Woodburn 2005; Widlok 2017). Property disputes did hardly arise. Nothing is ever completely over, so this type of sharing-without-ownership still sounds familiar. Sharing in the sharing economy, on the other hand, in most cases *presupposes* private property. It is an illusion to assume that property is not involved in practices of sharing (the food at the dinner table is provided by *somebody*, even if it is shared by the dinner guests). The things shared need to belong to *somebody*, so sharing itself is no alternative to property as such, but does offer alternative uses of it. But private property can be used and shared in different ways. Therefore, it is necessary to distinguish how private property can be involved in sharing, because this releases the different dynamics we encounter in the practices. In the following I will take carsharing as an example.

7. Not All Sharing is the Same: Types and Effects of Ownership involved in Car Sharing

Different ownership structures have different practical *effects*, and this could partly explain why sharing can turn out to be both "good" or "bad" (Loske 2015, 2019). A shared car may serve as an example here. So let us consider the various ways of jointly using a car.

(a) The counter-example against which sharing is often contrasted is the proto-typical exclusive use of private property: someone owns something and excludes others from using it. It is my car, only I am allowed to use it. The typical effect is that others are excluded—not only from using this particular car, but also from the use of the public space occupied by it when driving on public roads or parking in public space (Notz 2017). But this exclusion is not necessary, as things like cars can easily be shared. Most cars carry at least four passengers. But what types of sharing can we distinguish?

(b) Individual property can be used by different people, as in families, between friends ("Baby you can drive my car") or in carpools. Family cars are the norm in many cases (Heine et al. 2001, 39 ff.): not only does the family head (mostly the father) drive it to work, but one may drive on vacation together, take the children to sports or to school, and so on. While family cars are often shared simultaneously (several people in the same car at the same time), acquaintances tend to do so sequentially. The practical downside of this is evident: if there is one owner, but several users, there is a power differential that may lead to subordination. Families are hierarchical by their very nature. One way to solve this problem in many families was simply to buy another car. Thus, buying more and more cars promised not only freedom of movement, but also freedom from domination (an emancipation). But this is a dead end: it leads to more consumption, overspending, and traffic jams. Another way to equalize the relation of users is to share not only in the use of things, but also in the ownership (which also levels the playing field) of the used thing.

(c) In groups outside the family, sharing may extend to the ownership itself, if people share the costs as well as the use. Imagine a shared flat that also shares a car. At some point the question will arise why only one person should shoulder the cost of a car that is used by everybody, and the solution here is to share the burdens together with the benefits. If users share the ownership of the things used in common, legally this is still considered "private" (as in associations or a shared apartment). But friendship circles cannot grow arbitrarily large, and diverging plans can lead to disputes (if two persons need the car at the same time or someone parked it too far away). Therefore, this type of sharing is again intrinsically unstable, as it leads to conflict and high coordination costs—in terms of time and nerve. If every time you wish to use a car it is either taken, or you need to debate for hours, people will tend to opt out sooner or later. Therefore, ownership can eventually be outsourced to larger entities outside of the group itself to minimize organization costs. Here we face a bifurcation, as the third entity can once again have different ownership structures.

(d) It can be turned over into cooperative or municipal ownership, which is still rare in the field of car sharing (maybe because cities already have a public transportation system).[23] Here, group property enters a somewhat larger and more formalized scale. However, if a cooperative can no longer thrive on voluntary work and starts to pay people for the work they throw in (which is a matter of fairness), it joins the formal economy.

(e) It can also be turned into a small company that takes care of organizational matters and aims to refinance itself through fees or municipal support. Thus, private companies for the common good have emerged from citizens' initiatives, as in the case of TeilAuto or Cambio. This allows for more flexibility and reliability: if something does not work out in a cooperative, you might expect heart-warming excuses or endless discussions. If something goes wrong in a company, you get your money back. This is one advantage of becoming professional: things are organized more factually. This type of car sharing is often station-based, so there are always reliable parking spaces on returning the car.

---

23 One example is StattAuto in Northern Germany.

The main goal of these citizen-companies is not making profit by increasing their market share, but rather to reduce traffic and enhance the quality of life in their respective cities. However, some of them have grown, as demand for alternatives to the ownership model is on the rise. Indeed, the economy of scale is an advantage: dividing one car among four users is more complicated than dividing ten cars among forty users or 100 among 400. But this leads to a paradox: on the one hand, the aim of these companies is to reduce traffic and the number of cars in the streets. On the other hand, we see a constant drive towards expansion: small companies can easily be outcompeted or ruined even by minor economic irregularities; and users enjoy more choice and more range if the carsharing company is larger or active in different cities. This quantitative growth runs the risk of turning into a qualitative shift, as we have seen it in the commercialisation of sharing platforms (Airbnb, couchsurfing etc.).

(f) Finally, larger profit-oriented private companies with a lot of capital (such as car companies) may enter what is now a market, once they see that there is money to be made. Large car producers have the necessary capital and even a fleet to spare in order to get a carsharing company going with the snap of a finger. Of course, car companies wish to sell cars, or put them to another profitable use, the more, the better. For them leasing or "sharing" cars out against money is just another way to make a profit. So, their motive no longer is a reduction of traffic; rather, they have an interest to increase traffic and the number of cars, sold or rented out. This invalidates the ecological argument for sharing—if more cars are sold and used through sharing rather than less, the effect is reversed and turned into greenwashing. Studies have shown that cars from these free-floating fleets are often used on top of a car at home, so it does not reduce private cars, but rather public transport. Where profit becomes the end, the ecological subtext shrinks to a matter of marketing.

This ecological difference between (e) (reduction of traffic) and (f) (increase of traffic) can not only be attributed to different economic interests embodied by different types of firms (common good vs. for profit). It also works through different incentives for the users. Studies show that smaller providers (e) make it easier to say goodbye to cars, because in typical cases (trips to the hardware store, to the lake, to the grandparents) one can fall back on one without having to buy it (BCS 2016; Schreier et al. 2018; Öko-Institut 2018). If one uses shared cars *instead* of one's own, reduction occurs. The lever is the cost structure: if your own car has already swallowed up a lot

Ownership structure	a) private property used individually	b) private property used together	c) group property	d) cooperative or communal property	e) private property of small non-profit firms	f) private property of large for-profit firms
Type of sharing	(-)	Sharing within a small group	Sharing within a small group	Sharing in a community	Sharing in a town	Sharing in a city
Practical effect	Exclusion	Risk of domination	High coordination costs	Reduction of traffic	Reduction of traffic	Increase of traffic

Table 3: Effects of the Ownership Structure

of money before use, this encourages as many journeys as possible. But if each journey costs extra, that encourages people to drive less.

On the other hand, the low access-threshold of free-floating models is particularly tempting: you no longer have to go to the counter of a rental station, and the time of use is shorter and cheaper thanks to quick booking via smartphone (the car is paid for by the minute or by the mile). This cheap and easy comfort seduces to *additional* trips for people who already have a car at home and are used to it, but are on a trip somewhere without it, and also people who aspire to drive a fancy car. This leads to an addition to traffic, because the use is at the expense of public transport (if you missed the local train, quickly fetch a car).

Indirectly, this easy availability has further advantages for the industry: it socializes into driving even those people who cannot (yet) afford a car. The cheap and easy availability of cars socialises young people with a limited budget into car-junkies and also promotes the industry's newest models. It is a perfect advertising mechanism: it binds users to brands and provides "greenwashing" for companies with damaged reputations (think of the diesel scandal in Germany). This can be seen in the fact that free-floating also provides SUVs, sports or luxury cars that are meant to incite fun driving and boasting. Or think of business travellers who drive shared cars instead of public transport when they travel, or car owners who park their cars outside the city and use shared cars inside the city. Thus, more cars are driven, not fewer. Here, the whole point of sharing is reversed and turned into just another business with hardly any effect on social or ecological sustainability.

This comparison illustrates that sharing and private property are not at all mutually exclusive, that sharing is not per se an alternative to property. But sharing is not simply an extension of private property or practices of exchange. Some sharing practices *limit* the power of private property: they preserve the use-value-promises of private cars (flexibility and independence) without allowing private property to proliferate into profit-oriented exchange value and consumer fetishism (where the car turns into a symbol of distinction and status, and a sacred cow of economic policy). In order to grasp the differences, it is central to differentiate property structures involved in practices of sharing and their effects on the *Weltbeziehungen* of the users.

Works cited

Ameli, Najine (2020). *Die neue Share Economy: Bibliotheken der Dinge. Gemeinschaftliche Nutzungen für eine nachhaltige Stadtentwicklung*. Bielefeld: Transcript.

Banner, Stuart (2007). *How the Indians lost their Land. Law and Power on the Frontier*. Cambridge, MA: Belknap Press of Harvard.

Barbrook, Richard, and Andy Cameron (1995). *The Californian Ideology*. August 1995, online: www.imaginaryfutures.net/2007/04/17/the-californianideology.

Bendix, Reinhard (1960). *Herrschaft und Industriearbeit: Untersuchungen über Liberalismus und Autokratie in der Geschichte der Industrialisierung*. Frankfurt a. M.: EVA.

Botsman, Rachel, and Roo Rogers (2010). *What's Mine Is Yours: The Rise of Collaborative Consumption*. New York: Harper Business.

BCS (Bundesverband Carsharing) (2016). Mehr Platz zum Leben—wie CarSharing Städte entlastet, *Endbericht Berlin*. 02.05.2023 https://carsharing.de/alles-ueber-carsharing/carsharing-fact-sheets/bcs-studie-mehr-platz-zum-leben-carsharing-staedte.

Cesnuityte, Vida et al. (2022). *The Sharing Economy in Europe: Developments, Practices, and Contradictions*. Cham: Palgrave.

Chafkin, Max (2021). *The Contrarian: Peter Thiel and Silicon Valley's Pursuit of Power*. New York: Penguin.

Dardot, Pierre, and Christian Laval (2019). *Common: On Revolution in the 21th Century*. London: Bloomsbury.

Edelman, Benjamin et al. (2017). Racial Discrimination in the Sharing Economy: Evidence from a Field Experiment, *American Economic Journal: Applied Economics* 9.2, 1–22.

Fraser, Nancy (2019). *The old is dying and the new cannot be born: From progressive neoliberalism to Trump and beyond*. London: Verso.

Gerlach, Philipp (2017). The games economists play: Why economics students behave more selfishly than other students, *PLoS One*, 12.9, e0183814. doi: 10.1371/journal.pone.0183814.

Greer, Allan (2018). *Property and Dispossession. Natives, Empires and land in early modern North America*. New York: Oxford University Press.

Hegel, G.W.F (1991 [1821]). *Elements of the Philosophy of Right*. Cambridge: Cambridge University Press.

Heine, Hartwig et al. (eds.) (2001). *Mobilität im Alltag: Warum wir nicht vom Auto lassen*. Frankfurt a.. M.: Campus.

Helfrich, Silke, and David Bollier (2020). *Frei, fair und lebendig: Die Macht der Commons*. Bielefeld: transcript.

Henning, Christoph (2023). Poverty and Free Trade. In Geroge Ritzer (ed.). *The Blackwell Encyclopedia of Sociology*. Oxford: Blackwell (in print).

Henning, Christoph (2022). The Social Life of Things According to Marx and Lukács: The Critique of Reification Defended against Consumerist and Actor–Network Theories, *Metodo: International Studies in Phenomenology and Philosophie*, 9.2 (June 2022), 1–34.

Henning, Christoph (2021a). Befremdliche Nähe: Der Gabendiskurs in der neueren Diskussion, in: *Zeitschrift für Wirtschafts- und Unternehmensethik*, 1/2021, 123–39.

Henning, Christoph (2021b). Von Autos und Pflanzen lernen: Warum technische Perfektionierung Entfremdung verstärkt, und was das mit Arbeit zu tun hat. In Christoph Türke, and Oliver Decker (eds.). *Enhancement. Reihe Kritische Theorie und Psychoanalyse*, 115–36. Gießen: Psychosozial.

Henning, Christoph (2021c). Wirtschaft als Weltbeziehung: Earth Overshoot und die Macht des Teilens. In Universität Erfurt (ed.). *Globalisierung & Weltbeziehungen. Forschungsperspektiven aus der Universität Erfurt*, 31–32. Erfurt.

Henning, Christoph (2020). *Theorien der Entfremdung zur Einführung*. Hamburg: Junius.

Hochschild, Arlie (2003). *The Commercialization of Intimate Life. Notes from Home and Work*. Berkeley, CA: University of California Press.

Klein, Naomi (2007). *The Shock Doctrine: The Rise of Disaster Capitalism*. New York: Metropolitan.

Loske, Reinhard (2019). Die Doppelgesichtigkeit der Sharing Economy. Vorschläge zu ihrer gemeinwohlorientierten Regulierung, *WSI-Mitteilungen*, 72.1, 64–70.

Loske, Reinhard (2015). Sharing Economy: Gutes Teilen, schlechtes Teilen? *Blätter für deutsche und internationale Politik*, 11/2015, 89–98.

MEW: Marx, Karl, and Friedrich Engels (1956 ff.). *Werke*. Berlin: Dietz.

Notz, Jos Nino (2017). *Die Privatisierung öffentlichen Raums durch parkende Kfz: Von der Tragödie eine Allmende*. Discussion Paper TU Berlin.

Öko-Institut e.V. Freiburg (2018). *Share—wissenschaftliche Begleitforschung zu car2go mit batterieelektrischen und konventionellen Fahrzeugen*. Berlin.

Ostrom, Elinor (2015): *Governing the Commons: The Evolution of Institutions for Collective Action*. Cambridge: Cambridge University Press, reprint.

Peukert, Helge (2018). *Makroökonomische Lehrbücher: Wissenschaft oder Ideologie?* Marburg: Metropolis.

Pistor, Katharina (2019). *Code of Capital: How the Law Creates Wealth and Inequality*. Princeton, NJ: Princeton University Press.

Putnam, Robert (2000). *Bowling Alone: The Collapse and Revival of American Community*. New York: Simon and Schuster.

Ravenelle, Alexandrea (2019). *Hustle and Gig: Struggling and Surviving in the Sharing Economy*. Oakland: University of California Press.

Rid, Wolfgang et al. (2018). *Carsharing in Deutschland: Potenziale und Herausforderungen, Geschäftsmodelle und Elektromobilität*. Wiesbaden: Springer.

Ritsert, Jürgen (2017). *Zur Philosophie des Gesellschaftsbegriffs: Studien über eine undurchsichtige Kategorie*. Weinheim: Beltz.

Sahlins, Marshal (2004 [1972]). *Stone Age Economics*. New York: Routledge.

Sandel, Michael (2012). *What Money can't buy: the Moral limits to Markets*. New York: Farrar.

Satz, Debora (2010). *Why some things should not be for sale: the moral limits of markets*. Oxford: Oxford University Press.

Schor, Juliet (2020). *After the Gig: How the Sharing Economy got hijacked and how to win it back*, Oakland: University of California Press.

Schreier, Hannes et al. (2018). *Analyse der Auswirkungen des Carsharing in Bremen: Endbericht*, Team Red. 02.05.2023 https://www.bauumwelt.bremen.de/sixcms/media.php/13/2017-Analyse-zur-Auswirkung-des-Car-Sharing-in-Bremen_Team-Red-Endbericht.pdf.

Schreyer, Jasmin (2020). Sharing ≠ Sharing Economy: Ausprägungen der digitalen Sharing Economy im Lebensmittelsekto, *SOI Discussion Paper*, No. 2020–03, Stuttgart.

Simmel, Georg (1992 [1908]). *Soziologie: Untersuchung über die Formen der Vergesellschaftung*, Gesamtausgabe Bd. 2, Frankfurt a. M.: Suhrkamp.

Simmel, Georg (2004 [1900]). *Philosophy of Money*. London: Routledge.

Smith, Adam ([1776]). *An Inquiry Into the Nature and Causes of the Wealth of Nations* (Cannan ed.), vol. 1. Methuen. 02.05.2023 https://oll.libertyfund.org/title/smith-an-inquiry-into-the-nature-and-causes-of-the-wealth-of-nations-cannan-ed-vol-1.

Standing, Guy (2019). *Plunder of the Commons: A Manifesto for Sharing Public Wealth*. London: Penguin.

Sundararajan, Arun (2017). *The Sharing Economy: The End of Employment and the Rise of crowd-based Capitalism*. Cambridge, MA: MIT Press.

Turkle, Sherry (2011). *Alone Together: Why we expect more from Technology and less from each other*. New York: Basic Books.

Wallerstein, Immanuel (1974). *The Modern World System: Capitalist Agriculture and the Origins of the European World-Economy in the sixteenth Century*. New York: Acad. Press.

Walzer, Michael (1983). *Spheres of Justice: A Defence of Pluralism and Equality*. New York: Basic Books.

Weber, Max (1980 [1922]). *Wirtschaft und Gesellschaft: Grundriss der verstehenden Soziologie*. Tübingen: Winckelmann.

Widlok, Thomas (2017). *Anthropology and the Economy of Sharing*. London/New York: Routledge.

Woodburn, James (2005). Egalitarian Societies Revisited. In Thomas Widlok and Wolde Tadessa (eds.). *Property and Equality* 1, 18–31. New York and Oxford: Berghahn.

Zuboff, Shoshana (2019). *The Age of Surveillance Capitalism: The Fight for a Human Future at the new Frontier of Power*. London: Profile.

The Transformation of the Refugee Category and the Dialectics of Solidarity in Europe[1]

Nancy Alhachem

Trains are a fascinating place of being, that being of in-between. Often what we hear and witness on these moving platforms reflect in a way the society in a nutshell, with its different classes, races, and genders. I will briefly relate a small anecdote from last February: a week after Putin's invasion of Ukraine, sitting in a train on the way to Vienna, I overheard two men laughing about the effectiveness of the sanctions. One of them started talking about a colleague he worked with "who was a refugee". This passenger describes how his co-worker discovered that the salami on the pizza they were eating was pork, and was shocked about it, as the man affirms in German in this short conversation:

Passenger A: "I explained to him that it is pork meat, he was shocked he is not used to salami made out of pork, and I explained to him, *hier bei uns* it is pork, it is like that!"

Passenger B: "Ach! But salami is always pork!"

The narrator seemed thrilled telling this to his fellow traveller, as if he is recounting the story of an exciting adventure. A few moments pass, the two exchange thoughts on different matters, and start talking about Ukrainians' mass displacement, then suddenly shout:

Passenger A: *"Weiße Geflüchtete! Wie kam das?"* [White refugees! How did that happen?]

---

1 © The author/s 2023, published by Campus Verlag, Open Access: CC BY-SA 4.0
 Bettina Hollstein, Hartmut Rosa, Jörg Rüpke (eds.), "Weltbeziehung"
 DOI: 10.12907/978-3-593-45587-7_012

Indeed *"wie kam das,"* can refugees be "white"? For scholars familiar with the subject, it might seem like an absurd question to ask; however, looking at the discourses that shape the German-European post-migrant societies, one can understand how such bewilderment arose in the public. This is not a new categorization: already the nations that produce "the other," do so on a principle of differentiation, of "us" against "them." After all, isn't the "refugee" always that one who has a different skin colour, does not eat pork, and comes from a faraway land?

Truly *wie kam das*? Although Europe's transformation between the twentieth and the twenty-first century has been conditioned by migration, its history and impact on public affairs remains marginal. Displacement is often seen as moments of exception, rather than the condition of modern states. As if refugees are either threatening masses knocking on Europe's door, or invisible individuals living in "ghettos" of micro-societies on the margins of the dominant one. This is not an exclusively European matter; the Jewish refugees to the United States in the aftermath of the Second World War suffered such representations, before they were "adopted" in the "white" category (Brodkin 1999).[2] Hannah Arendt, in her short essay *We Refugees*, portrayed clearly how refugees exist outside political theory, even outside a legal representation which gives the *right to have rights*, wishing at one and the same time to belong, and to break away from this category (Arendt 1943). Although written in the mid twentieth century, the international legal rights guaranteed to refugees are still ambiguous and dependent on the benevolence of individual states. The 1951 UN Geneva Convention gives the following legal definition of a "refugee":

"[A]ny person who: [...] owing to well-founded fear of being persecuted for reasons of race, religion, nationality, membership of a particular social group or political opinion, is outside the country of his nationality and is unable or, owing to such fear, is unwilling to avail himself of the protection of that country; or who, not having a nationality and being outside the country of his former habitual residence as a result of such events, is unable or, owing to such fear, is unwilling to return to it."[3]

---

2 A study by Karen Brodkin (1999), using her own family history, shows how the whiteness of Jews was negotiated and constructed in post-World War II in the United States in contrast to Blackness and other immigrants.

3 Article 1 (A.2), Convention and Protocol Relating to the Status of Refugees, 1951 Convention, 1967 Protocol, access to the full text: https://www.unhcr.org/3b66c2aa10.

Every article, book, or research on forced migration relies on this definition. But how did displacement function prior to this point? Were "refugees" completely absent from social reality before the Second World War? If not, how did a legal framework emerge from the historical development of migration? In the following, I will look at the historical and social aspects of refugeehood, and how, after the emergence of a legal definition (1951), the concept of "refugee" became influenced by preconceptions on skin colour.

In *Les Exclus*, Michael Marrus (1994) tells us that the category of "refugee" in English emerged towards the end of the 17th century in reference to Protestants forced to exit from the Kingdom of France. Known as Huguenots, historians speak of Protestants' exile dating back as early as 1560. Along these lines, the "first refugees" were religious exiles. Calvin himself spoke of exile in terms of religious virtue by encouraging his followers to escape persecution (Pitkin 2020): "that those who believe that they do not have the strength to testify to their faith go into exile." Even in his interpretation of the Prophet Isaiah's book, Calvin investigates the Church across the centuries as a refugee community; as Barbara Pitkin argues this demonstration served the same as a mirror to the own experiences of the exiled of the 16th century and provided a comforting metaphor (Pitkin 2020). Without going into details of the early modern period, the Calvinist exiles present the first major movements of displacement in Europe. Settling mostly in Switzerland, Geneva, England, and parts of Germany, their host countries faced the same challenges of our times: fear of competition, protectionism, and cultural opposition.[4] The question of integration, despite a shared religion, and geographical proximity, was a tormenting task for the Ancien Régime. An immediate assimilation was desired, like the status of *Schutzverwandte* [person entitled under state law to live in a community but who could not own land and had limited rights] accorded to the refugees who ended up in Sachsen (and parts of Hessen and Kassel). Germany saw in the Huguenots more the figure of the immigrant than asylum seekers, hence those new subjects were perceived as changing loyalties and were welcomed as *"Verwandte,"* while in Holland and Belgium social distinctions were made between migrants, intellectual elites and artisans.[5] The mosaic of integration in the hosting countries (or Empires at the time) was a mixture of political

---

4 A case study on the economic conditions in Switzerland and the Huguenots' installation can be found in Ducommun (1991).
5 On the German case see: Braun and Lachenicht (2007).

will, economic realities, and individual choices of the migrants. Proving that the origins of legal categories are seldomly innocent regulations, the Huguenots were variously seen as refugees, immigrants, trouble-makers, asylum seekers, émigrés, in-transit refugees, and settlers, depending on where and whom you asked (Yardeni 2002). On top of the expulsion of the Jews and the Moriscos in the late 1400s from Spain, the Huguenots were the third very poignant (forced) migration in early modern Europe. The similarity it holds to other waves of expulsion and movement is that migration was a question of minority survival, as maintaining a Calvinist identity after the Revocation of the Edict of Nantes and the Bartholomew Massacre proved to be impossible in Catholic France.

1. When *Thy Neighbour* Became a Problem: (Internally) Displaced People, the Nation State, and the Birth of the Ethnic Refugee

The early 19th century is the time of political exiles par excellence: as we have seen previously for most of the early modern period, migration was a matter of religious persecutions, unregulated, as well as unpredictable. With the turn of the tide in thoughts and ideas, exile started to take on a political connotation, until today the term "political exile" has a noble undertone to it, for it is intrinsically linked to the bourgeois revolutionary refugees fleeing the Ottoman, Habsburg, and Tsarist autocracies. Largely cheered in the streets of European cities in the aftermath of the revolutions of 1848, in places like Germany, Sweden, and Switzerland, political exiles were in the *Zeitgeist* of an emerging generation eager for freedom, and nationalist ideals. At least as long as they remained few in number and manageable by their European hosts, the view towards "refugees" was unproblematic in general during the mid-Victorian era, for if they came as religious exiles, they could be used as workers and tax payers, or if they were hosted for their political activities, the existing order was not deranged by their "exotic political views." Until the early third of the nineteenth century, there was no political consciousness of the "refugee" category in Europe.[6] As the term covered multiple situations,

---

6 Despite different small-scale movements throughout the early 19th century, migration was seen mostly as individuals choosing a different political path from their societies. Famous examples like Marx, Mazzini, and Engels who crossed to places like London and Geneva paved the way for others to follow: as Porter (2009) called them, "little bands of political exiles."

it was still not associated with a "problem" or "crisis." Some countries even took pride in welcoming those who fell under the Decree of *Proscrits*, as the conservative British Lord Malmesbury affirmed in 1852:

"[I] can well conceive the pleasure and happiness of a refugee, hunted from his native land, on approaching the shores of England, the joy with which he first catches sight of them; but they are not greater than the pleasure and happiness every Englishman feels on knowing that his country affords the refugee a home and safety" (Porter 2009, 2).

What was especially unusual in British policy at the time was not only its open door for all kinds of exiled (poor, aristocratic, French, Italian…), but also the absence of laws, and not much record was kept in following who entered and who left: not specifically because of bureaucratic deficiency, but rather the Crown's welcoming mentality (unless in extreme cases regarding treaties of expulsion). Being welcomed didn't mean, however, one could do as one pleased: freedom of movement didn't guarantee automatically all the civic rights enjoyed by Britons (unless naturalised). This hospitality was from a specific angle: those *aliens*, as British parliamentarians spoke, "were visitors" and didn't cause any social conflicts worthy of legal regulation. This disinterest in controlling immigration to the United Kingdom resides in the small numbers that had no big impact on the population at the time (Philip and Reboul 2019).[7]

2. So, when did the Honeymoon end?

Individual incidents of xenophobic, racist, and antisemitic violence were not unusual.[8]

It is beyond the scope of this chapter to go into Max Weber's cultural racism, and national ideology; many scholars have already discussed Weber's works in the light of a postcolonial theory. Yet the discourse on "seasonal workers"[9] and economic immigration, and the national anxieties that started to form in the heated political atmosphere of pre-Great War Europe, show us

---

7 See for example: Pooley and Turnbull 1998; Philip and Reboul 2019.
8 One example is the "pogrom" of Italian immigrants in France 1893, in Aigues-Mortes (Noiriel 2010; 2007; NY Times 1993).
9 See as one example Max Weber's address in Freiburg (May 1895) on the "Slav Flood" (Weber and Fowkes 1980). Concerning Weber's cultural racism and national ideology, see Boatcă 2013; Barbalet 2022; Hund 2014.

how the current narrative on migration has a long tradition in the formation of nationalism.[10] Furthermore, the exploitation of what are called "seasonal workers," and then turning against their presence is not only a *Junkers*' ritual of the Prussian times: during the Covid pandemic of 2020, Romanian workers faced the same fate in the UK and Germany.[11]

There is a continuity in the national anxieties that arise in the different time spans. Outsiders are created even when they are not strangers from a different geographical space. This process varies as I have shown above; it could be fostered by the media and politicians, or even academics, and sometimes it is the combination of all three that turns social solidarity into blood-spattered xenophobia. Events of the 1890s were a turning point on many levels: the angst over immigrant workers in Germany and France, xenophobia associated with economic crisis, the winds of war raging across the continent, and last but not least, antisemitism culminating in the Dreyfus Affair (1894).

So far, this contribution has given an overview on the development of the categorisation of "refugee" from religious exiles to political migrants, and how racism and nationalism grew through experiences with economic migration, changing the perspective on refugees. Hence the refugee/economic migrant dichotomy in approaching the questions of movement does not always meet the reality of the migrants' conditions. On an inter-European level, empires long before the birth of the nation-state produced mass displacement in different time periods (mid-Victorian era, early modern, and 19th century, etc.)[12], for political and religious reasons as discussed above. However, what was distinct until the 19th century is how the host societies dealt with displacement, without producing global or even regional legislation. It was either ignored, welcomed, or tolerated, depending on whether the exiles and the host countries shared a common religion, or political views (or sometimes mutual enemies). Beginning in the 19th century, economic migration and experiences with it had an impact on how

---

10 The "Character of the German East that should be protected" and "a dark future in which they will sink without a trace" (Weber and Fowkes 1980) connect wildly with conservative politics following the summer of 2015. This, in addition to the views on migration from the Middle-East that see in Islam a danger to "White Christian Europe," but not only. Racism towards Eastern-Europeans has its own history in Germany: even in the face of the atrocities in Ukraine, CSU head Friedrich Merz accused the Ukrainians of *Sozialtourismus*, wanting to "take advantage of the system."
11 Reports from the Guardian, Der Spiegel, and Sky News can be found online.
12 Not to mention the Middle-Ages persecutions and the Spanish Inquisition.

receiving societies reacted to the different circumstances of migration and changed the perspective on the notion of "refugees."

As we move into the 20th century, with the unprecedented scale of two World Wars, the fall of empires, and the rise of nationalism, we will see how "refugees" became the condition of modern states. In an inability to manage the pluralism of old Empires (Russia, Austria-Hungary, and Ottoman), emerging nations produced the *ethnic refugee*. As Jan Jansen and Simone Lässig (2020) argued, displacement became intrinsic with *ethnic cleansing*: in the aftermath of imperial systems the idea of the homogeneous nation-state was built on the ground of exclusionary politics.

Around the decades before and after the Great War, at the intersections of the Habsburg, Ottoman, and Russian empires, territorial expansions and ethnic cleansing pushed entire populations into mass flight: Orthodox Christian Bulgarians following the Crimean War, Muslims from the Caucasus (and Tatars), Serbians and Croatians against Ottoman persecutions. Soon the alliances and competitions between Vienna, the Sublime Porte, and Russia internationalized the conflict, thus the ethnic and religious population displacement. Supporting or disavowing the refugees took a sharp political stand: Hellenization, Turkification, and Balkanisation turned Christian and Muslim sensitivities into monopolistic wars on both sides of the continent. At the surge of the First World War hundreds of thousands were forcibly displaced, took refuge, or fled spontaneously (Akçam 2012); by 1918 the number of refugees was at 1.5 million (Gatrell 1999; Proctor 2010). Peter Gatrell characterized this era by the "Class Differentiation" of "refugees". A notable example is that of the WRC (War Refugees Committee) work in London—established to help refugees fleeing German invasions in Europe—which separated lower-class from better-off Belgian refugees by giving blue and pink cards to differentiate between them (the pink cards meant better transport and lodging). Although the events of the Great War led to the establishment of relief aids, humanitarian support, and the creation of NGOs to help and accommodate the displaced, it also imposed great economic challenges on the host societies (Gartell 2015). A rising feeling of impatience was spreading towards the newcomers (Purseigle 2007). Perceived as ungrateful or unwilling to integrate (especially in the work market), refugees' exploitation grew and intersected with "national myths" of suffering and martyrdom. In *A Whole Empire Walking*, Gatrell (1999) speaks of about six million wartime refugees in Russia alone, and alongside this tragedy, a jargon of "crisis," "catastrophe" and "disaster" started to take place in public representation like newsletters, and media. Soon mass displacement of minorities contributed to the formation of separate states, such as Poland and Latvia after the War. In the midst of these hardships, solidarity with the displaced, vengeance for national pride, and the birth of ethnic groups was a melting-pot of the War. The following passage of Debussy's (1915) famous poem "Christmas of the Homeless Children" summarizes the "spirit of the time"[13]:

We've no houses anymore!
The enemy have taken everything,
everything, everything,
even our little beds!
Of course! Daddy's at the war,
poor mother died! Before seeing all this.

What are we to do?
Noël, little Noël, don't visit them,
don't visit them ever again,
punish them!
Avenge the children of France!
The little Belgians, the little Serbs,
and also the little Poles!

If we've forgotten any, forgive us.
Noël! Noël! And above all, no toys,
try to give us back our daily bread.

Expressions of suffering were being produced by artists, the media, and ordinary people who were either themselves displaced, or witnessed the *refugees' experience*. But although this song was intended to be a call for solidarity with the victims of German invasions, it bears as well the legacy of the Great War, which in Gatrell's words, was the "Nationalization of the refugee" (Gatrell 2015, 50–51).

---

13 Translation by Richard Stokes.

3. The Myth of Homogeneity

What religion was to the pre-1918 world, "nation" became to the post-War period. The myth of "pure" nations, instrumentalised by the rising leaders of Fascism, Nazism, and Stalinism to hide their expansionist aspirations, was not new. The population "exchange" between Turkey, Greece, and to some extent Bulgaria as part of the Treaty of Lausanne (1923), after which about a million refugees entered Greece, and some hundred thousands were expelled to Turkey, on the principle of Turkification, and Hellenization of those countries, fuelled the desire to get rid of ethnic minorities. Accordingly, an imagined peaceful, prosperous, and international resolution to the problem of minorities was determined (Ladas 1932; Pentzopoulos 1962). Religious minorities in the time of Empires became refugees either because they were seen as dangerous to the established regimes, or were seeking better conditions under which they could practice their newly founded beliefs. The upswing of Nationalism in Europe, no longer dominated by religious rivalry, justified the displacement and abuse of ethnic minorities. With Hitler's rise to power, and the need to justify the creation of *Lebensraum* for ethnic Germans, on one hand, and the expansionist mentality of the Soviets and the Nazis competing over the East on the other hand, a repartition of *Volksdeutsche* took place between 1939 and 1941 (Ahonen et al 2008; Bryant 2007).

4. Jewish Refugee Crisis and the Creation of Statelessness

> The consul banged the table and said,
> "If you've got no passport you're officially dead"
> But we are still alive, my dear, but we are still alive.

> Went to a committee; they offered me a chair;
> Asked me politely to return next year:
> But where shall we go to-day, my dear, but where shall we go to-day?
> W. H. Auden, *Refugee Blues*. (1939)

Directly after the election of the Nazi regime in March 1933, 25,000 Jews left Germany, along with some other few thousands of political opponents.

While consolidating power, the Nazis worked on denaturalizing Jews, and first-generation immigrants, who were granted a *Fremdenpass* [foreigner's passport]. Until that point, the holders of the aforementioned document were granted protection from the state. The violent persecution of the Jews, which took a legal form with the 1935 Nuremberg Law in creating the exclusionary category of "Aryan," led to a campaign of stigmatizing, identifying, and isolating Jews in the German society. By 1939, Jews leaving Germany and Austria for neighbouring countries attained an estimated number of 200,000. Despite a non-refoulement agreement among Western states, neither Belgium nor France were ready to share the burden of this migration. Mostly agreeing to a temporary stay and pushing toward overseas resettlement, the demand to find a solution for the increasing numbers fleeing Nazism started taking a transatlantic dimension. After the trauma and violence of the 1938 pogroms, even the most well off assimilated Jewish families realized the urgency to leave. Thereby, the Evian Conference of July 1938, called for by the American president at the time, thought to internationalize the management of the refugee question (Caestecker 2017). After nine days, with 32 representatives from different countries, and intergovernmental negotiations, solidarity died a bitter death. The only country which agreed to raise its quota of immigrants and indicated a willingness to accept up to a hundred thousand Jewish refugees was the Dominican Republic.[14] The context of the late 1930s is a complex one, different factors were in play: aftershocks of the Depression, colonialism, Zionism, antisemitism, and the newly emerging international organizations. The scholarship on the Intergovernmental Committee on Refugees (ICR) indicates that Western countries were seriously considering Madagascar and British Guiana as potential homelands for the Jews. In the meantime, the bordering countries such as Switzerland, Denmark, Sweden, and the Netherlands, that had an open travel regime with Germany, required technical means by which they could distinguish between German Jews and German (Aryan) tourists, for exclusionary practices. Thus, the Nazis launched new passports with a red "J" to denote the Jews, making it easier for the border countries to practice a racial policy towards migration. With the legal borders being closed for German Jews, illegal routes had to be taken, hence traffickers'

---

14 Not out of goodwill towards the Jewish refugees but rather as an attempt to turn away attention from the massacres that the Dominican dictator ordered against an estimated number of 25,000 Haitians (Turits 2002).

and smugglers' business flourished considerably. Neither the US, nor the European countries were willing to make legal means for the resettlement of the refugees fleeing Nazism, coupling their policy with xenophobic and antisemitic discourses by which the Jews were portrayed as troublemakers, and undesired rivalry (Caestecker 2017).

Despite the Conference failure in protecting and securing the Jewish refugees, it was a key point in international relations, and the individualisation of the "refugee" category. As it led to the establishment of the ICR, and paved the way for a legal definition of "refugee," it also pointed out the exceptionality of this category.

5. 1951: Point Zero in International Refugee Policy?

The beginning of the internationalisation of refugee policy can be traced to 1921, when a collaboration between the International Red Cross and the League of Nations established a High Commissioner for Refugees to help stateless people from Russia. Rebecca Hamlin, a researcher in Legal and Political Sciences, argues that since its very beginning the international refugee system was built on unequal sovereignties. As the League of Nations worked on resettling Assyrians and Armenians in the Middle East, which was under European mandates, it gave the receiving countries little to no say in this resettlement agenda. We have seen above that the question of Jewish refugees was also being handled within the framework of existing colonial regimes, in which the major European forces decided repatriation beyond their borders. Hence, the prevailing international refugee policy is the legacy of a colonial system that continues to influence migration management between the Global South and North to the present moment (Hamlin 2021). Before moving to the contemporary period, it is essential to recognize the context in which the 1951 UN Convention was adopted, and how the modern refugee regime was built on unequal and exploited solidarities.

After the Second World War, the displacement and death of millions, and the displacement crisis of 1945–1946, international efforts emerged more willing to solve the pan-European refugee problem. The creation of the United Nations Relief and Rehabilitation Administration (UNRRA 1943), and the War Refugee Board (1944), both in Washington, were envisioned as solutions not only to displacement but also to the shortage of labour; once again refugees were being transformed into potential immigrants for sustaining national interest. Along the lines of Gatrell, the 20th century marked the internationalisation of the responses to the nationalisation of refugees. With the end of world war II and the strengthening of an east/west division, the 1950s marked the formation of a new consciousness in regard to the "refugee" figure. The ideological war between the United States and the Soviet Union pushed the social dimensions of mobility into a political-ideology-focused sphere. Hence, people fleeing the USSR countries were portrayed as heroic anti-communist fighters: for example, the Hungarian war of 1956 came to prove the openness of the democratic Western societies to the freedom fighters claiming the status of refugees. Regardless of the economic and social realities, international refugee law claimed to develop a humanitarian vocabulary in response to Soviet critique of the United Nations institutions and responses to migrant emergencies. Although the Global South was also experiencing different waves of movement when the 1951 Convention was put in place, this was not of equal importance to the international organisations, in comparison to the political value given to the refugees from the USSR in the war of ideologies (Chimni 1998).

After the collapse of the USSR, another conflict erupted in Europe and put the values of the post-War world to test. Between 1991 and 2002 a series of ethnic clashes led to the collapse of the Yugoslav federations, producing an estimated 1.4 million refugees, and an ethnic cleansing targeting the Muslim Bosnians (Walker 2010). Germany and Austria were among the first European countries to take in 650,000 refugees seeking "temporal protection."[15] Nevertheless, both countries, despite the high numbers of *Gastarbeiter* [guest workers] who had settled in the 1950s-1960s and the new numbers of asylum seekers, didn't think of themselves as *Einwanderungsland* [immigration countries]. The migration and citizenship policies which were in place had a very ethnic undertone and being a citizen was still based on *jus sanguinis*. The status of Bosnians and other refugees from the former USSR, didn't include access to the legal rights guaranteed by the 1951 Convention and the United Nations Declaration of Human Rights. Instead, something called Temporary Protection Status (TPS) was put in place, in the hope of an eventual repatriation of these refugees. Thus, the Dayton Agreement was negotiated in Ohio

---

15 350,000 in Germany.

on the 19th of November 1995, and officially signed in Paris a month later.[16] Arguably, the Agreement enabled restitution and reconciliation, and became an important legislative action for redressing war destitutions. In reality, most of the returnees had to move "back" to places other than their original homes, and remained internally displaced. Therefore, the Dayton policy is more a product of the harsh asylum legislations of the European host countries, and less of a humanitarian solution for the displaced people themselves (Koser and Black 1999). Often the returnees had to settle in places where they became minorities (Serbia and Croatia), and hence the Agreement reproduced the ethnic divisions of the state, which originally were the cause of the ethnic-nationalist war itself (Franz 2010). In addition, the institutions put in place by the United Nations and the European Union, such as the OHR (Office of the High Representative), to implement the Dayton Agreement and foster reconciliation, functioned through a high level of corruption, and led to a surge in black market activities. As a result of the complicity of the government, politicians, and international organisations, Bosnians trusted neither their representatives, nor the international agencies (ibid.). Such sentiments would persist and grow, especially after the 2000s, and the growing industry of pushbacks and the complicity of many organisations in criminalizing solidarity and the help of displaced people. The following section will present an overview of the migration regime put in place following the summer of 2015, and the ambiguous *Willkomenskultur* [welcoming culture] in the wake of the Afghan and Ukrainian wars.

6. The Age of Camps, Pushbacks, and Double Standards

As the interventionist case in the Balkans showed, the international (and European) community involvement in (post) conflict areas has contributed to the production of displacement, as subsequent cases in Iraq, Yemen, Libya, and Afghanistan have shown. Yet these countries have taken very little (and ambiguous) responsibility for their political and military actions. The

---

16 The Dayton Agreement was intended as a peace Accord, to end the three and half years of war between Bosnia and Herzegovina. Under Clinton's administration, the peace agreement was seen as a triumph of United States diplomacy following policy slogans such "ending war by diplomacy."

big empires of the past, today in the form of nations, continue to act and engage with a colonialist mentality around the globe.[17]

According to the OECD (Organisation for Economic Co-operation and Development) estimations, South-South migration amounts to 82 million people, of which more than 63 million are internally displaced. If we follow UNHCR statistics, 83 percent of the world's refugees are hosted in low- and middle-income countries (top four being: Turkey 3.8 million, Colombia 1.8 million, Uganda 1.5 million, Pakistan 1.5 million).[18] Yet the European Union's budget for Frontex, for the year 2022 alone, was 754 million euros. Frontex, the European Border and Coast Guard Agency, created in 2004 supposedly to protect the European Union's external borders, will have a fund of more than 5 billion euros by 2027.[19] The European Union's obsessive discourse on border control in relation to migration mirrors a distorted reality in which the Global South is seen as the exporter of masses threatening the welfare states of the North. Yet as the numbers above demonstrate this is a far from reality narrative, that contributes to regenerating the policies that are themselves producing these dramas. Migration, whether forced, voluntary, or a mix of both, by legal and illegal means has become an industry in itself. The reasons why Tunisian migrants flee in small boats are complicated: economic situation, restriction of freedoms, etc. However, their means of "flight" (boats crossing the Mediterranean risking their lives) is considered "illegal." On the other hand, there are for example Syrian migrants who entered Europe on work or study visas (because they could and/or because they did not want to deal with the asylum process): legally they are immigrants, socially they are seen and treated as refugees. Hence, the reality of migration shows that it is rarely an either/or case of being voluntary or forced. Often it is a mix of both, and the legal systems adopt absurd measures that widen the abyss between refugee/immigrant. With billions being invested yearly, either by states that pay to keep refugees out, or migrants who give everything they have to cross borders, movement is turned into a lucrative dehumanized business, for smugglers, traffickers, externalization agencies, as well as transit and host

---

17 I don't suggest a simple continuity between colonialist rules and national interventions, rather the persistence of a *colonial gaze* in the relation between the North/South. (On the persistence of coloniality: Gregory 2004)
18 UNHCR statistics available on: https://www.unhcr.org/figures-at-a-glance.html.
19 Details of the fund can be found on the European Commission Website: https://commission.europa.eu/funding-tenders/find-funding/eu-funding-programmes/integrated-border-management-fund_en.

countries.[20] A quick look into the media portrayal of refugees arriving in the EU—packed boats, crowds trying to push down fences, tumultuous scenes from reception camps—reveals apocalyptic scenarios. Little is presented to the public on the dangers, and the money spent in taking those journeys, not to mention the criminal acts of European Union agencies, in forbidding any assistance to border crossers, for example by turning off boats' radios when distress signals are sent from the ships carrying refugees (Mannik 2016). The Mediterranean Sea is turning into a graveyard, with unofficial numbers speaking of more than 25,000 lost lives since 2014.[21] Other ethnographic work from "fortress Europe" and accounts from the Polish-Belarussian borders speak of militarized zones, where dozens of Iraqi and Syrian migrants have died in the last few years. Poland, promising in 2021 to build a wall all across their border to stop Middle Eastern and African refugees from crossing, had a quick change of heart after Putin's invasion of Ukraine in February 2022 and is now hosting more than 1.5 million Ukrainian refugees. NGOs reporting from the borders have reported that African and Middle Eastern people who were working or studying in Ukraine before the war, and had to flee, were subject to racist and discriminatory measures, and were often denied asylum, on the claim that the European Union's welcoming measures concern Ukrainian nationals only. Although the solidarity with Ukrainians in the first few months after the invasion was euphoric on the social and political levels, we witness today a turn of the tide, and what is often called "solidarity fatigue." As I mentioned earlier in this chapter, complaints, such as those by CDU/CSU politician Friedrich Merz, that Ukrainian refugees are "social tourists who move freely and enjoy the economic benefits" guaranteed by the German system, are contributing to a polarization in the society regarding support for Ukrainians. Inflation and global instability are also fuelling the conservative xenophobic rhetoric on migration, and pushing towards more and more divisions within and between the European communities.

    I tried in this contribution to present a historical overview on the development of the "refugee" category, from the early modern period to the present day. Although each period has and deserves a study of its own, I stress the im-

---

20 According to the refugees/migrants themselves the costs of illegal migration varies between 1300 USD being the minimum and 25,000 USD the highest. Often people have to pay twice or more for smugglers, to make the same trip (with safe arrival not being guaranteed).
21 According to Human Rights Watch.

portance of these developments, and the formation of solidarity in relation to economic conditions and political changes. I have shown that the "refugee" categorization process has subsumed different connotations according to the political atmospheres in the welcoming states. In the last section, I open, instead of conclude, a discussion on migration and solidarity that could transcend the politics of economy. By addressing the global needs of refugees in terms of resonant *Weltbeziehungen*, we can say that healthy *Weltbeziehungen* require political and legal measures for refugees that take into account the realities of the migrant experience, where the line between forced and voluntary migration is not always clear. Hence the importance of solidarity beyond national borders: not only in our relation to each other and the world we inhabit, but also in the research that could enable the bridging of social theory, migration studies, and political sciences. These fields could benefit greatly from an interdisciplinary study of movement and social dynamics, in place of rigid academic borders that still concern themselves with national limitations.

7. Instead of a Conclusion: Solidarity with Refugees as a Way of Repairing our *Weltbeziehungen*

> When he rebels, a man identifies himself with other men and so surpasses himself, and from this point of view, human solidarity is metaphysical.
>
> (Albert Camus, *The Rebel* (1951))

In philosophical discourse, from Aristotle to Hume, solidarity has been understood as a form of sympathy, a cement that keeps *a society* held together and knitting a sense of "us." Consequently, if there is "us" then there is "them," making solidarity exclusive and bounded by how far the circle of *a society* can be stretched. In anxious nationalism, as the experience of the 19th and 20th centuries have demonstrated, "us" as well can be divided into sub-groups. Instead of understanding solidarity as a form of binding, I ally with Camus' words: to a view on solidarity as an act of rebellion, in which a human "surpasses himself." Rebellion in this regard applies to any form of injustice, and is not exclusive to a certain group (refugees, or women, or trans people, etc.). Only by replacing the "or" with "and" can there be a form of solidarity that works against making sub-groups of humans, and thus against dehumanizing those who are not part of "us." If solidarity is an act of charity, that societies can afford only when they are doing well economically, then it becomes part of egocentric politics, a benevolence card that can be taken back whenever the GDP of a nation drops. As the election results in Italy, Denmark, and Sweden have recently shown, the prevailing view on migration (in all its forms) is still very intimately linked with the excuses of economic growth.

A suitable understanding of solidarity in the lines of my argument here can be examined in Axel Honneth's work on "recognition." In Honneth's argument, solidarity is possible as "an interactive relationship in which subjects mutually sympathise with their various different ways of life because, among themselves, they esteem each other symmetrically" (Honneth 1995). There are three key elements here that can help establish solidarity beyond a form of general passive tolerance: interactive relationship, mutual sympathy for different ways of life, and symmetrical respect. If we look at the context of migration in Europe these elements seem absent or only very partially applicable. Migrants who came to the European countries after the Second World War, either as "guest workers" or asylum seekers, are now mostly living in ghettoised neighbourhoods, which the other groups of the society visit as exotic oases, where they can taste the "authentic food of cultural diversity." In reality, the people living in these segregated areas have little to no interaction with the rest of the population, mostly work and frequent places that are owned by other migrants, and often "stay amongst each other." As for the newcomers, especially those who are still going through the asylum process, they are living in camps away from the rest of society, and have little access to the outside world. On this level, interactive relationship is basically absent between the migrant/refugee and the other citizens. Now if we look at the second point, concerning mutual sympathy for different ways of life, there are problems on both sides. On the one hand, integration is understood in political and public discourse as complete assimilation or even effacement in the new environment, and on the other hand, the migrant groups from different religious or cultural background refuse to negotiate certain traits of identity, because they fear a total disappearance of their different characteristics. The third element is a supplement to the last one: symmetrical respect. Many conservative and far-right politicians are making this an impossible task, especially in the rhetoric on Islam. An extreme example here is that of the Danish politician Rasmus Paludan (of the far-right party *Stram Kurs*/Hard Line), who on different occasions burnt copies of the Quran, in a public display with police protection, claiming that this is part of his "freedom of expression."

In this last analysis, I have tried to advocate for a solidarity that can become a form of repairing one's *Weltbeziehung*, against ethnic, national, and gender boundaries. This ought to be recognized as the individual's rebellion on injustices in the first place. However, if this cannot be maintained on the intimate, personal level, the state has a decisive role in maintaining and fostering social dynamics. As the recent pandemic revealed, state policies still maintain a powerful influence on society's responses to major changes. Migration is part of human life in general, but also of all countries' mutations, in the face of atrocities like war, and environmental catastrophes. In this sense, the discourse on migration needs a two-dimensional transformation: first to disentangle solidarity from the view on a nation's economy; and second to replace the dialectics of "crisis" with those of "chance" and "opportunity." For that, international cooperation is a necessity, as it cannot be possible to ask from one nation to "open its doors" as the others shut theirs. Migration can be tackled in the same way as climate change, on both global and individual levels, as part of a common future in which our *Weltbeziehungen* to each other are built on surpassing narcissistic needs. This requires rebelling not only against unjust policies, but also against the narratives that see in the human condition only narcissistic and egocentric potential for action.

Works Cited

Arendt, Hannah (1943). We Refugees. *Menorah Journal*, 31, 69–77.

Ahonen, Pertti (et al.). (2008). *People on the Move: Forced Population Movements in Europe in the Second World War and Its Aftermath*. London: Routledge.

Akçam, Taner (2012). *The Young Turks' Crime Against Humanity: The Armenian Genocide and Ethnic Cleansing in the Ottoman Empire*. Princeton: Princeton University Press.

Brodkin, Karen (1999). *How Jews Became White Folks and What That Says About Race in America*. New Jersey: Rutgers University Press.

Braun, Guido, and Susanne Lachenicht (eds.). (2007). *Hugenotten und Deutsche Territorialstaaten: Immigrationspolitik und Integrationsprozesse*. München: R. Oldenbourg Verlag.

Bryant, Chad (2007). *Prague in Black: Nazi Rule and Czech Nationalism*. Cambridge: Harvard University Press.

Barbalet, Jack (2022). Race and its reformulation in Max Weber: Cultural Germanism as political imperialism. *Journal of Classical Sociology*, 0, 0. https://doi.org/10.1177/1468795X221083684

Chimni, Bhupinder S. (1998). The Geopolitics of Refugee Studies: A View from the South. *Journal of Refugee Studies*, 11, 350–374.

Caestecker, Frank (2017). How the Refugees Crisis from Nazi Germany Got (Partly) Solved through International Concertation. *Comparativ*, 27, 39–59. https://doi.org/10.26014/j.comp.2017.01.03.

Ducommun, Marie-Jeanne, and Dominique Quadroni (eds.). (1991). *Le Refuge Protestant dans le Pays de Vaud (fin XVIIe – Début XVIIIe s.) Aspects d'une Migration*. Genève: Droz.

Franz, Barbara (2010). Returnees, Remittances, and Reconstruction. *The Whitehead Journal of Diplomacy and International Relations*, 11, 49–62.

Gatrell, Peter (1999). *A Whole Empire Walking. Refugees in Russia Durin World War I*. Bloomington: Indiana University Press.

Gatrell, Peter (2015). *The Making of the Modern Refugee*. Oxford: Oxford University Press.

Gatrell, Peter (2019). *The Unsettling of Europe: The Great Migration, 1945 to the Present*. London: Allen Lane.

Gregory, Derek (2004). *The Colonial Present*. Oxford: Blackwell Publishing.

Gubman, Boris T. (2007). Cultural Dialogue and Human Solidarity: The Rorty—Habermas-Debate Revisited in the Light of Wittgenstein's Philosophy. In Christian Kanzian and Edmund Runggaldier (eds.), *Cultures. Conflict – Analysis – Dialogue: Proceedings of the 29th International Ludwig Wittgenstein-Symposium in Kirchberg, Austria*. Berlin, Boston: De Gruyter. https://doi.org/10.1515/9783110328936.59.

Howden, Daniel (2022). Europe has Rediscovered Compassion for Refugees—But Only if They're White. *The Guardian*. 10 March 2022. https://www.theguardian.com/world/commentisfree/2022/mar/10/europe-compassion-refugees-white-european.

Hund, WD, and Alana Lentin (eds.). (2014). *Racism and Sociology*. Berlin: LIT Verlag.

Honneth, Axel (1995). *The Struggle for Recognition: The Moral Grammar of Social Conflicts*. Cambridge: Massachusetts Institute of Technology Press.

Jansen, Jan C., and Simone Lässig (eds.). (2020). *Refugee Crises, 1945–2000: Political and Societal Responses in International Comparison*. Cambridge: Cambridge University Press.

Koser, Khalid and Richard Black (2003). Limits to Harmonization: The "Temporary Protection" of Refugees in the European Union. *International Migration*, 37, 521–43, https://doi.org/10.1111/1468-2435.00082.

Ladas, Stephen P. (1932). *The Exchange of Minorities Bulgaria, Greece and Turkey*. New York: The Macmillan Company.

Mannik, Lynda (ed.). (2016). *Migration by Boat: Discourses of Trauma, Exclusion, and Survival*. New York: Berghahn Books.

Marrus, Michael R. (1994). *Les Exclus. Les Réfugiés Européens au XXe Siècle*. Paris: Calmann-Lévy.

Noiriel, Gérard (2010). *Le Massacre des Italiens. Aigues-Mortes*. Paris: Fayard.

Noiriel, Gérard (2007). *Immigration, antisémitisme et racisme en France (XIXe-XXe siècle): Discours Publics, Humiliations Privées*. Paris: Fayard.

NY times archive (1993). *1893: Job Riots kill 20*. 28.04.2023 https://www.nytimes.com/1993/08/19/opinion/IHT-1893-job-riots-kill-20-in-our-pages100-75-and-50-years-ago.html.

Pitkin, Barbara (2020). *Calvin, the Bible, and History*. Oxford: Oxford University Press.

Porter, Bernard (2009). *The Refugee Question in Mid-Victorian Politics*. Cambridge: Cambridge University Press.

Pooley, Colin G., and Jean Turnbull (1998). *Migration and Mobility in Britain Since the Eighteenth Century*. London: Routledge.

Philip, Laure, and Juliette Reboul (eds.). (2019). *French Emigrants in Revolutionised Europe: Connected Histories and Memories*. London: Palgrave Macmillan.

Proctor, Tammy M. (2010). *Civilians in a World at War 1914-1918*. New York: New York University Press.

Purseigle, Pierre (2007). "A Wave on to Our Shores": The Exile and Resettlement of Refugees from the Western Front, 1914–1918. *Contemporary European History*, 16, 427–44. http://www.jstor.org/stable/20081376.

Pentzopoulos, Dimitri (1962). *The Balkan Exchange of Minorities and Its Impact Upon Greece*. Paris: De Gruyter Mouton.

Rorty, Richard (1989). *Contingency, Irony, and Solidarity*. Cambridge: Cambridge University Press.

Rosa, Hartmut (2019). *Resonance: A Sociology of Our Relationship to the World*. Cambridge: Polity Press.

Turits, Richard Lee (2002). A World Destroyed, A Nation Imposed: The 1937 Haitian Massacre in the Dominican Republic. *Hispanic American Historical Review*, 82, 589–635. doi: https://doi.org/10.1215/00182168-82-3-589.

Weber, Max (1980). *The National State and Economic Policy Freiburg address*. Translated by Ben Fowkes. Economy and Society, 9: 4, 428–49.

Wilde, Lawrence (2013). *Global Solidarity*. Edinburgh: Edinburgh University Press.

Wils, Jean-Pierre (ed.). (2018). *Resonanz: Im interdisziplinären Gespräch mit Hartmut Rosa*. Baden-Baden: Nomos.

Yardeni, Myriam (2002). *Le Refuge Huguenot. Assimilation et Culture*. Paris: Honoré Champion.

Living World Relations—Institutes for Advanced Study as places for resonant relationships[1]

Bettina Hollstein

1. Introduction

Creativity and innovation are conditions for the emergence of knowledge, a key resource in modern societies that are more and more based on knowledge. In the light of current crises, creative ideas are not only necessary with regard to technical progress and innovation, but even more with regard to cultural and social innovations.

"But our knowledge society (as opposed to an information society) needs strong education, especially strong universities able to offer orientational Bildung. [...] The nature of the university is autonomous research and teaching within the framework of Bildung (i.e. an orienting, non-vocational education). Without Bildung, our open society, which expects and lauds innovation and mobility, will become paralysed by its own expectations, since it will be choked by a reign of technological specialists unable to offer society any universal orientation." (Mittelstraß 2006, Abstract)

Science policy concepts designed to improve the university system used and are still using Institutes for Advanced Study (IAS) with a universal orientation towards *"Bildung"* in order to create spaces to develop creative and innovative ideas.

In this contribution, I want to analyse which sort of *Weltbeziehung* is created through IAS. Using the theoretical concepts of Hans Joas (creativity of action) and Hartmut Rosa (resonance theory), I would like to look at the conditions for success in enabling creative inquiry through the creation of living

---

[1] © The author/s 2023, published by Campus Verlag, Open Access: CC BY-SA 4.0
Bettina Hollstein, Hartmut Rosa, Jörg Rüpke (eds.), "Weltbeziehung"
DOI: 10.12907/978-3-593-45587-7_013

relationships in Institutes for Advanced Study. The Max-Weber-Kolleg will be used as an empirical example.[2]

In the first section, I will give a short overview of the goals intended by the creation of IAS. Then I will clarify the specific characteristics of IAS. In the next sections, I will describe my theoretical tools, the action theory of Hans Joas, the creativity of action, and the resonance theory of Hartmut Rosa. Then I will present my case study of the Max-Weber-Kolleg. In the last section, I will draw some practical conclusions from the theoretical considerations concerning the conditions for success of IAS.

2. What are IAS good for?

In recent decades, Institutes for Advanced Study (IAS) have evolved worldwide from an exceptional phenomenon to a distinctive type of institution in the science system.[3] Starting from the historical models—such as the Princeton IAS—today, a wide variety of functions and forms have been developed under this umbrella (WR 2021, 6). Two motives in particular were important in Germany: the further internationalisation of research communication, and the enabling of cutting-edge research. Internationally, these developments are primarily due to an overall increase in the mobility of scholars as well as the possibility to conduct research and exchange research ideas even without physical contact (ibid., 10). As Britta Padberg has shown, IAS are both products and driving forces of the globalization of research and are closely intertwined with different trends of global science policies (Padberg 2020).

In science policy debates, the reason for establishing IAS is often given as the increasing efficiency- and management-oriented operationalisation of research and teaching at universities, which has considerably limited the time available to scientists for knowledge-oriented basic research and academic exchange. In this context, IAS are expected to provide free space for research and academic discourse in both the literal and the figurative sense.

---

2 I treat the Max-Weber-Kolleg as an IAS within the framework of this international institution, but for historical reasons I will have to deal mainly with the German context.

3 Britta Padberg estimates that there are approximately 100–150 such institutions in all regions of the world (Padberg 2020, 120). For a short history of the development of IAS see Wittrock (n. d.).

IAS have long been regarded as privileged places for the original "idea of the university" (Mittelstraß 2008, 11)[4] open to a circle of outstanding researchers. In this sense, ideally speaking, IAS realised "free intellectual meeting places and [...] places where scholarly serendipity and curiosity are respected and given the conditions to flourish" (Wittrock n. d., 4) in a science system that is characterised by the expansion of tertiary education, third-party-funded research that is increasingly oriented towards a certainty of expectations, and indicator-based allocation of funds (WR 2021, 11). IAS are thus a reaction to acceleration and growth processes at universities as well as to an increasing orientation towards efficiency standards.

IAS foundations were initiated with the Institute for Advanced Study in Princeton, New Jersey (USA), which was established in the 1930s at the suggestion of the US educator Abraham Flexner and is still considered the "model" of the IAS today. Flexner, influenced by the Humboldtian ideal, is regarded as a strict advocate of the ideal of purposeless and independent research. He impressively describes the structure and tasks of the Princeton IAS:

"The Institute should be small and plastic (that is flexible); it should be a haven where scholars and scientists could regard the world and its phenomena as their laboratory, without being carried off in the maelstrom of the immediate; it should be simple, comfortable, quiet without being monastic or remote; it should be afraid of no issue; yet it should be under no pressure from any side which might tend to force its scholars to be prejudiced either for or against any particular solution of the problems under study; and it should provide the facilities, the tranquility, and the time requisite to fundamental inquiry into the unknown. Its scholars should enjoy complete intellectual liberty and be absolutely free from administrative responsibilities or concerns." (Flexner 1930)

---

4 This "original" idea is influenced by Wilhelm von Humboldt: "Kern der Humboldschen Idee der Universität war die Vorstellung, dass Forschung und Lehre, die Lehrenden und die Lernenden um der Wissenschaft willen, um ihres Wirklichwerdens willen, da sind; Kern der idealistischen Theorie der Universität war die systematische und organisatorische Realisierung dieser Idee, in der sich ein traditioneller Bildungsauftrag der Universität nunmehr mit der Idee des autonomen Subjekts verbinden sollte." (Mittelstraß 2008: 11) ("At the core of Humboldt's idea of the university was the notion that research and teaching, the teachers and the learners, exist for the sake of science, for the sake of its becoming real; at the core of the idealist theory of the university was the systematic and organisational realisation of this idea, in which a traditional educational mission of the university was now to be combined with the idea of the autonomous subject.") (My translation)

Flexner combined his considerations regarding academic freedom and institutional reforms with fundamental ideas on the progress of science. It was not merely deliberations about usefulness and application in science that led to innovative solutions. Rather, these would emerge from the curiosity-driven basic research (Padberg 2020, 121). In 1939, Flexner published *The Usefulness of Useless Knowledge*, relating basic research and "intellectual and spiritual life" to innovation and creative solutions of problems in the world—"a sorry and confused sort of place" (Flexner 1939, 544). Seeing the political situation of his time—"In certain large areas—Germany and Italy especially—the effort is now being made to clamp down the freedom of the human spirit." (ibid., 550)—Flexner advocates for a plural and tolerant research community, interested in differences and new perspectives, and not restricted to functional issues:

"Justification of spiritual freedom goes, however, much farther than originality whether in the realm of science or humanism, for it implies tolerance throughout the range of human dissimilarities." (Flexner 1939, 550)

It follows from this that the creation of the IAS was not only a reaction to functional problems of the science system, but beyond that it was linked to a normative ideal that assigns a special role to the recognition of humanity, plurality, and tolerance.

In 1968, the first university-based IAS was established in Germany: The Center for Interdisciplinary Research (ZiF) in Bielefeld. In contrast to the IAS in Princeton, the ZiF was conceptualized as an integral part of the newly built University of Bielefeld (Padberg 2020, 125). The main goals intended with the establishment of the ZiF were defined by the philosopher and sociologist Helmut Schelsky (1912–1984), who saw the emerging expansion of the higher education sector as potentially endangering the primacy of research. His goals were:

(1) enhance the primacy of research,

(2) interdisciplinarity, necessary to scientific progress, and

(3) internationality, required to bring together different experts to work on innovative research topics (Padberg 2020, 126, with reference to Schelsky 1967a).

Schelsky recognised the functional differentiation of the university system and the need for research institutes organised in an efficiency-oriented operational form as core cells of the university *("betriebsförmig organisierte Forschungsinstitut"* (Schelsky 1967b, 38), but he also saw a danger in this, which he wanted to counteract with the founding of the ZiF.

In sum, the goals of IAS in their funding phase are strongly related to ideals of *"Bildung,"* freedom of research, humanism, and tolerance on the one side and, on the other side, the attempt to counteract the problems associated with the growth and acceleration imperatives and efficiency orientation in the academic system with an alternative design named IAS.

3. Characteristics of IAS

As we can already see from the described goals for IAS, they share some characteristics that should be mentioned here:

First of all, they bring researchers together in a defined space outside of their regular academic institutions. I would like to refer to this point as *collegiality*, which relates to the creation of a community of researchers centered around an interest in excellent research for a specific time in a specific place, the IAS.

Furthermore, IAS intend to allow excellent research by providing good working conditions, free from bureaucratic workload. I would like to call this aspect *tranquility*, an aspect that is often emphasized in relation with refugees, since IAS (especially Princeton) played a crucial role in providing an institutional home for some of the most famous intellectual refugees, among them Albert Einstein, John von Neumann, and Kurt Gödel (Wittrock n. d., 1). As seen above concerning Princeton, the first model-building IAS foundation, the aim is to create the best possible working conditions, above all by relieving the funded scientists and academics from other official duties and obligations for a certain period of time (WR 2021, 22).

The next aspect that seems important is the interest in bringing different perspectives together, either through interdisciplinarity, internationality or intergenerationality.[5] I would like to name this as *inter-relationality*, because

---

[5] This concept grasps the idea to bring together researchers with different research experiences (senior and junior researchers).

what seems to be important is the creation of some sorts of relations between different disciplines, cultures, ages/duration of research experience etc., not in the sense to integrate everything, but more in the sense to acknowledge and value differences in order to create ideal learning experiences (Joas/Kippenberg 2005). The majority of IAS promote the exchange of scientists from different disciplines, in some cases also with committed personalities from the arts, culture, as well as civil society. In dialogue, scientists reflect on their own foundations and their relationship to the living world *(Weltbeziehungen)*. The exchange between researchers and the public also serves to promote understanding between science and society (WR 2021, 22).

All in all, the characteristics of IAS describe institutions that create specific relations to the world of knowledge. These relations are oriented towards a common inquiry or collegial curiosity. They are based in a situation providing tranquility and security. And finally, IAS create productive tensions through the valuing of differences. The aim of these relations is to enable creative research. The question is now, how can an institution create relations or enhance creativity? In order to understand this in a deeper way, I will turn first to an action theoretical approach, that is centered around the concept of situated creativity by Hans Joas on the one hand, and then use the resonance theory of Hartmut Rosa on the other.

4. The creativity of action

Based on the assumption that creative research is based on action, I focus on an action theoretical approach. In this section, I would like to show the usefulness of a pragmatist theory of action as developed by Hans Joas (1996): *The Creativity of Action*. Three points are of particular relevance (Hollstein 2020, 1663 f.):

a) The embeddedness of human thinking in human practices means that human beings are constantly in interaction with their natural and social environment. Ends are never fixed independently from action but are developed in a creative way while persons are acting.

b) Human subjects are concrete embodied persons with corporeality and emotions living in concrete social structures and acting in a specific lifeworld sharing common experiences.

c) Since every action has an essentially social character, subjects have the possibility to communicate, discuss and give reasons for norms and ethical practices, opening up the possibility for mutual understanding.

The first aspect (a) is central to understanding processes of creative action adaptation. Action takes place predominantly according to well-rehearsed routines and habits. Only when disturbances occur does the need arise to rethink the routine and—taking into account the specific situation, interests, values and ideas of the good—to creatively adapt actions and establish new routines.

The stay at an IAS is a stop in the academic routine. Changing location, meeting new colleagues, organizing life in a new city disturbs the normal routine of researchers. They have to adapt creatively to the new situation. Even if they have established a work plan and developed a research project they intend to pursue, the interaction with other researchers may challenge these plans, question the prefigured outcomes and lead to new questions. Pragmatist action theory helps to conceptualise these challenges as chances for creative reinterpretation of the situation in order to find new solutions. The capacity of researchers to listen to others and to find new solutions is central for creative innovations. Therefore, IAS try to institutionalise procedures for questioning research in a mutual way and to install habits that help to develop joint solutions in a creative way, therefore reinterpreting and readjusting goals and means. Since all action is embedded in routines, the conceptualisation, creation and embodying of virtues[6], role models and attitudes play an important role and are part of a lived corporate identity of IAS.

The second aspect (b), the corporeality of action, points to the role of emotions and narrations. Taking researchers seriously in their physicality, their vulnerability and with their interests, values and emotions means turning away from a strategy that focuses solely on rationally acting actors.

IAS already acknowledge this in the aspect I have called tranquility. The articulation of experienced feelings and their interpretation in the light of conceptions of the good motivate action. Pragmatist action theory points here on the one side to the specific role of emotions on the level of the individuals and their motivation within and for academic institutions. On the other side, interpretative narrations and historical contextualisation of nor-

---

[6] Concerning the role of virtues see the contribution of Beier and Mieth in this volume.

mative propositions, as the search for scientific excellence or truth, can help to highlight such universal validity claims.

Finally, the sociality of action (c), the need for communication, deliberation, and critique, is obviously central for IAS. Public debates in which plural ideas and value claims are articulated and discussed are, according to John Dewey, central to realizing the life form of democracy. For him, "democracy is more than a form of government; it is primarily a mode of associated living, of conjoint communicated experience" (Dewey 2002 [1916], 101). In this respect, the community of inquiry of researchers in IAS appears to be one field of application for the pragmatist approach to democracy.

In sum, looking at pragmatist action theory is helpful to better understand processes of creative action in IAS and to get a deeper insight of the conditions necessary for these processes to become successful.

5. Resonance theory

The action theory of Joas is based on a concept of *situated* creativity. Therefore, it is central to understand how situations are perceived by the actors, how they experience themselves placed in the world and locate themselves in the material world as well as in the world of ideas. These aspects are discussed in the resonance theory of *Weltbeziehung* as developed by Hartmut Rosa, which describes resonance as a mode of being in the world characterised by four elements (Rosa 2019, 174):

1. Affection, which means being touched or moved by someone or something;
2. Emotion, meaning a response that bestows a sense of self-efficacy to the agent. This bi-directional process of mutual "touch and response" leads to
3. Transformation of those involved;
4. Unpredictability or uncontrollability (Rosa 2020), which carries the double meaning that resonance cannot be enforced, ensured or controlled and that it is open-ended in terms of its results.

Resonant relationships of individuals are grounded in a stable self-relationship that locates personal identity within a narratively developed moral topography. In this process, the individuals orient themselves to particular ideas of the good life that shape their identity and the way they lead their life, ideas which will be continuously updated over the course of their life (Taylor 1989). When collective actors are involved, such ideas of the good life must be interpreted in terms of a "common good." Researchers as well as institutions, such as IAS, need a conception of their purpose in relation to a vision of the good life or the common good. Narratives formulating the goals in a purely instrumental way (for example making cutting edge research to acquire third-party funding) lose the connection to the ideal of academic life and hinder the development of resonant relations in relation to the objects of research and the goals of IAS as mentioned above.

Resonance theory can be used to describe not only the relations of individual subjects to the world, but also those of universities, which are under constraints of acceleration imperatives as descripted in terms of growing numbers of students, of doctorates, growing amounts of third-party funding etc.[7] The members of the academic system mostly experience an increasing pace of life.

IAS are institutions that seem to fight this acceleration pressure by trying to create a resonant workplace and resonant relations between researchers in order to provide motivation as well as creativity. According to resonance theory, resonant institutions develop axes of resonance across three dimensions (Rosa 2019, 195 ff.):

- Social resonance is created by maintaining resonant relationships with colleagues as well as with the general public interested in research results.
- Material resonance describes resonant relationships with elements of material reality such as books, empirical data and artefacts, the physical workplace, and ecosystems.
- Existential resonance refers to broader encompassing realities, whether those be nature, history, life, the universe, or something like the world of ideas or the space of inquiry. This kind of resonant relationship with the world as a whole is an essential requirement for any viable conception of the good life.

---

[7] This can be illustrated by the target and performance agreements (*Ziel- und Leistungsvereinbarungen*) between the state of Thuringia and the state's universities. These can be found on the website of the Ministry for Economy, Science and Digital Society (TMWWDG 2023).

Thus, resonance theory provides us with an integrating perspective on institutions like IAS and the challenges they face as a result of processes of acceleration and different modes of approaching the world.

6. The case of the Max-Weber-Kolleg

In order to analyse which sorts of living relations are created at IAS, I would like to exemplify this by using the case of the Max-Weber-Kolleg as a concrete example. I will use the two theoretical approaches presented above to identify more deeply criteria relevant to establishing good living relations in an IAS. This is a kind of reflexive experiment not aiming to provide generalizable evidence but insights to make intuitions plausible, using theoretical ideas developed by colleagues in order to analyse a situational context I am part of.[8]

The Max Weber Centre for Advanced Cultural and Social Studies of the University of Erfurt (Max-Weber-Kolleg), founded in 1998, is unique in combining an IAS with permanent graduate and post-graduate programmes. It shows all the characteristics mentioned in the section above, such as collegiality, tranquility and inter-relationality and was clearly also founded as a counter-design to the measurement of success in the sciences based on quantitative criteria (Langewiesche 2005, 15).[9]

As can be read on its website: "Internationally renowned scholars from various disciplines are appointed as fellows for set periods of time. These fellows work on their individual research projects related to the Weberian research programme and simultaneously advise and create networks with junior researchers (PhD candidates and postdocs). In this way, the Max-Weber-Kolleg brings together scholars of different generations, so that fellows benefit from the innovative ideas of the junior researchers, who in turn ben-

---

[8] I started to work at the Max-Weber-Kolleg at its foundation in April 1998 and remain there today.
[9] "Nur was groß und teuer ist, gilt heute in Deutschland als gut und wirksam. Die Tonnage zählt: Drittmitteltonnage, Zahl der Forscher, die an einem Themenbereich arbeiten, Zahl der Publikationen in referierten Zeitschriften" (Langewiesche 2005, 15) ("Only what is big and expensive is considered good and effective in Germany today. Numbers count: amount of third-party funding, number of researchers working on a topic area, number of publications in peer-reviewed journals"). (My translation) (Dieter Langewiesche was one of the first fellows of the Max-Weber-Kolleg and founding vice-president of the University of Erfurt.)

efit from the experience and contacts of the fellows." (University of Erfurt 2023)

In addition to the mentioned aspects of collegiality,[10] tranquility, and inter-relationality,[11] the Max-Weber-Kolleg shows a specificity, namely its Weberian research programme. "Research in the cultural and social sciences at the Max-Weber-Kolleg is historical and comparative. The focus is on the interdisciplinary linking of the disciplines represented at the Kolleg, which were influenced in a special way by Max Weber: Sociology, History, Religious Studies, Economics, Law, Philosophy and Theology" (ibid.). Establishing an institution with a social and cultural science orientation in 1998 acted as a step against the spirit of the time *(Zeitgeist)*, because the humanities appeared to be significantly less important than supposedly future-oriented sciences such as the life sciences, computer science etc. (Langewiesche 2005, 13).

The Weberian research programme can be briefly characterised as interdisciplinary and comparative social sciences with great historical depth and an interest in normative questions. This is not a fixed research programme, but evolves over time. In the founding and development phase of the Max-Weber-Kolleg, the Weberian research programme was directed towards the following problem areas:

- religion, science, and law as powers of interpretation and control
- interactions between cultures, social orders, and mentalities in radical change
- action-theoretical foundations of cultural and social sciences and their relationship to normative, especially ethical questions (Max-Weber-Kolleg 2005, 2).

---

10 "Sie [die Konzeption des Max-Weber-Kollegs] sieht eine Kommunität von Forschern vor, die sich gemeinsam auf Zeit einem bestimmten Themenfeld widmen" (Langewiesche 2005, 16) ("It [the concept of the Max-Weber-Kolleg] envisages a community of researchers who devote themselves together for a certain period of time to a specific thematic field"). (My translation)

11 "Sie [die Fellows] werden [...] von ihren normalen Verpflichtungen auf Zeit ganz oder teilweise frei gestellt, um sich am Max-Weber-Kolleg einer Form von Forschung und Lehre zu widmen, die ich mit Einsamkeit und Gespräch umschreiben." (Langewiesche 2005, 18) ("They [the fellows] are [...] in whole or partly released from their normal temporary obligations to devote themselves at the Max-Weber-Kolleg to a form of research and teaching that I describe as solitude and conversation.") (My translation)

In its present phase the Weberian research programme is described as a comparative cultural analysis of *Weltbeziehungen*. Under this headline, the Max-Weber-Kolleg has defined its current three thematic foci:

- normativity and social critique
- space-time regimes and the order of the social
- religion as innovation (Max-Weber-Kolleg 2022, 47).

But regardless of the naming of the respective focal points, common questions remain significant, which can only be dealt with in an interdisciplinary way and must each be updated anew in their own time. These include questions of action theory, the role of corporeality and materiality, the significance of normative dimensions and the contingency and unavailability of social change (Joas 2005, 90 f.).

In the following, the aspects to which the creativity of action and the resonance theory draw attention will be confronted with the situation at the Max-Weber-Kolleg in order to clarify the conditions for success as well as the problems.

The two alumni-evaluations conducted so far by the Max-Weber-Kolleg serve as the basis for the assessment. In the first alumni-evaluation (published in 2011), 26 of 44 former junior researchers (59 percent) and 22 of 36 former fellows (61 percent) responded. In the second alumni-evaluation (published in 2019), 29 of 121 former junior researchers (24 percent) and 26 of 114 former fellows (23 percent) responded. In general, the results are very positive. Here, I will try to concentrate on critical aspects in order to develop criteria to improve the performance of Max-Weber-Kolleg as an IAS.

The stay at the Max-Weber-Kolleg is normally a stop in the routine of academic life. This is important for creative adaptation, also in terms of research, and most of the time, this seems to be successful. Overall, the increase in their own productivity was emphasized by the alumni fellows, particularly in qualitative terms—e.g., with regard to the development of new research questions in an interdisciplinary context and the expansion of their own research to include aspects from other disciplines (Max-Weber-Kolleg 2011, 15). The different comments that came from the disciplinarily mixed circle of fellows and junior researchers and that contribute the most diverse aspects are positively emphasized by junior researchers. One of them writes: "the atmosphere as well as the debate on content was very fruitful and engaging—and I say this also with a view to comparable structures in the international context in which I have worked since then" (ibid., 5).

In the vast majority of cases, the structure or interdisciplinary orientation of the Max-Weber-Kolleg is praised as beneficial, stimulating and enriching (86 percent describe the interdisciplinary structure as very helpful or helpful) (Max-Weber-Kolleg 2019, 2). The reasons given for the furthering of their research are above all the stimulating and enriching interdisciplinary exchange with fellows and junior researchers about their own projects ("The mix of old and young, of specialists of the ancient world to modern times, I have always found very inspiring") as well as the discussions at a high professional level in a collegial atmosphere (ibid., 12). As can be seen, living and resonant relations were created between very different researchers, proving the fruitfulness of communality and inter-relationality.

Critique was articulated concerning ongoing tasks and administrative duties at the home university, so that there was not enough freedom for research (Max-Weber-Kolleg 2011, 15). This means, that the stop in academic routines was not always realized as expected. Especially part-time fellowships are therefore critical, since it seems more difficult for (junior) fellows to really interrupt the academic routine at their home institution.

The Max-Weber-Kolleg grew considerably in the time between the two evaluation reports. This can also be seen in some critiques articulated in the second evaluation: One person regretted, compared to a previous stay, above all a fragmentation of the discussions into smaller groups because the total number of researchers involved has increased so much. Another person criticised the sometimes sparse attendance, and one person felt that there was too little contact beyond the colloquia and supervisory discussions. It was also mentioned that the fellows did not always use the opportunities for exchange as well as they could (Max-Weber-Kolleg 2019, 12). All these comments relate to difficulties in creating living and resonant relationships—for example simply because you cannot meet each other when you are not at the same place—such that meeting occasions appear more or less automatically. Therefore, attendance and meeting opportunities beyond research groups are important issues to make living relationships possible.

One other aspect that changed from the first to the second evaluation is a growing internationalisation. Especially through participation in the institutionalisation of the Merian Centre in Delhi (ICAS:MP), funded by means of the German federal state, contacts on eye-level with Indian partners were established. This is helping to challenge Eurocentric perspectives and also decentralizing theoretical approaches in social and cultural sciences at Max-

Weber-Kolleg.[12] However, administrative challenges related to internationalization require professionalization and more administrative staff to handle these problems.

Corporeal aspects are not directly addressed by the evaluation reports. We find only that the optimal support by the staff of the Max-Weber-Kolleg and the good infrastructure (including library service) are praised (Max-Weber-Kolleg 2011, 15). In the second evaluation we find the demand for a cafeteria or a common room (Max-Weber-Kolleg 2019, 11, 14). This highlights that the evaluation reports pay too little attention to these aspects which should be addressed more explicitly in further evaluations.

As resonance theory emphasizes, resonant relationships transform the subjects involved. In addition to the substantive benefits for scientific work due to the experience of the interdisciplinary field and for finding one's way in complex research fields, junior researchers mentioned their own intellectual development as a result of their stay at Max-Weber-Kolleg. The Max-Weber-Kolleg was also positively highlighted with regard to the development of one's own personality, among other things as a place where one could meet interesting people and gain important experience. The creation of scientific and personal networks were positively emphasized (Max-Weber-Kolleg 2011, 10). "The cooperation was never characterised by authoritarianism or paternalism, but was always collegial and solely dedicated to the cause. A great, stimulating togetherness!" as mentioned one alumnus (Max-Weber-Kolleg 2019, 16).

Max-Weber-Kolleg is, for one former fellow, a successful institution. "The only recommendation is: always seek and choose the best scholars and guests, and the best students; aim at excellence and rigorous scientific investigation above anything else; seek equal opportunities, fairness, transparence, and inclusion; and foster interdisciplinary collaboration that enlarges our perspectives and invaluably enriches our research" (ibid., 19).

As can been seen from these responses, Max-Weber-Kolleg created at least in some cases resonant relationships, but as emphasized by Rosa, these cannot be enforced, but are always unpredictable. From the critical remarks as well as from the positive assessments, we can learn that for establishing creative and resonant relations in IAS the constant reinterpretation of the constituent characteristics of IAS (collegiality, tranquility, and inter-rela-

---

12 For more details, see the contribution of Fuchs, Linkenbach and Renzi in this volume.

tionality) in the respective current situation is of central importance—but always remains unpredictable.

Conclusion

In this contribution IAS as institutions aiming to offer a space for creativity and innovation and oriented to an ideal of 'Bildung' including freedom, autonomy, tolerance and democracy were characterized by three key concepts referenced here as collegiality, tranquillity and inter-relationality. Using the theoretical means provided by Joas and Rosa action-theoretical aspects (interruption of routines, corporeality and sociality) and resonance-theoretical ones (being moved by others, express oneself, being transformed and unpredictability) were discussed in general and then applied to the case of the Max-Weber-Kolleg. The discussion of the evaluation reports of alumni fellows and junior researchers showed that resonant relationships were created, but that there are still aspects to improve, because enabling resonant living world relations remains an enduring task that must always be tackled anew without guaranty of success. This self-reflexive exercise should therefore be understood as a reminder of the goals and characteristics of IAS that are in danger of being lost in the day-to-day business and as an encouragement to uphold the ideal of IAS against the imperatives of growth and acceleration.

Works cited

Dewey, John (2002 [1916]). *Democracy and Education. An Introduction to the Philosophy of Education*. Bristol: Thoemmes Press.
Flexner, Abraham (1930). *Vision*, cited according to the Website of IAS Princeton. 12.01.2023 https://www.ias.edu/about/mission-history.
Flexner, Abraham (1939). The Usefulness of Useless Knowledge. *Harpers*, 179, June/November 1939, 544–52.
Hollstein, Bettina (2020). Role of Corporations in the Great Transformation to Achieve Global Sustainable Development Goals: A Pragmatist Perspective. In Jacob Dahl Rendtorff (ed.). *Handbook of Business Legitimacy. Responsibility, Ethics and Society*, 1661–69. Cham: Springer.
Joas, Hans (1996). *The Creativity of Action*. Chicago: Chicago University Press.

Joas, Hans, and Hans Kippenberg (2005). Einleitung. Interdisziplinarität als Lernprozeß. In Hans Joas, and Hans Kippenberg (eds.). *Interdisziplinarität als Lernprozeß. Erfahrungen mit einem handlungstheoretischen Forschungsprogramm*, 7–11. Göttingen: Wallstein.

Langewiesche, Dieter (2005). Einsamkeit und Gespräch. Hoffnungen eines Geisteswissenschaftlers bei der Gründung des Max-Weber-Kollegs. In Hans Joas and Hans Kippenberg (eds.). *Interdisziplinarität als Lernprozeß. Erfahrungen mit einem handlungstheoretischen Forschungsprogramm*, 13–21. Göttingen: Wallstein.

Max-Weber-Kolleg für kultur- und sozialwissenschaftliche Studien (2005). *Nachrichten*, 5, Sommer 2005.

Max-Weber-Kolleg für kultur- und sozialwissenschaftliche Studien (2022). *Jahresnachrichten*, 23, Winter 2022/23. 14.01.2023 https://www.uni-erfurt.de/fileadmin/fakultaet/max-weber-kolleg/Forschung/Publikationen/Broschueren/newsletter_2022-23_netzversion_lowres.pdf.

Mittelstraß, Jürgen (2006). The Future of the University and the Credibility of Science and Scholarship. *Ethical Perspectives*, 13, 2, 171–89. 12.01.2023 DOI: 10.2143/EP.13.2.2016629.

Mittelstraß, Jürgen (2008). Die Universität zwischen Anspruch und Anpassung. Denkströme. *Journal der Sächsischen Akademie der Wissenschaften*, 1, 11–23. 12.01.2023 http://repo.saw-leipzig.de:80/pubman/item/escidoc:16002/component/escidoc:16001/denkstroeme-heft1_11-23_mittelstrass.pdf.

Padberg, Britta (2020). The Global Diversity of Institutes for Advanced Study. *Sociologica*, 14, 1, 119–61. 12.01.2023 https://doi.org/10.6092/issn.1971-8853/9839.

Rosa, Hartmut (2019). *Resonance. A Sociology of Our Relationship to the World*. Cambridge: Polity Press.

Rosa, Hartmut (2020). *The Uncontrollability of the World*. Cambridge: Polity Press.

Schelsky, Helmut (1967a). Grundzüge einer neuen Universität. Eine Denkschrift. In Paul Mikat and Helmut Schelsky (eds.). *Grundzüge einer neuen Universität. Zur Planung einer Hochschule in Ostwestfalen*, 35–70. Gütersloh: C. Bertelsmann Verlag. 14.01.2023 https://www.uni-bielefeld.de/(de)/ZiF/Allgemeines/Schelsky_2.pdf.

Schelsky, Helmut (1967b). Das Zentrum für interdisziplinäre Forschung. Eine Denkschrift. In Paul Mikat and Helmut Schelsky (eds.). *Grundzüge einer neuen Universität. Zur Planung einer Hochschule in Ostwestfalen*, 71–88. Gütersloh: C. Bertelsmann Verlag. 14.01.2023 https://www.uni-bielefeld.de/(de)/ZiF/Allgemeines/Schelsky.pdf.

Taylor, Charles (1989). *Sources of the Self. The Making of Modern Identity*. Cambridge, MA: Harvard University Press.

Thüringer Ministerium für Wirtschaft, Wissenschaft und Digitale Gesellschaft (TMWWDG) (2023). Website *Hochschulentwicklung und Finanzierung, Ziel- und Leistungsvereinbarungen*. 14.01.2023 https://wirtschaft.thueringen.de/wissenschaft/hochschulentwicklung.

University of Erfurt (2023). *Website of the Max-Weber-Kolleg*. 12.01.2023 https://www.uni-erfurt.de/en/max-weber-kolleg/forschung/webersches-forschungsprogramm/the-research-programme-of-the-max-weber-kolleg-erfurt.

Wissenschaftsrat (WR) (2021). *Entwicklungsperspektiven von Institutes for Advanced Studies (IAS) in Deutschland*, Drs. 8958–21, Köln 22.04.2021. 12.01.2023 https://www.wissenschaftsrat.de/download/2021/8958-21.html.

Wittrock, Björn (n. d.). *A Brief History of Institutes for Advanced Study*. 12.01.2023 https://cas.oslo.no/getfile.php/137422-1457965964/CAS_publications/Jubilee%20booklets/PDF/HIstory_of_institutes.pdf.